THE
REFLEXIVE THESIS

THE
REFLEXIVE THESIS

WRIGHTING SOCIOLOGY OF SCIENTIFIC KNOWLEDGE

MALCOLM ASHMORE

Foreword by Steve Woolgar

 The University of Chicago Press
Chicago and London

Malcolm Ashmore is a lecturer in sociology at Manchester Polytechnic.

The University of Chicago Press, Chicago 60637
The University of Chicago Press, Ltd., London
© 1989 by The University of Chicago
All rights reserved. Published 1989
Printed in the United States of America

98 97 96 95 94 93 92 91 90 89   5 4 3 2 1

Library of Congress Cataloging-in-Publication Data

Ashmore, Malcolm.
  The reflexive thesis : wrighting sociology of scientific knowledge
  Malcolm Ashmore ; foreword by Steve Woolgar.
     p.   cm.
  Bibliography: p.
  Includes index.
  ISBN 0-226-02968-9 (alk. paper)
    1. Knowledge, Sociology of.   2. Self-knowledge, Theory of.
I. Title.
BD175.A85   1989
121—dc19   89-4728
                                                    CIP

⊗ The paper used in this publication meets the minimum
requirements of the American National Standard for Information
Sciences—Permanence of Paper for Printed Library Materials,
ANSI Z39.48-1984.

To Alison, who really doesn't have to read it

CONTENTS

CHAPTER FOUR

The Six Stages: The Life and Opinions of a Replication Claim

CHAPTER FIVE

Analysts' Variability Talk: The Levels of Discourse Analysis

CHAPTER SIX
The Critical Problems of Writing the
Problem: A Double Text   169

CHAPTER SEVEN

The Fiction of the Candidate (Summer 1985)   194

APPENDIX

Nonbibliographic Sources and Other Secrets   221

Notes   227

ABBREVIATIONS AND PUNCTUATION

CSSSK	Core Set of Sociologists of Scientific Knowledge
ESRC	Economic and Social Research Council
NLF	New Literary Forms
R-awareness	Reflexivity as self-knowledge
R-circularity	Reflexivity as mutual constitution
R-reference	Reflexivity as self-reference
SOBER	Spirit Of BErtrand Russell
SSK	Sociology of Scientific Knowledge
SSRC	Social Science Research Council
TRASP	True Rational Successful Progressive (science from rationalism from SSK)
TRT	*The Reflexive Thesis*
WSB	"Warranting Scientific Belief"
6S	"The Six Stages"

( )	In interview transcripts parentheses enclose uncertain hearings, laughter, or pauses. Elsewhere they enclose parenthetical comments and references.
[ ]	In interview transcripts brackets enclose interpretations or interpolations. In quoted material they enclose interpolations. In invented dialogue they enclose authorial additions, such as references, which are not spoken.
. . . .	In interview transcripts and quoted material four dots indicate substantial omissions.
. . .	In quoted material three dots indicate brief omissions as they do in interview transcripts when they occur inside a turn. When they occur at the end of a speaker's turn in interview transcripts and in invented dialogue they indicate the continuation of the speech in that speaker's next turn, while their occurrence at the beginning of a turn indicates that the speech is a continuation of the speaker's last turn. Throughout the text they also indicate incomplete or interrupted passages.

FOREWORD

Doug Mitchell, Senior Editor
University of Chicago Press.

Dear Doug,
Here is my idea for a foreword:

FOREWORD

Doug Mitchell, Senior Editor
University of Chicago Press.

Dear Doug,
Many thanks for sending me the Ashmore manuscript. I have to say this is one of the most impressive manuscripts I have read in a long time: carefully researched and documented, highly unusual in its format, an important and serious contribution to a key topic, yet witty and clever throughout. It is without doubt an important contribution.

The subject matter of the manuscript is the "problem" of reflexivity, specifically as it arises in the sociology of scientific knowledge (SSK). SSK is a vigorous (some would say virulent) subdiscipline, as energetic in its research production as it is contentious in its epistemological predelictions, which has become increasingly influential both within the history and philosophy of science and in sociology and social science more generally. The central achievement of SSK has been the demonstration that even the most esoteric features of scientific and mathematical knowledge can be understood as social constructs; that scientific facts are not so much reflections of the world as persuasive texts, accomplished within and shaped by a complex of contingencies and circumstances. This is a significant achievement because it shows that no kind of knowledge need be exempt from critical scrutiny: in particular, scientific knowledge need not be considered a special case.

Ashmore asks what happens when the power and success of SSK is turned upon itself. Appropriately enough, the deconstructers of the "hardest possible case" of knowledge production (natural science) themselves become the target for deconstruction. But, far from the commonly envisaged spectre of self-destruction, Ashmore demonstrates how this approach makes possible a whole new area of exploration. In this treatment, the deconstruction of deconstruction does not just "cancel things out" but enables us to grasp the enormity of the consequences of scepticism relentlessly and authentically pursued. SSK's challenge to the realist presumptions of natural scientific practice throws doubt upon the notion of an objective world; the challenge to SSK in this exploration of reflexivity poses far-reaching questions about the very distinction between "practice" and "world." By this route, also, we see a way of recovering some of the initial excitement of early work in SSK, now beginning to wane somewhat as SSK settles into a self-confident institutionalised explanatory format.

Reflexivity has a salience for areas of thought far beyond the relatively narrow confines of the sociology of scientific knowledge. The grounds for knowledge have come under increasing challenge within a wide range of disciplines—anthropology, psychology, sociology, philosophy—and more recently in a number of intellectual movements which share a concern for the "problem" of representation and which cut across traditionally defined disciplinary boundaries—poststructuralism, postmodernism, literary theory, and so on. The general thrust of Ashmore's thesis will resonate with and give support to the concerns of these areas. The main difference is that Ashmore treats similar issues with extraordinary attention to detail. Whereas many existing discussions of reflexivity are unhelpfully abstract, Ashmore adopts features of the "case study" approach—a characteristic of SSK itself—to provide discussion and analysis based on close attention to transcribed interview responses, detailed documentary evidence, and so on. Far from the aporia sometimes imagined to follow the adoption of a form in order to study that form (as if recourse to a more abstract level of discussion might somehow immunise the author from contamination), Ashmore's approach opens up a whole wealth of imaginative possibilities for the treatment of profound aspects of representation.

Above all, Ashmore shows that reflexivity need not be conceived of as a "problem." Classically, the struggle of all phenomenologically inclined inquiry has been to deal with the accusation that the contingent basis of all perception and representation applies as much to the analyst's own determinations as to those of the subject. Under hard-nosed positivism, such objections are finessed by construing them as matters of methodic or technical adequacy. But phenomenology reveals its deeper commitment to mundane ontology (Pollner 1987) when it worries about the possibility of securing grounds which are more adequate than those of the subjects being analysed. The approach followed by Ashmore suggests a way of moving beyond this. The problem is in conceiving of reflexivity as a problem in the first place; as if it was at all profitable to seek an escape from realist ontology once we have committed to conventions of representation which buttress just that particular ontology. The strategy is to sustain and explore the paradoxes which arise when we attempt to escape the inescapable, not to attempt their resolution.

Of course, this perspective on reflexivity is bound to require modifications to expectations about what counts as an adequate ("useful") answer and, in particular, what counts as a serious approach to the problem in the first place. Ashmore eschews the heavy hand of earnest theoretical abstraction. And yet he shows how one can be entertaining and witty without losing any of the seriousness.

In sum, I think the manuscript should unquestionably be published. It will attract a wider than usual readership both because it deals with topics with a very wide range of significance and because it does this in a way which, with very few exceptions, has really not been tried before.

However, it follows from the above, Doug, that the *form* of Ashmore's argument is absolutely crucial to its effect. It is precisely the form of thesis which Ashmore exploits and interrogates to such devastating effect: the play between thesis-as-argument and thesis-as-an-occasioned-academic-product. Now I know there is a widespread feeling among academic publishers that what gets submitted as a (doctoral) thesis needs to be "turned into a book." Indeed, the convention seems to be that all traces of thesis-ness be exorcised. I'm not sure what the rationale is for this viewpoint (perhaps the arcane style of many theses simply doesn't make for good marketing), but I strongly recommend you resist this tendency in this particular case. The thesis should be presented "as is."

The interesting paradox, of course, is that you need to make clear that what you publish as a book is in fact a thesis, even though it *appears* to be a book. Perhaps you could try to get this point across by including some kind of spoof foreword? Obviously, a number of literary devices are available, well known to writers like Umberto Eco, which seek to situate the origins of the *contents* of the book in relation to the particular *form* in which it appears. Eco has a foreword in which he tells of the discovery of the manuscript of his *The Name of the Rose* in a monastery. That won't work here, of course, but you might use the occasion of a foreword to solicit an appreciative endorsement from some eminent figure in the field. S/he can then give some brief progressivist account of the pressing intellectual issues of the day, using this to provide a rationale for the significance of the manuscript, and hence explaining why and how the content (the thesis) must be apprehended in terms other than its circumstantial appearance (as a book).

I realise that by following this path, one necessarily flouts convention and will raise eyebrows in many academic publishing circles. Indeed, I would expect lesser publishers to baulk at the prospect of taking on this kind of project. This more conservative reaction does not (and perhaps cannot) see the interesting potential of a publishing project which attends to the central features of the argument being published. This is why the conventional publisher's reaction is to ask the author to re-present the "same content" differently. Through their lack of imagination, these publishers will have lost out. I am confident that Ashmore's thesis will benefit substantially from its handling by a bold publisher and, in particular, by an editor with a not inconsiderable amount of flair. I look forward to receiving my cheque.

Best wishes,
Steve Woolgar
Wolvercote, August 1988

ACKNOWLEDGMENTS

Intellectually, I am most indebted to the collective work of the sociology of scientific knowledge, and especially the writings of Collins, Latour, Mulkay, Barnes, and Woolgar. I also owe much to the work of such diverse reflexive enthusiasts as John Barth, Mary Douglas, Alex McHoul, Jorge Luis Borges, Alvin Gouldner, David Caute, Ray Holland, Douglas Hofstadter, Paul Feyerabend, Stanislaw Lem, Bernard Sharratt, Jacques Derrida, and Lawrence Sterne.

As a thesis, this book owes most to my supervisor, Michael Mulkay. Supervising is hardly an appropriate term for Mike's contribution. As friend, colleague, mentor, and intellectual sparring partner, he has no equal. Let me just say that this writing has developed as a product of and a contribution to a mutual dialogue of a rare kind. Thank you, Mike.

My interest in the problems of relativism—and my fascination with those outrageous writers who described themselves unashamedly as relativists—started in Malcolm Vout's course in the philosophy of the social sciences at Trent Polytechnic. A bold thinker and excellent teacher, Malcolm has since become a close friend and a firm supporter of the reflexive cause. Thanks, Malcolm.

And thanks also to Trevor Pinch, who as my other supervisor and internal examiner and lately as my research colleague and friend has always treated my arguments with patience and generosity even when he totally disagreed with them.

I would like to thank all the sociologists of scientific knowledge who generously gave of their time and energy to take part in the research. In particular, Harry Collins for disagreeing with me so creatively and for reading and commenting on the first draft of Chapter Four; Andy Pickering for putting me up, and putting up with me, in Edinburgh and recently in Urbana; Jonathan Potter, for many stimulating talks and whiskies and for the longest interview of them all; Steve Woolgar, for *really* understanding what it was all about, and lately for trying so hard to keep me off the streets; David Bloor, for so intriguingly refusing to be interviewed; and of course Michael Mulkay and Trevor Pinch whom I have thanked already.

I want to thank the British SSRC/ESRC for funding my studentship; everybody in the Department of Sociology at the University of York; and all contributors to the Discourse and Reflexivity workshops.

For helping to produce the thesis as a material object I have to thank Jean Pover, the computing facilities at Trent Polytechnic, and especially Andy Oldfield.

For their unstinting encouragement, enthusiasm, and financial assistance I am deeply indebted to my parents, Tom and Joan Ashmore: many, many thanks.

As a book, this thesis owes a great deal to the encouragement I have had from the generous reactions of such readers as Arthur Brittan, Kay Oehler, Graham Watson, and Don McCloskey as well as many of the people I have mentioned already including Pinch, Potter, Latour, and Woolgar. Indeed, to Steve Woolgar I owe not only the idea of sending my manuscript to the University of Chicago Press but also of contributing the Foreword.

To my editor, the anonymous publisher's readers, and all the staff at the Press who have done so much to help transform a thesis into a thesis, I owe especial thanks.

The production of the most beautiful (electronic) manuscript in the history of the world was managed with consummate skill by Vivienne Taylor. To her, and all at Computype (241 Hull Road, York YO1 3LA, U.K.), many thanks.

An earlier version of Chapter Four, "The Six Stages: The Life and Opinions of a Replication Claim," has appeared in Steve Woolgar, ed., *Knowledge and Reflexivity* (1988a) under the title "The Life and Opinions of a Replication Claim: Reflexivity and Symmetry in the Sociology of Scientific Knowledge." I acknowledge the permission of Sage Publications to reproduce it here.

Finally, then, to Alison Lindsay; without whom, nowt.

ABSTRACT

This thesis is an inquiry into the problems and possibilities of a reflexive sociology of (scientific) knowledge. Starting from a recognition of the inherently self-referential character of modern sociology of scientific knowledge which is due to the strong reflexive tie between its subject and its method (the explanation of explanation, the replication of replication), the study proceeds to examine the various ways in which practitioners conceive and subsequently manage the reflexivity of their practice. The management strategies identified vary from outright rejection through in principle acceptance to explicit attempts at celebration. It is to the development of this last strategy that the book itself aims to contribute. It tries not to be a metastudy; it wishes to write *in* its topic rather than *on* it.

The bulk of the text is taken up by a series of case studies in each of which a particular aspect of the discourse of sociology of scientific knowledge (and, in an early chapter, Kuhnian historiography and ethnomethodology) is interrogated self-referentially: What does it mean to make replication claims for studies which deconstruct replication claims? Is the claim of high variability in accounts self-exemplifying and what are the conclusions to be drawn from finding out? Is the very articulation of the methodological horrors subject to them, and if so does this matter?

A prominent aspect of the thesis, in keeping with its topical interest in reflexivity, is its concern with its own status as thesis, study, book, text, sociology, knowledge, etcetera. The problem of combining this necessary reflexivity with the book's equally necessary analytical concerns is recognised in and by a series of experimental textual forms ranging from the fundamental feature of the fictional framing of the first and final chapters to alliteration and the visible display of the three-hundred word limit in this

INTRODUCTION

Introductory Pre-Texts

Is there any knowledge in that subdiscipline which is called "sociology of scientific knowledge?"

> Alex Dolby (Letter, undated 1982)

It behoves a sceptical science to adopt an attitude of scepticism towards its own ascetic ideals.

> Theodor Adorno (1976:252)

It, too, must dance to its own music.

> Alvin Gouldner (1976:xvi)

An important task for the sociologist is to show that the construction of reality should not be itself reified.

> Bruno Latour and Steve Woolgar (1979:179)

Sociology may now have overcome its "imprinting" on mistaken parent figures—the natural and physical sciences—so enabling it to recover its history, its subject matter and most powerful analytical tools: it has come of age. The condition of this emergence is a strong sociology of knowledge capable of turning sociology upon itself in continuous criticism and collective self-reflection—reflexivity at last.

> Ray Holland (1977:271)

Don't kid yourself. If you are reading this you are going precisely nowhere. Let us continue to play with ourselves.

> David Caute (1971:78)

And start to speak.

> Jacques Derrida (1978:32)

TASKS AND REGULATIONS

The first chapter of the thesis shall be preceded by an introduction, so headed, defining the relation of the thesis to other work in the same field and referring appropriately to any findings, propositions or new discoveries contained in the thesis and to any important points about sources or treatment. (University of York 1983/84:59)

The first task of my Introduction is to introduce my readers into my text: You're welcome. The text is now yours. The second task of your Introduction is to consider whether what follows (preceding the first chapter of the thesis) is a contravention of the Regulation quoted above. Clearly, the formal aspect of the Regulation is here adhered to. The first chapter of the thesis is definitely preceded by an Introduction, so headed. The problem, I suspect, is to do with the content.

However, this second task will naturally have to wait until the Introduction has been completed. Unfortunately, at that point the Introduction will have been completed without having included the considerations that are its second task. Alternatively, if at some point preceding the first chapter of the thesis, such considerations are attended to, should they themselves be understood as a genuine part of the Introduction? To put this incipient dilemma another way: Can a discussion of the Introduction take place in the Introduction? Or is such a discussion inevitably something else; something that is outside and perhaps "above" the Introduction itself? Something we might perhaps call a Metaintroduction? If so, then the second task of your Introduction is vain: a simple impossibility. This concludes one "important point about . . . treatment" in the form of a definition of "the relation of the thesis to other work in the same field."

The third task of your Introduction is to explain why this text takes the form it does rather than . . . but I must not prejudge the second task. Let me put it differently: in order to be an authentic Introduction to (in) this text, it must strive both to talk about the world—in this case the thesis—to avoid "pathological navel-gazing" (Gouldner); and to talk of itself—in this case the Introduction—in the conviction that it is "a part of the very order that it describes" (Brannigan). To put it metaphorically—or, in this case, literally—it must carry out both the Regulation and the tasks. The Problem, of course, is how to do this successfully. The form—which is to say the content—of this Introduction is a small attempt at doing so. In this paragraph I have been "referring appropriately to [some of the] findings [and] propositions . . . contained in the thesis and to [some] important points about sources [and] treatment."

On the assumption that some of our readers remain unconvinced that I have now covered the full range of material (with the exception of "new discoveries" which is hardly likely) as specified in the Regulation, the fourth task of your Introduction is to introduce you in detail to the full range of introductions that are to be found in the text.

Introductions to the Thesis-as-a-Whole

There are two of these. The first you are still reading. The second is Chapter Two, ASHMORE, which gives a detailed, chapter-by-chapter account of the type you, perhaps, expected to find here.

Introductions to the Substantive Topic

Chapter One introduces the sociology of scientific knowledge by means of an introductory lecture, after which the core-set of sociologists of scientific knowledge introduce themselves. Chapter Two includes introductions to some of the work of some of these sociologists including Barnes, Bloor, Latour, and Pinch. The work of Harry Collins's "empirical programme of relativism" on scientific replication is introduced in Chapter Four; Chapter Five provides an introduction to Michael Mulkay's "discourse analysis" and particularly the claim for high variability in accounts; Chapter Six introduces Steve Woolgar's attempts to deconstruct the main features of metascience argument concentrating on the use he makes of the in principle/in practice dichotomy.

Introductions to the Thematic Topic

The thesis stands as a general introduction to reflexivity. A variety of writings on this topic are introduced in Chapter Two. Chapter Three introduces the problems of reflexivity. The problems of reflexive writing (practice) are introduced in the Introduction, in Chapter One, "Unsatisfactory Answers," and in Chapters Three, Six, and Seven.

Introductions to the Relations between the Topics

The relation between the sociology of scientific knowledge and reflexivity is introduced in Chapter One; in Chapter Two, especially in the entries for GRUENBERG, BARNES, BLOOR, COLLINS, LATOUR, MULKAY, PINCH, S. WOOLGAR, and ASHMORE; and in Chapters Four, Five, Six, and Seven.

Miscellaneous Introductions

Various other things are introduced in the thesis including the writing of fiction for serious analytic purposes (Chapters One and Seven), Bertrand Russell and self-reference (Chapter Two, PARADOX, and Chapter Five, " . . . a Dialogue . . . ," metahistory (Chapter Three), ethnomethodology (Chapters Three and Six), sameness/difference (Chapters Four and Six), the character of critical discourse (Chapter Six), the problem of the "meta" (Introduction, Chapters Three and Five), originality and copying (Chapters Four, Six, and Seven), the truths of fiction and the lies of fact (Chapter Seven), the problem of writing introductions (Introduction), and I could continue but I will resist the temptation; except to mention that the issue of when enough is enough is introduced in the "Miscellaneous Introductions" section of the Introduction and also in Chapter Four, "Stage Six," as well as somewhere in Chapter Five.

I think we can say, with confidence, that all the tasks of your Introduction have now been completed and that the Regulations of the University of York have not been frivolously dispensed with (or made mock of) in favour of indulging in some irresponsible reflexive game.

THE SIGNIFICANCE OF THE THESIS OF THE BOOK

I think the manuscript would benefit from an introduction which [briefly] states the significance of the argument for those outside of the social studies of science. (Reader 2 [TRT]:3)

Reflexivity is an issue which has salience for a wide range of intellectual concerns from literature to logic and from physics to photography. In fact, it is an issue with potential relevance for all modes of representational practice (Woolgar, forthcoming). To some it is a threat. To others it is a critical tool for use only against others. And yet to others still it is an opportunity. The interest in exploring the role of reflexivity in the sociology of scientific knowledge is that all three of these management strategies coexist. What accounts for this is the immediacy of reflexivity in this discursive arena. As a discourse which, much to the distress of some of its practitioners, is routinely treated as inherently and supremely critical of its object—an object which is routinely treated as uniquely capable of producing valid knowledge—it is not surprising that those who wish to defend the status of science respond to its critique by turning the critical discourse of the sociology of scientific knowledge onto itself. And thus some practitioners experience reflexivity—the move of "turning it onto itself"—as a threat. My argument in this book is that the reflexive move is double-edged. In that it entails a process of re-it-eration (the "it" being that which is actively being deployed in the "turning" as well as that which is the passive recipient of such deployment), reflexivity acts as much to preserve as to destroy. This book sets out to reevaluate reflexivity, to defuse its problematic reputation, and to show how a positive assessment of the phenomenon can open up new areas for scholarly inquiry (Woolgar 1988a).

Thus, the significance of the argument for readers outside of the social studies of science who perceive reflexivity as a threat is clear. This category of readers would likely include social scientists who are attracted to a relativistic, or constructivist, or postempiricist approach to their range of phenomena, but who find the prospect of understanding their own discursive practices in such terms rather disconcerting.

The intellectual tradition within which reflexivity and self-reference have been the objects of the most intensive study is undoubtedly philosophical logic. There have been periods in this extensive tradition when the self-referential and the paradoxical have been treated in a positive fashion (Fuller 1986). But the approach, at least in the Anglo-American world, which has been dominant throughout the modernist era (Nelson, Megill, and McCloskey 1987), is to treat such phenomena as paradigmatically destructive of rationality. As the guardians of the rational, philosophers and logicians have attempted, with much rigour and sophistication, though without much success, to rid us of the infection of reflexivity (Priest 1987). Interestingly, when rationalists are confronted with work that suggests that the most rational of practices—mathematics and science—are shot through and through with informal, rhetorical, practical reason, their most frequent response to such work involves *deploying* reflexivity in countercritical "tu quoque" arguments (Trigg 1980). The significance of the argument for rationalists is that it shows, by pointing to this kind of double standard, that their treasured rhetoric of consistency cannot consistently be deployed. However, for those philosophers (and others) who are concerned with the problem of knowledge, but who have ceased to believe in the traditional epistemological quest for foundations and justifications, the significance of the argument is that it suggests that we are indeed better off without them.

The history of reflexivity in the arts and humanities is as extensive as it is in philosophy. The difference is that the phenomenon has here been more frequently thought of as liberating than as threatening. Reflexivity promises a release, however temporary, from the constraints of representational realism. Experimentation with self-referential techniques has been a staple of the twentieth century avant gardes in literature, painting, drama, and film. The significance of the form of the book for those interested in such experiments is that their use in this serious scholarly context indicates that they need not be limited to the production of cultural products labelled as art or entertainment; in short, to fictions. Arguments are stories. Serious purposes can be addressed with nonserious means. Scholarly/scientific, nonfiction discourse is another form of rhetorical fiction; or so the argument runs.

For readers who are interested in texts—literary critics, discourse analysts, semioticians, rhetoricians, communications scholars—the significance of this text is . . . well, no doubt you will decide what it is in your various ways.

The significance of the argument, the significance of the form, the significance of the text; for social scientists wary of self-reference, for philosophers bored with foundations and prescriptions, for avant garde artists and post-everything textualists—can all be summed up in just one word: **wrighting.** But I wouldn't advise it (Ashmore 1989).

CHAPTER ONE

THE FICTION OF
THE LECTURER
(Winter 1983)

WHAT IS THE SOCIOLOGY OF SCIENTIFIC KNOWLEDGE?—A LECTURE

Lecturer: The sociology of scientific knowledge [SSK] is a fairly young
subfield of sociology, having been in self-conscious existence for less
than fifteen years (and possibly less than ten). One consequence of its
youth is that attempts at summary such as this lecture is claiming to
be—I'm sorry, I should have mentioned at the start that this talk has a
very specific title. It is the question: What is the sociology of scientific
knowledge? Anyway, I was saying that efforts to encapsulate our topic
are bedevilled by the fact that its history is continually in the process
of being written, unwritten, and rewritten by its various practitioners,
commentators, and critics, all of whom tend to claim for it different
origins, precursors, and lines of development as well as differing problematics, achievements, and findings. Which is not to say, as some of
you may be thinking, that there *is* no answer to the question we are
concerned with this morning. If you are thinking such thoughts, you
are also presumably thinking that I am cheating you: having inveigled
you here under the pretext of answering a question, I proceed immediately to claim that there is no answer. Well, of course I haven't
claimed that: at least not quite and at least not yet. All I have implied
is that there is no *one* answer—at the present. The story I will tell
you—*my* answer—is, I am afraid, only a version. To speak of versions in this way—a way that implies the principled nonexistence of
correct, best, or even better versions in any absolute sense—is, as you
will realise, to embrace a form of *relativism*. Our second fact of the
morning is that the sociology of scientific knowledge is itself a relativist discourse. The first fact, of course, was its age—or rather its youth.
This, as I have implied, has a bearing on the current availability—or
rather unavailability—of reliable facts about our topic.

1

One way to talk of what we might term the fluidity of conceptions of the sociology of scientific knowledge is by entering its discourse and speaking its language. Thus we can say that the character
of the sociology of scientific knowledge is a matter that is *socially
constructed*—these metaphors are very important and very prevalent
and I advise those of you who are interested to take note. Right; as I
was saying, what the sociology of scientific knowledge is (or rather
will turn out to be and to have been all along), is a matter that will be
settled, or socially constructed, by a process of *negotiation* among the
discipline's practitioners, commentators, and critics. At the same time,
such negotiations are also about just who is to count as a recognised
practitioner or commentator or critic of the sociology of scientific
knowledge. Furthermore, and this is the crux of the matter, there is a
third aspect of such social negotiations: the settlement of these apparently quite trivial social and historical questions—for example, X is a
true member; Y is a serious critic; *that* is the true history of the field;
these are its correct concerns—all these results *also* and *simultaneously* determine the *relevant existence* and the *real character* of the
discipline's realm of empirical phenomena. In the case of the sociology of scientific knowledge this realm is, of course, scientific knowledge itself.

What I have just said about the social processes of negotiation
and their outcomes is a paraphrase and an extension of the conclusion
to a paper by a sociologist at the University of Bath called Harry Collins. The paper, published in 1975, had the interesting title: "The
Seven Sexes: A Study in the Sociology of a Phenomenon or the Replication of Experiments in Physics." Collins's topic was a controversy
about the experimental manifestation of phenomena known as gravity
waves. (I would very much recommend that you read this paper, by
the way. It is listed in the Bibliography which I will give you at the
end.) Anyway, to continue—*our* topic is the production of knowledge
in a new sociological specialty. In principle—that is, if the theory can
be generalised—both topics can be illuminated by talking in terms of
social negotiation in the way that we have been doing. This means that
the sociology of scientific knowledge has, potentially, the interesting
property of being *self-exemplifying*. Let me explain: the concepts,
methods, and findings of the sociology of scientific knowledge—
which of course are about the concepts, methods, and findings of
(natural) science—can be *turned back* on themselves. Which is to
say that . . . Look, let's take an example. Let's take Collins's notion
of social negotiation amongst physicists. He claims in "The Seven
Sexes" that this process is responsible for the establishment or non-
establishment of physical phenomena. Right. That was published in
1975. Here we are, eight years later, and I am quoting his claim to you

as an established finding in the sociology of scientific knowledge. What has given it this status? There are many indicators that it does have this status among interested parties, by the way. Several sociologists claim to be influenced by it, and to have modelled their research and their own writings upon it. In fact, Collins himself claims that some of this secondary research has replicated his original findings. Barry Barnes, whose work should be relatively well known to students in this course, claims that he teaches Collins's work to his own students in a quite straightforward way. "The Seven Sexes" has recently been reprinted in two sociology of science readers. (These are Latour 1982 and Barnes and Edge 1982.) All of the major reviews of the subject treat Collins's findings as part-of-what-we-now-know: as, for instance, Mulkay does in his book *Science and the Sociology of Knowledge* [1979a]. So, how can we make sense of all this? One way, I suggest, is by making use of Collins's own findings about the processes of social negotiation. If we want to know how the sociology of scientific knowledge comes to know about scientific knowledge, we can use its own findings as a resource by applying them to *this* case of knowledge creation. Now, it is frequently considered that there is something rather *odd* about such a procedure. It would appear to be blatantly *circular*. It would also appear to introduce the spectre of the infinite regress: how would *our* investigation of *their* investigation (of scientists' investigations) be investigated, and so on, and on. All of these apparent consequences of the self-exemplifying character of the sociology of scientific knowledge can be expressed as "the problem of reflexivity." My own particular research is concerned with the differing perceptions of this problem and the different strategies and responses put forward to cope with it by practitioners of the discipline.

This lecture, on the other hand, will largely proceed as if this problem did not exist. This means that I shall *not* be paying attention to the problematic nature of imparting information, making knowledge-claims and, indeed, of lecturing as I do these things. Instead, I will tell you all about the sociology of scientific knowledge.

It started in Britain in the early 1970s—or perhaps in 1969 [Barnes 1969; Mulkay 1969]. People who described themselves as doing this thing—not that they all use the label I have given them: indeed many do not, preferring social studies of science or sociology of science or social history of science or anthropology of science or no label at all; it doesn't really matter, they say—anyway, those who started to do whatever it is or who advocated its being done, required, we can say with the benefit of hindsight, both *originality* and *importance* for their emerging enterprise.

Originality was claimed by a strategy of dissociating their new research programme from others. One such programme that they dissociated themselves from in the early seventies was the mainly American, functionalist sociological specialty dominated by the work and students of Robert Merton, known as the sociology of science. This body of work was claimed to be either irrelevant, or to be wrong, or to be in need of drastic modification and supplementation. One of those who currently claims the irrelevance of the Mertonian programme is Collins, who writes of it thus, and I quote:

A crucial feature . . . is the assumption that the ultimate answers to the question are Nature's, mankind being only a mediator . . . . This program does not require sociological attention to the content of scientific answers [because] the answers become interesting to the sociologist only if they are wholly men's answers rather than Nature's—that is to say, if they are not "properly" a part of scientific knowledge. [1983d:266–67]

The originality of the new programme . . . the *claimed* originality, rather; it has not remained uncontested. For instance, it has been disputed on behalf of Mertonianism by an American sociologist called Tom Gieryn. His paper, the replies, and his counterreply are all in the May 1982 edition of the journal *Social Studies of Science*. The references are: Gieryn 1982a and 1982b; Collins 1982d; Mulkay and Gilbert 1982c; and Krohn 1982. This is a particularly interesting debate, by the way, for those interested in how such disputes are rhetorically and argumentatively constructed. Anyway, I seem to be digressing again. As I was saying: the new programme's originality vis-à-vis Mertonian sociology of science was that it *was* interested in the content of scientific knowledge because it *does* believe that such knowledge consists of people's answers rather than Nature's. To the new programme, scientific knowledge was not going to be a "black box"—a phrase from Whitley's influential 1972 paper, meaning an unexamined given; a "fact," in other words. Thus, the sociology of scientific knowledge can consider itself a distinct enterprise from one that it *defines* as treating the content of science as unproblematic. Its originality, then, is based on the claim, in Collins's words, to be "concerned precisely with what comes to count as scientific knowledge and with how it comes so to count" [1983d:267].

The new subject also separated itself from the two mainstream traditions in the sociology of knowledge, the one proceeding from Mannheim (and from Marx) and the other from Durkheim. The claimed distinctiveness of the sociology of scientific knowledge from the work and traditions of these theorists is, however, far less dramatic than in the originality strategy we have just examined. It consists of freely taking up and modifying some of their analytic ideas while insisting that both Mannheim and Durkheim had mistakenly and illegitimately protected Science itself from sociology of knowledge analysis. Such a "failure," in quotes, can itself be understood in sociology of knowledge terms by, for instance, invoking the theorist's social context or social interests.

As for the positive borrowings from traditional sociology of knowledge, the invocation of "interests" as an explanatory resource, as in the work of Barnes and MacKenzie, for example, is essentially Mannheimian, whereas the notion of "social imagery"—the idea that natural knowledge is in effect a transposition of social arrangements and experience, and thus that the true origin of "Nature," in quotes, is in Culture and Society—*this* idea is fundamentally Durkheimian and has, for example, been used in Bloor's work. (References here: Barnes 1977; Barnes and MacKenzie 1979; MacKenzie 1978 and 1981a; Bloor 1973, 1976, and 1982a.)

A different strategy for claiming originality was necessitated by the explicit claim to be concerned with the content of science; such a claim brought the practitioners of our topic into direct competition with that part of the academic division of labour whose domain has traditionally been scientific knowledge: namely, philosophers of science and epistemologists. To claim distinction from Mertonian sociology of science or from Mannheimian sociology of knowledge involved a strategy that we might call topic-differentiation. To claim distinction from an area of academic practice that dealt with the same topic required a somewhat different strategy. This requirement was satisfied by claiming a different *method:* original, first-order, matter-of-fact, naturalistic, empirical research as opposed to the derivative, second-order, speculative, prescriptive, and prejudiced announcements of the armchair-bound professional philosopher. I don't think I have exaggerated these caricatures very much: they are prevalent in the literature—the *sociological* literature, that is. Philosophers, of course, describe things differently. For an example of both styles of polemic, have a look at a volume called *Rationality and Relativism* edited by Hollis and Lukes [1982], and especially the articles by Barnes and Bloor [1982] and by Hollis [1982].

To deal with the problem of the *status* of their work and its findings with regard to contemporary debates in philosophy, sociologists of scientific knowledge frequently tend to characterise their research, in the standard empiricist manner, as providing evidential *support* for those epistemological theories they approve of, such as the Duhem-Quine thesis of the underdetermination of theory by evidence and the thesis of the theory-ladenness of observation. I will explain these later if anyone wants me to and we have time. [Meantime, readers could consult Harding 1976 for the former theory, and Hesse 1980 for the latter.] Equally, the findings of the sociology of scientific knowledge are claimed to *disconfirm* less well-liked philosophical schemes, such as Popper's falsificationism and other forms of rationalism and empiricism.

The three strategies for claiming distinctiveness and originality that I have talked about so far can be presented schematically in this diagram I have put up on the board here. [See table 1.]

Now this is all very neat. Unfortunately, this pattern does not hold for the case of the history of science, where distinctions between its concerns and those of the sociology of scientific knowledge have been far more equivocal. While some of our sociologists have stressed the importance of concentrating on contemporary scientific episodes [Collins 1981a, 1983a] and have even written against the study of past science [Collins 1981f], others have always worked on historical materials [Barnes and Shapin 1979]. A problem here, of course, is the arbitrary nature of the contemporary and the historical: How do you categorise a piece of scientific research that took place, say, five years ago? Furthermore, it could be argued that however up-to-date one's topic might be, all research is necessarily past-orientated. Sociologists of scientific knowledge have tended to use the labels "history" and "sociology" as flexible resources for argument. One well-known writer in the field even told me that there was no point in interviewing him for my research, as he was a historian and not a sociologist at all. In terms of academic boundary creation and maintenance, history of science is seen as an area that is partly coextensive with the sociology of scientific knowledge—see for instance Shapin's review of a set of historical studies which has the revealing title: "History of Science and its Sociological Reconstructions" [1982]. The part of history of science that is not assimilated in this way is treated as sociologically incompetent—as history done in the wrong way.

The felt importance of the new subject can be understood as following from or accompanying the strategies of distinctiveness stroke originality that I have described. Oh yes, I've forgotten to mention the relation of the sociology of scientific knowledge to ordinary mainstream sociology. Well, perhaps it is not worth mentioning: not much notice has been taken of the subdiscipline by the major discipline, and vice versa. However, certain established sociological "schools"—for want of a better word—have moved into the study of science. I am thinking of Harold Garfinkel and his students who have done a series of ethnomethodological studies of the work of the sciences; and of John O'Neill and his students who have analysed science texts from a sort of "critical phenomenological" perspective. If you have a look at the contribution by Lynch, Livingston, and Garfinkel [1983] to the Knorr-Cetina and Mulkay reader called *Science Observed* [1983] (which should definitely be in the library), you will be able to pick up

Table 1   Three Strategies for Claiming Originality for the Sociology of
Scientific Knowledge

	From	Method		Topic	
1.	Mertonian	Sociology	of	Science	[Knowledge]
2.	Mannheimian/				
	Durkheimian	Sociology	of	[Scientific]	Knowledge
3.	Epistemology	Philosophy			
		[Sociology]	of	Scientific	Knowledge

Note: Points of difference stressed in each case are in [brackets].

the ethnomethodological work. For the O'Neill material see his 1981a
or 1981b.

I was about to tell you about the felt *importance* of our topic for
its practitioners. It went something like this: sociology—the lowliest
of the sciences—promised to be able to explain the roots of credibility
that sustain the self-evident and the obvious as well as the True, Rational, Successful, Progressive [TRASP; see Collins 1981e] pronouncements of natural science itself. If it could be shown that natural
scientific knowledge—whose status as *the* arbiter and standard for all
other knowledge activities, including sociology, is still extraordinarily
high, if not entirely unquestioned; if *this* kind of knowledge could be
described as resting on no foundation more impressive than the contingent social circumstances of groups of interested—in both senses—
human actors, then the consequences should be quite remarkable. For
instance, such a conclusion would appear to warrant a reevaluation of
the major epistemological thrust of Western philosophy since Des-
cartes. Second, if physics can be explained by sociology, this threatens
to invert the hierarchy of the sciences. Third, the project of the sociology of scientific knowledge has major and direct implications for the
practice—including the teaching and learning—of the social sciences.
Throughout your course you will have come into contact with versions
of natural science. In Economics, for example, an image of the natural
sciences probably forms an implicit backdrop to your studies while
acting as a taken-for-granted standard by which work in the discipline
is judged. Here in Philosophy and Methods—and probably also in
some of your Sociology and Psychology courses—an image of the
natural sciences is made explicit. This image then forms the basis for
the formulation of the longest-running and most serious methodological question in social science: Can and/or should the social sciences be
like the natural sciences? The sociology of scientific knowledge does
not pretend to *answer* this question; instead, it provides the materials
for an entirely different picture of what the natural sciences actually
are and of how they actually work. Should this new picture manage to
replace the old one—and there are signs that this is happening to a

limited extent—then the basis on which this perennial methodological dispute is formulated will be fundamentally changed. Good examples of this new approach to this old question are Knorr-Cetina 1981b, Latour 1981, and Toulmin 1982.

Fourth, and finally, the project of the sociology of scientific knowledge promised to produce a wealth of fascinating reflexive problems for some future PhD student to research. For instance, how does an explanation of credibility achieve credibility for itself? Will this be easier than other attempts, such as those it takes as its topic and describes in its research, because it *has* described them? In other words, will its knowledge of how knowledge is made enable it successfully to make its own knowledge? Or will its last act be a reflexive explanation of why and how it failed? Anyway, time is getting on, and I have promised to avoid such questions this morning.

Right. I was talking of the potentially earth-shattering consequences of a sociology of scientific knowledge. How was such a revolutionary project to proceed? Two authors offering early programmes were Barry Barnes and David Bloor. Presumably because both operate from the same institution—the Science Studies Unit at Edinburgh University—they have been frequently lumped together; and indeed it is certainly not difficult to extract a similar content from their writings, and to reconstruct what is *not* similar as merely differences in emphasis. For our purposes here today, however, I will separate them. Barnes, in his *Scientific Knowledge and Sociological Theory* [1974], calls for a programme that treats science as a form of culture just like any other. The techniques of cultural analysis, as developed in cultural sociology and social anthropology, should be applied in a matter-of-fact way—meaning without any epistemological misgivings—to the cultural institution of science and its cultural product of scientific knowledge.

Bloor's programme is perhaps the best-known artifact so far to have come out of the sociology of scientific knowledge. I would suggest that this is due to its presentation in his book *Knowledge and Social Imagery* [1976] as an explicitly labelled *programme* consisting of four brief (and therefore quotable) tenets. Actually this programme appeared earlier in a slightly different form in Bloor's 1973 paper entitled "Wittgenstein and Mannheim on the Sociology of Mathematics," and was also discussed in John Law's "Is Epistemology Redundant?" [1975]. Anyway, here are the tenets of the strong programme in the sociology of knowledge as given in Bloor's book [1976:4–5]:

1. [Causality] It would be caused, that is, concerned with the condition which bring about belief or states of knowledge. Naturally there will be other

types of causes apart from social ones which will co-operate in bringing about belief.

2. [Impartiality] It would be impartial with respect to truth and falsity, rationality or irrationality, success or failure. Both sides of these dichotomies will require explanation.

3. [Symmetry] It would be symmetrical in its style of explanation. The same types of cause would explain, say, true and false beliefs.

4. [Reflexivity] It would be reflexive. In principle its patterns of explanation would have to be applicable to sociology itself. Like the requirement of symmetry, this is a response to the need to seek for general explanations. It is an obvious requirement of principle because otherwise sociology would be a standing refutation of its own theories.

What, perhaps, is most noticeable about these statements is their tone of "optimistic scientism." This is Bloor's own phrase. He claims to be, quote, "more than happy to see sociology resting on the same foundations and assumptions as other sciences" [1976:144]. Actually, almost nothing of subsequent work in the sociology of scientific knowledge has followed the strong programme in its entirety—and this includes Bloor's own studies in the sociology of mathematics [1973, 1978]. It is generally the causality tenet and the scientism that is implicitly or explicitly rejected. For instance, Collins prefers to talk of explanation rather than cause [1981e:216], and Latour, who pioneered the "laboratory study" style of research (for the results, see Latour and Woolgar's *Laboratory Life* [1979]); Latour exhorts those who study science to be "agnostic" and to "do everything to make clear that we do not want and do not intend to be scientists . . . . It would be unethical for a student of science to ask for the garment, status and role of a scientist" [1981:212]. (I should mention that Collins also rejects Bloor's reflexivity tenet, but I will resist the temptation to expound on *that* topic for the moment.) Perhaps the implicit rejection of Bloor's scientistic stance by most sociologists of scientific knowledge has to do with their affinity with the interpretive and antipositivist movement in current social science. Such affinities can be gauged by enumerating the variously claimed influences on and precursors of the subject. These include the later Wittgenstein [1958], the earlier Lakatos (of *Proofs and Refutations* [1976], if you know that work; it's well worth reading if you don't). Feyerabend [1975, 1978]. Uh, who else? The idealist philosopher of history, Collingwood [1946]. Mary Douglas [1975], the radical Durkheimian anthropologist, and Mary Hesse [1974], the postempiricist philosopher; both of whom have intellectual relationships with, especially, Barnes and Bloor which amount to mutual involvement rather than one-way influence [Douglas 1982; Hesse 1980]. Peter Winch [1958] and the so-called rationality debate; the best book for all that is Bryan Wilson's *Ratio-nality* [1970]. And of course Thomas Kuhn—the earlier Kuhn, that is, of *The Structure of Scientific Revolutions* [1970a], before he recanted his radical relativism. Kuhn, by the way, is often credited with the (re)discovery of the work of Ludwik Fleck [1979] as first published in 1935. Fleck is far and away the best candidate for true SSK precursor-ship yet found. Finally, from the ethnomethodological input we can note the influence of Schutz [1967] and Garfinkel [1967]. It's interest-ing to note the large number of philosophers and the small number of professional sociologists in this list. If all its members have a "family resemblance"—to quote Wittgenstein [1958]—it would appear to be something to do with relativism. And, to get back to Bloor's strong programme, it is its relativistic nature, as implied in the impartiality, symmetry, and reflexivity tenets, which has been the focus for most of the *philosophical* criticism that it has received.

Relativism is indeed a feature of any investigation that translates "knowledge" into "whatever counts as knowledge" in any particular society, culture, period, language, discipline, group, and so on. *Not* so to translate, say cognitive relativists, is to fall prey to an ethnocentric view: it is to operate under the illusion that one can *really* know which beliefs are *really* true and/or *really* false. In practice, such a stance merely ends up by denigrating the beliefs of others and celebrating one's own [Dean 1978:287]. Virtually all self-described sociologists of scientific knowledge hold to some form of cognitive relativism, as I mentioned earlier. It was our second fact of the morning, as I recall. However, they differ in the strength of the variety held and the enthusi-asm with which they hold it. Some feel that it is something to which it is reluctantly necessary to admit [Knorr-Cetina 1982:135], "as if it were a crime rather than a necessity" [Bloor 1976:143]. Others like Bloor, whom I have just quoted on crime and necessity, feel the need, nevertheless, to qualify their relativism with soothing adjectives like "methodological" [Bloor 1976:142, 1982d]. Some take it for granted, as Mulkay claims to do [in interview: MM17], while others explicitly celebrate it as Collins does when he labels his version of sociology of scientific knowledge, "an empirical relativist programme" [1983a]. Collins has also cowritten a theoretical defence of relativism: Collins and Cox 1976. Whatever variety of relativism is claimed, practitioners in the field are unanimous in arguing—or simply assuming—that their variant is able to circumvent the usual philosophical critiques of this theory of knowledge. At this point, I don't want to go into what these are. If you don't know, and want to find out, by all means ask me; I will be happy to come back to them later on, if we have time. [Readers may turn straightaway to Chapter Two, BLOOR, COLLINS and GRUENBERG for discussions of these critiques.]

What I want to do now, in the little time remaining to us—I appear to have run on a bit. Never mind, it's better to have too much to say than too little. Or perhaps you don't agree. Anyway, I will finish this talk with a glimpse of the current state of play in the sociology of scientific knowledge, in order to give you some idea of the large variety of work that has been done under this title. The scholars concerned include not only undergraduate-trained sociologists but also ex-physicists, ex-mathematicians, ex-philosophers, ex-astronomers, ex-psychologists, and ex-anthropologists. The academic bases of these practitioners include not only ordinary university sociology departments such as at York or at Keele, but also interdisciplinary Science Studies departments such as at the universities of Manchester, Edinburgh, and recently Bath. The sociology of scientific knowledge is no longer confined to Britain (if it ever was). Scholars in France, the Netherlands, Germany, Australia, Canada, and even the United States are now involved.

The literature has been growing and diversifying at such a rate that an influential reviewer—David Edge, director of the Science Studies Unit at Edinburgh and joint founder and editor of the subject's house journal, *Social Studies of Science*—Edge had to ask: "Is There Too Much Sociology of Science?" [1983]. There have been studies of controversies that are internal to science [Collins 1975; Travis 1980a, 1981; Kemp 1977; Wynne 1976; Dean 1979] and ones that have gone public [Markle and Petersen 1980; Dolby 1975; Wynne 1982; Nelkin 1979], as well as studies of consensus-formation [Collins 1981c; Pickering 1981a; Harvey 1981]. Studies have been done of the influence of science on society [Shapin 1980] and the influence of society on science. What "society" means in the phrase "the influence of society on science" has been formulated in both macro-sociopolitical terms [Forman 1971; Cooter 1979; Shapin 1979; Harwood 1977] and micro-intradisciplinary terms [Harvey 1980; Pinch 1980; Edge and Mulkay 1976; Harwood 1976]. Attempts have also been made to connect these two levels of analysis [MacKenzie 1978; Douglas 1982; Knorr-Cetina and Cicourel 1982]. There have been studies of whole scientific specialties which have included models of their inception, growth, and decay [Lemaine et al. 1976; Mulkay 1975; Edge and Mulkay 1976]; studies of small networks of scientists concerned with a particular issue or involved in a particular episode—Collins [1981d] calls such networks "core-sets" [Collins 1974, 1981a; Collins and Pinch 1979, 1982; Gilbert and Mulkay 1984a]; and studies of a single laboratory [Latour and Woolgar 1979; Knorr-Cetina 1981a; Lynch 1985].

Theoretical concerns, while similar in the ways I have described—namely, a dominant interest in the content of science coupled with a relativist or constructivist or contextualist approach to re-

search—can be seen nevertheless to vary from a traditional sociology
of knowledge approach which explains the outcome of scientific episodes in terms of the interests of the scientists involved [Barnes and
MacKenzie 1979; MacKenzie 1981a; Pickering 1980a; Shapin 1979]
to a more ethnomethodological approach which is concerned with the
microprocesses of practical reasoning in the laboratory [Garfinkel,
Lynch, and Livingston 1981; Lynch 1982; Woolgar 1983c]. The researcher may take great pains to become conversant with the technical
details of the area of science in question [Gilbert and Mulkay 1984a;
MacKenzie 1981a; Lynch 1985; Collins and Pinch 1982] in order to
achieve "participant comprehension" [Collins 1983a], or may prefer to
take a stance of anthropological strangeness in order to avoid believing
in the science in question [Latour and Woolgar 1979; Latour 1981].
Sociologists of scientific knowledge variously take the "Science" of
science to reside in esoteric technical procedures [Shapin 1979; Lynch
1982; Collins and Harrison 1975], or formal scientific papers [Gilbert
1976a; Bazerman 1981; Woolgar 1980; Morrison 1981; Law and Williams 1982; Myers, forthcoming], or in informal discussion and "negotiation" [Collins 1975; Collins and Pinch 1979; Pinch 1981; Mulkay
and Gilbert 1982a], or nowhere at all [Latour 1981]. The methodology
employed might be documentary historical research [Barnes and
Shapin 1979; Rudwick 1986; Garfinkel, Lynch, and Livingston 1981;
MacKenzie 1978, 1981a; Latour 1983; Wynne 1976], the rhetorical
analysis of scientific texts [Gusfield 1976; Mullins 1977; Yearley
1981a; Myers 1985; Anderson 1978; O'Neill 1981b; Mulkay, Pinch,
and Ashmore 1987], the analysis of conference data [Potter 1983],
participant observation [Lynch 1985; Collins and Pinch 1982; Knorr-
Cetina 1981a; Zenzen and Restivo 1982; Latour 1978], informal and
informed depth interviewing as a substitute for participant observation
[Collins 1975, 1981a; Edge and Mulkay 1976], or interviewing with
the aim of collecting data not as evidence for what went on but simply
as material that can be analysed to display the patterned forms of scientific talk itself [Gilbert and Mulkay 1984a; Potter and Mulkay 1985].
In Kuhnian terms, the research topic might be normal science [Collins
1974; Knorr-Cetina 1981a; Law and Williams 1982; Latour and Woolgar 1979] or it might be extraordinary, or potentially revolutionary,
science [Dolby 1975; Collins and Pinch 1982]. There are also studies
of historically accepted scientific revolutions [Shapin and Schaffer
1985; Frankel 1976; Farley and Geison 1974; Latour 1983; Forman
1971; Young 1981]. Similarly, the topic might be in the scientific
mainstream [Collins 1981a; Knorr, Krohn, and Whitley 1980] or it
may be "on the margins of science" [Wallis 1979; Nowotny and Rose
1979; Hanen, Osler, and Weyant 1980].

The sociology of scientific knowledge has frequently concerned itself with "deconstructing" the folk-terminology of scientific method [Latour 1980a:53]. The terms that have received such treatment include discovery [Woolgar 1976b, 1980; Brannigan 1981; Mulkay 1985], proof [Bloor 1978; Pinch 1977], replication [Collins 1975, 1976; Travis 1981; Ashmore 1983, 1985, 1988, 1989; Mulkay 1984a, 1985], problem [Callon 1980], fact [Latour 1980a; Latour and Woolgar 1979; Law and Williams 1982], observation [Latour 1978; Shapin 1979; Woolgar 1988b; Pinch 1985], and application [Potter 1982; Ashmore, Mulkay, and Pinch 1989].

The range of sciences investigated includes particle physics [Pickering 1980a, 1981a, 1981b, 1984], quantum mechanics [Harvey 1980, 1981; Pinch 1976, 1977], parapsychology [Collins 1976, 1985; Collins and Pinch 1979, 1982; Wynne 1979], phrenology [Shapin 1979; Cooter 1979; Gieryn 1987], twentieth-century genetics [MacKenzie 1981d; Brannigan 1979; Harwood 1980b], nineteenth-century geometry [Bloor 1976, 1978; Barnes and Law 1976], eighteenth-century geology [Rudwick 1982a, 1986; Yearley 1981a, 1981b], artificial intelligence [Collins 1987a, 1987c; Woolgar 1985, 1987; Bloomfield 1987b; Fleck 1980], biochemistry [Latour and Woolgar 1979; Kemp 1977; Gilbert and Mulkay 1984a], radio astronomy [Garfinkel, Lynch, and Livingston 1981; Edge and Mulkay 1976; Gilbert 1976b; Woolgar 1976a, 1976b], the classification of species in botany [Dean 1979], the classification of species in anthropology [Barnes 1981b], economics [Whitley 1986; Colvin 1985; Ashmore, Mulkay, and Pinch 1989], the physiological psychology of worms [Travis 1980a, 1981], the "designing of the dinosaur" [Desmond 1979; Latour 1980b], the field study of primates [Wieder 1980; Latour 1978], the social psychology of personal constructs [Potter 1983, 1988], sedimentology [Law 1980], astrophysics [Pinch 1980, 1981, 1986], laser building [Collins 1974, 1985; Collins and Harrison 1975], intelligence testing [Harwood 1976, 1977, 1980a], the sociology of scientific knowledge [Ashmore 1985, 1989; Pinch and Pinch 1988; Woolgar 1981b, 1983a; Collins 1983d; Mulkay, Potter, and Yearley 1983; Mulkay 1984a; Oehler 1983], and many, many others.

In the next few years, the major developments in the field are likely to be in the analysis of the social construction of technological artifacts and systems [Pinch and Bijker 1984; Bijker, Hughes and Pinch 1987; MacKenzie and Wajcman 1985], the investigation of various aspects of science in public [Collins 1987b; Silverstone 1985; Ashmore, Mulkay, and Pinch 1989], and the theoretical and empirical articulation of the "actor-network" approach [Callon, Law, and Rip 1986; Law 1986; Latour 1987]. Perhaps we may also see some sustained interest in reflexivity [Mulkay 1985; Oehler and Mullins 1986; Fuhrman and Oehler 1986, 1987; Potter 1987; McKinlay 1986; Fuller 1986; Woolgar 1988a; Ashmore 1989].

To sum all this up is not easy. There are several versions of what all this activity amounts to. Each new review [Mulkay 1980a; Bloor 1982c; Shapin 1982; Collins 1983d; Whitley 1983; Brown 1984; Pinch 1988; Woolgar and Ashmore 1988; Ashmore 1989, ch.1; Lynch, forthcoming] claims that the *important* message is something rather different than every other review claims. Of course, the writing of such reviews, along with the conducting of debates and polemics, and the formulating of programmes for future research, is as much a part of the activity of the field as is the research I have been enumerating. Participants tend to see such activity as peripheral; as talking about the sociology of scientific knowledge rather than doing it [Collins 1983a: 102]. However, one of the things that the sociology of scientific knowledge teaches us is that such activities are not only indispensable to the construction and maintenance of the discipline as a definite and distinctive entity but also, and more important, that they are essential to the construction and maintenance of its product as a coherent piece of credible sociology.

So what then, you may well be asking, *is* the product of all this welter of activity? One answer, which is not as frivolous as it may sound is: a lot of paper and a lot of print. On second thought, such a reply is not staggeringly helpful. But if we put it another way and say the product is a series of "texts"—whether written or spoken, formal or informal, or even verbal or nonverbal; a text being here an ensemble of interpretables—if we put it like that, then we have a principled way of avoiding the sort of answer that is implied in asking for a product: namely, a neat list of actual findings about scientific knowledge which constitutes the coherent piece of credible sociology that is the sociology of scientific knowledge. If we talk in the postmodern fashion of texts rather than findings—a way of talking which, as such luminaries as Richard Bernstein [1983], Clifford Geertz [1980], Paul Ricoeur [1971], and Richard Rorty [1982] have recently reminded us, is becoming perhaps the dominant discourse heard in the interstices of philosophy, social science, and literary studies—this sensitises us to the permanently interpretable and reinterpretable nature of all such cultural products. But such a reinterpretation is outside the scope of this lecture. I see my time is now up. All that it remains for me to do is to encourage you to read the texts—in the conventional sense—that constitute the fascinating and paradoxical enterprise of the sociology of scientific knowledge. Are there any questions?

PROFESSOR GEEZER'S AWKWARD QUESTION

From the back of the room someone rises and speaks.

"A Plump Bald-headed Old Geezer" [Mulkay 1984b]:[1] My dear young
man, I found your talk most interesting. As an academic of many
years' experience, who prides himself (not excessively I hope) on the
width of his intellectual interests, I had become aware to a limited extent of the trend in sociological studies of science which you have described so clearly, yet in such brief span. Your talk has enabled me
more fully to appreciate (as an outsider, albeit one who has, may I say,
an almost "vested" interest in such issues) the central objectives of
these so-called sociologists of scientific knowledge and their supposed
achievements. What surprised me most of all in your historical account was the lack of humility of those involved. Do they really believe that, in ten short years, they have been able to dismantle all the
main accomplishments of Western culture? Surely this smacks of hu-
bris? Moreover, they seem blithely unaware of the paradox on which
their conclusions are built. Having deconstructed scientific knowledge,
they insist that we accept their arguments because they have been scientifically demonstrated. What nonsense! I take it that this problem
arises under the heading of "reflexivity," about which you did not talk
today. My question is also a challenge, namely: Can you successfully
resolve this paradox in their and your own position? [Mulkay 1984c][2]

He resumes his seat with (as the Lecturer thinks) an air of smug self-
satisfaction.

Lecturer [to himself]: How did he get in here?[3] This lecture was supposed to
be for students [and readers ignorant of SSK] only. I was supposed
to be this week's Expert, expected to expound on an important and
interesting topic for their edification and instruction. Naturally, I
would expect and welcome questions from the audience; the process
of education should always aim at achieving a state of mutual dialogue. But to be faced with such a question—or as the man so rightly
puts it, such a challenge—is, in this particular social context, something of a problem. I suppose that I could simply refer him to my
thesis; after all, it advertises itself as dealing with reflexivity in the
sociology of scientific knowledge. The trouble—apart from such an
answer being considered both arrogant and evasive—is that the thesis
has hardly begun. So how *am* I going to answer him?

If you are wondering why the Lecturer does not simply answer the question, here and now, straightforwardly, without further prevarication: I can tell

you that he is most unhappy about the task. He understands that "to respond to the question 'seriously' is to buy into the auspices of the question" (Lynch, letter, 8 November 1983) as one of his correspondents will shortly be reminding him. The question asks him to accept that the appropriate thing to do with paradoxes is to (try to) resolve them. He knows that this is a form of destruction and he feels reluctant to join in. Eccentrically as he often thinks, he finds he enjoys paradoxes, even to the extent of taking pleasure in increasing their number. But let us rejoin his ruminations at the point where they are about to be replaced by his attempt at an answer to the question which questions the question's auspices, much as I have been doing here. The Lecturer's very mouth is formed for his very opening word when—lo and behold!—he perceives that the audience now includes the Core Set (Collins 1981d) of Sociologists of Scientific Knowledge (CSSSK).[4]

Introducing the Core Set of Sociologists of Scientific Knowledge

Lecturer [unfortunately silent once more and increasingly paranoid]: How did they get in here? Anyway, I'm not sorry they missed my lecture. They would only have disagreed with me and with each other, perhaps especially about my stress on the current lack of consensus in the field. My playing the role of "SSK expert" in such company would be bound to lack a certain degree of credibility. But as it is, my colleagues have transpired in the nick of time. The Old Geezer is bound to prefer an answer straight from the horses' mouths, as it were. And it is also possible that their reflexive reflections may not be heard as entirely satisfactory, in which case the answer I was about to give may well seem less obscurantist and more to the point.

> *[Out loud, and at last addressing himself to the Plump Bald-headed Old Geezer]:* Well, Professor Er . . . , it seems that by a fortunate circumstance a number of my colleagues in the sociology of scientific knowledge are present. Perhaps they could introduce themselves and then perhaps you might care to put your question to them.

Professor Geezer: An excellent notion.

CSSSK: Right. We will introduce ourselves in alphabetical order so that any implications of a hierarchy are minimised.[5]

Ashmore: My name is Malcolm Ashmore. I am a student of Michael Mulkay's at the University of York where my research is a reflexive study in/on SSK. My current interests concern the nature of reflexivity and its maintenance through the use of more flexible literary modes, such as the thesis. In the future I will study the discursive practices of applied social science while getting my thesis published.

Barnes: My name is Barry Barnes. I work in the Science Studies Unit at Edinburgh University. My special interests are scientific culture and

cognition. I don't believe in labels and I am a relativist, an instrumentalist, and a finitist. I am currently working on the nature of self-
reference. I will shortly develop a new sociological analysis of power.

Bloor: My name is David Bloor. I too work at the Science Studies Unit in
Edinburgh. I have cause to be interested in the strong programme and
the sociology of mathematics. My present and future scientific concerns are with grid/group analysis and a sociological interpretation of
Wittgenstein.

Collins: The name's Harry Collins and I'm the director of the Science Studies Centre at the University of Bath. I have investigated contemporary
scientific controversies in physics and parapsychology. My discovery
of the permeability of replication has been replicated. Currently, I am
developing my empirical programme of relativism as a tool for science
policy. Later, I will become interested in artificial intelligence and the
way science is presented in public.

Gilbert: Nigel Gilbert. Sociology of science is just one of my many interests, but in this field I have worked on the growth and decline of research specialties and have recently been involved in the analysis of
biochemists' discourse. I am based in the Sociology Department at
Surrey University and am an ex-student of Mike Mulkay's.

Harvey: My name is Bill Harvey. I have done research in the sociology of
quantum mechanics at the Science Studies Unit, Edinburgh. I am now
teaching physics and making sure that Ohm's Law is never violated by
the social contingency of my pupils' experimental incompetence.

Harwood: Jon Harwood here. I am based at the University of Manchester.
My research has been largely concerned with the "hard case" of argumentation in social science and social policy over the nature of intelligence. I was previously a student at the SSU in Edinburgh. In a few
years I will become involved in a study of academic engineering.

Knorr-Cetina: I am Karin Knorr-Cetina and am currently at Bielefeld University in Germany. Since I began the first laboratory study I have
been involved in doing and writing about laboratory ethnography from
a constructivist, opportunisticist, idiosyncraticist, transepistemic perspective. In the future I will move several times.

Latour: I am named Bruno Latour and I work in Paris. I did the first laboratory study and developed the notion of inscription devices to explain
the material embodiment of ideas and scientists' obsession with writing. I am an agnostic about science though this may change. Now, I
am interested in the laboratory as a social actor which I will develop
through a study of Pasteur.

Lynch: Hi! I'm Mike Lynch. I have collaborated with Garfinkel on the ethnomethodological study of scientists' technical practices, as well as
doing a similar study independently which will soon be published.

After finally getting a job at Boston University, I will continue to work on scientists' representational practices.

MacKenzie: I'm Donald MacKenzie. I work in the Sociology Department at Edinburgh. Most of my research in SSK has been concerned with the social interests of statisticians. Some of my work has been in collaboration with Barry Barnes who supervised my postgraduate studies in the Science Studies Unit. My current interest is in applying the SSK approach to military technology; this interest will later extend to analysing the "social shaping" of information and communication technologies.

Mulkay: My name is Michael Mulkay. I am based in the Department of Sociology at York. I have published far too many books and articles and have researched radio astronomy and bioenergetics. I am currently elaborating the programme of discourse analysis into a form that is capable of recognising its own textuality. I am soon to become head of the department and will compensate by writing about humour and the application of social science.

Pickering: I'm Andy Pickering. I am doing research in the unit at Edinburgh on the high energy physics community. I am one of the few really *committed* relativists in the field. When my PhD is published, I will work in the United States and become a pragmatist.

Pinch: This is Trevor Pinch. Most of my research has been done at Bath, some with Harry Collins and some, on the sociology of the sun, independently. I am currently at York, where I am extending the empirical programme of relativism to the analysis of technological artifacts. Having done this, I will attend many conferences while researching everyday economic reasoning and the practical application of economics.

Potter: Jonathan Potter. I'm really only a social psychologist, or so my colleagues in the Psychology Department at St. Andrews think. My work in SSK has been on the analysis of social psychologists' discourse, which I carried out while a student of Mike Mulkay's at York. I will later become the only serious discourse analyst in the field and will move south to the University of Loughborough.

Travis: My name is David Travis. I work in the Sociology Department at North London Polytechnic. While a student of Harry Collins's at Bath I started my PhD research on the "memory transfer" controversy in worm running, which is a serious branch of animal psychology. At some time in the future I will complete my thesis and return to Bath to work on a science policy project.

Woolgar: This is Steve Woolgar and I work in the Department of Sociology—later Human Sciences—at Brunel, the University of West London. I started in this field as another of Mike Mulkay's students and did research on accounts of the discovery of pulsars. I am interested in studying the phenomena of practical reasoning, including the phenomena of practical reasoning *about* the phenomena of practical reasoning. This interest will continue, as will my interests in reflexivity and the ethnographic method. I will also become very concerned with computing software.

Yearley: My name is Steven Yearley. I am at Queen's University, Belfast. My main research in SSK was pursued at York under the supervision of Michael Mulkay and was concerned with the analysis of evaluation arguments in earth science texts. I am now writing the philosophy of social science. Research into these matters will proceed, together with a new interest in Irish science policy.

CSSSK: That's it, we're afraid. Of the several possible absentees, John Law is too busy, Steven Shapin says "sorry, but I'm only an historian," David Edge is greatly missed, Brian Wynne couldn't be contacted, Alex Dolby's most relevant comment appears elsewhere, Richard Whitley wasn't certain about his membership status, Daryl Chubin, Sal Restivo, and Tom Gieryn send fraternal greetings from the States as do Michel Callon from France, Wiebe Bijker from the Netherlands, and Gus Brannigan from Canada. Various other analysts have unfortunately been overlooked. But not to worry, I'm sure that between us we can put you right on any points, Professor Er . . . , that you may care to raise.

Professor Geezer: Well, I'm sure I speak for us all when I say that I am most grateful for this unusual opportunity. I'm sure that our young Lecturer here won't take offence, but I think it is not entirely untrue to hint that he was making rather heavy weather of a question of mine when you er, turned up. So perhaps I can prevail upon you to step into the breech? I was asking an admittedly somewhat tricky and provocative question about—as I see it—the apparently rather paradoxical basis of your enterprise. We would appreciate it so much if you would enlighten us on the nature of your "reflexive problematic," if I may so put it.

CSSSK: Groans. Mutters. An air of discomfort. Exchanges of "oh no, not *this* again"-type glances. Etcetera.

Professor Geezer: Oh dear, I seem to have . . . Well, let's put that one on the back burner, as an époche, so to speak. Nevertheless, the nature of this unique and remarkable occasion encourages me to press you on a not unrelated matter. As sociologists we are more often than not engaged directly or indirectly with the investigation of *others*. I think it would be fascinating to hear your views on our Lecturer's reflexive project which, ha ha, puts as it were, the boot on the other foot. If, of course, he wouldn't mind?

Lecturer: No, no, not at all. I would just like to request that we start with a friendly witness. Mike?[6]

But *I* would just like to request that we first avail ourselves of the following

Discouraging Pre-Texts

What science ever discouraged self-scrutiny by its own methods?
A. W. McHoul (1981:114)

It is a paradox that while the "radical doubt" of relativism has posed the most challenging questions of recent sociology, this doubt is a "theoretical" and not a "practical" possibility, whether the practice is "doing sociology," teaching or anything else.
Michael Young (1973:213)

While professional philosophers acquire by their special training the difficult skill of bootstrapping just near, but never beyond the edge of solipsism, [sociologists] are ill-equipped to cope with such ventures.
W. Baldamus (1976:204)

One needs to write about the least prestigious members of a scientific community in the same terms as the most prestigious. Where contemporaneous studies are involved this can upset one's peers.
Harry Collins (1981e:223)

In one sense this entire [section] can be taken as commentary on the frequent utterance of our participants: "That's **[un]interesting.**" [7]
Bruno Latour and Steve Woolgar (1979:232)

Unsatisfactory Answers

Mulkay: When you came along I was not receptive to your original suggestions, was I? I kept trying to persuade you to do something else and used all the same old stale arguments that, uh, our colleagues have used in other places in response to your project. [MM 8101–03]

Bloor: I am afraid I feel that it is a bad choice of subject. Like introspection you can do too much of it. It's all pots and pans and no pudding. [Letter, undated 1982]

Collins: It can be paralysing because you spend so much time looking up your own anus, as it were, that you never get on and do what seems to me to be **interesting** things. [HC 0503–04]

Harvey: It's nice to sort of say, "Right, I'm going to try to do this about people who are trying to do this about other people." But I can see

there might be problems about that, that you end up contemplating
your navel and . . . bogged down in a vicious circle. [BH 0116–18]
Pinch: My feeling generally about reflexivity is that certainly there's a general problem, but in terms of actually doing concrete research it's debilitating to actually think about problems of reflexivity . . . . You just
start to sit there, you don't actually do anything. [TP 1106–09]
Knorr-Cetina: It would get kind of incestuous, wouldn't it? [Letter, 22 July
1983]
Barnes: Not a topic I'd choose for myself. [BB 0102]
Collins: If you're going to put all this effort into it, let's do it on an area of
science that is intrinsically more **interesting** . . . . I wouldn't dream of
researching a social science. [HC 0206–09]
Pinch: I myself find natural science more **interesting,** but that's just my
taste. [Letter, 12 February 1982]
Bloor: I suppose there is no accounting for taste. Why not try a first-order
study? [Letter, undated 1982]
Latour: Taking your complicated case as a proof that knowledge is socially
fabricated seems to me quite unnecessary because your readers will
take that as hair splitting. If it is a subset of daily activity take a *daily*
activity! [Letter, 14 June 1982]
Collins: I don't see it as a very hard case and I don't see that much is
going to come out of it of *general* application. [HC 0210–11]
Harwood: I'm sure you *can* do a sociology of SSK, but, as you note yourself, who will be surprised by it? (By contrast *many* are surprised/
provoked by a sociology of scientific knowledge.) [Letter, 13 August
1982]
MacKenzie: The point of the discipline is explaining the world in some way,
um, and I think too much—*some* degree of focus on the internal social
relations and intellectual constructions of the discipline's a good thing
but too much is a bad . . . . It's getting too internally fascinated. [DM
3020–24, 3016]
Pickering: You're going to find everybody you interview is going to say,
"Yes, we are reflexive," and they're all going to ask you where it's
going to get you. I can't imagine how you can write a very **interesting**
thesis on it. [AP 0103–05]
Barnes: I see nothing more or less **interesting** in studying the group you
have picked just because it happens to be engaged in the same sort of
work as yourself. I *don't* accept your point in fact that it is a peculiarly
well-chosen subject just *because* of the reflexivity involved. [BB
0109–15]
Collins: I honestly see you know, I'm sorry, but I see this as a kind of waste
of resources. [HC 0506–07]
Harwood [getting up to leave]: I am not willing to take time to provide the

kinds of documents which your project requires . . . . There are other things which I am desperately keen to do which must take priority. [Letter, 13 August 1982]

Bloor [at the door]: I am afraid that I am going to refuse to be interviewed. [Letter, 4 May 1983]

Pinch: It presents peculiar "political" problems since the audience for your work will be the people you study. Be warned—you are bound to make an enemy of everyone! [Letter, 12 February 1982]

Knorr-Cetina: And end in a blood bath, n'est pas? [Letter, 22 July 1983]

Gilbert: My initial reaction, I must confess, was extremely negative. I'm getting more adjusted to the idea. [NG 4514]

Pinch: I think your project is a good idea . . . . It would be a very worthwhile contribution. [Letter, 12 February 1982]

Ashmore: That's what I thought [all of] you were going to say.[8] [Interviewer: SY 2051]

Professor Geezer: Tut, tut. I can understand your pique, but I'm not sure that this serious academic discussion is either the time or the place for it. And anyway, it would appear from the last few remarks that you might be winning them over. Perhaps, therefore, this may be an opportune moment to readdress my original question to this eminent gathering. So, lady and gentlemen, how do you manage the problem of the paradox of reflexivity?

CSSSK: What problem?

Yearley: I think we're already stuffed full enough of paradoxes that reflexivity, if it is a paradox, isn't too much of a consternation. [SY 3145]

Gilbert: I'm somewhat impatient of people winding themselves up into knots on these kinds of issues. [NG 4220–22]

Barnes: [My position on reflexivity] is one of indifference. [BB 0103–04]

Gilbert: Nobody has anything **interesting** to say about reflexivity. [NG 4421]

Collins: I can't see what you can do with it. And I can't see what *use* it is. [HC 0219–20]

MacKenzie: In principle, reflexivity is always there. I must admit never to have been terribly worried by [it]. [DM 2366–67]

Lynch: Some order of reflexivity is inevitable and hardly something to claim to justify the validity of one's own inquiry. [Letter, 8 November 1983]

Collins: I just ban reflexivity! [HC 1514]

Professor Geezer [to the Lecturer]: Well now. Your colleagues don't seem exactly convinced that "reflexivity" names anything worth their, or your own, attention. With the exception of Dr Collins, whose desire to ban it altogether suggests that it cannot be *entirely* unproblematic, one would think we were discussing . . . er . . . well, I can't think of an appropriate analogy. But anyway, something which is certainly not worth such *concentration*.

Lecturer: If my colleagues would oblige us with some brief renditions of

THE FICTION OF THE LECTURER   23

their usual approach to their own practice, followed by a few descriptions of occasions where reflexive work has been undertaken by members of the field, we may begin to glimpse the nature of the *practical* barrier that appears to prevent any successful combination of empirical study with what I am convinced is the highly **interesting** practice of reflexive inquiry. I think Dr Collins might start us off. Harry?

Collins: My advice to scientists, for instance, is "for Christ's sake, don't take relativism seriously. You'll never do another piece of decent work in your life." [HC 2007–09]

Pickering: [Scientists] often wonder why I'm doing it. [But they] don't reflect very much on their practice. They have a very kind of naive view of what they do when they come to articulate it. [AP 0605–07]

Collins: I can't see what difference it's supposed to make to *my* practice. Just as I don't expect my studies to make any difference to them, to the *scientists'* practice. I'm not trying to change physics. So I can't see that a study of the sociology of science of the same sort would necessarily have an impact on the way sociology of science is practised; would or should. [HC 0401–07]

Harvey: We may have displayed that scientists, when they talk about scientific method producing facts, are suffering from [false consciousness], and we show that, we show that some people—that, uh, what they're doing is not that and we tell them what they're doing. And you seem to be implying that we've got the same problem. [BH 3609–12]

Barnes: Sociology of science, sociology of scientific knowledge have definitely grown in an unusual way outside of the mainstream. And I *don't* understand why, um, why it has happened . . . . And of course through the seventies people got together far more and started defining themselves and being talked about, and I very much see the idea of the field as it were, growing up after the fact which I've never taken much **interest** in. I'm afraid I'm not **interested** in what happened. [BB 1413–16, 0310–13]

Knorr-Cetina: Frankly, I love and know my colleagues in science studies too much to wish to read too much of them, not to mention *about* them. [Letter, 22 July 1983]

Gilbert: I was worrying about reflexivity when I was doing studies on the growth and decline of research specialties. I wanted to know where I really was in sociology of science, reflexively. Was I in the "up" period, in which case I should stay in the area, or in a "down" period, in which case I should go and do something else fast! [NG 4399–4404]

Travis: I've tended to sort of, to wander off into side issues [like] can sociology of science explain itself? . . . At one time I indulged myself in going off on these things. [DT 1110, 1208]

Harvey: Within the limits of a paper you address yourself either to these methodological issues or you present empirical data. I have presented empirical data but OK, there is a problem there certainly. [BH 2608–10]

Pinch: The funny thing is that I get **interested** in the problem of reflexivity when I'm not doing empirical work. When I'm doing empirical work and I've got interviews to analyse, scientists to interview, going on ahead, starting to produce theories of scientific consensus, I'm not **interested** in reflexivity. But then when I'm not doing that—about two years ago I wasn't doing that, I sat back and thought, "Well, what problems can I look at?" And I actually thought I'd write a paper about reflexivity arguing against Harry and I haven't—I've got it somewhere half-written and someday I'll probably come back to that again.[9] I just see there's more pressing problems than reflexivity. [TP 1206–12]

Travis: These questions of self-understanding and self-reference . . . I may not have any answers to these things. I have, uh, some empirical material and, uh, some half worked-out things that I would love to be able to get back to but, uh, for the moment it's just impossible. [DT 1206–08]

Professor Geezer: Well, well, well! I was under the impression that this last set of speeches was supposed to begin to show the utility of a reflexive stance. And yet here we are, having arrived at a point where such a concern is represented as practically impossible. To put it as dramatically as I can, I wonder if I may quote from one of your texts, Monsieur? "Given the pressure of a scientific career, reflexivity is equivalent to suicide" [Latour 1978:24, n.14]. May we assume, young man, that you have found some way out of this impasse?

Lecturer [weary now; this was all taking a long time]: Why don't we listen to my colleagues one more time. After all, the concern is at least as much theirs as it is mine.

Harvey: In practice and certainly in print, you take it back to a reasonable level to show your concern about the issues, and we all know it's a problem and that's as far as you go. [BH 2917–3001]

Collins: You're going to have even more reflexive problems, if you like, because for the purposes of this study you're going to have to treat the sociology of scientific knowledge as completely constructed, and having no kind of reality at all, with it kind of being totally negotiated. And yet, boy, you're going to have to assume that your findings have got some objectivity, have an out-there-ness. That's going to be even harder to pull off than the tricks that I do! [HC 1815–20]

Pickering: If you ask me "am I reflexive?" the answer is "yes I am." I analyse the way people tell stories and I tell stories myself. I'm not really sure what more you can do apart from document the fact that I analyse other people's stories and I assure you that I'm telling a story myself. [AP 0107–09]

Yearley: What I think is **interesting** about reflexivity is the way that people evade the implications of the paradox, and I think it's other people's evasion that is **interesting** and instructive rather than that we should create an experience out of facing the anxiety itself. So why I seem to run down reflexivity is because with these paradoxes my feeling is that the best thing to do is *not* to confront them face on as somehow I feel that you're trying to do, but to see how they are an achieved accomplishment. So that always to look at them at one remove, but perhaps if you want to take the problem seriously to say, "Well, I must do it much like other people do." But not—I'm not sure that you can get anywhere by taking it on for yourself as a real-worldly problem. [SY 3240–53]

Potter: How do you deal with the issue of forever contextualised attributions of reflexivity? [Letter, undated 1982]

Latour: I think [our] friend Steve Woolgar would be much more of a help for you because he loves convoluted subjects! [Letter, 14 June 1982]

Woolgar: But the second dimension [we] produce *must* be that you're making the reader think about what's involved in talk; what's involved in reporting; what's involved in telling tales about the world. Now there's a danger that, um, to the extent that you—it's a question of balance—to the extent that you push [this dimension] the whole enterprise could be read as, um, reflexive games, um, which is silence. Right? [SW 5801–06]

And silence there was. Briefly. Just as the Lecturer was thinking that a smattering of Woolgar-silence would be something to be welcomed after the noise of this serious academic debate, he glimpsed the Old Geezer getting to his feet once more. The Lecturer was determined to forestall him.

A Vote of Thanks and a Suggestion for Further Reading

Lecturer: May I say, before we all finally leave, how much I have enjoyed both the questions and the answers that we have had today. However, it seems that none of us so far has satisfactorily answered Professor Er . . . 's original question. Today's exchange is only the first part of a possible "answer"—if that is any longer the appropriate term. However, I am in the process of preparing an Encyclopedia of Reflexivity and Knowledge which will eventually cover every aspect of our topic.[10] Although at present it is woefully incomplete,[11] you are all welcome to consult it. Thank you for your attention.

[Reader, or] Member of the Audience: But where can we find this Encyclopedia of yours?

Lecturer: Did I say mine? No matter. You have only to turn the page . . .

CHAPTER TWO

AN ENCYCLOPEDIA
OF REFLEXIVITY
AND KNOWLEDGE

An Encyclopedic Pre-Text

There could be infinite sayings about reflexivity, and still reflexivity would not be captured. Reflexivity will exhaust us long before we exhaust it.

Hugh Mehan and Houston Wood (1975:159)

ASHMORE

Reflexivity is the major topic of Malcolm Ashmore's theses (1985, 1989) which he explores by focusing on various aspects of the discourse of sociology of scientific knowledge. SSK is a particularly apposite focus for the study because of the reflexive tie between its findings about science and the "scientific" methodology that constructs them. Among the major practitioners of SSK, there is a great diversity of views on the proper role of reflexivity. Some (e.g., COLLINS and PINCH) seek to outlaw it, seeing it as a paralysing influence on their practice and seeing the assumption of similarity between the object and the method of investigation upon which a reflexive stance rests as "arbitrary, unnecessary and undesirable" (Collins and Pinch 1982:190). Others (e.g., BARNES, BLOOR, and LAW) accept reflexivity in principle, usually on the grounds of full generality or of self-consistency. However, such programmatic advocacy is largely sterile and has little noticeable effects on the output of these practitioners. Others still (e.g., LATOUR, WOOLGAR, and MULKAY) have made various attempts to incorporate the serious recognition of reflexivity into their analytic practices. It is to this last enterprise which Ashmore's thesis claims to contribute by attempting to develop, articulate, and utilise a series of "new literary forms" in and by which reflexivity can be permanently sustained *without* the analysis thereby degenerating into a form of "stagnatory autotelicism" (McHoul 1982:102).

Chapter One consists of a fictional Lecture, as given by, perhaps, the author to, perhaps, undergraduate social science students, with the title "What Is the Sociology of Scientific Knowledge?" This straightforward and entirely unreflexive—in Ashmore's sense—exposition is designed as an introduction to the substantive topic of the thesis and serves the purpose usually served by an introductory literature review (which, of course, it is). The lecture is followed by an awkward question about the apparently absurd consequence of the reflexive application of SSK's findings to SSK, which the Lecturer finds difficulty in answering despite the intervention of many of the practitioners of the subject, who proceed to give an informal commentary on reflexivity which seems designed largely to debunk the Lecturer/author's overblown and rather obsessive (as they see it) concern with reflexivity. (This section consists mainly of a collage of SSK participants' statements taken from correspondence and interviews.) Despite the Lecturer's best endeavours the awkward question does not receive a satisfactory answer.

To aid the understanding of the members of the audience, the Lecturer invites them to consult his unfinished Encyclopedia of Reflexivity and Knowledge which constitutes Chapter Two. The material in this chapter is wideranging both in form and in content. The entries vary from cross-references to brief essays on major figures in SSK (Barnes, Bloor, Latour, Pinch) including, of course, those practitioners with the most direct relevance to the rest of the thesis (Collins, Mulkay, Woolgar, Ashmore). The content, while centred on SSK, ranges over general sociology, ethnomethodology, anthropology, psychology, Marxist science studies, philosophy, fiction and literary study, and even strays into logic and metamathematics. Also included is an analysis of the terminological confusions apparent in the variety of usages of the word.

Chapter Three is concerned to elucidate and display the meaning of reflexive practice by an examination of the uses and limitations of "tu quoque" arguments. These arguments use the idea of self-reference for critical purposes. A major and relevant example is the antirelativist self-refutation argument. The chapter shows, by looking at two cases of the use of the tu quoque (in Kuhnian historiology and in the ethnomethodological problem of the "reflexivity of reflexivity"), that the negative conclusions of these arguments, such as self-refutation, are neither singular nor necessary. Ashmore's thesis, on the contrary, is that the reflexive self-reference that the tu quoque correctly points to can be celebrated rather than avoided. In the pursuit of this ideal, the chapter (and the thesis as a whole) attempts to show the positive benefits of self-reference both by defusing its supposed traps—the infinite regress of metadiscourse, the impossibility of being both a participant and an analyst at once, the inevitable self-destructiveness of a self-referential approach—and by adopting an attitude of serious nonseriousness toward the writing's own paradoxical nature.

Chapters Four, Five, and Six are applications to SSK topics of the kind of analysis developed in Chapter Three's investigations of Kuhnian and ethnomethodological discourse. Chapter Four is concerned with the work of Harry Collins on replication in science. Recently Collins has claimed that his own original studies of this phenomenon have themselves been independently replicated and that because of this the findings of (all) these studies are now validated. In general terms, the original findings claim to show that what is, or is not, counted as a replication is the contingent outcome of complex social negotiations and thus that replication cannot act as an unproblematic criterion capable of validating the existence of a phenomenon. Using an adapted version of one of Collins's original replication studies (1976), Ashmore examines his replication claim and the disjuncture between its auspices and the findings that are its object. This chapter includes material from interviews conducted with those analysts most closely associated with the claim at issue. It also incorporates dialogues between the Author and Collins, and between a Critic and a Friend of the replication claim. The chapter also includes a reflexive treatment of its own replication candidacy vis-à-vis Collins's original studies. In terms of SSK theoretics, the chapter, most particularly in the Friend-Critic dialogue, is concerned with the nature of "symmetry" (Bloor 1976): Can a symmetrical approach be sustained in practice, most especially when the roles of participant and analyst are inextricably (con)fused, as they are in this case? The chapter concludes with a conclusively inconclusive conclusion.

Chapter Five takes as its topic the programme of discourse analysis as developed by Michael Mulkay and his collaborators. One major empirical claim of this programme is that participants' accounts on any given topic are subject to high variability. Ashmore's interest in this claim is to ask whether it is self-exemplifying. If it is, this would mean that analysts' claims about levels of account variability would vary greatly. If it is not, this would entail a low degree of variation in such accounts. Taking his cue from a particularly strong and unusually explicit high variability claim (Gilbert and Mulkay 1984a:11), Ashmore carries out his reflexive inquiry in terms of the three types of variability isolated by Gilbert and Mulkay. These are between the accounts of different speakers, between the same speaker's accounts in different contexts, and between accounts from the same speaker in the same context. The upshot of Ashmore's detailed analytical exercise is the finding of a massive *in*variability in these accounts; in other words the claim for high variability is found not to be self-exemplifying. The final sections of the chapter deal with a paradox produced by the analysis, namely, the paradoxical "metaconclusion" of the simultaneous support and lack of support for the claim entailed in finding either that it is self-exemplifying or that it is not. The chapter concludes, as befits the complex findings of its analysis, with two contradictory endings which are designed *not* to be read as alternatives.

Theoretically, the chapter is mainly concerned with the "participant/ analyst dialectic" and the related issue of the connectedness of levels of analysis, both of which were raised in Chapter Three. Ashmore's concern throughout is to deconstruct the theory and practice of level separation. His use of a variety of new literary forms including "strange loops" (Hofstadter 1980), dialogue, and parody aids this deconstructive project.

The topic of Chapter Six is Steve Woolgar's studies in the explanatory and argumentative strategies of SSK discourse. Perhaps because of the intensely reflexive nature of this topic—Woolgar's texts are doing the same thing (and facing the same problems) as Ashmore's text is doing (and facing)—the experiments in form which play a relatively minor role in previous chapters are here all-pervasive. The chapter is structured as a "double text" of which the First is a conventional analysis of the ways in which Woolgar's texts variously deploy the in principle/in practice dichotomy which structures Woolgar's formulation of ethnomethodology. The Second Text is made up of a series of commentaries, interior monologues, digressive analyses, and other miscellaneous materials most of which attempt to address the problems of writing The Problem; "The Problem" being one of Woolgar's terms for the fundamental uncertainty of discourse. These problems are dramatically displayed by the regular breakdown of the First Text occasioned by its continual failure to deal adequately, by conventional analytical means, with its own reflexive nature. By the device of the double text, then, Ashmore seeks "at the level of textual representation" (Woolgar 1984) to deal *directly,* as topic, programmatic, and method, with reflexive writing itself.

Chapter Seven is Ashmore's final chapter and, as is usually the case with final chapters, its topic is the thesis itself. This is explored in a "novel" way by means of a "fictional" oral examination of a "fictional" thesis and its "author," both of which bear a strong resemblance to the "real" ones. The bulk of the "chapter" consists of a "factual document" which is the "transcript" of the "recording" of the "examination." This "section" is introduced by three "author's notes," all of which "disagree" as to the precise fictional or factual "status" of the "transcript."

The major themes of Chapter Seven are the links between facts and fictions, the problems of reflexive conclusions, the benefits and penalties of games playing, and the nature of originality. The topics from the rest of the thesis that are discussed in the greatest depth are the status of the Lecture as a textual form, the problem of readings, "research programme construction," and the various gains and losses of self-studies in general and the reflexive study of SSK in particular.

The fictional form (or forms) of this concluding chapter is the most sustained attempt in the thesis to do scholarly work by nonscholarly means. The new literary forms advocated and practised throughout are here put to their most extensive and intensive use. Ashmore clearly considered that the rigidity and irreflexiveness of the standard conclusion was such that only its total and uncompromising replacement by a radically different textual form could hope to prevent the production of a reflexive thesis ruined by a nonre-flexive conclusion.

Ashmore's prime concern, then, is with the development of a sustain-able reflexive practice. The aim, it seems, is to show that Reflexive Sociology can be something other—and something more—than a slogan, a moral stance, or even a thesis. Through the practice of "wrighting," the articulation of reflexive concerns may become a practical possibility for social science inquiry in general. That, at any rate, is Ashmore's thesis.

See also CANDIDATE.

ATTENDING TO TERMINOLOGY

The term "reflexivity" is used in a variety of ways. Before we look at these directly, we should do some etymology.[1] The prefix "re-" implies back, again, against, reversed. The Latin root of the main body of the word is *flectere,* to bend. So we have "to bend again" or "to bend back." Perhaps even here we can glimpse a disturbing sense of redirection and even reversal that implies some disruption of the normal course of things. From this basis, we can detect a splitting into the two main (if overlapping) forms of *reflect* and *reflex,* both of which can be further differentiated as follows.

Reflect

The Discourses of Seeing: The Image of/in the Mirror
Optics. Reflection of light; laws of reflection; angle of reflection.
Microscopy. Reflecting microscope—image produced by mirrors not lenses.
Telescopy. Reflecting telescope—image produced by concave mirror and magnified by eye piece.
Lens manufacture. Reflex[2] light—lens with a reflecting back, visible when a light shines upon it.
Photography. Reflex[3] camera—type in which reflected image can be seen up to moment of exposure.
Painting. Reflected light—an area painted as if illuminated by light from another part of the picture.
Shakespearean language. To reflect—to cast a light.

The Discourses of Thought and Intellection
Reflect on/upon—to think deeply and deliberately upon a topic.
Reflection—the above process.

The Discourses of Morality: Ethics and Politics
Reflect on/upon—to censure or reproach.
Reflection—a censure or a reproach; that which is responsible for discredit.
To reflect—to bring harmful results.

Reflex

The Discourses of Automatism
Biology, physiology, psychology. Reflex action—one which occurs automatically as a response to an external stimulus.

Behaviorist psychology. Conditioned reflex—a "learned" automatic response to an arbitrary stimulus.

The Discourses of Self-Reference
Grammar. Reflexive form—indicating that the action turns back upon itself; reflexive verb—indicating the identity of subject and object; reflexive pronoun, etcetera—referring to subject.

Logic. Reflexive (of paradox)—synonym for self-referential.

Linguistic philosophy. Reflexive relation—that which a term must have to itself if it also has it to something else; irreflexive relation—that which a term cannot have to itself; nonreflexive relation—that which a term may or may not have to itself.

Miscellaneous Discourses
Geometry. Reflex angle—an angle greater than 180 degrees and less than 360 degrees.

Radio. Reflex wireless set—one which uses the same valve for both low and high frequency amplification.

Botany. Reflexed—bent abruptly backward or downward.

Shakespearean language. To reflex—to direct or project.

With an etymological background as complex as this, it is not surprising that uses of "reflexive" and "reflexivity" in social science discourse tend to be subject to unsystematic variation. What are we supposed to understand by reflexive sociology (Gouldner 1970; O'Neill 1972a), or reflexive and dialectical analysis or theorizing (Roche 1975), or reflexive practice (Ashmore 1985, 1989)? What does it mean for reflexivity to be put forward as a criterion for good work in the human sciences (Bloor 1973, 1976; Oliver and Landfield 1962; Scholte 1972; Holland 1977; Phillips 1976; Snizek, Fuhrman, and Miller 1979)? Is there a difference, and if so what is it, between Gruenberg's (1978) problem of reflexivity and the problems of reflexivity described by Sandywell et al. (1975)? What is meant by reflexive individual, reflexive interpretative procedures, reflexive use of knowledge systems, and reflexive practical accomplishments (all phrases from Chua 1974)? When Blum claims that sociology studies and exemplifies reflexivity (1974:201) and Chua claims that sociologists neglect reflexivity (1974:243), do these authors disagree? Does McHugh's (1970) discussion of truth as reflex (a variety of positivism) have anything to do with reflexivity? Does Woolgar's (1983a) reflective position on the relation between accounts and reality? And what of reflectivity

(Sjoberg and Vaughan 1979)? What, finally, can it mean to say that reflexiveness is the reflexive feature of reflectiveness (Blum 1970:315)?

Reflexivity as Self-Reference

Social science can be considered an implicitly self-referential discourse in that if it is about humans and their social arrangements then it is (also) about those humans in those social arrangements who are responsible for the production of social science (see ETHNOGRAPHY, GRUENBERG, PSYCHOLOGY, SOCIOLOGY, MERTON AND THE MERTONIANS). However, in most social science, and indeed in the majority of discourses of all kinds, this self-referential aspect is latent, in that it has no obvious or immediate consequences. But in metascience, and especially in SSK (see LATOUR, COLLINS, S. WOOLGAR, GRUENBERG), the consequences of self-reference are manifest. Reflexivity as self-reference is also found in its acute form in psychology, literary study, and in logic and mathematics (see PSYCHOLOGY, DISCOURSE ANALYSIS, ETHNOGRAPHY, FICTION, PARADOX, SELF-EXEMPLARY TEXTS). For our distinctive purposes we will designate this form of reflexivity "R-reference."

Reflexivity as Self-Awareness

When used in this fashion, designated "R-awareness," reflexivity is rarely problematic. What is recommended through the advocacy of self-awareness is a simple "benign introspection" (Woolgar 1984:10); we are merely exhorted to think more deeply about what we do. Now, clearly, such thoughts could lead one in more problematic and more interesting directions, as they did Gouldner (see SOCIOLOGY), but this is by no means a necessary, or even particularly likely, consequence of being self-aware (see BLOOR, COLLINS).

Reflexivity as the Constitutive Circularity of Accounts

In this usage, reflexivity is a technical term in ethnomethodology. It refers to a general and universal feature of accounting procedures. The essential reflexivity of accounts, as the phrase goes, is taken to reside in the mutually constitutive nature of accounts and reality. In order to make sense of an account one must, in a sense, already know what it is that the account refers to; and in order to know that, one must have already made sense of the account. Woolgar describes this reflexive process, by and through which all interpretation is said to take place, as a going "back-and-forth" (1981a:12). I see it as more of a circular process. And hence we have "R-circularity."

These three interpretations of the phenomenon of reflexivity are no more mutually exclusive than they are entirely comprehensive, but I wish to leave the reader to form her own connections.

BARNES

"A Necessary and Satisfying Reflexivity"

> The ontological and epistemological implications of the foregoing arguments have so far been set aside. Indeed they have been studiously avoided since the issues they raise are so vexatious that they could have impeded the execution of the main task of the monograph.[4] Since, however, they are not entirely irrelevant to the concerns of the practising sociologist, they are considered very briefly here apart from the main text. (Barnes 1974:153)

Thus begins the epilogue to Barry Barnes's *Scientific Knowledge and Sociological Theory*. Evidently, the matters considered therein are of minimal importance in comparison to the substantive content of the main text. Significantly, they are entirely concerned with a reflexive evaluation of that content; that is, the epilogue addresses the question of how the text itself stands in relation to its own arguments about knowledge. The answer that Barnes gives is unequivocal: his text can and should be evaluated as a self-exemplification of its own arguments. Such an answer can be understood as the advocacy of reflexive consistency, in the spirit of Bloor's reflexive tenet (1973, 1976): "The account of knowledge offered here must accordingly claim no special status for itself; it must be fully reflexive" (Barnes 1974:154).

Barnes proceeds to identify the three major reflexively applicable conclusions of his inquiry:

> It has been claimed that knowledge grows through the development and extension of models and metaphors, that the process can be understood deterministically, and that claims to validity throughout remain contingent, since any "context of justification" must always rest upon negotiated conventions and shared exemplars. (1974:154)

Next, Barnes briefly reviews the different degrees of difficulty involved in the reflexive application of each of these three claims. The first is unproblematic because "no attempt has been made to conceal the metaphors upon which the argument depends" (1974:154–55). And, indeed, the only mention of reflexivity prior to the epilogue is in the following metaphorical footnote:

> We may say that the sociologist metaphorically redescribes theoretical accounts as metaphorical redescription. This is a necessary and satisfying reflexivity. (1974:166, n.11)

The second claim (deterministic understanding) is as easily dealt with. Barnes sees his work as very plausibly a product of its time and thus as being potentially subject to external sociology of knowledge-type explanations which, however, "need make no difference in evaluating the claims which are made"

(1974:156). It is the claim that knowledge is only contingently valid which is "likely to be found the most troublesome. Why, it will be said, if the preceding account makes no claim to being the best account we have in a fully objective sense, should anybody accord it credibility?" (1974:156). As Barnes comments, this is a version of the classic self-refutation argument against relativism. (See also TU QUOQUE ARGUMENTS and BLOOR.) Barnes's counter to this hypothetical charge is simply to declare that the text's justification lies within itself. To bolster this somewhat bald (and somewhat "internalist") assertion, Barnes claims, again reflexively, that such a justification is only likely to be convincing to those sharing at least some of his own cultural predispositions. This final point (which is a version of Hesse's (1980) counter to the "absolutist" variant of the self-refutation argument) solves, according to Barnes, "what have been regarded as the epistemological problems of the sociology of knowledge" (1974:157).

The Pervasiveness of Self-Reference and the Importance of Epistemological Moderation

In his paper "Social Life as Bootstrapped Induction" (1983), Barnes extends his sociological articulation of Hesse's (1974) network theory of knowledge into the area of self-reference. To Barnes, self-reference is a subset of reference understood as "the relationship between our speech and that which is spoken of" (1983:524).[5] If certain speech acts cannot be said to refer to anything outside of (other) speech acts, then "one will be unable to identify speech acts and their referents as independent sets of phenomena: it will not be possible to specify what the community has knowledge of independently of what the community knows of it . . . . Its knowledge includes a self-referential component" (1983:524).

The existence of this component causes a problem for Barnes. If cognitively differentiated societies such as ours can be characterised as operating with a discourse that is significantly self-referential at the level of the whole "array" of speech acts, how can this be squared with our individual experience as members of a society in which successful learning through inductive inference appears to take place all the time? Or as Barnes puts it, how is "bootstrapped induction" possible? The answer is that

individual inductions concern the operation of the array itself. Each separate individual learns about the whole, a whole of which his own learning is a part, but so small a part that his inductions remain reliable for most practical purposes . . . . The inductive inferences involved are not notably dissimilar to *other kinds,* but the products of the inferences are cycled back via a feedback loop to become distinctive inputs to the inductive processes themselves. [This describes] bootstrapped induction. (1983:533, 535; my emphasis)

I have emphasised "other kinds" in the above quotation to introduce the question of Barnes's position relative to other contemporary theories of knowledge. At the end of his paper, Barnes discusses these other theories in terms of how they stand on the question of self-referential discourse. Some theorists treat its occurrence as (implicitly) rare and (explicitly) pathological—Barnes's example here is Merton. In other theories such as ethnomethodology, it is treated as so pervasive that the very possibility of "other [than self-referring] kinds" of inference is rejected. In arguing against the former set of theories (which we might call the "epistemological right"), Barnes points to the work of SSK in particular as evidence that it is not feasible to consider even natural science as an area uncontaminated by bootstrapped induction:

Natural science is the crucial case as far as the distribution of bootstrapped inferences is concerned. Their pervasive role in social life generally is clearly evident; [as] they pervade science also . . . then they are present everywhere. (1983:540)[6]

In arguing against the latter set of theories (the "epistemological left") Barnes pursues a different strategy. He makes no equivalent attempt to specify where and when one might find instances of *non*–self-referring inference. Indeed, it would be hard for him to do so as the arguments he puts forward against the epistemological right tend themselves to rely on a general case against the existence of non–self-referring discourse. This case can be argued from Wittgenstein's (1958) analysis of following a rule, or from the sameness/difference argument (Ashmore 1989, ch.4; Barnes 1981b, 1982a; Mulkay 1985, ch.5), or from the metaphor/analogy argument (Hesse 1963; Pickering 1980a, 1980b; Barnes 1974), or from the nondetermining role of norms and values (Law 1974; Mulkay 1976, 1980b). What all these arguments point to is the formal impossibility of pure routine. They stress that every new candidate instance encountered by an agent must be *actively* interpreted as an instance of a class rather than passively (routinely) assigned to a class on the basis of some inherent essence of the particular in question (Barnes 1983:540). Barnes pursues his case against the epistemological left by means of satire—"Trees are nothing more nor less than what are called trees, electrons what are called electrons" (1983:540)—and by an argument from the consequences of accepting such a theory. He complains that it has been used to justify "an exclusive concentration upon the study of speech or discourse" and that pressed into this kind of service, the theory becomes "an empty rationalization of . . . methodological prejudices" (1983:540). Barnes accuses those ethnomethodologists and discourse analysts who use the theory for this purpose of not taking it far enough. "If we cannot properly and routinely identify external particulars, then on the same argument we cannot identify speech-acts, and we cannot re-identify particulars to which we have attached pattern by speech-acts" (1983:540). Having pressed the argument to this point, Barnes asks:

Should we then lapse into silence as a result of this? (1983:541)

The answer to this fundamental question appears to depend on what "basic model or metaphor" underlays our self-understanding. A Barnesian no-nonsense theorist of empiricist/pragmatist bent will not despair, as a rationalist might, because she never believed that cognition should be a logical process anyway. Instead, such a person will cheerfully proceed to equate human cognition with the operation of an egg-sorter which, after all, *does* routinely, if unreliably, manage to sort particulars (eggs) into classes (small, large, or medium) (1983:541). With this model, and the assertion that there is no a priori reason why non–self-referential speech acts should *not* occur, Barnes feels able to occupy the "epistemological centre" after all. Considering the weakness of his arguments against the left, it is tempting to suggest that Barnes simply finds it more congenial in the middle.[7] Here is his judicious summing-up:

I am myself satisfied that there are finite sequences of acts of concept application which are satisfactorily analogous to the operation of the egg-sorter, just as I am equally satisfied that continuing concept application, even in specifically delineated contexts, cannot be fully made intelligible in terms of this conception. Accordingly, I do not accept the assertion that reference reduces to self-reference, but treat it on a par with the alternative scientistic claim which wrongly discounts self-reference altogether. (1983:541)

See also BLOOR, GRUENBERG.

BARTHES

Because it *stages* language, instead of simply using it, literature [text, writing] feeds knowledge into the machinery of infinite reflexivity. Through writing, knowledge ceaselessly reflects on knowledge, in terms of a discourse which is no longer epistemological, but dramatic. (Roland Barthes 1983:464)

BLOOR

The Strong Programme and Self-Refutation

David Bloor insists that his "strong programme in the sociology of knowledge" should be reflexive.

In principle its patterns of explanation would have to be applicable to sociology itself. Like the requirement of symmetry this is a response to the need to seek for general explanations. It is an obvious requirement of principle because otherwise sociology would be a standing refutation of its own theories. (1976:5)

This formulation is the fourth tenet of the programme as given in *Knowledge and Social Imagery.* There seem to be two grounds for reflexivity given here, both of them "requirements of principle." The first is generality: if everything is to be explained, then sociology, inasmuch as it is a part of everything, must (also) be explained. This says nothing about any specific characteristic of sociology which might make it a particularly strong candidate for explanation. The second ground attends to this lack of specificity with the negative argument that were sociology not to be such a candidate for (its own) explanation it would refute itself; and indeed, judging by Bloor's terminology—"*standing* refutation"—sociology would then constitute a (Popperian) falsifying instance.

The inverted positive form of this argument states that a reflexive sociology of knowledge does *not* refute itself. Thus Bloor's account reverses the causal connections between reflexivity and self-refutation that are implied in the tu quoque argument from self-refutation which states that a reflexively consistent sociology of knowledge *must* refute itself. In *Knowledge and Social Imagery,* Bloor addresses and counters the determinism version of this classic self-refutation argument, with the observation that it relies for its effect on illegitimately equating determined belief with false belief.

Bloor's advocacy of reflexivity can thus be interpreted as solving one interpretative problem (consistency) and as setting up another (classic self-refutation).[8] This strategy effectively prevents his rationalist critics from being able triumphantly to unmask any dishonest covering-over of his perceivedly absurd (because self-refuting) position. As one of these critics puts it, Bloor

is honest in this, but . . . the admission that sociological explanations are probably only the product of the social milieu of those putting them forward undermines their authority. Why should anyone in those circumstances pay any more attention to sociologists than, say, witch doctors? (Trigg 1978:291)

Bloor, as I have mentioned, deals with the accusation that he has undermined himself with the formulation: (social) causation does not imply error. It would seem, then, that the causality tenet of the strong programme is an important interpretative prop for this sequence of moves. It is only after he shows that the self-refutation argument is premised on the assumption that (social) causation does imply error—a premise that Bloor dismisses as a "gratuitous assumption and an unrealistic demand" (1976:14)—that he is able to announce the disposal of such arguments along with their premise.

One of the characteristics of self-refutation arguments that Bloor comments on and complains of is that they "have become so taken for granted

[that] their formulation has become abbreviated and routine" (1976:14). Interestingly, Bloor encourages just this kind of "unmodalised" (Latour and Woolgar 1979) language with respect to the *counter*arguments; apparently they should (have) become so taken for granted that their discussion is no longer necessary.[9] For instance, in a 1982 paper coauthored with Barnes entitled "Relativism, Rationalism and the Sociology of Knowledge"—a paper explicitly concerned with issues of a "methodological and philosophical character" (Barnes and Bloor 1982:25)—the only reference to the self-refutation argument is a footnote citing its thorough discussion and thorough demolition by Hesse (1980, ch.2).[10] And that is that. So now we know. A similarly brusque attitude is evident (again in a footnote) in another article from the same year, namely, "Reply to Gerd Buchdal" (Bloor 1982b; see also 1982a and Buchdal 1982) in which Bloor declares, "I shall not discuss the argument from self-refutation [citation of Bloor 1976 and Hesse 1980]. (Perhaps it is time that this venerable issue was finally laid to rest.)" (Bloor 1982b:310).[11]

In an article in the *Dictionary of the History of Science* (Bynum and Porter 1982) on "Relativism (Methodological)," Bloor uses another tactic to dispose of the issue. This consists of splitting relativism into the "more sophisticated" methodological variety (which he defends) on the one hand, and the "vulgar" variety (which he does not defend) on the other. Of the second type, he writes that a proponent would say that "any opinion is as good as any other and, perhaps, that the use of evaluative words was pointless. It is frequently argued that such a position is self-refuting" (1982d:369). This splitting procedure enables Bloor simply to deny that accusations of self-refutation can be legitimately levelled at *his* version of relativism. With such a tactic there is no longer any need even to cite counterarguments, let alone to argue them.

Bloor's Critics on Reflexivity

Bloor's work, and especially *Knowledge and Social Imagery* has been frequently criticised by sociologists (Pawson and Tilley 1982; Turner 1981; McNeil 1978; Carrier 1977), historians (Manier 1980; Buchdal 1982; Millstone 1978), and especially philosophers (Boon 1979; Freudenthal 1979; Worrall 1979; Meynell 1977; Trigg 1978; Laudan 1981, 1982b; Lukes 1982; Hollis 1982; Flew 1982; Hesse 1980, ch.2; Manicas and Rosenberg 1985, 1987).[12] I will take three examples of critics' responses to Bloor's advocacy of reflexivity in order to show the variety of reactions that it has engendered. (Perhaps the most common reaction is indifference as most of his critics ignore the issue altogether.)

Laudan's response is indeed rather close to indifference. He finds reflexivity to be "redundant" (1981:181) as it is "a virtual corollary of the thesis of causality"; thus it is "every bit as sound and every bit as uncontroversial" as the causality thesis. Reflexivity has no "teeth" (1981:184).

In total contrast, Hollis treats reflexivity as the latest and greatest absurdity of an absurd programme. A reflexive relativism produces the "fiasco [of] the social destruction of reality" (1982:80). In the older Durkheimian/deterministic sociologies of knowledge, continues Hollis, "self-reference is an embarrassment, not a selling-point" (1982:81). In the newer "actionist" versions, reflexivity cannot be avoided and, fears Hollis, "it spreads a dry rot too vicious for anyone's comfort . . . . What set off as an insight into the construction of social objects ends as the sceptical destruction of reality" (1982:82–83).

Millstone is more concerned with what reflexivity might mean in practical terms. In his gloss of Bloor's (1973) programmatics he argues that, just because "there can be no a priori exclusion of the beliefs of the sociologist from scrutiny by the discipline of the sociology of knowledge," this does *not* "confer a specific obligation upon sociologists to examine the social relations of their own beliefs" (1978:115). Millstone's attitude to such a nonobligatory procedure is evident from his ironic comments on the prospect of the sociology of knowledge taking the emergence of its own discipline as a topic:

The sociology of knowledge can make a contribution by explaining why people ever came to believe that the sociological study of beliefs is possible and desirable, and what good it is supposed to do, for whom. (1978:116)

Bloor's Reflexivity: An Interpretation

Bloor has not carried out, or encouraged the carrying out of, any reflexive study in or of SSK.[13] Reflexivity to Bloor is purely, and merely, an in principle programmatic advocated on grounds of generality and/or consistency. Even at this level, Bloor has "retreated"; the version of the strong programme from 1976 is noticeably less reflexive than that from 1973 (see note 8). Since 1976, Bloor has not to my knowledge discussed, let alone practised, his reflexivity. It would indeed appear to be "redundant" (Laudan 1981:181). So how can we account for Bloor's advocacy of a programmatic that he is so clearly unprepared to take at his own word? I think the answer may lie in a rather peculiar form of self-confidence, or "epistemological complacency" (1976:72), which he advocates, notices in others, but perhaps has failed to fully develop for himself:

Kuhn studies something that he appears to take utterly for granted, and he studies it by methods which he takes utterly for granted. It is not unusual for historians to achieve this self-confidence. For example, they often apply their historical techniques to work of past historical scholars . . . . Historians do not tremble for history when they realise that their discipline can be reflexive . . . . The desired stance might be called a natural, unselfconscious form of self-consciousness. (1976:71–72)[14]

In this passage, Bloor opposes disciplinary reflexivity to personal reflexivity; the former is celebrated, the latter denigrated. If "to take utterly for granted" is to be personally *un*reflexive, it would seem that the successful development of reflexive disciplines is dependent upon, in Bloor's formulation, a radical lack of personal reflexivity; which, minimally, consists of not taking one's own practice for granted. If I may be permitted a personal comment, I sincerely hope that Bloor is as wrong on this important matter as I hope he is.

See also COLLINS, BARNES, SELF-REFUTATION ARGUMENTS, TU QUOQUE ARGUMENTS, GRUENBERG, PSYCHOLOGY, S. WOOLGAR.

CANDIDATE

D. Phil Candidate is a rather mysterious character who, according to Ashmore's PhD thesis, "A Question of Reflexivity: Wrighting Sociology of Scientific Knowledge" (1985), is the author of a dissertation entitled "Wrighting Knowledge in Sociological Science by Reflexive Questioning" (Candidate 1985a). There is to my knowledge no further mention of Candidate in the literature, with the exception of a citation in Ashmore's new book, *The Reflexive Thesis: Wrighting Sociology of Scientific Knowledge* (1989). In this text Candidate appears as the author of yet another thesis—or could it be the same one with a different title?—called "Wrighting Knowledge: The Scientific Thesis of Reflexive Sociology" (1985b).

In the final chapter of *The Reflexive Thesis*, Ashmore quotes the following passage, which he claims is taken from an introductory section of Candidate's "Wrighting Knowledge":

Among the major practitioners of SSK, there is a great diversity of views on the proper role of reflexivity. Some (e.g., Collins . . .) seek to outlaw it, seeing it as a paralysing influence on their practice and . . .

With this passage as evidence, Candidate is promptly accused of plagiarising Ashmore's own work! Of course, I should point out that all of this occurs within a so-called fiction which Ashmore claims to have devised for some reflexive purpose or other. In the terms of this "fiction," we are asked to believe, not in the highly unlikely and rather paranoid idea of this wholesale plagiary, but rather in the actual nonexistence of D. Phil Candidate and all his works.

Unfortunately for Ashmore, who as usual has overestimated the naivety of his readers (Latour 1988), his strategy of actually *quoting* from the supposedly fictional Candidate's thesis in order to warrant the charge of plagiarism seems to have backfired. For the charge to work (as a part of the "fiction") Ashmore would need to establish that the quoted passage was his own work in the first place. This he has failed to do. In Ashmore's later text (1989) the passage in question occurs three times—twice in Chapter Two and once in Chapter Seven—and in not one of these cases is it at all clear that Ashmore is its author.

The first occurrence is in a description of Ashmore's work, written in the third person, in the form of an encyclopedia entry. The second is in another encyclopedia entry, this time on Candidate, in which it is stressed that the passage is from Candidate's work. The third occurrence of the passage, which is the one I quoted above, is in the "fiction" we have been discussing in which the passage purports to be a quotation from one or other of the earlier contexts. It is clear that the question of its authorship is radically unclear. This casts doubt on the fictional account of Candidate's plagiarism; Ashmore is surely an equally plausible candidate for such a charge. More important, it introduces the possibility that the story we are asked to accept—that D. Phil Candidate is a fictional character invented by Ashmore—is itself a fiction invented, quite possibly, by Candidate's own fictional character, Malcolm Ashmore.

COLLINS

Antireflexivity

Harry Collins has repeatedly argued that reflexivity is a Bad Thing. With the exception of Pinch, Collins is the only SSK participant to have articulated such a view in print. Collins's antireflexive arguments are not all of a piece, however. They are interestingly at variance with one another.[15].

In a footnote in *Frames of Meaning* (Collins and Pinch 1982:190) the authors claim that

the reflexive argument rests on the prescription "treat sociological knowledge as being like scientific knowledge" and this seems an arbitrary, unnecessary and undesirable prescription.

Collins's paper entitled "What Is TRASP? The Radical Programme as a Methodological Imperative" (1981e) is cited for expansion of this point. Here the argument takes the form of a denial of competence or, to be more accurate, a demarcation of appropriate tasks:

The question of whether the patterns of explanation applied by sociologists *to science* are equally applicable *to sociology* is not a question to be answered by those sociologists who are looking at [*sic*] the sociology of science. (1981e:216)

(The phrase "looking at" is surely a slip and should presumably be something like "working in." It is a rather Freudian one, however, considering Collins's next recommendation.) Instead, such questions are only of concern to a putative " 'sociologist of sociology of scientific knowledge' " (1981e:216) whose role is to be reflexive on behalf of SSK, leaving its practitioners free to get on with the job without having to worry about self-referential questions.

Leaving this unlikely role aside for a moment, how does Collins recommend other sociologists of science to act? The answer is "special relativism," a doctrine that can be traced from its first expression in "What Is TRASP?" (1981e), where it is called the Radical Programme, through "Special Relativism: The Natural Attitude" (1982c) to "Appendix 1: Special Relativism" (1983a:101–3).

In interview, according to Ashmore (1985:88, 1989:42), Collins has characterised the antireflexive arguments in these texts as responses to the proreflexive arguments of others: the first as a response to Bloor's fourth tenet (see BLOOR), the second as a reply to Laudan's (1982a) criticism of the studies published as *Knowledge and Controversy* (Collins 1981a), and the third as a critique of the perceived reflexivity of Mulkay and Gilbert's programme of discourse analysis. Now, while Collins's conclusions are similar in all three of his texts, the positions to which he responds are not. While both Bloor and Mulkay and Gilbert can be read as advocating a positive reflexivity, Laudan's comments use reflexivity for critical purposes in a tu quoque argument. Laudan accuses Collins of reflexive inconsistency because he

aims to show *by empirical research* that the facts of the matter have no bearing on our beliefs . . . . If the world puts no constraint on our beliefs, *empirical* sociology is a gratuitous exercise. (Laudan 1982a:132)

Collins responds to this argument with two interpretative moves.[16] First, he invokes special relativism (which will shortly be explained) to block the reflexive inference from (Collins's) statements about the natural world to (Laudan's) statements about these statements themselves. Second, he does a "meta tu quoque"[17] on philosophers like Laudan: "Perhaps the most curious thing about [this sort of point] is that it should be applied to sociological work while leaving philosophers untroubled about the reflexive possibilities within their own discipline" (1983a:101). It can be seen that Collins understands the reflexive argument as a way of making trouble. (This is, of course, precisely the way that Laudan uses it.) Therefore, to advocate a self-reflexive stance is, to Collins, merely a way of making trouble *for oneself*. And, naturally, this should be avoided! The following arguments may best be understood as attempts to do so.

Strong Special Relativism and the Hard Case Argument

Collins's special relativism, in its strong form, is a dualist doctrine that insists on a separation of the Natural and the Social. The natural world, as well as scientists' knowledge of it, is to be treated relativistically. The "natural attitude" to natural scientific knowledge must be suspended. This allows the social scientist to "observe the way that an apparently fixed reality is built up in the community of the natural scientist" (1982c:140). However, "it is only the natural world which should be held in doubt" (1983a:102). The social world, on the contrary, should be treated "as real and as something about which we can have sound data" (1981e:217) and "as a relatively well-behaved external entity which yields replicable observations" (1982c:141). So, "the everyday work of the sociologist of science" (1982c:140) involves two forms of the natural attitude: "In suspending his natural attitude to the natural world he is maintaining his natural attitude to the social world" (1982c:140).

Collins himself can be seen constantly to override this distinction between the natural world and the social world, and between "questions of sociological methodology and questions of the construction of natural scientific knowledge" (1982c:142). One example arises as a direct result of the original formulation of the special relativism thesis in "What Is TRASP?" Consider the following advice to SSK practitioners which is presented as an alternative to "worrying" about the question of "whether or not the knowledge produced by the sociologist of scientific knowledge [is] like the knowledge produced by the scientist" (1981e:216):

It seems more sensible . . . to assume that the things that he or she finds out about scientific knowledge are "objective"—that is, he or she should go about finding out things about the social world of the scientist in the same spirit as the scientist goes about finding out things about the natural world.

Not only does this recommendation to be objective itself transcend the boundary between Sociology and Science (by appropriating the scientific category of objectivity for sociology) but it also seems to constitute an answer to the very question that it was designed to avoid. Inasmuch as the sociologist works "in the same spirit as the scientist," then their respective forms of knowledge *are* alike.

The recommendation that sociologists of science should follow the Way of the Scientist becomes increasingly problematic when Collins's characterisation of the results of the scientific enterprise is taken into account. The knowledge of the natural world produced by the scientist is described as "problematic—a social construct rather than something real" (1981e:217). SSK's knowledge is that Science's knowledge is a form of false consciousness; Science is deceived in its unproblematic realism. Collins's call to mimic such an approach becomes a call for a paradoxically self-conscious false consciousness.

Collins also overrides the distinctions of special relativism in his programmatic statements on the larger aims of his work. Collins characterises "the relativist school" as being "primarily concerned with the nature of human knowledge . . . . The relativists' *constitutive* question is . . . about knowledge in general, not about scientific knowledge in particular" (1982d: 300). He sees "the mainstream concern of the sociology of scientific knowledge as being the *sociology of knowledge* and . . . the exploration of ideas about knowledge in general" (1983a:87). Thus, according to these general programmatics, a reflexive sociology of SSK is a simple extension of the programme; or it is if SSK can be considered a part of human knowledge.

Unfortunately, warrant for maintaining the distinctions of special relativism is given by Collins's main rhetorical justification for his exclusive concentration on natural science: the hard case argument.

If one wants to prove a general thesis you endeavour to prove it for the case where the thesis seems *least likely to hold* . . . it is fair to generalise to cases when it seems more likely to hold whereas one has no warrant for generalising in the other direction. (1982c:142)

The hard case is hard science. To reveal the social construction of physics is more impressive than revealing the social construction of sociology. Everybody always knew that sociology has no brute facts and no real reality. The success of the programme depends on deconstructing the really brutal facts of physics. So, while the hard case argument makes it possible to draw reflexive conclusions about the production of SSK by generalising from SSK conclusions about the production of natural science—a move which the natural/ social dualism of strong special relativism disallows—the argument also trivialises any reflexive investigation of SSK since no conclusions relevant to "knowledge in general" may legitimately be drawn from such a project.

Weak Special Relativism and the Critical Status of SSK

Let us turn, then, to the last of Collins's arguments against reflexivity which I call weak special relativism. In contrast to the strong version (but in concert with the hard case argument) weak special relativism works by appealing to the *triviality* of reflexive concerns. (This, of course, makes it exceedingly difficult to rebut; arguments from triviality always seem rhetorically powerful. However, such considerations are of little relevance in this strictly informational and analytical context.) To show the skill with which this argument is built it is necessary to have a lengthy quotation.

One of the things that sociologists of scientific knowledge are becoming very skilled at is suspending taken-for-granted ways of seeing. As we have learned to suspend more and more the subject has advanced . . . . The same abilities can be used to re-examine the basis of our own subject *of course*. Indeed it must be *obvious* that this type of analysis can be applied to *any* sort of generalising ability . . . . Because of the *universal applicability* of this type of analysis, it ought to be clear that the mere demonstrability of the socially analysable nature of any explanatory category should not be allowed to count, by itself, as a criticism of the use of that category. It amounts to no more than being "more reflexive than thou." A criticism that can be so easily applied to everything is not really a criticism of anything . . . . An awareness of one's own procedures is a valuable methodological astringent, but when we are doing the sociology of science, as opposed to talking about it, it is as well not to suspend the taken-for-granted rules of the method of sociological research adopted. It is only the natural world which should be held in doubt (special relativism). (1983a:101–2; my emphases)

In this passage, the version of special relativism we are presented with seems to be very different from the strong version we have discussed so far. Here there is no juggling with the natural/social dichotomy and little talk of quite different natural attitudes and their suspension and/or maintenance. The message, however, remains the same: reflexivity is wrong. Considering the magnitude of the change in the argument that is involved, this is a considerable achievement. So what is this change? Instead of declaring that, for the SSK practitioner, it is illegitimate even to broach the question of the status of one's own practice, here Collins accepts that possibility wholeheartedly. In itself, this is a large concession to reflexivity. However, Collins's skilful interpretative moves makes this very concession into yet another reason *not* to engage in it. Suddenly, "of course" it is possible; this "must be obvious"; and precisely because of the "universal applicability" of analyses that suspend the taken-for-granted, applications are unwarranted if they involve criticism and/ or if they are applied to one's own procedures in any more radical fashion than as a sort of "methodological Brut."

If analyses of this kind really require a noncritical status to be adequate, it may be that such a criterion would rule out Collins's own studies along with most other relativist/constructivist work. According to Woolgar:

The mere fact that [the analyst] points to the possibility of another account can be taken to suggest that there is something inadequate about the original. The humble sociologist may claim that he is merely outlining another way of looking at the same reality, and that he intends no discredit to the original account . . . . Notwithstanding the declared intentions . . . the proffered alternative account will be heard as a comment on the adequacy of the original account . . . . One might better understand the ironicising of science if it was [not] frequently accompanied by . . . statements of respect for its achievements and declarations of impartiality.[18] (1983a:253–54)

If Woolgar is on the right lines here, then the problem is not so much that universal criticism is no criticism but rather that the criticism universally implied by relativist/constructivist analyses should be so regularly denied. Let me illustrate this point, and end this entry, by quoting an anonymous SSK participant who, in interview with a putative sociologist of sociology of scientific knowledge, expresses both a recognition of the critical function of his work and a desire to deny its existence (Ashmore 1985:96–97).

> . . . you give papers in the sociology of scientific knowledge debunking some
> area—not debunking some area—showing that, showing that some area
> could be understood—cancel "debunking"—can be understood as a so-
> cial construct . . .

See also PINCH, OEHLER.[19]

DISCOURSE ANALYSIS

Although reflexivity is virtually an absent concept in the early work of the
SSK discourse analysts (Gilbert and Mulkay 1984a; Potter 1983; Yearley
1981b), this work can nevertheless be interpreted as entertaining an implicit
reflexivity. Because discourse analysts treat discourse as an entity in itself,
there are no obvious distinctions of either a social kind (between the scientist
and the sociologist) or an epistemological kind (between the level of the analyst and that of the participant) to prevent either the analysis of "traditional"
analysts' discourse (Mulkay, Potter, and Yearley 1983; Gilbert and Mulkay
1983; Yearley 1982) or, even more reflexively, the analysis of discourse analysts' discourse (Ashmore 1985, ch.4; 1989, ch.5).

Moreover, the concern with discourse as such—how it is managed and
how it functions—has led some analysts to attempt to analyse their own discourse and textual practices as an integral part of their project (Wynne 1988;
Mulkay 1985, 1988; Potter 1988; Ashmore 1988, 1989). Fuhrman and Oehler
(1986, 1987) have critically, though sympathetically, reviewed this approach.
They argue that the exclusive concern with writing reflexive texts, that is,
texts which display their own modes of construction, reflects a narrow and
limited conception of reflexivity. Their version of the phenomenon, drawn
from Gouldner (1976; see SOCIOLOGY) is broader: "A reflexive sociological
study . . . depends on exploring the limits of the sociologist's self-understanding of the sociological project. [It] must pay attention to the social structures
and processes under which knowledge is produced and legitimated; such a
focus precludes analyzing texts alone" (Fuhrman and Oehler 1986:304–5).

In the course of their critique, Fuhrman and Oehler suggest that, for the
analysts they discuss, reflexivity has become the arbiter of progress in SSK
(see also Woolgar and Ashmore 1988). Potter (1988) rejects this particular
story of SSK. Instead, he portrays the writing of reflexive texts as just one
way to proceed which should be complementary to both nondiscourse analytical work and to "traditional" discourse analysis (see also Potter and Wetherell 1987). He also provides a complex analysis of the reading of readings
and suggests that such work must, if it is to succeed, display the constructive
process of analysis "on the page." Discourse analytical work is already, then,
a form of reflexive writing.

See also MULKAY, NEW LITERARY FORMS.

ENCYCLOPEDIA ENTRIES

The promise of the term "encyclopedia" can never be fulfilled. All such texts, whether general (*Britannica*) or subject-bound (*Asimov's Biographical Encyclopedia of Science and Technology* [1975]) will be inevitably incomplete or nonencyclopedic. This present Encyclopedia of Reflexivity and Knowledge is no exception. However, it is probable that this particular example of the genre will seem more incomplete, and less encyclopedic, than most (see OMISSIONS for details). I want to suggest that certain formal aspects of this text are to blame. In order to do so I must (temporarily) "jump out of the system" (Hofstadter 1980) of encyclopedia entry and . . .

[reenter the thesis-as-such in which this encyclopedia is, in a way, a fictitious entity, apparently written—or collected, or edited—by the Lecturer, who, in turn, is a fictitious character created by myself and the author of this text for our reflexive purposes. It is only in this fiction that the encyclopedia is an independent, bounded text. In the Real Text of the thesis, it is just a part: Chapter Two, to be precise. The functions of this chapter include displaying the author's scholarly erudition, displaying the width and depth of the author's reading, acting as a general introduction to the main topic of the thesis, acting as a series of specific introductions to the reflexive claims made by those SSK participants discussed in greater detail in subsequent chapters, acting as a series of substitute analyses of the reflexive claims of those SSK participants *not* discussed in greater detail in subsequent chapters. As just one chapter, the Lecturer's ambition of "completion" is, of course, simply not practical (as well as being impossible). The length of even a pragmatically complete encyclopedia on the topic of reflexivity would be prohibitive and would tend to unbalance the text as a whole.

The status of the encyclopedia as a part of another text also accounts for some of the (otherwise eccentric) headings and the order in which some of the entries occur. The major distinguishing formal feature of encyclopedias is the alphabetical ordering of the constituent parts. This text, as you have probably noticed, is no exception. However, because it is (also) only a single chapter of a thesis my task has been to manipulate the strict-but-arbitrary alphabetical order so that it could be read in a coherent fashion. This requirement was most pressing at the beginning and at the end of the encyclopedia because, obviously, these are the points where it connects with the rest of the text. Luckily, the alphabet was not too recalcitrant, although I have had to label the anthropological material ETHNOGRAPHY because I wanted the very first entry to be an explanation of what was going on and a guide to the rest of the text(s). The alphabetically fortuitous label ASHMORE provided the opportunity. Next, I felt, should come an attempt at codification and categorisation of the various ways in which "reflexivity" and its grammatical transforms are used. The heading for this entry provided an alphabetical problem which I have solved, rather inelegantly, with ATTENDING TO TERMINOLOGY.

I tried to deal with the problem at the end by having the final two entries explicitly link into the following text. Again, there was a certain amount of alphabetical luck: the letter "T" is close enough to the rear of the alphabet not to cause too many repositionings of those entries which might have appeared later than THE NEXT ENTRY and TU QUOQUE ARGUMENTS. In fact, the only noticeable victim of this policy is the entry for Woolgar which you will find under S. WOOLGAR.]

. . . having done so, complete this entry.

ENCYCLOPEDIAS OF REFLEXIVITY

I know of none, other than my own modest effort.[20] In order to fill this space, we will have to include, as members of this category, works which deal with the self-referential in more than a single context or in more than one way. For instance, anthologies:

Babcock (1980a) *Signs about Signs.* A collection of pieces on the semiotics of self-reference in ritual, diary, logic, and film.

Bartlett and Suber (1987) *Self-Reference.* An anthology covering formal and informal logic, pragmatics, "retortion" in the philosophies of Polanyi and Lonergan, cognitive relativism in sociology of science, and the literature of *Tristram Shandy.*

Falletta (1983) *The Paradoxicon.* A compendium of paradoxes and other self-referentialia; logical and amusing, verbal and visual.

Hughes and Brecht (1978) *Vicious Circles and Infinity.* Ditto.

Smullyan (1980) *This Book Needs No Title.* And ditto. There are many of this kind of thing. (See PARADOX.)

Woolgar (1988a) *Knowledge and Reflexivity.* A collection of widely ranging essays which discuss reflexivity within the broad area of SSK from the distinct perspectives of the Brunel, York, Bathist York, St Andrews, and Paris schools. Approaches to reflexivity vary from the positive to the ambivalent while the authors range from male to female and from English to French.

Wide-ranging discussions:

Babcock (1980b) "Reflexivity: Definitions and Discriminations." The myth of Narcissus and its positive reconstruction; mirroring cross-culturally; and the reflexive Self in Mead, Cooley, Schutz, Heraclitus, Merleau-Ponty, Montaigne, Rousseau, Durkheim, Lévi-Strauss, Geertz, Aristotle, etcetera. Discriminating, we have reflexivity as private or public, as individual or collective, internal or external, implicit or explicit, and partial or total.

Hofstadter (1980) *Gödel, Escher, Bach.* Reflexivity in metamathematics, visual art, music; and in AI, DNA, and Zen. Looping, levelling, nesting, and Carrolling.

Hofstadter (1985) *Metamagical Themas.* Self-answerability, -documentation, -entrenchment, -inventoryness, -modification, -propagation, -referentiality (as waste of time), -replication, -reproduction, -schedulability, -underminingness, -etcetera (Hofstadter 1985:845–46).

Myerhoff and Ruby (1982) "Introduction." Although mainly concerned with reflexivity in anthropology and ethnography (see ETHNOGRAPHY), this text also covers such areas of modern culture as literature, music, art, and journalism. Reflexivity is distinguished from personal self-reference, self-consciousness, and self-absorption. It is thought of, in the terms of communication theory, as the structuring of communicative products so as to display to the audience the coherent relation between producer, process, and product.

Woolgar (1988b) "Reflexivity Is the Ethnographer of the Text." Varieties of reflexivity are ranged on a continuum from "weak" benign introspection to "strong" radical constitutive reflexivity according to the way they manage the double bind involved in the relationship between (a) what is represented and (b) the way it is represented. The double bind consists of holding that while (a) and (b) are distinct they are also in some way similar. Weak reflexivity, while admitting some similarity between (a) and (b), will also maintain some distinction between them. Strong reflexivity, on the other hand, will deny any (relevant) distinction between (a) and (b) and will thus formulate their relation as essentially similar. Literary criticism, ethnography, and social studies of science are discussed in terms of these distinctions. (See S. WOOLGAR.)

Finally, we have annotated or classified bibliographies:

Ashmore (1989, ch.2) "Encyclopedias of Reflexivity." A very brief listing of some texts which treat reflexivity in a broader way than some others. The bibliography is divided into anthologies, wide-ranging discussions, and bibliographies.

Suber (1987) "A Bibliography of Works on Reflexivity." This is the most extensive reflexive bibliography I know, running as it does to well over 100 pages. It is divided into three sections: Introduction, Alphabetical List of Citations, and Cross-Reference Lists. This last section consists of twenty-eight topical subdivisions, such as "heterological," "Russell's paradox," and "self-justification." Although the range of topics

is said to be comprehensive, with sections on art, law, literature, re-
ligion, and science, the vast majority of the listed works are from
the field of logic. Suber cites two other bibliographies which he
used in constructing his own. Unfortunately, because both of these
are limited to a particular narrow topic, I cannot follow his example
here.

ETHNOGRAPHY

"Toward a Reflexive and Critical Anthropology"

Bob Scholte's essay of this title, published in 1972, was "motivated by a
sense of malaise" (Scholte 1972:430). It appears that the community of an-
thropologists, at least in the United States, was going through a period of
crisis and self-questioning that was rather similar to that experienced at the
same time by sociologists and social psychologists. Scholte's recommendations have much in common with Gouldner's (1970, 1973; see SOCIOLOGY)
and Holland's (1977; see PSYCHOLOGY).

Experimental Ethnographies as Texts

An emerging trend in reflexive anthropology is the joint project of writing
self-consciously experimental ethnography together with the study of ethnography as writing (Ruby 1982; Marcus and Cushman 1982; Clifford and Marcus 1986; Parkin 1982; Webster 1982; Babcock 1980a).

The major characteristic shared by experimental ethnographies is that they integrate,
within their interpretations, an explicit epistemological concern for how they have
constructed such interpretations and how they are representing them textually as objective discourse about subjects among whom research was conducted. (Marcus and
Cushman 1982:25)

Postmodern Ethnography—But Not Yet

The most interesting—and the most radically reflexive—of these new kinds
of anthropological writing are, as both Tyler (1986) and Watson (1987) make
clear, nonexistent; and even, perhaps, impossible. "The point anyway is not
how to create a post-modern ethnography or what form it ought to take. The
point is that it might . . . never be completely realised . . . . Transcendence
comes from imperfection not from perfection" (Tyler 1986:136); "an ethnography in which the writer continually confronts and displays his essential
reflexivity, thus prompting the reader to question his authority, is a contradiction in terms" (Watson 1987:37).

As an aside, it is interesting to note some interconnections between the
concerns, and the texts, of anthropology and SSK. Some advocates of reflex-

ivity in anthropology, such as Watson (1987) and Crick (1982), support their arguments with the sociology of scientific knowledge, while some advocates of reflexivity in SSK, such as Woolgar (1984, 1988b) and Ashmore (1989), do likewise with the reflexive writings of ethnographers.

See also FICTION, NEW LITERARY FORMS, SOCIOLOGY, S. WOOLGAR.

ETHNOMETHODOLOGY

See ATTENDING TO TERMINOLOGY, McHOUL, S. WOOLGAR.

FICTION

And what, you may ask, is an entry on fiction doing in this serious Encyclopedia of Reflexivity and Knowledge? (Actually, I doubt whether you would ask such a naive question, but to be on the safe side I will explain.) To start with, we are only concerned with *reflexive* fiction, one characteristic of which is the intertextual commingling of the real and the fictional (Rimbaud, forthcoming), and which therefore is intensely concerned with questions of knowledge and representation. Second, to talk of fiction is not (necessarily) to engage in it.

Literary-critical studies of reflexive fiction seem to constitute a minor industry. The scholars' most popular term for the genre is metafiction (Scholes 1979; M. Rose 1979; Christensen 1981; Hutcheon 1984; Waugh 1984), although such works are also described as self-conscious (Alter 1975; Waugh 1984), self-begetting (Kellman 1980), surfiction (Federman 1975), narcissistic (Hutcheon 1984), and even reflexive (Kawin 1982).

These writers are mainly concerned with modern—or perhaps postmodern—novelists who, in a variety of ways, attempt to subvert the conventions of the standard modes of writing and reading in our culture. The novelists and their novels include—this is just my own personal selection—John Barth for *Lost in the Funhouse* (1972) and *LETTERS* (1979), Jorge Luis Borges for *Labyrinths* (1970a), Italo Calvino for *If on a Winter's Night a Traveller* (1982), Robert Coover for *Pricksongs and Descants* (1969), John Fowles for *Mantissa* (1982), Stanislaw Lem for *A Perfect Vacuum* (1979), Mario Vargas Llosa for *Aunt Julia and the Scriptwriter* (1984), and Gilbert Sorrentino for *Mulligan Stew* (1979).

Reflexive fiction, though, is not exclusively a modern phenomenon. Limiting ourselves to the development of The Novel, reflexivity was there at its Birth in the eighteenth century. Cervantes' *Don Quixote* and Sterne's *The Life and Opinions of Tristram Shandy* are both reflexive, the latter intensely so. However, at least one critic has analysed Tristram Shandy's reflexiveness as a kind of prefiguration of the philosophic concerns of Husserl and Heidegger (Swearingen 1977) and of Nietzsche and Derrida (Swearingen 1987).

Reflexive fiction has been accused of being exclusively concerned with writing about writing (about writing). While this is by no means entirely true, it is undeniable; that such writing is heard as absurd though it possesses great charm: as in this brief and abridged extract from Salvador Elizondo's seminal, though possibly apocryphal work, *The Graphographer* (no date; quoted in Vargas Llosa [1984]).[21]

I write. I . . . that I am . . . . Mentally I see myself . . . that I am . . . and I can also see myself seeing that I am . . . . I remember . . . and also seeing myself . . . . And I see myself remembering that I see myself . . . and I remember seeing myself remembering that I was . . . and I . . . seeing myself . . . that I remember having seen myself . . . that I saw myself . . . that I was . . . and that I was . . . that I was . . . that I was . . . . I can also imagine myself . . . that I had already . . . that I would imagine myself . . . that I had . . . that I was imagining myself . . . that I see myself . . . that I am writing.

It is clear from this fragment that Elizondo is far more concerned with the mental processes of sight, memory, and imagination than he is with writing. In my opinion it is a work of introspective psychology.

One feature of the general reflexive tenor of recent literary practice and study is a move toward the blurring of genres (Geertz 1980), with the effect of deconstructing the distinction between, for instance, literary practice and literary study. For example, Lem's novel *A Perfect Vacuum* (1979) is designed in exactly the same way as Sharratt's work of literary criticism *The Literary Labyrinth* (1984). Both consist of a series of reviews of imaginary books; and both are as "fictional" as they are "critical" and vice versa.

The blurring of genres is evident, too, in the current interest across a whole variety of scholarly disciplines in the analysis of their rhetorics of inquiry. Indeed, it seems almost as if "rhetoric" is taking the place of epistemology as the all-purpose metadiscipline (Scott 1976). And, if only because the former is far less prescriptive than the latter, this can only be a development to be welcomed (Weimer 1977). Prominent in this area of work is McCloskey on economics (1985; see also Mirowski's marvellously titled review [1987]), Myers on biology (forthcoming), Edmondson on sociology (1984), Clifford and Marcus on anthropology (1986), and Nelson, Megill, and McCloskey on the human sciences in general (1987).

See also BARTHES, NEW LITERARY FORMS, SELF-EXEMPLARY TEXTS.

GOULDNER

See SOCIOLOGY; see also HYPER-REFLEXIVITY, DISCOURSE ANALYSIS.

GRUENBERG

Barry Gruenberg's "The Problem of Reflexivity in the Sociology of Science" (1978) is an unusually sympathetic philosophical analysis of the ways in which reflexivity differentially affects various kinds of sociology of science. According to Gruenberg, any sociology of science faces a "critical obstacle" (1978:321) in the shape of its self-referential aspect.

Because the sociologist of science is a social scientist, he is in the peculiar position of having to define "science" both as the object of his research and, at the same time, as the methods and procedures he employs in carrying out this research . . . . This leads to serious problems . . . . First, it undermines the capacity of the sociologist of science to define his subject matter independently of his methodology, so that the specification of a methodology presupposes an understanding of the subject matter which the methodology itself is intended to provide. In addition, the reflexive relation between subject and object in the sociology of science systematically precludes its capacity to maintain a critical stance towards its subject matter because any critical position would inevitably be self-congratulatory if positive while a negative assessment of science would undermine its own credibility and would therefore be self-defeating. (1978:321–2)

Gruenberg is quite correct to argue that the inquirer into inquiry cannot divorce the research object from the research method.[22] Consider the following products of such an enterprise: explanations of explanation,[23] descriptions of description, understandings of understanding, observations of observation, experiments on experiments,[24] and replications of replications.[25] However, Gruenberg clearly believes that this kind of nonindependence is both highly undesirable and avoidable. It is undesirable first because it precludes the justification of one's research practice in the idealised terms of an application of a topic-independent method onto a method-independent topic; and second because it prevents the practice of a critical sociology of science.

Gruenberg examines how three forms of sociology of science fail to overcome the obstacle of reflexivity. The empiricist variety (e.g., Ben-David 1971), which "treats science as an unalterable given that yields certified knowledge" (Gruenberg 1978:328) avoids the problem by simply denying its existence. Gruenberg demonstrates, with the application of the standard arguments from postempiricist philosophy, that this form of sociology of science is untenable, systematically immune to self-criticism and thus "particularly pernicious" (1978:328).[26]

The other two sociologies, though both described as relativist or Kuhnian, differ in their relation to the "norms and practices" of natural science and thus in their degree of independence from their object of research.[27] Relativist-causal sociology of science (e.g., Barnes 1974; Bloor 1976), which derives its own norms and practices from those of natural science, fails to provide a solution to the problem of reflexivity precisely because of this derivation: "It would hardly make sense to find our solution in a model of social science which itself presumes an adequate understanding of scientific method" (1978:330).

We are left then with the relativist-interpretative position which, because of its declared independence from natural scientific norms and practices, would seem on the face of it to provide Gruenberg's required solution.[28] In this mode of sociology of science

an adequate account of natural science [depends] upon the extent to which the communities of natural and social scientists agree that the sociological account: (1) makes natural scientific beliefs and practices comprehensible, i.e. internally coherent, and (2) is consistent with the natural scientific community's understanding of its own beliefs and purposes. There is, therefore, no problem of reflexivity in either the demarcation or the methodological tasks of the sociologist of science. (1978:334)

Gruenberg, however, is far from happy with this Winchean solution (Winch 1958; for a critique, see Gellner 1968) because interpretative sociology is deemed incapable of making any "distinction between rational and irrational beliefs and practices" (1978:336).

The remainder of Gruenberg's paper is taken up with a specification of the "critical sociology of science" which he believes entails the correct solution to the problems of reflexivity. It would solve the independence problem by grounding itself in a model of science culled from philosophy which would specify which particular scientific norms and practices were ideally rational. Armed with this standard, a Gruenbergian sociologist would be able to solve the demarcation problem by matching what scientists actually do with what scientists *should* actually do (as specified by the standard). When scientific activity does not come up to scratch, the Gruenbergian sociologist can designate it bad science or perhaps nonscience. This is being "critical." Gruenberg's solution is not a sociology of knowledge but a sociology of error (Bloor 1976). (Of course, the above is caricature. Gruenberg's ideal for a critical sociology is noble and hardly something to dispute. "According to the critical ideal, sociological knowledge is founded on a normative commitment by the social scientist to the value of alleviating human suffering" [1978:338].)

My objections to Gruenberg's arguments are of two kinds. First, his recommended solution to the problem of reflexivity is no solution at all. He claims that his critical sociology of science has a "methodology and epistemology made on independent philosophical grounds" (1978:324). One might question how independent of science such grounds really are. For instance, natural scientists regularly use these same philosophical grounds to justify their own practice (Travis 1981; Mulkay and Gilbert 1981a).[29] Moreover, the philosophy of science has gained its ideal of good science from a particular reading of scientific history (Kuhn 1977b; Barnes 1982a).[30] One might also question the kinds of "criticism" that such grounds allow. It seems to me that the only kind of criticism likely to be forthcoming from such a sociology of science is of those bits of scientific practice which fail to measure up to the particular ideal of the essence of scientificity specified in the model of science in use. What Gruenberg's programme would seem to outlaw is any criticism *of* that ideal. Moreover, the construction of the boundary between good and bad science could not become a topic of investigation and neither could the boundary between science and philosophy.[31] Finally, Gruenberg's programme could never investigate philosophy as a set of knowledge-making practices.

My second objection is that Gruenberg's whole idea of the problem of reflexivity is entirely misconceived (Ashmore 1989, ch.3). My arguments above on the critical limitations of Gruenberg's critical sociology of science assume his own premise that criticism depends on independence. *If* it does, then we may give it up as lost because, most especially in the study of science (Latour 1981), independence is not an option. However, there is no intrinsic reason why Gruenbergian independence is necessary for criticism. A relativistic (and reflexive) approach to knowledge is very well able to maintain a self-critical stance. As a prescription, relativism can also teach us to beware of epistemological positions like Gruenberg's:

Beware of theories that naively assume the truth of your own knowledge and the falsehood of everyone else's . . . . Ignore theories of knowledge that do not give proper explanation of why we believe what we believe, but merely "explain it away." (Dean 1978:287)

Finally, let me simply assert this (following Ashmore and McHoul):

Reflexivity is not a problem *for* a sociology of science but a constituent problem *of* it.
See also BARNES, LATOUR, PSYCHOLOGY, S. WOOLGAR.

HOFSTADTER

See PARADOX, NEW LITERARY FORMS, ENCYCLOPEDIAS OF REFLEXIVITY.

HOLLAND

See PSYCHOLOGY.

HYPER-REFLEXIVITY

For the new sociological relativism the metaphor must be that of the onion. First, reflexivity usefully peels the skin away, then hyper-reflexivity takes over and strips away the remaining layers until nothing—for an onion has no kernel—remains. (Rose 1979:287; Rose and Rose 1979:328)

Contemporary Marxist science studies in Britain appear to be split along similar lines to bourgeois studies of science; that is, into the (relatively) rationalistic/scientist wing exemplified by the work of Hilary and Steven Rose and other members of the British Society for Social Responsibility in Science, and the (relatively) relativistic group exemplified by Robert Young and his colleagues in the Radical Science Collective.

Analyses of the mutual relations of these groupings, both to each other, to SSK and to rationalist philosophy, sociology and history of science have been undertaken from the perspective of SSK by MacKenzie (1981c) and, from the point of view of relativistic Marxism, by Cooter (1980). What is of interest here is the use of "reflexivity" as a critical term by representatives of the rationalistic wing of the two Marxisms (cf. Gouldner 1980). The article by Hilary Rose from which the quotation above is taken is entitled "Hyper-Reflexivity—a New Danger for the Counter-Movements" (1979). As the quotation, with its metaphor of the empty onion implies, hyper-reflexivity is entirely destructive. It is not content with the deconstruction of those things one is *against* (in the Roses' case, IQism, sociobiology, scientific racism); it continues uncontrollably on its way, thoughtlessly eliminating even those things that one is *for* (in the Roses' case, correct genetics and genuine social science); and it doesn't stop until you are *really* confused.

Whilst we may begin by acknowledging the widespread retreat from the confident belief that progress in science and technology is associated with social progress, we find ourselves rapidly moving and being moved from a critique of others' knowledges to an autocritique of our own knowledge and on towards an escalating reflexivity . . . . As the new reflexivity, initially a welcome aid to the disenchantment of the sociological world spiralled through the discourses, it consumed not only "ideology" but "science" itself. The certainties of [that] distinction are to be obliterated, scientific knowledges are to be sociologised away, dissolved into social determinations and an equality of discourse. (Rose 1979:281–82; cf. Rose and Rose 1979:324)

The various perpetrators or "victims" of hyper-reflexivity selected for comment include not only Robert Young (especially as represented by his 1977 article, "Science *Is* Social Relations") but also Theodor Adorno, Paul Feyerabend ("published, for some unfathomable reason by New Left Books" [Rose 1979:282]), Barry Barnes, Luke Hodgkin, and Alfred Sohn-Rethel. Their critics object to games playing, to hipness and coolness, to the new authenticity, and to interpersonal subjectivism. The left critique of science is presented as having been corrupted by the philosophical relativism of the new sociology of knowledge. Fatally weakened by this contamination, the sociological relativists of the Radical Science Collective are disarmed in the face of ideological counterattack (Rose and Rose 1979:323–26; Rose 1979:282–85). The result is a tragedy for the victims:

The new relativists speak of a theory and practice based "in the end" on "personal commitment." Such sociological nihilism, which has gone beyond critique and autocritique, despite all its radical affirmation, reaches out with unseen hands towards an old enemy. (Rose 1979:288; cf. Rose and Rose 1979:328)

But of course one can choose instead to notice the deep affinities between the form and content of the Roses' attack on hyper-reflexivity, and those critiques levelled at the same or similar "victims"—Feyerabend, Garfinkel, Mannheim, Marcuse, Habermas, Nietzsche, Lévi-Strauss, Derrida, Kuhn, SSK, etcetera, etcetera—which emanate from such impeccably radical sources as Popper, Gellner, Trigg, Hollis, and Flew. (For some of these, see BLOOR.) And we can conclude thus:

The new rationalists speak of a theory and practice based "here and now" on "objective certainty." Such philosophical positivism, which refuses both critique and auto-critique, despite all its radical affirmation, reaches out with unseen hands towards an old enemy.

LATOUR

"The Three Little Dinosaurs or a Sociologist's Nightmare"

Once upon a time there were three little dinosaurs. The first one was called Realsaur, the second Scientaur and the third Popsaur. They were of unknown origin and a sociologist was hired to disentangle the complicated genetics of their incestuous relationships . . . . Which dinosaur generated the others? (Latour 1980b:79)

Thus opens this text by an eminent sociologist/anthropologist of scientific knowledge which is published in the eminent journal *Fundamenta Scientiae*. What is going on? Perhaps we can find out by paying attention to those trivial textual elements that frame and contextualise the average published article. This is what the opening page looks like:

Fundamenta Scientiae Vol. 1, 79–85   [some numbers]
©Pergamon Press Ltd, 1980. Printed in Great Britain.
        The Three Little Dinosaurs or a Sociologist's Nightmare
                                    BRUNO LATOUR*
Fable dedicated to the Unknown Relativist**
[Text]
*15, rue Damremont, 75018 Paris, France
**This text is due in part to a long discussion with Professor Rom Harré and Dr
    Karin Knorr in Vienna.

At the top left we learn the title of the journal, the volume and page numbers, and the name of the publisher to whom the copyright belongs, and the year and country of publication. At the top right, we learn very little. Then moving down, we have the title and the author's name which has an asterisk by it, which we learn at the bottom of the page is a pointer to what looks like the author's private address. Wouldn't we normally expect an *institutional* address? This could be significant. But I am ahead of myself. Going back up the page, we discover, immediately before the text, an apparent description of the contents. It is a "fable" dedicated to "the Unknown Relativist." This, apart from the title itself, is the first clear readers' indication that this is "not serious." The Unknown Relativist is, it would seem, a joke. And the genre of the fable, while certainly possessing an honourable didactic history (from the New Testament parables and Aesop's moral tales) is certainly not the type of textual form deemed suitable for the presentation of one's work to one's professional colleagues and coworkers; in short, to discursive equals. The double asterisk once more takes us to the bottom of the page where we read what looks like an acknowledgment to Harré and Knorr of their coauthorship. (Can Vienna be significant?)[32] The claim that the text is due, in part, to a discussion, and thus not to real research, also tends to have a trivialising effect: a mere game arising out of mere talk.

If we turn now to the end of the article we find this:

> *Acknowledgments*—This work was supported by a NSF Fellowship No. 18676; a grant from the Relativist Constructivist Workers of the Proof Union No. 234567, and a special endowment from Save the Dinosaurs Movement (S.D.M.). I wish to thank John Stewart and Patricia Coupard for their help in revising this fable.
> *References*
> [Text of references 1–13]
> 14. For an apparently more serious version of this argument see [Latour and Woolgar 1979, ch.4].

In the Acknowledgments, five further agencies are listed (to add to Harré, Knorr, and perhaps Vienna) who have some responsibility for the text. Three of these five are providers of funds, while two are people credited with rather more direct responsibility for the text. Now, it is of course quite obvious that the first grant agency is serious while the second and third are not. These "jokey" acknowledgments are another clear indication that the text is not for serious attention. However, when we come to a consideration of Reference 14 we find that all of these previous indications of the text's nonseriousness are thrown in doubt. In this reference we are informed that a version of "this argument" may be found in another text (Latour and Woolgar 1979). As Reference 14 is appended to the summary (p.88) it seems reasonable to suppose that "this argument" refers to the argument of the whole text. Whereas before it seemed that we were dealing with a "fable," now it appears that the text consists of an "argument." However, we are also told that the version of the argument in the other text is only *apparently* more serious. This suggests that neither text is really serious, the difference between the two being merely a matter of appearance: Latour and Woolgar 1979, chapter 4, may *look* serious but it isn't really. Consequently the question arises of the coherence of any such distinction as that between the *essential* and the *apparent*. After all, we have been looking, in our examination of the textual indicators surrounding Latour's (?) text, at appearances of nonseriousness, not essences of it. If the quality of nonseriousness is produced, as I claim, by the textual manipulation of appearance, then it would seem that the quality of seriousness must be the result of a similar process.[33] And this means, in turn, that there is no intrinsic distinction between the serious and the nonserious. Finally then, let me persuade you that Latour's fable has the appearance of nonseriousness for fundamentally serious reasons and is thus really a deeply serious text, which, through its appearance, that is, its (new literary) form, is able to cope with Latour's reflexive concerns which are discussed next.

The Reflexive Relation of Observer and Observed

In sociology of science, the observer and the informant are doing exactly the same thing: fabricating information into a scientific field. This situation, unique in social sciences, warrants a unique methodology: observer and "observed" work together on their own practice. (Latour 1978:3)

The theme of an "isomorphism of practice" between science and metascience (observed and observer) is a constant in Latour's work, though its various formulations show interesting variations in the way that he uses it as a persuasive technique. Consider the following two quotations, the first from a study of primate field studies and the second from a study in a peptide laboratory.

When analysing the construction of a peptidic sequence in a laboratory, the sociologist is not directly related to the content of the operation [but] when he studies people making sense of field notes . . . that is also what *he is doing*. A direct approach . . . is thus possible. (Latour 1978:21)

Outside observers appear to be in a position essentially similar to scientists in that they are also confronted with the task of constructing an ordered account out of a disordered array of observations . . . . [This means] the observer can better understand . . . scientific activity. (Latour and Woolgar 1979:34)

In both quotations the argument is the same: what makes this a good study is that I am doing the same as those whom I study. However, in the first extract Latour contrasts the greater reflexivity gained in studying primatology with the lesser reflexivity to be had from studying peptide chemistry, while in the second the activities involved in the study of peptide chemistry are characterised as (equally) reflexive. Lynch, in his (1982) critique of *Laboratory Life*, finds this "isomorphic" version of reflexivity objectionable. What Lynch objects to are accounts of the relationship between the practices of the investigator and the investigated that attribute an illegitimate similarity to them.

Lynch prefers such accounts to recognise the essential difference between what he claims are "separate orders of practice" (1982:530). In fact, the only form of sameness that Lynch seems prepared to recognise (on the basis of his reading of Garfinkel's [1967] reflexivity) is a total identity: for an account of a practice to be *legitimately* reflexive, the competence that produces the account must be identical to that which produces the practice.[34]

"Insiders and Outsiders in the Sociology of Science"

In this text, Latour argues that sociology of science requires a distinct mode of enquiry. In this area of study, because the standard set of methodological problems are inverted, the standard solutions are peculiarly inappropriate.

When such a fundamental inversion of the usual methodological principles occurs, we have evidently neared [their] reference point . . . . All the methodological advice points toward what one may metaphorically style the magnetic pole of Exact Science [where] all compasses go wild . . . . Those who want to travel toward this pole need to find another way of orienting themselves. (Latour 1981:201)

It is a pity that so few sociologists of science (Latour prominent among this few) have tried.

Metareflexivity and Infrareflexivity

In a recent text (1988) Latour distinguishes two forms of reflexive writing: the metareflexive, which is the attempt to avoid a literal reading, and the infrareflexive, which is "the attempt to avoid a text *not* being believed by its readers" (Latour 1988:166). Examples of metareflexive texts include Derridean deconstruction, Garfinkelian ethnomethodology and those who use "new literary forms" for reflexive purposes in SSK (Mulkay, Woolgar, Ashmore). Metareflexive writers are obsessed with methodology to the exclusion of all else, overexcited about having the "Author" as a character, and hung up on loops and levels and degrees. The dire result is their unreadability and, much worse, their retention of a naive belief in "the possibility of writing truer texts" (1988:168).

For infrareflexive writing, on the other hand, you "just offer the lived world and write" (1988:170). The necessary reflexivity is achieved by applying "principles of analysis which are self-exemplifying" (1988:171), by multiplying genres, by getting on the side of the known (1988:173), by gaining explanatory equality with those we study, and by refusing to build a metalanguage (1988:174). It would really be very simple if it wasn't quite impossible. As "a story, just another story" (1988:171) Latour's tale of infrareflexivity is a romance; and I've seldom read a better one.

See also S. WOOLGAR.

LAUDAN

See BLOOR, COLLINS, SELF-REFUTATION ARGUMENTS.

LAW

The

Reflexivity in the law and in legal argument is not covered in this encyclopedia. Except that according to Suber (1987) the main topic is the circularity of liens (see note 20).

John

In his "Theories and Methods in the Sociology of Science" (1974), John Law advocates a kind of methodological reflexiveness involving "careful study of the status of sociological methods" (1974:228) as an important feature of his recommended interpretative approach to the study of science. However, the purpose of this reflexivity is to enable interpretivism to avoid the kind of essential reflexivity (R-circularity) said to be an ineradicable feature of the normative approach (Merton, etcetera) to which Law is opposed. In short, one form of reflexivity is recommended as the cure for another.

See also OMISSIONS, MULKAY, BARNES.

LAWSON

See PHILOSOPHY AND POSTMODERNITY.

LOGIC AND METAMATHEMATICS

See PARADOX.

LYNCH

See LATOUR, S. WOOLGAR.

McHOUL

Alex McHoul is an ethnomethodologist whose substantive topic is the social practice called reading (1980, 1982). McHoul is concerned to develop a reflexive practice based on a vision of relativistic discourses as essentially non–self-privileged. The term "relativism" is used to designate

any mode of investigation in social science which does not ascribe privilege to any particular order of discourse (*particularly itself*) vis-à-vis that order of discourse's capacities for representing other such orders. (McHoul 1981:107; my emphasis)

MERTON AND THE MERTONIANS

Otsogery

Defined by Robert Merton in his *On The Shoulders Of Giants* (1965:275) as, and I quote word for word, "the general practice of otsog [a close-knit narrative that pays its respects to scholarship and its dues to pedantry; also, an exceedingly diversified (and thoroughly parenthesised [footnote: and heavily footnoted]) piece of dedicated scholarship] -type scholarship (as distinct from a particular specimen, let alone a minute piece [which is an otsogism])." Merton's most well-known specimen of the art of otsogery is, of course, *On The Shoulders Of Giants* itself, of course, which is ostensibly many things including a letter to a friend, an inquiry into the life and opinions of Newton's Aphorism ("if I have seen further it is because I stood on the shoulders of giants"—or something like that), an impressive piece of historical research, a rare example of the Compleat Shandean historiographical method in action—complete, that is, with all the impedimenta of the digressiveness, the bookishness, the reflexiveness, the wittiness, the circulatoriness, the ambulatoriness, and the humanness; in short, the entire otsogalore (cf. ibid.) of the (un)Sterneist mode—yet, in happy actuality is nothing less than an excellent joke. Unless it is, (perhaps as well—or perhaps not) a treatise in the sociology of science on priority, plagiary, and originalism (cf. Weinsheimer 1984).

The Self-Fulfilling Prophecy

The specious validity of the self-fulfilling prophesy perpetuates a reign of error. (Merton 1968:477)

As his main example of a self-fulfilling prophecy, Merton uses a run on a bank. Customers know that further withdrawals will weaken the bank and perhaps bring it down. They also know that lack of confidence in the bank inspires withdrawal. In such circumstances, the "rational" course of action would be not to withdraw—except of course that everybody else would also have to come to this conclusion. In practice, the most likely situation is that each customer will calculate that their best interest lies in withdrawing, thus "knowingly" contributing to the very event, the possibility of which inspired such a course in the first place. In Merton's analysis, according to Barnes (1983:537), the self-fulfilling prophecy is a "pathological pattern of inference. The banks it destroyed *really* were sound and were brought down by mistaken inference. Conversely, whatever beliefs and practices it sustained were errors and fantasies . . . . Merton identified [the self-fulfilling prophecy] in order to condemn it, and eliminate it." Further commentary on self-fulfilling prophecies and related phenomena can be found in Popper 1966, Henshel 1982, and Krishna 1971.

Self-Exemplification

That the findings of the sociology of science can also apply to itself has not escaped Merton and his colleagues. Considering the usual characterisation of the Mertonian programme found in SSK [see Chapter One], the willingness on the part of these sociologists of science to acknowledge the reflexive nature of their practice may seem slightly surprising. However, if we notice the lack of epistemological consequences following from this acknowledgment—at least of the kind which plague, or benefit, SSK—this small puzzle dissolves. The reason for this lack is because, in the Mertonian tradition, epistemology is entirely anodyne. Mertonians already know what Knowledge is; and thus they do not question it. As Pinch (1982b:20) has put it, they "are happy to leave the roots of scientific knowledge in the real (Natural) world and thus they share the epistemological views held by most scientists." Pinch aptly terms this attitude "laissez-faire realism" (1982b:20). Because there is little or no sense of a *critical* aspect to their writings on science, the idea that what they say about "science X" may also be said about their own "science" comes not so much as a shock, but more as a positive reinforcement of their noncritical, essentially complacent view of knowledge practices.

Let us take a very brief look at an example of the Mertonian approach to self-exemplification.

The sociology of science is curiously self-exemplifying . . . . It was not until a few sociologists began to study science as a social institution that serious inquiry into the growth and differentiation of specialties began . . . . The emergence of scientific specialties became interesting only when a new scientific specialty came into being. (Cole and Zuckerman 1975:139)

Here, then, the topic and the field are one and the same, namely, the sociology of scientific specialties. But this self-reference has no consequence beyond the strategic (Cole and Zuckerman 1975:140). While it is clear that in this case "the reflexivity of social science is . . . not at all vicious in that [it has no] implications for its adequacy" (Gruenberg 1978:323), it is also clear that "those who employ [Mertonian methods] suffer from complete identification with the ethos of science. At no point [not even with the aid of reflexivity] is this identification taken as the problem to be studied" (Latour 1981:203).

MULKAY

"Methodology in the Sociology of Science"

The concluding paragraph of this paper could be written in at least two quite different ways. Let me present them both. I can see no convincing grounds for preferring one rather than the other. (Mulkay 1974:118)

In fact, of course, the concluding paragraph of Michael Mulkay's paper is written in only one way, which begins with "The concluding paragraph of this paper" and continues with, first, the presentation of "Ending one" and, second, the presentation of "Ending two." I wish to make two points about this staggeringly obvious ordering. First, there is only one ending to the paper despite the author's declaration to the contrary. This is, of course, ending two. It seems reasonable to suppose, in the absence of any commentary, that the ending the author chooses to present last will tend to be read as more conclusive than the other. My second point is that the device of presenting two alternative and mutually exclusive endings is, for the reader, equivalent to a nonending. Because the two endings seem both to cancel each other out and to be equally preferable, the reader is unable, finally, to choose between them. The author's aim of presenting the reader with *alternatives* is thus subverted by his mode of presentation. (My first point asserts that ending two is the real ending; my second point, in contrast, claims that there is no real ending at all. I can see no convincing grounds for preferring one rather than the other.)

Mulkay's doubled conclusion is about the implications of his analysis of the nature of sociological research methods for the future conduct of sociological research. Essentially, he claims that the lack of explicit methodological theories which duly acknowledge the social and interactive processes of gathering and interpreting data means that either (ending one) . . .

sociological analysis . . . is faced with an irresolvable dilemma . . . . Findings cannot be regarded as valid until we have satisfactory methodological theories. But [these] are no different in principle from other sociological theories [in that] they . . . need the support of firm methodological theories. We appear, therefore, to be caught in an infinite regression which effectively prevents any form of intellectual advance.[35] (1974:118)

. . . or alternatively (ending two) . . .

in the sociology of scientific development . . . we have the opportunity of constructing explicit methodological theories . . . from the start . . . . In practice it will often be necessary to make "reasonable assessments" of partially inconsistent data and to introduce speculative ex post facto methodological theories. But . . . they will be open to scrutiny and to improvement. This procedure appears to be directly analogous to "pulling oneself up by the bootstraps." (1974:118–19)

These two conclusions can be interpreted as pointing to aspects of Mulkay's later work. The first ending, with its thoroughly pessimistic outlook on the intellectual prospects of sociological research, can (with hindsight and an inappropriately Whiggish view of history)[36] be said to prefigure Mulkay's move away from the "traditional" analysis of action and belief and into the analysis of discourse.[37] (See DISCOURSE ANALYSIS.) The second ending points toward the kind of concern with sociological methods evident both in discourse analysis and in Mulkay's later reflexive turn (1984a, 1985, 1988).

"The Scientist Talks Back"

The reflexive turn in Mulkay's work takes full shape in this one-act play, with a moral, about replication in science and reflexivity in sociology (1984a; 1985, ch.5). As the substantive concerns of this text are replication and reflexivity, it is tempting to speculate on the provenance of the evident similarity of these themes to those of Ashmore's "The Six Stages" (1983; cf. 1985, ch.3; 1988; 1989, ch.4).[38] But let us bypass this trivial matter and move on to a brief interrogation of Mulkay's text.

Why a play?

I wanted to bring the scientists, from whom we obtain our knowledge about science, into my secondary, sociological discourse as active participants [to] challenge some of the accounts of scientific action . . . in the recent sociological literature. (1984a:265)

I see. So that the scientist can talk back, then. But why a *play?*

I want to draw attention to . . . interpretative reciprocity . . . [in] that participants and analysts deal with the same topics, . . . their interpretative resources merge, and . . . both parties take over each other's discourse. (1984a:266)

I can see that trying to deal with the interpretative reciprocity between analysts and participants is an important reflexive undertaking. But I still don't understand about this drama business.

A second concern . . . is how to display the interpretative work carried out by analysts, including myself. [By] construct[ing] an imaginary dramatic confrontation . . . I have sought to emphasise the interpretative, creative character of my own, as well as of participants', discourse. (1984a:266)

Yes, I can see that the standard research report is an inappropriate vehicle for the display of one's own interpretative work, and I can also see that such a display would become an important issue for a discourse analyst attempting to be reflexive. Am I right?

I am trying to . . . explore seriously the issue of reflexivity in the sociology of science and in sociology generally . . .

But I still don't understand why writing a play should necessarily assist such an exploration.

. . . and to find out whether new forms of analysis and presentation can help us to make our research practice appropriately reflexive. If we accept that our own discourse, as analysts, is a flexible and contingent accomplishment, and . . . that our readings of participants' discourse are potentially multiple and open-ended, then it . . . . may be possible, through an awareness of, and a creative approach to, our own discourse, to devise ways of accepting, coping with, even celebrating, reflexivity. (1984a:266–67)

I see. So the play is one of these new forms of analysis for celebrating reflexivity. I wonder what other forms there might be . . .
    See also DISCOURSE ANALYSIS, NEW LITERARY FORMS.

NEW LITERARY FORMS

The idea is that the format of the standard empiricist research report inhibits the development of any serious and sustainable reflexive practice, and that therefore other alternative formats are to be preferred. This conception of the promise of "new literary forms" appears to have been developed at a recent series of Discourse and Reflexivity Workshops. It has been advocated in Mulkay 1984a, 1985; Woolgar 1982, 1988a; Ashmore 1989; and Woolgar and Ashmore 1988. The various experimental forms include the play (Mulkay 1984a; Heaton 1985), the limerick ([Collins; published anonymously] 1984a), the parody (Mulkay 1985, ch.8; Ashmore 1989, ch.5), the parable (Latour 1980b), the dialogue (Mulkay 1985; Ashmore 1989; Pinch and Pinch 1988; Ashmore, Mulkay, and Pinch 1989), the antipreface (Mulkay 1985), the anti-introduction (Woolgar and Ashmore 1988), the parallel text—analytical and meta-analytical—(Wynne 1988; Ashmore 1989, ch.6; Woolgar 1983c), the narrative collage (Ashmore 1989, ch.1; Ashmore, Mulkay, and Pinch 1989), the lecture (Ashmore 1989, ch.1), the encyclopedia (Ashmore 1989, ch.2), the examination (Ashmore 1989, ch.7), and the press report (Ashmore, Mulkay, and Pinch 1989). In addition to all these, occasional use has also been made of such self-referential devices as the self-engulfing photograph and self-referring footnote (Woolgar 1984, 1988b) and Hofstadter's (1980) "strange loop" (Mulkay 1984a; Ashmore 1989, ch.5). Criticisms of such efforts include Walker 1986, Wynne 1986, Oehler and Mullins 1986, Pinch and Pinch 1988, Latour 1988, and Halfpenny 1988.
    What characterises many of these experiments is their use of explicitly fictional forms of writing. This aspect of these new literary forms implies a critique of the distinction between the fictional and the factual; a distinction which constitutes the most basic interpretative prop for the production of scholarly/scientific (nonfiction) discourse. For the social scientist, as Krieger comments, "fiction is a temptation which repeatedly must be refused" (1984:271); there are, however, a handful of ethnographic writers who have embraced the temptation (Krieger 1983; Bluebond-Langer 1978).

Of course, epistemologically sophisticated analysts of scientific knowledge are unlikely to accept the analytic validity of a crude disjunction between fact and fiction; however, the majority practise their trade as if the distinction held. The importance of experiments in fictionalising in this area of discourse is, therefore, to show the inadequacy of the distinction in practice.

See also DISCOURSE ANALYSIS, ETHNOGRAPHY, FICTION, PINCH.

OEHLER

See COLLINS, DISCOURSE ANALYSIS.

OMISSIONS

No account whatsoever has been taken in this encyclopedia of the following crucial areas:

O'NEILL

See SOCIOLOGY.

PARADOX

Paradox, antinomy, aporia, insolubilium, double bind; logical, syntactic, semantic, pragmatic; self-referential, non–self-referential; in metamathematics, in logic, in physics, in economics, in communication, in law, in literature, in aesthetics, in metascience; classical, Megarian, medieval, modern; of the liar, of the truth-teller, of the noncommunicator, of the barber; of omnipotence and of implication; the prediction, the surprise quiz, the unexpected examination, the hangman's; the strengthened and generalised and possible Liar (or Epimenides or Eubulides'); Russell's, Grelling's, Cantor's, Richard's, Berry's, Newcomb's, Curry's, Drange's, Burali-Forti's, Arrow's, Kleene and Rosser's; the Zermelo-König, the Löwenheim-Skolem, the Einstein-Podolsky-Rosen.

In Logic and Metamathematics

Let me tell you a story. For ninety years or so logicians and metamathematicians have been engaged in a research programme called "solve the paradox." Although paradoxes in bewildering variety have been known for thousands of years, the "solve the paradox" programme only got going in earnest at the turn of the twentieth century under the impetus of developments in formal logic and set theory.

It all started, let us imagine, with the sober-hearted Bertrand Russell seated at his desk staring at a blank sheet of paper from dawn to dusk for nigh on a year during 1901, 1903, and 1904. He was trying to solve an extremely obdurate set-theoretical paradox which threatened the complete frustration of his work with Alfred North Whitehead to systematise the whole of mathematics in what was to become the *Principia Mathematica* (Russell and Whitehead 1910). "What made it the more annoying," Russell complained in his autobiography, "was that the contradictions were trivial, and that my time was spent in considering matters that seemed unworthy of serious attention" (Russell 1967:151). Russell's trivial contradictions included a puzzle about classes (or sets) which turned on the classes of classes which are, and are not, members of themselves. Considering the class of classes which are not members of themselves, Russell asked whether this class was a member of itself or not. If it is a member of itself then it must possess the defining property of the class, namely, that it is not a member of itself. On the other hand, if it is not a member of itself then it cannot possess the defining property of not being a member of itself, in which case it must be a member of itself. Both answers, then, produce a paradox: if it is a member of itself then it is not a member of itself, and vice versa.

The linguistic version of this puzzle is known as Grelling's Paradox. Some adjectives apply to, or describe, themselves: awkwardnessful, neologistical, English, pentasyllabic. Others—the majority—do not: long, German, bisyllabic. If we invent the adjectives "autological" to describe self-descriptive adjectives, and "heterological" to describe the ordinary variety, Russell's question then becomes: Is "heterological" autological or heterological? Once again we find that if it is the one it must also be the other.

Russell set out to banish such self-referential paradoxes with his theory of types. This is how it worked: a set (or class) of the lowest type could contain only objects and not sets. A set of the next highest type could contain only objects or sets of the lowest type. In general a set of a given type could only contain sets of a lower type, or objects. Every set would belong to only one specific type. In this system, no set could be a member of itself for if it was then it would belong to two types at once and this was not allowed. Furthermore, the "set of all sets which are not members of themselves" is also outlawed as it cannot belong to any finite type.

The banishment of self-reference was attempted in the domain of language by the logical positivist movement. But the stratification of this domain into an object language and various distinct metalanguages succeeded in getting rid of Grelling's and similar self-referential paradoxes—by declaring such formulations as "heterological" meaningless—at the immense cost of outlawing *all* linguistic self-reference, whether paradoxical or not. The ban extends to such innocent formulations as "In this entry I discuss the theory of types." In the context of this entry, talk of "this entry" is a transgression: it should only take place in a metaentry. Moreover, I mention "I"; what could be more self-referential? The final irony of the scheme is that all discussions of it are, in its own terms, meaningless, because they could not take place in any of the levels of language "internal" to the scheme.

Throughout the ninety-year research programme, ironies of this kind have kept occurring. The problem lies in the basic assumption of the programme that no contradiction can be true and hence that the reasonings which result in the paradoxes must be fallacious. But there is an alternative: accept the adequacy of the reasoning which leads to paradox and embrace the category of *dialetheia;* some things just *are* both true and false. The end.

My thanks are due to Quine 1962, van Heijenoort 1966, Russell 1967, Martin 1970, Hughes and Brecht 1978, Hofstadter 1985, and Suber 1987; and most especially to Hofstadter 1980 and Priest 1987 from whom I have borrowed shamelessly.

PHILOSOPHY AND POSTMODERNITY

The End of the Beginning

Our story begins with a crisis. It is the crisis of nihilism. Rationalism, the discourse of truth, destroys itself in two stages: relativism (nothing is certain; truth is relative) and reflexivity (nothing is certain, not even this; "truth is relative" is relatively true). We are living in abnormal times. The postmodern condition is after truth. If the "essence" of modern nihilism is the destructive moment of reflexivity, what is left but cynicism and disillusion? Back to the dreams of rationalism? But they are just dreams. Reenter the cosy world of relativism? But it is an illusion. Because, after truth, we should not think of reflexivity as a "problem." It has no conceivable solution. It has to do with the structure of our thought.

So what do we have and what shall we do? Beyond truth and falsity there are many truths which are fictions. Some work and some do not. Fictions are stories, and though the character of a story is to be limited it always contains limitlessness within it. We will cultivate this limitlessness in a new pragmatical pluralism: a pluralism which recognises itself. The strategies of invention will help us create powerful stories after the constraints of truth. From the disorder of modern nihilism the postmodern pluralist resolves to act to maximise not happiness but intensity. Everything is left as it is and a whole world is at stake.

We have told the story that the story of stories cannot be told (The Second of January Group 1986).[39]

The Beginning of the End

Why are some philosophers so difficult? It is because they face reflexivity head on. Nietzsche, Heidegger, and Derrida constantly confront the negative, paradoxical, destructive face of reflexivity and, while using it as a weapon against the enterprise of Knowledge, attempt to transform the phenomenon into something positive. They are difficult because this project is difficult. They reject the easy alternatives of avoiding reflexivity or eradicating it.

The move from Nietzsche through Heidegger to Derrida is a move from the subject to the text. The strategies they use for confronting their reflexivity are, in order, anarchic assertion, endless postponement, and perpetual unravelling. Closure is the enemy, the lover, the seduction, the trap. Their ground is the denial of the possibility of a final account; their preoccupation is, Is this denial the final account? (Lawson 1985).

Other accounts of the problems and prospects of the postmodern predicament include Lyotard 1984; Tyler 1986; and Lawson and Appignanesi, forthcoming.

PINCH

Naive, Debilitating, and Dangerous

In his summing-up address to the 1982 conference of the European Association for the Study of Science and Technology, Henk Verhoog asked himself, with reference to several papers presented at the conference, "What would happen if the author of the paper applied his analytical approach to his own research?" (Verhoog 1982:10). Trevor Pinch, who was one of the authors in question, undertook to answer Verhoog's query by suggesting that it would be best left unasked.

The recent concern . . . with reflexivity is naive, can be debilitating to the carrying out of empirical research and can be dangerously misleading. Thus . . . researchers should, where ever possible, avoid reflexivity. (Pinch 1982c:6)

Let us take these three points one by one.

Naivety
Reflexivity . . . confuses the *social* construction of knowledge with the individual awareness of [it]. Just because something can be understood as a social construct does not necessarily mean there are any implications for individual awareness or action. (1982c:6)

While as an abstract point this is unobjectionable, when the (socially constructed) practice in question is precisely the practice of understanding practices as social constructs, the "implications for individual awareness" become so strong as to be hard to avoid. Which is why, of course, Pinch had to go to the lengths of writing an article explicitly to recommend the avoidance "where ever possible" of such obvious reflexive implications.

Debilitation
If [physicists] really could be made aware of the social construction of their knowledge it would be difficult for them to continue their research . . . . There would be a tendency to say, "what is the point . . . since it just reflects our own social commitments?" (1982c:7)

Pinch is quick to point out that some scientists do manage to continue their work despite awareness of its social provenance. However, in a field such as SSK which is less "confident" than the natural sciences, Pinch maintains that it is "desirable to hold some sort of view that one has privileged access to some domain or that one is finding out something about [social] reality to keep going" (1982c:7). So for Pinch, the debilitating consequences are greater in SSK than they are in the natural sciences.[40] But what exactly are these dreadful consequences of, in the case of SSK, a reflexive self-understanding? What is it that is so disheartening about the statement, "My knowledge is a social construct?" Just why does Pinch expect that, upon such a realisation, sociologists of knowledge would feel compelled to give it all up and try pig farming instead? Maybe Pinch is appealing to a version of the rationalist demarcation: that there is objective, asocial, pure Knowledge on the one hand; and on the other (inter)subjective, socially contaminated Belief or Opinion. In other words, that Pinch understands the social as the dangerous virus which corrupts the purity of Truth, Rationality, Science, and Progress.

Danger/No Danger

But of course not. On the contrary. Relativist sociology of scientific knowledge, of which Pinch is a fully paid-up member, has spent a decade of theoretical and empirical endeavour in efforts to refute all versions of the Demarcationist Philosophy. The social is *not* antithetical to knowledge or reality:

The obsession with reflexivity can even be dangerous . . . because it mistakenly assumes that something which can be shown to be a social construct is somehow now less than it was . . . . Quarks are not any less real or any less important for being shown to be social constructs—neither . . . are the findings of [SSK] researchers. (1982c:7)

The problem for Pinch is that if this argument is correct, then a reflexive understanding could do SSK no harm whatever. This contradiction between his debilitation and his "no danger" arguments is given a final twist in Pinch's penultimate paragraph:

In my work I do describe the "reality" of science and this is certainly the purpose of the work . . . . However . . . someone could show that what I take to be the reality of science is actually a social construct. Such a demonstration would have no more impact on my work or aims than my claim that natural science is a social construct has upon the work of the scientists I study. (1982c:7)

The first two sentences display the contradictory relation between the two arguments, and especially the way in which each argument deploys the concepts of the social and the real, in a particularly acute form. In the first sentence the term "reality" refers to whatever it is that Pinch makes of science. What Pinch makes of science, as we know, is that it is a social construct. In the second sentence this reality (that science is a social construct) appears to be contrasted with someone's demonstration that the reality of science is "actually a social construct." Alternatively, the intended contrast could be between Pinch's description of the reality of science (as a social construct) and someone's demonstration that this description itself was a social construct, and thus not a reality. On this reading, the opposition between the socially constructed and the real that underpins the debilitation argument is resurrected. However, in the present context, the opposite conclusion is drawn. A hypothetical demonstration of Pinch's social constructions is predicted to have no debilitating effect whatsoever on Pinch's work or aims.

So what conclusions can we reach from this brief analysis of Pinch's antireflexive arguments? Perhaps these: that a reflexive concern in SSK cannot be held to be naive, given that the nature of the discourse makes it virtually unavoidable; that a reflexive concern cannot be successfully avoided on the grounds that it is both debilitating and that it has no adverse effects; and finally, that reflexivity must unfortunately be held to be "essentially uninteresting" (Garfinkel 1967) to at least some SSK practitioners . . .

Reservations, Devils, and Good Tunes

. . . but not to Trevor Pinch and Trevor Pinch, whose recent spirited defence of reflexive concerns pursued through new literary forms (1988) is a fine example of this mini genre. Although supposedly ambiguous—its title suggests criticism while its dialogic form and self-referential character imply sympathy (and indeed participation)—the Pinches' text is a clear demonstration of the validity of this kind of reflexive practice. Constructed in the form of a debate between a supporter and a critic of these developments, the text cleverly appears to have the critic win the argument. In order to do so, however, the critic has to dispose of his alter ego and revert to monologue, thus exemplifying the argument of his "defeated" colleague that a viable reflexive practice requires alternative textual forms.

. . . and Trevor Pinch shows why in his recent spirited critique of reflexive writings (Pinch and Pinch 1988). Although apparently ambiguous—Pinch's title and major arguments show his critical intentions while the dialogic structure and reflexive trappings suggest a measure of sympathy (or at least understanding)—Pinch's text is a clear demonstration of the absurdities of this kind of "reflexive practice." Couched in the form of a debate between a critic and a supporter of these developments, Pinch shows the validity of the critic's arguments by "killing off" the junior author (the supporter) and reverting to the time-honoured monologic format. By "exemplifying" the position of the critic in this way, Pinch neatly turns the tables on his reflexive opponents.

See also COLLINS, NEW LITERARY FORMS.

PSYCHOLOGY

Advocacy

What is to be accounted for must be accounted for, else the venture is a failure; and any psychological venture is a failure if in its accounting it fails, or refuses, to take into account its own accounting. (Oliver and Landfield 1962:123)

The psychologist must face the reflexivity of her practice; if she is unable or unwilling to do so, she pays "the penalty of falling into the paradoxes of self-reference" (1962:122).

This early call for psychologists to take reflexivity seriously is echoed by Ray Holland; though his reasons for doing so are rather less logicist than Oliver and Landfield's. In *Self and Social Context* (1977), Holland argues that reflexivity should act as a criterion of the adequacy of theories, not only in social psychology but throughout the human sciences. This "entails the requirement that . . . the activity of producing the theory must at least be consistent with the theory itself . . . . A new standpoint in the human sciences must *explain itself*" (1977:267–68). Holland cites Freud,[41] Marx, and Husserl as adequately self-reflexive theorists (1977:268).

A second reason for advocating reflexivity, which goes beyond assessments of adequacy, is its utility—in its negative mode (Fuller 1986)—as a critical instrument. By "making a theory answer to itself, a critique of considerable power can be constructed; a critique which uses the rigorously drawn conclusions of a theory against the theory itself" (1977:268). This describes a practice of critical reflexive analysis which is very different from, for instance, Gruenberg's idea of criticism. Holland cites as practitioners Althusser (Althusser and Balibar 1977) turning Marx on Marx, Lacan (1968) turning Freud on the psychoanalytic community, and Wilden (1968) turning Lacan on Lacan. We can add Holland (1977) turning theorists of the Self on themselves, Ashmore (1985, 1989) turning SSK on SSK, McHoul (1981) turning ethnomethodology on ethnomethodology, Douglas (1975) turning Durkheim on Durkheim, and Bloor (1976) turning Popper on Popper. What Holland is advocating and practising is a form of tu quoque argumentation. Bearing in mind Ashmore's (1989, ch.3) strictures on the use of the tu quoque, let me tentatively suggest that it is best used by critics who are themselves discursive insiders and who, therefore, "use the resources of a theory to criticise and *develop* it" (Holland 1977:268; my emphasis). With the exception of Bloor, who is hardly a Popperian, all the analysts in the above list conform to this insider criterion.

Holland, let me add, thinks highly of Bloor's *Knowledge and Social Imagery* (1976) which he treats as the exemplar for a strong sociology of knowledge. With more of this kind of work, hopes Holland (but see BLOOR), "sociology might . . . become *reflexive* and therefore radically self-critical as a discipline" (1977:265).

Practice

George Kelly's (1955) psychology of Personal Constructs is said by enthusiastic practitioners such as Don Bannister (1970) to be the only theory of the person which succeeds in explaining its own construction in its own terms and which is thus adequately reflexive. The theory is able to account for itself because its theory of the person is of the person as a theorist. (But see Shotter 1975; but see Stringer 1985.)

Another form of reflexive practice in psychology is the work concerned with investigating the social psychology of the psychological experiment (Orne 1962; Adair 1973). This includes Orne's studies of the demand characteristics of experimental designs (1959) and Rosenthal's enquiries into the "experimenter effect" (Rosenthal 1966; Rosenthal and Rosnow 1969). A commentator notes an interesting consequence of the reflexivity of Rosenthal's experiments on experiments. Critics who deny the existence of the experimenter effect tend to explain Rosenthal's results as "artifacts due to [Rosenthal's] experimenter bias" (Westland 1978:26).

See also BLOOR, SOCIOLOGY, TU QUOQUE ARGUMENTS.

REFLEXIVE MOMENTS AND MENTIONS

Moments: In Brief But Serious

The suggestion is that the winning side does not possess truth, but rather that it has monopolised plausibility . . . . I believe my findings support this viewpoint, but . . . the reader must judge the plausibility of *my* arguments for himself. (Harvey 1981:124)

In writing this paper we have quite naturally considered the possible influence of external factors on our interpretation of the spontaneous generation debate, and it seems only proper to examine this issue in closing. (Farley and Geison 1974:198)

We must attempt to understand [the actor's] interpretations—that is, his changing cognitions. To do this, of course, we too are engaged in interpretative work, like every other actor. (Law 1974:223)

There is nowhere any account of the research that could be something more than a fiction. We constantly make sense of the world and build paths leading . . . to one another and convince people that a particular path is more straightforward than any other. It is useless to [deny] that the . . . present account obey[s] the same mechanism. (Latour 1980a:69)

Mentions: Jokes, Exclamations, Brackets, Of Courses, Footnotes, Tu Quoques

—always remembering, however, that our position will achieve only contingent success! (Law 1977:371)

(Indeed, our own argument when fully developed, implies its own lack of finality!) (Barnes and Law 1976:223)

(The following account is itself, of course, a gloss.) (Barnes and Law 1976:229)

I am, of course, aware that my analysis also applies to the present paper! (Star 1983:228, n.39)

There are far too many references on citations to cite here! (Edge 1979:128, n.5)

The two approaches [to "interests" in SSK represented by Woolgar 1981b and by MacKenzie 1978] are directed by different (dare we say it?) interests. (Callon and Law 1982:616)

It is difficult to by-pass the natural ability of scientists to provide good grounds, after the event, for their decisions, and the natural ability of the sociologist to see the ulterior or functional/ideological reasons for precisely the same thing. It is not only the observations of natural scientists which are theory-laden! (Yearley 1981b:39)

The sceptical might be forgiven for suggesting that the Popperian tradition has, itself, all the characteristics of a degenerating research programme! (Law 1975:325)

In view of their sophisticated awareness of their own role as "ethnographers," however, it is surprising that both Knorr and Latour . . . refer to themselves as "observers," thereby appearing to adopt the unthinking empiricism that they criticise when they find it in the scientists they are studying! (Rudwick 1982b:628)

REFLEXIVITY

See every entry; see also OMISSIONS.

REFLEXOLOGY

Therapeutic foot massage. Not to be confused with anything else discussed here. An excellent illustrated manual, or pedual, is by Kaye and Matchan (1979).

RHETORIC

See FICTION.

RUSSELL

See PARADOX.

SELF-EXEMPLARY TEXTS

Texts in which what is said is exemplified by the way in which it is said, or in which the form echoes the content, are rare; and works in which total self-reference is achieved are even rarer.

I know of only the following attempts:

Aldo Spinelli (1976) *Loopings*.
John Hollander (1981) *Rhyme's Reason*.
Joel Weinsheimer (1984) *Imitation*.
R. R. Wilson (1985) "This Is Not a Meta-Review of Three Books on Meta-fiction, But What Account Should Be Given of a Self-Referential Title."
Douglas Hofstadter (1980) *Gödel, Escher, Bach;* the tortoise and Achilles dialogues.

See also FICTION, NEW LITERARY FORMS, MERTON AND THE MERTONIANS.

SELF-REFUTATION ARGUMENTS

The self-refutation argument is a particular, and very prevalent, form of anti-relativist argument. In structure it follows the format of the tu quoque in that it uses reflexivity purely for the critical purpose of convicting relativisms of being self-refuting. Two of the most popular substantive grounds for self-refutation arguments are determinism and absolutism/universalism. The latter is encountered in two forms. All three of these versions have their own coun-terarguments as follows:

Determinism
Relativism states that all beliefs are determined. If all beliefs are determined then the belief "all beliefs are determined" is determined. Thus, relativism is self-refuting.

The Counter
This argument makes the mistaken assumption that determined beliefs are there-fore false. Without this assumption the self-refutation fails.

Absolutism/Universalism One

Relativism states that there are no universal standards of truth. If this statement is asserted to be universally true, then it contradicts itself. It is self-refuting.

The Counter

Relativism is not asserting a universal truth. Its assertion is necessarily relative to its own local culture, time, class, or language.

Absolutism/Universalism Two

Relativism states that there are no universal standards of truth. If to be consistent the statement is not asserted to be (universally) true, then it must be asserting its own falsity. It therefore refutes itself.

The Counter

This version, while recognising that relativism can be consistently locally asserted, assumes that local truth is equivalent to universal falsity. As relativism denies this latter category it cannot legitimately be used to convict relativism of self-refutation.

Self-refutation arguments are deployed in one of two ways, depending on the perceived level of self-reflexiveness of the relativist discourse in question. If this level is low or nonexistent, the self-refutation argument proceeds by first pointing out the reflexively inconsistent nature of the target discourse as a prelude to convicting it of refuting itself by virtue of the undermining character of its newly unmasked self-referentiality. An example of this strategy is Laudan's critique of Collins (see COLLINS. A rare example of the unmasking of reflexive inconsistency for purposes of preserving rather than attacking the relativist discourse concerned can be found in Ashmore 1989, ch.4). The second strategy, for use against reflexive relativisms, consists of simply passing the sentence of self-refutation alone. An example is Trigg's critique of Bloor (see BLOOR).

For a formal logical analysis of this class of argument, see Mackie (1964). For an informal logical analysis, see Walton (1985).

See also GRUENBERG, BLOOR, TU QUOQUE ARGUMENTS.

SOCIOLOGY

The Coming Crisis: Reflexive Sociology in the Seventies

Alvin Gouldner is the most famous advocate of reflexive sociology, most famously for *The Coming Crisis of Western Sociology* (1970), which is a five-hundred-page sociological study of the work of social theory. The famous section which deals with a reflexive sociology is, however, merely an epilogue of thirty pages. Gouldner advocates that the community of sociologists should take steps to "know itself." This is to be achieved by the promotion of a radical sociology of sociology together with the idea that the personal duty of each sociologist is to come to terms with his (*sic*) own circumstances before allowing himself the arrogant luxury of disengaged pronouncement on the circumstances of others. Gouldner clearly desires a sociology that recognises its own implication in the social world. However, in this brief epilogue, Gouldner does little in the way of theorising the nature and the consequences of this reflexive implication.

Gouldner goes further in his reply to his critics (1973), who predictably accused him of (advocating) narcissism, pathological navel-gazing, egoistic subjectivism and the rest.[42] In response, he writes: "The ridicule of 'navel-gazing' expresses an uneasiness with all efforts at self-knowing and self-*reflection*. It is false consciousness's effort to protect itself from change" (1973:124). Gouldner proceeds to historicise and sociologise the idea of self-knowledge:

Knowing who you are in our society is in part knowing that you are part of a tradition in which knowing who you are is important and which is committed to this quest. A sociology of sociology and a critique of social theory is simply part of this tradition and an effort to enact it under special contemporary conditions. (1973:124)

In *The Dialectic of Ideology and Technology* (1976), Gouldner treats reflexivity as a constituent part of that "grammar of rationality" by which we are bound (1976:55). This grammar is constituted by the two competitive norms of *reflexivity* and *autonomy*. The norm of reflexivity is

the capacity to make problematic what had hitherto been treated as given; to bring into reflection what before had only been used; to transform resource into topic; to examine critically the life we lead. [It] is thus located in meta-communication. [This norm is] limited by that other norm of rationality which seeks to make discourse autonomous, either from the language in which it takes place or from the social conditions on which it rests. This criterion of self-groundedness . . . generates systematic silences about those substantial conditions, in language and society, on which the conduct of that discourse depends. It thus produces . . . that pathology of cognition called "objectivism" . . . . Objectivism and the critique of objectivism, then, are *both* produced by the grammar of modern rationality, and are symptomatic of its internal contradictions. (1976:49–50)

Autonomy, then, limits reflexivity; but reflexivity similarly limits autonomy—and it is autonomy that is most commonly seen as the more important. All forms of rationalism essentially appeal to the overriding importance of the self-grounded ideal—that which insists that the speaker be able to articulate the necessary and sufficient premises for his argument and his conclusion. This regulative ideal fosters cognitive security: all the cards *can* be on the table. But it also fosters "false consciousness"—a fact that is regularly pointed out in discourse animated by the ideal of reflexivity. Critiques of this kind, however, tend to be systematically ambiguous with respect to the ideal of autonomy. In unmasking false claims to autonomy they celebrate the ideal itself; but in emphasising the force of external influences and the power of society they tend to deny the very possibility of autonomous speech (Gouldner 1976:52). The consequence of this denial are often seen as very grave: as opening the floodgates to the forces of irrationalism, mysticism, and nihilism; which lead, as is well known, to decadence (Bloom 1987) or to totalitarianism (Popper 1961).

Gouldner, of course, is not so absurd. He does, however, recognise that the mere realisation of a limitation to the autonomy of discourse has its own dangers; it can often be "an opening to a positivistic accommodation to the sheer fact of limits on rationality . . . . It does not yet pose systematically the question of what may be done to *overcome,* to pierce, stretch, struggle against and at least limit these limits themselves, if not remove them" (1976:52). According to Gouldner, then, the reflexive critique of objectivism does not yet go far enough if it remains content with revealing that objectivist discourses fail to live up to their own standards, that is, if the critique *stops* with this tu quoque argument. One way of going beyond this stage is Gouldner's attempt to "limit the limits." Another, is to treat reflexivity in a more specifically self-referential fashion. An example is Gouldner's claim that the historical move from the critique of ideology to Mannheim's sociology of knowledge—a move from "a partial view to one that regards the views of *all* groups as grounded socially" (1976:281)—was

not a true step toward acceptance of *one's own concrete cognitive* limits. It is simply a vague and general admission that "we are all human," but not a specification of our own concrete "guilt." (This remains visible in "normal" sociology's common unwillingness to apply the "sociology of knowledge" to *itself* and in its knee-jerk hostility to a "sociology of sociology.") (1976:281)

Apart from Gouldner's work, the most influential reflexive sociology to emerge in the seventies was Robert Friedrichs' *A Sociology of Sociology* (1970) and John O'Neill's *Sociology as a Skin Trade* (1972a). O'Neill, although a critic of Gouldner's (1970) version of reflexive sociology—he describes it as a self-portrait and complains that it is "an abuse of the task of reflexive sociology to confuse it with one's sociological memoirs" (O'Neill 1972c:216)—is sympathetic nevertheless to the larger purpose of such an enterprise. From O'Neill's perspective of critical phenomenology, the importance of "the phenomenological institution of reflexivity is that it grounds critique in membership and tradition. Thus the critic's auspices are the same

as those of anyone working in a community of language, work and politics"
(O'Neill 1972b:234).

This talk of "auspices" leads us naturally to . . .

Analysis/Theorizing: The Work of Blum, McHugh, Foss, Raffel, Sandywell, Silverman, Roche, Filmer, Phillipson, Walsh, Jenks, and Colleagues

I have no intention of analysing or theorizing this corpus of texts. After reading them awhile, one gets the feeling that any attempt at crude categorical analysis or even at simple literary interpretation is to transgress their auspices. One is invited to actively read/write these texts and then to use them (if that is not too crudely utilitarian) to re-cover, re-trieve and re-member one's Self and one's Tradition: the Logos of the Occident via Plato, Nietzsche and Heidegger—and Aristotle, Marx, and Sartre. "And this is sociology?" I hear you ask incredulously. "But most definitely Yes. The authentic Being of sociology is our topic and our deepest ground. But then again, most certainly No. Our Writing is written *against* contemporary sociology and its piffling technocratic, positivist pseudo-tradition"; such is my reply on behalf of this corpus.

Despite the transgression involved in so doing, let me state that the members of the American group (the first four names above; although Raffel is not American) are commonly thought of as (ex)ethnomethodologists who have taken an opposed route to that taken by conversation analysts in response to the ethnomethodological problem of the reflexivity of reflexivity. (For this see Ashmore 1989, ch.3.) This group are responsible—I choose my words carefully—for McHugh 1970; McHugh et al. 1974; Blum 1970, 1974; Raffel 1979; Blum and McHugh 1984. The British contingent are spiritually based at Goldsmith College, London, and have put their names to these texts: Filmer et al. 1972; Sandywell et al. 1975; Jenks 1977; Silverman 1974, 1975a, 1975b; Roche 1972.

One way of describing their project is as a series of attempts to prove Gouldner wrong when he complained that there is "absolutely no case on record in the history of sociology in which a sociologist is known to have systematically pondered the meaning of 'is'. This is simply not his job, he says" (1973:110). Let us, then, interrogate these texts.

How is reflexive writing to be done?

A model of reflexive writing must itself become an occasion to exemplify the invariant grounds of its production—as an occasion to retrieve one's own method, to interrogate the wonder of the Concept, one's way of transforming text into world and vice versa but without objectivitying it within the writing. Showing one's method then becomes tantamount to showing one's responsibility for the writing—the moral commitment of the text. (Sandywell et al. 1975:32)

Is this reflexive project deconstructive?

Reflexive and dialectical theorizing doesn't deconstitute the thing but commits itself to think the thinghood of the thing. (Sandywell et al. 1975:135)

But surely it is critical of scientific discourse?

The embeddedness of scientific discourse in the grammar of market speech . . . conceals the form of life that locates it. Like the bourgeois society it expresses, it can admit everything except its own character. (Silverman 1975b:168)

And of normal sociology?

[Reflexive sociologists] would not be doing sociology as it is traditionally understood, precisely because to be doing reflexive sociology is to be rendering problematical, and thus the central topic of inquiry, that very tradition in whose (unexplicated) terms sociology is understood as what it is. (Sandywell et al. 1975:155)

And even of ordinary speech?

Everywhere, speech seems to strive to express itself as yet another instance of the unwritten text of non-reflexive language. (Silverman 1974:357)

Are you talking of self-reflection or of something deeper?

The reflexive turn which essentially characterises theorizing treats the ordinary formulation of objects in the world as concrete insofar as the method of formulating is itself unheeded in the formulation of the object. The concrete grasp of the world does not include itself (its act of grasping) as a topic of inquiry. Thus, reflexiveness is not a mere suspension of the natural attitude; rather it constitutes an expansion of the possibilities inherent in ordinary looking in order to include such ordinary looking within its purview. This reflexive feature of reflectiveness, then, includes reflectiveness and its achievements and grounds as objects of reflection. (Blum 1970:315)

I see. But somehow I'm still not sure about the relation between sociology and reflexivity.

Sociology studies and exemplifies reflexivity, but it is the reflexivity of the practical interest: which means that sociology declares that it owns as topic the concern that all other topics gloss. (Blum 1974:201)

This sounds so suffocatingly serious. Have you no truck with reflexive games? Is laughing at yourself entirely inappropriate?

Rather than eliminate "bias," we celebrate it, refashion it, carry it to its limits, and provide materials for its production. (Blum 1970:308)

That sounds promising.

Within the polarities of literalism-totalitarianism and playfulness-solipsism, reflexive and dialectical reading searches for itself, for its tradition. (Sandywell et al. 1975:116)

That doesn't. What is so wrong with playfulness?

Reflexive and dialectical theorizing is answerable to life and death; it is answerable to the question of the nature and intelligibility of the persisting presence and present which form the situation of theorizing and the theorist. (Sandywell et al. 1975:135)

I apologise for my frivolity. A final wise word would be welcome.

Then "ultimately," how (and why) do we seek for unity, reason and tradition in the self-comprehension of a reflexive and dialectical analytical enterprise? (Sandywell et al. 1975:117)

Against Reflexive Sociology: A Caricature

Bell and Newby (1981) argue that even in Britain things got out of hand in the 1970s. Disappointed and disillusioned sociologists, retreating from the failures and the expectations of the sixties, shut themselves up in the tarnished ivory towers of the new universities and proceeded to amuse themselves by talking to, and of, each other. Rampant reflexivities, in the guises of "speculative theorising, a regard for epistemology and the growth of a 'sociology of sociology'" has led to "the threat of immobilism" (Bell and Newby 1981:7). What was, perhaps, a usefully corrective reflexiveness in relation to the joint hegemony of grand theory and statistical manipulation in the fifties and sixties has now overstayed its welcome. The culprits include the influential, yet hopelessly relativistic, Kuhnian reconstructions of a Friedrichs (1970) or a Ritzer (1975); the spread of a narcissistic culture of self-awareness (Hougan 1976; Schur 1976); and, we must suppose, the general demoralisation of the Thatcher years.

The cure? Just get on and do it and *stop worrying*.

SUPERVISOR'S SUGGESTIONS

1. That the incompleteness of the encyclopedia is inevitable and a positive factor.
2. That suggestion 1 should be explained in an entry entitled ENCYCLOPEDIA ENTRIES.
3. That suggestion 2 should be explained in an entry entitled SUPERVISOR'S SUGGESTIONS.
4. That the encyclopedia should display a higher level of internal self-reference.

S. WOOLGAR

Steve Woolgar is probably the most consistent advocate of reflexivity in SSK. However, this concern has appeared in his work in a variety of guises, including the practice of methodological reflection, a concern with the essential (ethnomethodological concept of) reflexivity of accounts, and most recently the advocacy of new literary forms as an essential aid to an authentic reflexive practice.

Methodological Reflection

It is possible to characterise virtually all of Woolgar's writings as the practice of methodological reflection. His earliest published work (1976a, 1976b, 1979), which stemmed from his PhD research into the discovery of pulsars (1978), was largely concerned with showing how the problems he had faced in this research provided in themselves further fruitful lines of sociological inquiry, directed toward the mutual and reflexive understanding of those methods of practical reasoning shared by sociologists (of scientific knowledge) and scientists. In "Changing Perspectives: A Chronicle of Research Development in the Sociology of Science" (1979), Woolgar labels this strategy "methodological transposition"

whereby the researcher makes explicit the essential similarity between the methods he uses for overcoming inferential problems and those used by his subjects. Rather than attempt to resolve any such problem the researcher can fruitfully ask: In what sense might this be a problem for participants themselves? What methods do participants use to overcome this problem? (1979:437; cf. 1978:221)

It is clear that this recommendation that researchers pay attention to *participants'* inferential problems is rather more than merely a rhetorical device for legitimating reflexive study (Ashmore 1989, ch.6), as Woolgar himself has since written on the inferential practices of solid state physicists (1983c), artificial intelligence researchers (1985) and their sociological critics (1987), metaethnographers (1984, 1988b), peptide chemists (Latour and Woolgar 1979), and social problems sociologists (Woolgar and Pawluch 1985). Nevertheless, Woolgar has also carried out methodologically reflexive studies on the discourse of his own community.[43] These cover the debate between rationalists and strong programmers (1980), the benefits of an ethnomethodological approach to the study of science (1981a, 1981c), the structure of interests explanations (1981b, 1981c), reviews of laboratory studies (1982, 1983b) and the "instrumentally ironic" character of SSK discourse (1983a). A constant critical theme of these texts is the complaint that the social study of science exhibits an inappropriately low level of reflexivity:

It might be reasonable to expect scholars concerned with the production of science to have begun to examine the basis for their own production of findings. Yet the best of these scholars remain mute on their own methods and conditions of production. (Latour and Woolgar 1979:18)

At the very least, one would expect a high level of reflexive awareness in any attempt to construct an account of scientists' constructive work . . . . Unfortunately *The Manufacture of Knowledge* [Knorr-Cetina 1981a] ignores this issue altogether.[44] (Woolgar 1983b:468)

There have been some programmatic declarations that the kind of epistemological strictures made with respect to science can in principle apply to sociology. But . . . this declaration operates at a *programmatic* rather than a *practical* level . . . . The reflexivity alluded to in the strong programme is disjointed; the analysis of scientific knowledge is separate from, and precedes, the possible analysis of the analysis. (1982:492)

Garfinkel Good, Bloor Bad

In "Science and Ethnomethodology" (1981a), Woolgar's critique of the reflexivity of the strong programme takes a rather different form to the argument presented in the last quotation. In the earlier text, Woolgar contrasts Bloor's version of reflexivity with Garfinkel's (1967). In the course of this exposition, the strong programme is described as "an analytical scheme which is . . . 'reflexive' in the sense that [it] could equally well apply to sociological knowledge" (1981a:11). Bloor's reflexivity is doubly ironicised in this formulation: it is presented in scare quotes while Garfinkel's is presented straight; and while Bloor's version appears to be a matter of contingent choice, Garfinkel's appears as a completely general and a priori feature of practical reasoning in which "members' accounts are constituent features of the settings they make observable" (Garfinkel 1967:8).

Practical Constitutive Reflexivity

In "Reflexivity Is the Ethnographer of the Text" (1988b; see also 1984), Woolgar combines ethnomethodological reflexivity (R-circularity) with the self-referential variety (R-reference) in an analysis of systems of representation in which reflexivity refers to

the perceived relationship between our system of representation and the properties of the represented object. The adequacy of representation can be said to depend on: 1. the *distinction* between representation (image) and research object (reality) and 2. the *similarity* of these separate entities. (1988b:20).

With this formulation Woolgar is able to assert that the constitutive reflexivity of foundational ethnomethodology is the most radical form of reflexivity because it "amounts to a denial of distinction and a strong affirmation of similarity; representation and object are not distinct, they are intimately inter-connected" (1988b:22). This radical constitutive reflexivity is directly relevant to SSK, Woolgar claims, because in this field,

the researcher is required to participate, *in the course of her research,* in activities which are also the object of that research. She produces knowledge claims about the production of knowledge claims; she aims to explain how explanation is done, to understand how understanding is produced, and so on. (1988b:23)

So, finally, how is this insight to be translated into a form of research practice? In this paper, Woolgar suggests that one way is by

juxtaposing textual elements such that no single (comfortable) interpretation is readily available. In this scheme, different elements manifest a self-referring or even contra-dictory relation with one another. (1988b:30)

Woolgar himself incorporates two examples—the self-engulfing photograph and the self-referring footnotes mentioned in NEW LITERARY FORMS—but comments that this kind of device "isolated within an ostensibly traditional form of reportage, may seem sufficiently strange that it is not taken seriously" (1984:22–23).

Perhaps something more sustainable is required in addition? Here is some additional advice:

I would advise in addition the eschewal of overt and self-conscious discussion of the narrative process. I would advise in addition the eschewal of overt and self-conscious discussion of the narrative process. (Barth 1972:122–23)

See also NEW LITERARY FORMS, LATOUR, ATTENDING TO TERMI-NOLOGY, MULKAY, ASHMORE.

THE FINAL ENTRY

See THE NEXT ENTRY. (See the next entry.)

THE NEXT ENTRY

The next entry is the last in this encyclopedia. It is called TU QUOQUE AR-GUMENTS and serves as an introduction to the next chapter which deals with tu quoque arguments and how to get beyond them, and why.

TU QUOQUE ARGUMENTS

The tu quoque is a type of argument that uses reflexivity for critical purposes. The basic format is as follows:

This position (theory, argument) is incoherent (illegitimate, mistaken) because when reflexively applied to itself the result is an absurdity: self-contradiction (-refutation, -destruction, -defeat, -undermining).

The tu quoque strategy thus uses and to that extent implicitly acknowledges the rhetorical power of self-reflexive consistency in discourse. But it only uses reflexivity *against* the discourses it seeks to attack and its unmasking of reflexive inconsistency is, finally, only a strategic move played to discredit the target discourse on grounds other than reflexive inconsistency itself. These grounds are more often than not scepticism and/or relativism. On the latter ground, SSK is frequently the target for tu quoque arguments.

This sense of the term "tu quoque" can be found in Habermas (1975), Weimer (1977), Govier (1981), Walton (1985), Teichmann (1987), and apparently in Aristotle. However, the most extensive examination of the tu quoque is probably Ashmore's (1989, ch.3) in which the author attempts to get (us all) "beyond the tu quoque" by following through all the problematics of a reflexive stance, as prefigured in the self-contradictory conclusion of the tu quoque, in order to achieve a rhetorical grounding for his recommended reflexive practice. His aim is to encourage assent to these final exhortations:

The tu quoque is not a problem *for* a reflexive practice but a constituent problem *of* it.

But also:

The problem of reflexivity turns out to be the preserver of relativism *for* relativism and not its destroyer.

See also BLOOR, COLLINS, GRUENBERG, SELF-REFUTATION ARGU-MENTS, THE NEXT ENTRY; see also the next chapter; see also the next page.

CHAPTER THREE

BEYOND THE
TU QUOQUE
*The Dissolution of
Reflexive Critique*

Pre-Texts for Beyond

Given that the word "Reflexive" merely labels a complex of questions, problems, topics and that there are degrees, levels, gradations of reflexivity relative to specific practices, what *preliminary* directions should the analyst of semio-praxis take? What would constitute a provisional path toward reflexive analysis?

Barry Sandywell (no date:3)

One redeeming feature of the sociological perspective is that relativizing analysis, in being pushed to its final consequence, bends back upon itself. The relativizers are relativized, the debunkers are debunked—indeed, relativization itself is somehow liquidated. What follows is *not*, as some of the early sociologists of knowledge feared, a total paralysis of thought.

Peter Berger (1969:59)

In order to decide the dispute which has arisen about the criterion, we must first possess an accepted criterion by which we shall be able to judge the dispute; and in order to possess an accepted criterion, the dispute about the criterion must first be decided.

Sextus Empiricus (no date:II.e.xx)

The structure of the area in which we are operating here calls for a strategy that is complex and tortuous, involuted and full of artifice.

Jacques Derrida (1977:192)

To fling oneself into the abyss—rather than slipping in—would require abandoning the notion of self-abandon itself in favour of a model more intent on control.

William Ray (1984:185)

THE POWER OF TU QUOQUE ARGUMENTS

One of the most well-known instances of the power of tu quoque arguments is this supposedly decisive observation against the claims of logical positivism:

Logical positivism demarcates meaningless from meaningful statements by the principle of empirical verification: if a statement cannot (in principle) be empirically verified, then it is meaningless; if it can be, it is meaningful. Unfortunately [or rather fortunately], a statement of the verification principle cannot *itself* be so verified and is therefore meaningless. (Ashmore 1985:159)

Now, I have no intention of *arguing* with this wonderful piece of irony—for those who live by logic to die by logic is an eminently satisfying state of affairs; even if, as our sociological intuitions insist, we cannot quite believe in the historical myth which suggests that logical positivism simply ceased to be as a result of this utterance. After all, as Gellner comments, "making an exception on one's own behalf, having difficulty in accounting for oneself, is the professional ailment of philosophies, and is virtually written into the terms of reference under which they work" (Gellner 1974:49). The power of the tu quoque cannot reside in its logic, however perfect, because logic *in itself* does not compel (Barnes 1974, 1982a; Bloor 1976). My point in pointing to such arguments is therefore certainly not to suggest that their existence disproves the positions that they attack. If this were the case, then SSK would certainly have died (or perhaps would never have been born) and I would have no topic; its relativism crushed under the weight of arguments from self-refutation—a classic tu quoque indeed.

But neither is my purpose to put forward counterarguments. Getting beyond the tu quoque is not and cannot be simply a matter of producing equal-and-opposite arguments that attempt to escape from the charge by alleging faulty reasoning in the tu quoque. Nor can this be done by using the same form of argument as a counteraccusation or meta tu quoque. Such self-protective strategies are, I feel, both pointless and counterproductive. Pointless, because arguments of the tu quoque type seem to be subject to a Law of Eternal Recurrence; and counterproductive, because such reactions involve two fundamental complicit *agreements* with the tu quoque: that the upshot of this kind of argument (self-contradiction or whatever) is *unavoidable;* and that it must have a *negative evaluation.* In effect, both the tu quoque and its counter share a logicians' prejudice against paradox grounded in a magical belief in its evil power.

My approach, on the other hand, suggests that reflexive self-reference can be worked with—investigated as a topic and used as a resource—with the aim of celebrating "the monster" (Woolgar 1982:489).[1] Such a project involves simultaneously increasing and decreasing the degree of respect usually accorded to the phenomenon. Inasmuch as I am determined to look it in the eye, I have to take it seriously; but because I refuse to be afraid of it, it presents no "paralysing difficulties" (Collins 1981e:215)—it is only the gaze of the evil eye that has a convincing reputation for inducing paralysis.

THE NEW HISTORIOGRAPHY APPLIED TO ITSELF

The literature on Kuhn is very large and is about to be increased.[2] It includes internal criticism and commentary mainly from within the largely rationalist philosophy of science community;[3] attempts to portray various nonnatural science disciplines in Kuhnian terms;[4] efforts in the sociology of science to operationalise and empirically confirm the Kuhnian scheme;[5] and the portrayal of *The Structure of Scientific Revolutions* (Kuhn 1970a) as an exemplar for SSK.[6]

The major relevant features of Kuhn's historiography are familiar. Scientific knowledge is nonaccumulative across successive paradigms and is therefore historically and cognitively limited; however, this insight is generally unavailable to members of scientific communities working at their "puzzle solving," embedded in their "disciplinary matrices" and articulating their particular "exemplars." This is because the historical succession of paradigms is made invisible. Each paradigm institutes a rewriting of scientific history such that previous science done under previous paradigms appears as mistaken and yet historically inevitable: as the necessary path which has been travelled on the way from yesterday's ignorance and error to today's (relative) knowledge and truth. In short, the history of science of paradigm-embedded participants is progressive. Kuhn is at pains to emphasise that this situation of historical false consciousness is beneficial and indeed necessary for the very existence of the practice of science as we know it.

This historiography is, then, a Romantic theory of traditions (Bloor 1976, ch.4). As such, it can be treated self-referentially. By ascending to a metalevel we can treat this Kuhnian *historiography* (the writing of history) as a topic for a Kuhnian *historiology* (the doctrine or science of historical writings; Naess 1972:20). Historiologies can take many forms, but the one we are concerned with here is a history of histories (of science) couched in terms of cognitive nonaccumulation over incommensurable traditions.[7]

The first point to notice for a Kuhnian historiology is the sheer variety of historiographies all of which carry out the task of writing history in different ways. The Kuhnian metahistorian—let us call her Metakuhn—understands them as relatively self-contained traditions. As each historiographic tradition N is superceded by N + 1 the image of N, which during N's dominance is a self-image and therefore more or less correct, is redefined by N + 1 as being more or less mistaken in comparison to the new (self-)image, composed of the approach, methods, results and conclusions of N + 1 (Naess 1972:115). We can say that each new historiography rewrites the history of historiographies in a progressivist fashion and that "the exposition and criticism of the old is an essential part of the new" (1972:114).

How do Kuhn and other writers in the new historiography of science talk of their immediate predecessors' tradition and its way of doing history? They describe it pejoratively as the practice of "Whig history" (Butterfield 1931) which is glossed as "the progressive eradication of error and revelation of truth" (Thomas 1979:175). Kuhn himself characterises the achievements of the old, bad practice as "a chronology of accumulating positive achievement in a technical specialty defined by hindsight" (1977d:107). While as an exposition this is undoubtedly critical, it pales beside the following characterisation from Barnes's *T. S. Kuhn and Social Science* (1982a). Whig history sets the past

into a false relation with the present. It was almost as though the present was a cause of historical change, pulling the past in conformity to it by some magnetic attraction, or perhaps pre-existing like some genetic code in the developing social organism, telling it the final perfected form into which it had to grow. (Barnes 1982a:4)

This is good hard-hitting rhetoric which Barnes provides with a perfectly straight face. There seems no hint of reflexive irony when he describes the alternative Kuhnian mode as "the modern professional approach which sets this to rights" (1982a:4), or when he claims that it simply *is* "good historical method" (1982a:5). Although Barnes has claimed to be self-reflexive (see Chapter Two, BARNES), here we notice him reproducing his version of the Whig historian's approach to the past in the very act of condemning Whig history and commending its modern professional alternative. The new historiographers and their supporters turn out to be Whig historiologists. As Naess comments,

An uncritical reading of the new, contemporary historiographers' exposition and criticism of the old dominant trend gives one, more or less inevitably, the impression that the new trend is more correct. (1972:113)

Now why should this be? Why should this impression be inevitable? In commenting on historiographies and historians, the historian is simply a participant—in Kuhn's terms is paradigm-bound. In analysing scientific knowledge and scientists, however, historians are able to tell us that what they see is not visible to scientist-participants. According to Naess, this means that "the new historiographers of science can . . . transcend their own historical situation, revealing what is hidden to others" (1972:118). But perhaps the trick of the new historiographers has a simpler and more prosaic explanation than historical transcendence; perhaps, after all, they are merely exercising the time-honoured privilege of the accredited and competent observer: the right and ability to look at things in perspective, to take the big picture, to tell the wood from the trees. But the credibility of observer privilege depends on bringing off a distinction between the realm of the observer and the realm of the observed. Let me suggest, then, that Kuhn's insistence on limiting his thesis to physics and similarly "mature" sciences acts to preserve the boundary between his own practice and the practice that he observes.[8]

Kuhn's boundary-work may explain why, when discussing his own practice, his comments display a certain lack of reflexive awareness, even when he seems to be setting the stage for self-referential comment.[9] For instance, in the first few pages of *The Structure*, Kuhn describes the outcome of the reaction against Whig history as a "historiographic revolution in the study of science" (1970a:2). It is very tempting explicitly to relate such comments to the Kuhnian scheme—as Naess does. However, Kuhn himself does not.[10] Were he to do so—were he, that is, to write as a Kuhnian historiologist—he would not be found engaging in polemic against the old historiography. Rather, he would treat it in its own terms and would say of it what he says (originally about old science) in the following extract:

If these out-of-date beliefs are to be called myths, then myths can be produced by the same sorts of methods and held for the same sorts of reasons that now lead to [histori-cal] knowledge. If, on the other hand, they are to be called [history], then [history] has included bodies of belief quite incompatible with the ones we hold today. Given these alternatives, the [meta]historian must choose the latter. (1970a:2)

To Metakuhn, our Kuhnian historiologist, the fact that Kuhn does *not* write in this vein is just what she would expect of those, like Kuhn, who share a paradigm (Naess 1972:116). Similarly, Metakuhn would find it perfectly ex-plicable that Kuhn can claim that the concept of science in *The Structure* emerges "from the historical record of the research activity itself" (1970a:1). As Naess comments, this "tendency to pretend that scientific theories some-how emerge from the facts" (1972:116) is characteristic, according to the new Kuhnian historiography, of the old prekuhnian way of talking about science.

So what does all this metacommentary amount to? According to Naess, and to Metakuhn, it constitutes a tu quoque argument. It seems that there must be something wrong with the Kuhnian scheme. If one is a Kuhn fan, as many social scientists and most sociologists of scientific knowledge seem to be, then this conclusion must seem less than welcome. Perhaps the aggrieved reaction from such quarters may be the suggestion that if the only result is trouble, why not leave well alone? The answer of course is that we are only following Kuhn in our insistence on *not* leaving well alone. The good Kuhn-ian can only, in all consistency, convict Kuhn in the ways suggested by Naess in the following formulations of the tu quoque:

[Kuhn's doctrine] contains a fair proportion of potential self-destructiveness. (1972:114)

[Kuhn] is caught in his own relativism [because] the new historiography cannot, on Kuhn's premisses, properly claim any special status in relation to other historiographies. (1972:117)

The historiographer cannot at the same time be both inside and outside. (1972:116)

The application of the new historiography . . . to itself *hebt sie auf,* suspends it. But suspension *(Aufhebung)* is not identical with refutation, and not necessarily an argument for abandonment of its research programme. (1972:119)

There is, however, another way to look at the situation. Those who only use reflexive argumentation in the tu quoque manner see only one side of the coin. They see refutation or self-destruction or undermining. My argument is that the self-same sequence of moves (until the final one) can lead to an opposed evaluation of the consequences of the reflexive application of relativist discourse. Minimally, we can argue that the application of the new historiography to itself is *an* application and therefore can act as a demonstration of its increased generality. More generally, we can simply argue that self-reflexivity is an abstract Good. And, of course, we can point to the substantive conclusions (however brief, sketchy, and unsubstantiated they may be) of the new historiology. For example, it has provided us with explanations for Kuhn's Whiggism in his exposition and criticism of Whig history; for his lack of historical reflexivity; and for his historiographical empiricism.

These points taken together are designed to go some way toward counteracting the power of the tu quoque reading which insists that "self-reference is an embarrassment not a selling-point" (Hollis 1982:81). But this is not nearly enough to show that the reflexive self-reference that the tu quoque articulates can be celebrated rather than shunned.

THE REFLEXIVITY OF REFLEXIVITY:
MANAGING THE TU QUOQUE IN ETHNOMETHODOLOGY

Ethnomethodological Reflexivity

The process whereby members of the social world engage in practical reasoning—interpreting, inferring, making reference to, reasoning, negotiating, pointing out, accounting for, etcetera; in general, making connections between documents and underlying patterns (Woolgar 1981a)—is interpreted, referred to, accounted for, etcetera, in ethnomethodology as members' use of the "documentary method of interpretation" (Garfinkel 1967; cf. Mannheim 1952). The relationship between a document and an underlying pattern (or: appearance and reality, signifier and signified, word and world, account and accounted) that is achieved in and by this process is *reflexive* in that the sense of the former is elaborated by drawing on "knowledge of" the latter; at the same time the sense of the latter is elaborated by what is known about the former . . . . The establishment of a connection between document and underlying reality is thus a back-and-forth process. (Woolgar 1981a:12)

And thus it is a circular process. The independence of word and world that is both a basic feature of "mundane reasoning" (Pollner 1974, 1987) and the minimal necessity for an adequate rationality would appear to be compromised by ethnomethodological reflexivity.[11] (Interestingly, it is just this property of practical reasoning that is said to produce and sustain the appearance of independence. On this account, then, the facticity of the world—its out-thereness—is a paradoxical product of reflexive and circular interpretive procedures.) Within the discourse of ethnomethodology, then, the reality of True knowledge and Correct reasoning is denied: these "entities" are the Appearance and are only real-for-members. Behind the Appearance is the Reality of the ethnomethodological "entities" of reflexivity, indexical expressions, ad hocing, defeasibility, scenic practices, turn-taking rules, and the rest. The question is: What is the epistemological or ontological status of these theoretic objects themselves? Is reflexivity a reality? Or is it "part of the very order which it describes" (Brannigan 1981:171)?

The Problem of the Reflexivity of Reflexivity as a Tu Quoque

In *The Reality of Ethnomethodology* (1975), Mehan and Wood discuss at length a problem for ethnomethodology which they call "the reflexivity of reflexivity."[12] Having previously arrived at the formulation "upon analysis" to describe the reflexivity of research, they notice the following trouble:

The finding that all realities justify themselves only reflexively casts doubt on the reality of reflexivity. What kind of ontological claim can be made for ethnomethodological studies if their discoveries arise only upon analysis? (Mehan and Wood 1975:162)

The recurrence of the "only" phrase ("only reflexively"; "only upon analysis") and the authors' clear desire to be able to make an ontological claim for the reality of the reflexivity phenomenon suggest that they read the reflexivity of reflexivity as a problematic tu quoque threatening their natural attitude to the practice of ethnomethodology.[13] What the reflexivity of reflexivity appears to do is to make ethnomethodology just another form of life and its practitioners just another group of members. As Silverman and Torode put it, "Most practitioners turn their backs on the murky prospect of a *mundane* science, in favour of the beckoning pastures of a *science* of the mundane" (1980:331). That these practitioners should find this position so uncomfortable is both interesting and seemly. If ethnomethodologists are unable to live in an eth-nomethodological world, what right do they have for criticising others, such as "normal sociologists," for not doing so?

Management Strategies

Avoidance—the Puritan Mode

One might think as a naive outsider that, simply due to the subject matter of ethnomethodology—the organised methods by which anything gets done—a position which denies that ethnomethodology can or should be turned back on the organised methods by which *it* gets done would be unsus-tainable from the start. However, this appears not to be the case. Indeed, the very extent of ethnomethodology's empirical domain helps to sustain such a position. First, there is an infinitude of topics to choose from; practitioners can be kept busy researching others' ethnomethods for as long as it takes. Sec-ond, because *any* set of practices can be topicalised, including the professional and the scientific, ethnomethodology can understand itself as "descriptor-in-the-last-resort of (even) those discursive orders which cast themselves as meta-discourses (semiotics, psychoanalysis, generative grammar [and SSK])" (McHoul 1981:117). Moreover, although ethnomethodology tends to level all discourses to the status of the ordinary and thus renders them a disprivileging service, this is only achieved "by counter-position with, and by permission of, [ethnomethodology] itself as the fully-fledged form of professional de-scriptivism" (McHoul 1981:116). And playing the role of the final descriptor can *only* work, according to McHoul, by avoiding the reflexivity of reflexivity which requires ethnomethodology "to identify its 'object' domain as but an effect of its discursive practice" (1981:117).

The most extreme strategy for avoiding the reflexivity of reflexivity is the proposal that ethnomethodology should separate itself entirely from its object domain. While most shouts of Positivism! in contemporary social sci-ence are little more than cheap insults, the occasional claim from normal sociology that ethnomethodology is positivistic (Lally 1976:72; Giddens 1976:133; Barnes 1982a:97) is more interesting than most and certainly more so than ethnomethodology's similar claim about sociology (e.g. Filmer et al. 1972). Indeed, the interest of the former claim is that it is a comment on a particular response in ethnomethodology to the latter. Having discovered that sociology was only a "folk-discipline" contaminated through and through with ordinary members' knowledge—and that therefore its claim to meta-status was both unjustified and a product of unreflexive reification; and thus that sociology was positivistic—this particular ethnomethodological response was to reject the prospect of such contamination: ethnomethodology's claim to metastatus *should* be justified. One feature of this rejection was a distrust of theory and a concomitant radical empirical stance. Another was the pro-posal for a strict separation between topic and resource. In the case of one such proposal the similarity to the programme of the logical positivists is remarkable:

Nothing we take as subject can appear as part of our descriptive apparatus unless it itself has been described. (Sacks 1963:2)

This injunction seems as impossible to fulfil as the logical positivists' attempt to construct a neutral observation language; and indeed Quine's marvellous description of that chimera—a "fancifully fancyless medium of unvarnished news" (quoted in Giddens 1976:135)—is equally apt for a totally described language of description. The attitude that can formulate such a programme I call "puritan." It distrusts the messiness and muddiness of ordinary language and, desiring clarity and certainty, imagines it can be a purely outsider discourse, even to the extent of being outside society and outside language. In milder forms, this puritanism is a hallmark (although reflexively constructed on each occasion of its recognition) of much ethnomethodological-type discourse.[14]

An interesting example of an avoidance strategy occurs in Brannigan's ethnomethodological SSK study of *The Social Basis of Scientific Discoveries* (1981). Brannigan puts forward a new theory of discovery—the attributional theory[15]—which he claims does not suffer from the defects of others, whether lay or professional, "mentalist" or based on "cultural maturation," or produced by scientists or metascientists. The inadequacy of many of these other theories, and specifically Kuhn's, is that they are not truly explanatory because those features which are displayed in the theory as *conditions for* discovery are, upon Brannigan's analysis, found to be implicated in the theorist's *definition of* discovery (Brannigan 1981:25). Thus, such theories are found to be tautological rather than explanatory.

According to the general ethnomethodological account of universal practical reasoning, tautology is impossible to avoid. Reflexive circularity is the ground and condition of all forms of sense-making. To find (upon analysis) that, for instance, Kuhn reasons in a circle is not, then, surprising. But to criticise his theory because of this circularity *is,* especially when the criticism is accompanied by Brannigan's confident claim that his own attributional theory is exempt from the contamination of reflexive constitution (1981:82–3). Brannigan deals with this unwelcome possibility, and thus avoids the reflexivity of reflexivity, by making a strict and "imperative" separation between the levels of analysis of the member and of the analyst.

The members' domain is one with its objective discoveries and their relevant features, while the analyst's domain is the criteria used by members of society to attribute and reflexively uncover those phenomena . . . . The use of the criteria is teleological, circular or reflexive; however, the position which accounts for the occurrence of discoveries . . . is causal. (1981:83)

Is the analyst's domain exempt from reflexive constitution? This question is not intended naturalistically. That is, it is not itself claimed to be free from the reflexivity of accounts. It is formulated from within the language game which holds to the thesis of necessary and inevitable reflexivity (as reflexively discovered on analysis). The answer to the question is, of course, No. Brannigan's claim for the causality of his explanations has precisely the same analytical status as have (Brannigan's) members' claims for the objectivity of discoveries. Which is to say that it can be analytically deconstructed: the attributional theory can be found (upon analysis) to have been found upon analysis.[16]

Management strategies of avoidance, then, have two features, the first of which is shared by most of the following solution strategies. This is the tu quoque reading of the reflexivity of reflexivity in which the phenomenon is understood as a criticism of ethnomethodology and thus as a problem for it. The other feature consists of the various ways in which the relevance of the problem for this-particular-case is denied. Study policies that involve a strict separation of topic from resource, or of the members' domain from the analyst's domain, can be considered attempts to immunise such studies from the effects of their own analytical findings.

The Solution of Nonpuritan Realism

Ethnomethodologists are not exempt from using common sense knowledge in their studies of how it is used by others. The major difference between ethnomethodology and sociology is that for the ethnomethodologist, common sense knowledge is a topic of study as well as a resource. (Leiter 1980:93)

This statement illustrates the nonpuritan mode in ethnomethodology. As a solution to the reflexivity of reflexivity, however, it is problematic. The price paid for "using common sense knowledge" is a total surrender to realism. In this mode, ethnomethodology becomes just another form of realist study with its own set of real-world objects for its descriptions to match. "If we pose, a priori, *any* ontological existents . . . then there is no need to hold to the principle of the reflexive constitution of (social) objects in the first place. If 're-flexivity' can be given a place in the world, then so can suicides" (McHoul 1981:113).

The Californian Solution

Once an ethnomethodologist has encountered the reflexivity of reflexivity, he knows nothing. This experience is only initiatory. Each ethnomethodologist must go beyond that spectre to find his own unique way. (Mehan and Wood 1975:167)

This seems a rather inappropriate way of talking of "a concerted and collective step in social science method" (McHoul 1981:113).

The Solution of Turning the Problem into a Topic

An extremely popular solution to any problematics in ethnomethodology is to treat the troublesome object as a topic of investigation. The reflexivity of reflexivity is no exception.

In all accounts (including ethnomethodology) the gloss we use to describe the world confirms our view of it. The only obvious path away from the abyss is to treat the glossing activity itself as the object of study. (Silverman 1972:200)

This is certainly not a path *away* from the abyss: the study of confirmatory glossing could produce only a confirmatory gloss. This is only a problem, however, for those seduced by the terminology of fear ("spectre"; "abyss"). For this abyss is a paper tiger. If the reflexivity of reflexivity *is* ethnomethodology's "most intriguing phenomenon" (Mehan and Wood 1975:19), then avoiding the abyss means throwing out the baby with the bath water. So we can at least say that topicalising the phenomenon, as I am doing here, is a step in the right direction: *toward* the abyss.

The Relax and Stop Worrying Solution

Another popular solution is to hold that our knowledge and our epistemology have no absolute grounds and do not suffer for their lack. We can then relax and get on with the job without concerning ourselves with insoluble methodological/epistemological/ontological conundrums, secure in the knowledge of a natural limit to our enquiries. Well, yes. The problem with this mode of response to paradoxical problems (very common in SSK) is that they get avoided by default. Because, rightly, it is believed that they cannot be solved, the likelihood is that they will never be addressed. Although we believe in *a* limit to our enquiries, we will never get to find out what it is. In ethnomethodology this approach would solve the reflexivity of reflexivity by default. Yet it is doubtful whether ethnomethodology, SSK, or any other deconstructive discourse could ever have got off the ground had such a worldy wise attitude prevailed. Relativisms are constantly in danger of re-becoming realisms (Knorr-Cetina 1982:134). In ethnomethodology, facing the reflexivity of reflexivity "acts as a mnemonic. It reminds us that we must not be tempted into according the privilege of correspondence to a real order of events or objects to our descriptions" (McHoul 1982:100).

The Solution of Re-Covering the Grounds of Speech

This is the strategy pursued by those doing Analysis/Theorizing (Blum 1970, 1974; McHugh et al. 1974; Sandywell et al. 1975; Jenks 1977; Raffel 1979; Blum and McHugh 1984). The response to the reflexivity of reflexivity which is displayed in the work of these theorists is to reject the form of life that throws up the problem, that is, empirical research. Instead, they seek the grounds or auspices of their discourse and generally find them in Plato, the Logos, the Tradition, or at least in Heidegger. They have certainly given up the project of matching their discourse to the real but at the expense of not bringing news of any kind.[17] But inasmuch as those engaged in Analysis/ Theorizing respond to the reflexivity of reflexivity with self-removal from the problematic site, they seek not so much to solve it as to avoid it. If, in ethnomethodology, Analysis/Theorizing is situated at the opposite end of (such useful fictions as) the idealist/realist and philosophic/scientific continuums from Sack's conversation analysis, both practices share the quest for the unproblematic life. (What appears to be a continuum is really a circle.)

The Dual Vision Solution

The most theoretically sophisticated solution strategy is McHoul's (1982) proposal for a dual vision in ethnomethodology (cf. for SSK, Collins 1981e, 1982c; and for general metascience, Elkana 1978). The proposal affirms the reflexivity of reflexivity and recognises that ethnomethodology can be a topic of investigation for itself. In this mode of operation—when it addresses itself as a phenomenon—"ethnomethodology can . . . hold that [the] objects and practices (which it takes as 'topic') in fact emerge as products of the concerted, reflexive work of the ethnomethodological tradition and discourse" (McHoul 1982:101). However, in its other mode of operation—its investigative mode—"ethnomethodology might usefully rely upon the research heuristic ('myth') that the phenomena it treats comprise a real order of events, that they are objects in an independently existing world" (1982:101). At this stage, then, McHoul's proposal looks like a pragmatic compromise. Moreover, it appears that the more authentic mode of the two is the self-referential because it is here that the reflexive constitution doctrine is taken seriously. In the other mode this doctrine is, however reluctantly, suspended for practical purposes and replaced by the " 'myth' " of realism. So far so fair. If the study project does require a realist natural attitude for its very existence (and this question is the very crux of the matter), then the dual vision solution, with its treatment of realism as a mere heuristic and its concomitant recognition of the self-referential moment as the site at which The True Ethnomethodology is preserved, would seem the best we can do.

Unfortunately, McHoul does not leave it at that. First, he argues that ethnomethodology has "a built in 'dual vision' of every phenomenon it addresses" (1982:102). By this he means that in recognising that members' phenomena are objective (for members), ethnomethodological study "preserves" the objectivity of these phenomena; but in showing how these phenomena come to be objective, it "dissects" their objective status. And, concludes McHoul, the reflexivity of reflexivity merely indicates that the same dual vision also applies to the phenomena of ethnomethodological discourse (1982:102). This seems to me highly disingenuous. Objectivities cannot be simultaneously "preserved" and "dissected." The discourse of ethnomethodology is deconstructive even if it doesn't want to be. To show how objectivities *become* objectivities is to show that they are *not* objectivities (cf. for SSK, Woolgar 1983a). On this revised account the relevance of the reflexivity of reflexivity is that it provides the means by which ethnomethodology can (paradoxically) deconstruct its own arrogant metadiscursive claims. Once again, however, McHoul invokes practical grounds to disallow this project. "To 'get things done' [ethnomethodology] (whether descriptive of itself or not) depends, like any other form of life, on the 'myth' that, for any given analytic occasion, this possibility will not be invoked" (1982:101). The point is that the reflexivity of reflexivity (whether as the site of authentic ethnomethodology or not) is rendered impotent if the practical exigencies of research require that on any (every) given analytic occasion the realist myth (which thus becomes no myth at all) is instated. The practical upshot of McHoul's dual vision is the reduction to William Blake's single vision. If the following stirring words are to be taken seriously—and I mean practically rather than piously—McHoul's dual vision solution must be rejected.

What [ethnomethodology] might have to fear is the possibility that reflexivity *cannot* be [or: is never going to be] "turned back" upon it—for then [ethnomethodological] theories would start to look like *actual* ontological existents independent of the method of their description and then [it] would have to claim to have discovered the first unequivocal sociological atoms. And this is precisely what it has most emphatically sought to avoid . . . . The "problem" of [the reflexivity of reflexivity] therefore turns out to be the preserver of [ethnomethodology] *for* [ethnomethodology] and not its destroyer. (McHoul 1981:114)

The Dis-Solution of Practical Reflexivity

Having dismissed all these efforts at managing the reflexivity of reflexivity, I should now present the correct meta-analytical solution to this and other similar self-referential problems. Unfortunately, I cannot fulfil this expectation. And, indeed, I would prefer to suggest that all of its terms are misconceived:

It is not a matter of authorial presentation.
It is not a matter of being correct.
It is not a matter of meta-analysis.
It is not a matter of solving a problem.

These negative injunctions do not arise solely as the inevitable result of my analytical practice; it is not simply that "even efforts to examine *how* it is [managed] are doomed in that they entail an attempt to [manage] it" (Woolgar 1982:489). Rather, they arise from the following series of interrogations of the assumption of the inevitability of "doom" in the first place.

THE NAESS TU QUOQUES

Self-Destructiveness, Self-Destruction, and
Relativism's Formulation Problem

[Kuhn's doctrine] contains a fair proportion of potential self-destructiveness. (Naess
1972:114)

Other than to reiterate that Naessian self-destructiveness is far from the
only result of the reflexive application of relativist discourse, I do not wish to
contest this statement. But if my purpose here is to develop (an argument for)
a research practice beyond the tu quoque, in which a positive and practical
reflexivity has a central place, how can this be possible or desirable given the
uncontested potential self-destructiveness of so doing? The initial answer to
this question is that self-destructiveness does not entail self-destruction. (Here
I am, still speaking.) For self-destruction, in this context, is the wilful abandonment of speech on the grounds that Clear speech is both highly desirable
and completely impossible. Self-destructiveness, however, points only to its
impossibility; relativists know that the charge of Unclarity can be brought
against all discourses, especially those whose speech seems Clearest, that is,
Realisms and Sciences. So, we can say that self-destruction is a management
strategy of an extreme avoidance kind for what is perceived as the threat of
self-destructiveness—the unclarity of one's own speech.[18] Deconstructive
relativisms, on this account, only *appear* to be uniquely self-destructive; and
perhaps they appear so only because this Naess tu quoque argument is Realism's way of countering Relativism's deconstructive attacks on its own treasured Clarity.

Or perhaps not. Perhaps relativist discourse suffers from greater and
more distinctive handicaps than this account admits. Let us review this possibility with an argument concerning the nature and limitations of propositional language and its role in the production of semantic paradoxes.
Propositional language, consisting of statements about the world, is inherently
a mode of assertion. Every statement *as* a statement is positive in that it can
be formally rendered with a prefix such as "It is true that . . ." To put it more
succinctly, every statement incorporates a metastatement that asserts the truth
of the statement. This is so even for those statements that, as far as the content of the assertion goes, are negative. "It is not true that X" can be formally written "It is true that it is not true that X." Problems of a paradoxical
kind arise with universal negative statements such as "Nothing is true." The
expansion of this is "It is true that nothing is true." The paradigm of such
semantic paradoxes is the paradox of the Liar. It is paradigmatic in that it
introduces explicitly the notion of lying; that is, it points to the usually implicit element of metastatement—"It is true that . . ."—in all statements.
There are then certain propositional statements that our language does not let

us make without contradicting the form in which all such statements must be made. For our purposes, the major class of such nonstatable statements are those that are sceptical, relativistic, or agnostic about claims to knowledge including (paradoxically but necessarily) their own.

This argument would suggest that the problem of relativism is basically linguistic. This is neither trivial nor resolvable; language is not an epiphenomenon that can be ignored or dispensed with in favour of more direct approaches to the (more) Real. However, accepting this linguistic diagnosis casts doubt on the warrant for the following kind of tu quoque argument made against SSK:

I shall try to show that truth is in a sense trans-social in character, by demonstrating the self-destructive nature of the contradictory position. (Meynell 1977:490)

To argue, as Meynell does here, that the assumptions of one epistemology must be accepted simply because the alternative suffers from a formulation problem is, apart from anything else, to deny the relevance of empirical investigation and evidence for *this* case of theory-choice. As Simonds remarked in defence of Karl Mannheim's sociology of knowledge,

to argue against [Mannheim] on the basis of an assumption of absolutism ("what I am saying is true") is clearly trivial, for self-referential consistency in such a sense is achieved only by taking as settled, without any reference to evidence, the very question which Mannheim proposes to investigate. (Simonds 1978:168)

The Question of Levels, the Status of Metadiscourse, and the Threat of Infinite Regress

[Kuhn] is caught in his own relativism [because] the new historiography cannot, on Kuhn's premises, properly claim any special status in relation to other historiographies. (Naess 1972:117)

[By the term relativism] I seek to designate any mode of investigation in social science which does not ascribe privilege to any particular order of discourse (particularly itself) vis-à-vis that order of discourse's capacities for representing other such orders. (McHoul 1981:107)

These two versions of relativism both express what we might term its relative powerlessness. For Naess, who talks of discursive power in the liberal terms of propriety and status, relativism's inability to claim a greater degree of credibility than its rivals is something to be regretted. For McHoul, however, who speaks of the power of discourse as a matter of privilege, relativism's refusal to ascribe privilege to itself is cause for congratulation.

Both Naess and McHoul agree, then, that relativism, when reflexively applied, is a discourse that has no firm grounding. And why is this? Because what this formulation says about relativist discourse is just what that discourse says about those others that are the topics of its talk. And this suggests that in the world according to relativist discourse *no* discourse has a firm grounding.

Relativity would seem to sum up all the threats to our cognitive security. Were truth and reality to be made context-dependent and culture-dependent by relativising philosophy, then the truth status of that philosophy is itself automatically destroyed. Therefore, anyone who would follow . . . must give up the comfort of stable anchorage for his cognitive efforts. (Douglas 1975: xvii)

I hope to persuade you that McHoul's nonprivileging and Douglas's cognitive precariousness is more interesting, more fruitful, more fun, more serious than the needless hankering for authority, status, and comfort that animates the tu quoque.[19] In order to do so I will have to deconstruct, not just the tu quoque but the way in which my own analysis appeals complicitly to a certain authority. I refer to the authority of the Higher Level, or of metadiscourse.

Let us see how both Naess's tu quoque and my own excursion into historiology depend on the privileging of the metalevel. The claim that Kuhn is "caught" in his relativism is a judgment about Kuhnian historiography made by Naess in the role of a Metakuhnian historiologist. But why stop the ascent of the levels here? On exactly the same basis a putative Metametakuhn with her metahistoriology could make similar judgments about Naess's historiology. The question I want to address concerns the cognitive status of those levels lower than the one being analysed. For instance, in the case of a Metakuhnian historiology (which finds Kuhn's historiography deficient in the ways we have examined), what becomes of the status of the level of natural scientific knowledge, the level that Kuhn finds deficient on the same grounds? If Naess's tu quoque is sustained, then it would seem we now have no warrant for trusting Kuhn. Thus, the level of natural science which Kuhnian historiography had so unjustly criticised can now be restored to its former glory.[20] (This would seem to fit the logic of the situation: the purpose or the consequence of producing anti-Kuhn and anti-SSK tu quoques is often to rescue science from relativist disrespect.)

Let us represent this process using numerals for the levels (2 for science, 3 for historiography, 4 for historiology, and so on) and the terms "deconstructs" and "resurrects" for what occurs at each level. Thus we get 4 deconstructs 3 and resurrects 2. Similarly, when we move to the next higher starting point (level 5: metahistoriology), we get 5 deconstructs 4 and resurrects 3 and deconstructs 2. The result of this little game is that each move to a higher level produces a domino effect on all the levels below such that, in the last example, Kuhnian historiography is born again and natural science is re-deconstructed. Naess's conclusion that Kuhn is "caught in his own relativism" thus gains all its credibility from the fact that Naess stopped at level 4; had he proceeded to level 5, he would have had to reverse his judgment. Of course, if he then proceeded to level 6 a reversal of the reversal would have been in order; but at level 7, once again . . .

But before we confront the infinite regress I want to venture a scandalous speculation about the fate of level 1 which represents, of course, the objects of science or, as I call them here, the World. According to our little model, 2 deconstructs 1 (science deconstructs the World). What can this mean? How can this be squared with an understanding of science, and science's self-understanding, as a matter of knowing and discovering the World? It seems to make equally little sense in terms of level 3's (e.g., SSK's) deconstruction of science's self-understanding. While no longer allowing science to be a matter of knowing and discovering, SSK's version of science as a process of construction and invention seems just as incompatible with the version we have arrived at here. Shortly, I will suggest that this incompatibility is only apparent. In order to see why, we have to take the formulation "science deconstructs the world" seriously.

What is really meant by deconstruction? Essentially it means the subversion of a Participant level self-understanding by a superior Analyst level meta-understanding. This is a very well-understood phenomenon invoked, for instance, in this well-known piece of folk methodology: Lord forgive them for they know not what they do. It simply represents the superior vantagepoint of the Observer or the superior knowledge of the Expert. In the context of natural science, however, talk of the superiority of the Observer seems to express a self-evidence so deep that its very *articulation,* never mind its denial, sounds distinctly odd. Does it? I hope so. In order to convince you that science can be understood as a deconstructive enterprise, it is necessary to disturb the deep self-evidence of statements such as these: the World is not a possible Participant—it has no discourse of its own that can be counterposed to science's discourse about it. The World simply *is* only an object—science's single vision is a simple necessity.

And yet people have not always and everywhere experienced the World in this way. Nonscientific cultures (if we believe *our* historical anthropology) lived *in* the World, not *off* it. People in such cultures were a part of the World in a way that we find it hard even to imagine. The World, to these Others, was not a dead realm of matter, moved but unmoving, incapable of Action; Science, understood as a broad historical and cultural project, makes it so; literally, makes it "it." We live in (or rather, apart from) a world of objects because this is the World for Science. The historical accident of the existence and success of the science project, fuelled, as it were, by an instrumental interest in prediction and control (Habermas 1971, 1972; Barnes 1977) has mutually constituted Man and World in a nondialectical opposition to each other.[21] The World as Object is the *result of* not the *warrant for* Science.

If this piece of speculative history seems to portray science more as a constructive enterprise than a deconstructive one, I would argue that successful constructions are simultaneously deconstructions, and vice versa. The old pre-science reality is deconstructed and replaced with a new construct, which, to science, has been there all along: the objective World. The phrases "science deconstructs the acting, participatory World" and "science constructs the objective World" describe the same historical process.

At this point, let's return to our numbers: 3 (metascience; SSK) deconstructs 2 (science) and resurrects 1 (the World). Here, then, is the scandalous speculation I promised. Nothing less than the Mission of the Millennium is entrusted to our intrepid little band of science deconstructors: the resurrection of the acting, participatory World!

In comparison with such a vision, the infamous infinite regress appears quite tractable. And it is—in practice. Infinity represents a phenomenon which cannot be experienced or known or reached. It is a purely "theoretical" term and does not name any-thing.[22] So why is it so frequently treated as a threat? Why so much talk of the spectre and the abyss?[23] Presumably, if the image of the abyss is anything to go by, such talk expresses the fear that once you start to fall you cannot stop because there is no bottom because the abyss is infinite: a fear of eternal death or a dream of Hell.

One circumstance that gives weight to the apparent reality of the infinite regress is that such phenomena can be produced in the world. An example is the effect produced in a mirror when it reflects the image of another mirror which reflects the image of the first mirror . . . repeatedly, with no theoretical end point to the process. However, the images do get smaller all the time, and, if you count them, you will stop quite soon. The *theoretically* infinite has a *practical* end. This point is brought out even more clearly with the cornflakes packet example. On your breakfast table is your packet of cornflakes and on your packet is a picture of the smiling Kellogg family at breakfast, and on their table is a picture of your packet which has a picture of the smiling Kellogg family, and so on, and so on (you know the one I mean). If you count how many packets there are the number will probably not be greater than the number accounted for in the last sentence, that is, four. Ah! you say, that is merely due to the limitations of the printing technology. And this, of course, is precisely my point.

If we return to Naess's arguments formulated from the apparent reality of a Kuhnian historiology, we can understand the relevant practical limitations which would prevent anything like an infinite metahistorical regress ever occurring.

Only the new historiographers of science can see through the epochs and tell us about their global character . . . . Those who, like [Naess], are not caught up in the act, but are simple, modest bystanders may . . . vaguely conceive its non-global character . . . .

But if the capacity to look at a string of historiographies from the outside should seem beyond him, who is left capable of discussing the issue at all? (Naess 1972:118–19)

Naess seems to be emphasising deficiencies in the capacity and capability of individual researchers as the relevant limitation. This does not seem convincing to me if he is suggesting that the interpretation of higher levels requires a correspondingly higher level of intellect. It is not a deficiency in the personal intellectual capacity of the potential researcher that makes metainquiry so comparatively rare and, perhaps, difficult. It is rather that there is always a comparative paucity of paradigmatic environments (in the Kuhnian sense) within which to undertake such inquiry. This is because metainquiry is parasitic upon its objects: it requires, for its existence, the prior development of the lower level(s). This is a purely pragmatic consideration, of course: the parasitism of metainquiry is no better or worse—because it is no different— than the parasitism of all Observer-privileged inquiry.

Perhaps the reader has got the worrying impression that I have been contradicting myself. How does my discussion of the pragmatic limitations to the infinite regress, which relies on the idea that in practice there is always a level at which metainquiry stops, square with my castigation of Naess for having stopped and my general advocacy of nonprivileging discourse?

First Answer: Contradiction Account

A discourse which refuses to privilege itself may justify the decision on the grounds of self-reflexive consistency with its insight into the falsely conscious nature of any and all discourses' claims for privilege. This insight is based on a recognition of the vulnerability of all discourses to metadiscursive deconstruction. And this recognition, in turn, relies on the imagery of the infinite regress for its plausibility. Therefore, to claim that the regress argument is irrelevant because of real world pragmatic limitations is to kick the major support out from under the carefully constructed arguments for nonprivileging discourse. (And so the whole house of cards collapses.) Moreover, an argument which stresses the importance of pragmatic limitations to the regress can itself be used for discourse-privileging purposes. Thus, there is indeed a contradiction.

Second Answer: Noncontradiction Account

The pragmatic limitation argument does not rule out any particular regress or metadiscursive deconstruction. Therefore, the argument for the essential vulnerability of discourse stands. This is, we can retain the notion of the infinite regress for purposes of justifying the refusal of privilege by reading it as a reference to the infinite *availability* of regress. At the same time we can use the pragmatic limitation argument to deconstruct the Hell and

Damnation imagery which manages, through its rhetoric of fear, to justify discursive privilege (however irrationally) by making any further ascents of the metalevels seem dangerous and, what is more, by making proposals to refuse privilege altogether seem equivalent to proposals to commit suicide. In short, there is no contradiction at all.

In pointing to a possible contradiction, addressing this possibility with the device of two contradictory accounts (contradiction versus noncontradiction) and thus setting up a new contradiction on the metalevel, it would seem that I am attempting to construct an insecure text that lacks discursive privilege. However, this appearance of textual insecurity is contradicted by the following consideration. If the text is claimed to exemplify nonprivileged discourse on the basis of a high contradiction count, this claim becomes problematic once we notice that it is not neutral with regard to some of these contradictions. That is, the claim contradicts the contradiction account contained in the First Answer (which contests the arguments for nonprivilege) and supports the noncontradiction account contained in the Second Answer (which is an argument in favour of nonprivilege). Interpolating the claim for nonprivilege (which originated as a claim *about* the text) "backwards" *into* the text in this way seems to contribute to a resolution of the possible contradiction with which we started: we now have good reason to reject the contradiction account and to accept the noncontradiction account. This result in turn annuls the metacontradiction; and we suddenly find ourselves without any contradictions at all. Unfortunately, it was the existence of all these contradictions that warranted the claim for a lack of textual privilege in the first place.

Perhaps all that need be said in conclusion to such convoluted and quite possibly contradictory considerations is, in agreement with McHoul, that " 'Pure' relativism [or nonprivileged discourse] is clearly an illusion" (1981: 107). In keeping with this modesty requirement, we shall continue our slow and digressive movement through the Naess tu quoques in pursuit of the impure reflexive discourse that will constitute a version of The One Best Way to Write.

The Necessity and the Impossibility of Being both Inside and Outside: The Participant/Analyst Dialectic and the Metascience Paradox

The historiographer cannot at the same time be both inside and outside. (Naess 1972:116)

Perhaps your most pressing initial question is, Why am I treating this apparently banal and obvious comment as a tu quoque? Surely Naess is merely repeating a truism rather than voicing a criticism? In one sense this is correct. On the version of inquiry that we have been talking of (and with) throughout—the version that relies in general on Observer-privilege and in particular on Metalevel-privilege—such a statement is indeed unremarkable. However, if it was really the case that insiderness and outsiderness were completely distinct realms, then reflexive argumentation, including the tu quoque itself, could have no purchase. Accusations of self-referentially consistent absurdity would be utterly idle if it was not possible (or, more weakly, not sensible) to understand a realm of practice in the terms that that practice uses to understand its realm of phenomena. If it is accepted that any tu quoque relies on the relevance of this interconnection, we seem to be back with the question with which this section started: How can I read a denial of this interconnection as a tu quoque? Frivolously, I could simply answer that I choose to do so; more responsibly, I have to acknowledge that it is not a well-formed example of the phenomenon. Despite its malformation it will be treated here as the most important obstacle that stands in the way of reflexive practice in general and my own project in particular. If it really is impossible to be inside and outside at the same time, then the project of working in/on SSK is likewise.

So far in this chapter we have been concerned with the outside. That is, we have been discussing modes of study and inquiry. Based on our interest in the possibility of a nonprivileging practice we found that ordinary nonreflexive inquiry is vitiated by its Observer-privilege. Using the availability of further metalevels to deconstruct this ordinary mode, we discovered that meta-inquiry itself is characterised by its privileging of the Higher Level—as is the tu quoque. Finally, through a consideration of the complexities of constructing a contradictory text, we arrived at the conclusion of the illusion of purity.

If the problems I have summarised here are the result of being outside, then perhaps we ought to investigate the other side of the coin: insiderness. Some of the fundamental features of the inside, the outside, and the relationship between them can be represented as and in a set of dichotomies.[24]

insiderness—outsiderness	lay—expert
internal—external	form of life—mode of inquiry
participant—analyst/observer	knowing how—knowing that
member—ethnomethodologist	subjective—objective
society—sociology	intuition—analysis
object—object language	implicit—explicit
object language—metalanguage	tacit knowledge—public knowledge
the World—science	unconscious—conscious
science—metascience	natural attitude—reflexive attitude

The items on the left of each pair are constructions of the items on the right, as are the latter themselves. This is the case almost by definition because the inside can only speak via the outside. For instance, to know that "knowing how" is an inside category is to engage in the outside category form of knowing, that is, "knowing that." It is not members who invent ethnomethodologists; ethnomethodologists are responsible for both members and ethnomethodologists.[25] The inside categories cannot be self-defining because the act of definition is only an outside category act. Once a "lay-participant-member" recognises herself as such she is doing "expert-analyst-ethnomethodologist" work. To describe even one's own skills as tacit knowledge is to produce public knowledge; and if this production is then itself described as another form of tacit knowledge, this latter description must again take the form of public knowledge. To sum up: the Inside is constructed by the Outside (which includes all forms of inquiry, reflection, thought, and discourse) to Name that which does not Name itself: Being, the Unthought, just livin'. On this deep phenomenological level we can surely agree with Naess that being inside and outside at the same time *is* impossible; if, that is, we desire to Speak. But of course Naess is concerned with the rather more superficial level of academic inquiry. If we turn his impossibilist assertion into the question, Can an analyst be inside and outside at the same time? what would be the grounds for rejecting his negative response?

The version of the inside/outside question which is concerned with the character of the participant/analyst dialectic can be formulated, Can one be an analyst and at the same time be a participant? The assumption behind the research practice of participant observation (or participant comprehension; Collins 1983a, 1983b, 1983c) is that this question has a positive answer. This form of research attempts to combine the requirements of an insider epistemology (Merton 1972) with those of an outsider epistemology. The former is based on the idea that the participant knows best. In some versions *only* the participant is capable of knowing anything. The problem for traditions of inquiry which accept the validity of this epistemology in any of its forms is that "inquiry" itself is predicated on the alternative outsider version of knowing. Participant observation is thus a balancing act between these two opposed ideals, each with its attendant dangers. Too much insiderness and one risks going native; too much outsiderness and one is in danger of mis-*Verstehen*-ing the situation. Can the contradictory loyalties of participant observers be successfully combined and thus transcended? Is it possible to practice in both modes simultaneously? What happens to the "hypothetical student of witchcraft practices, who returns from the field expecting both a PhD and recognition from fellow sorcerers" (Latour 1981:202)?

A rather more ambivalent form of the participant/analyst dialectic is presented by the highly paradoxical and highly relevant case of a science of science or an inquiry into inquiry. Insider epistemology has no credibility in (natural) science.

If you say to a biologist, "You cannot study a frog because you are not a frog," you will be laughed at. (Latour 1981:200)

Indeed, the hallmark of science is its belief in the virtue, and even the necessity, of the outsider stance. This is called objectivity. To study anything scientifically is thus to study it from the outside. If one wishes to study science scientifically—as, for example, Bloor does (1976:40)—one must therefore do so from the outside. But to be scientific is to practice science, and to practice science is to be a scientific insider. To study science scientifically is paradoxical because the only way to be scientifically objective is to abandon the practice of scientific objectivity. If considerations like these lead you to think that the solution lies in abandoning the objective of being scientific in science studies, in favour of being "agnostic" (Latour 1981), you will be sorely disappointed.

In order not to be scientific, one must be outside science; but to study science or anything else from the outside is to be scientific. Therefore, in order to study science unscientifically one must abandon objectivity and study it from the inside. But to be inside science means to be scientific. And therefore . . . well, I'm sure you take the point. Which is that this rather entertaining metascience paradox gives us an effective rejoinder to Naess's impossibilist tu quoque: in the study of science (and knowledge practices generally) the student *cannot avoid* being inside and outside at the same time. Another way of saying this is that the reflexivity of inquiry into inquiry is not a problem *for* that inquiry but a constituent problem *of* it (to paraphrase McHoul). All such work has to be written in as well as on its topic.

Naess, however, is concerned with a different matter. His formulation of the question, Can one be a participant and an analyst at once? would read: Can one be a participant in analytic practices and an analyst of these practices at the same time? In other words, is it possible to combine analysis and meta-analysis? Naess, of course, thinks not. Kuhn is simply *unable* to be a historiographer and a historiologist simultaneously.

Disregarding the issue of Thomas S. Kuhn's abilities—about which I have no relevant opinion—let us examine what the consequences could be of attempting analysis and meta-analysis simultaneously. Such a project appears to invite the dreaded infinite regress in which the fear is that "nothing (analytic) ever gets done" (McHoul 1982:100) because the analyst continually finds herself ascending the levels from meta- to metameta- to metametameta-analyses of each prior level with no justifiable or nonarbitrary point at which to stop. The result is thus a kind of paralysis (Collins 1981e:215). That Naess should find this prospect impossible (and Collins undesirable) is hardly surprising. I would argue, however, that the consequences of their type of negative response are equally unwelcome.

First, all that a negative response suggests is that meta-analysis not be undertaken as a part of the original analyst's analysis. It leaves the possibility of meta- (and metameta-) analysis by *others*—and thus the same threat of the regress—untouched. Any particular stopping-point will be just as arbitrary and unjustified; as is, for example, the third level meta-analysis of Kuhn by Naess from which the negative stipulation itself follows. Moreover, when meta-analysis is carried out as a standard practice only by others—as it is Today—higher levels of analysis can become institutionalised as disciplines (epistemology) or subdisciplines (historiology; sociology of sociology). Most important, if self-referential analysis could simply not be done, the book you are reading would not exist; along with every other conceivable write-able, its issues of practical reflexivity would be delegated—or relegated—to the meta-analyst as her "topic." As Collins says to Ashmore, and as Kuhn might wish to say to Naess:

> C: The reason it doesn't trouble me is that you're here. You're doing the job
>   of being reflexive for me.
> (HC 1515)

Both Naess's inside/outside tu quoque and the positive alternative to its negative stipulation share the same image of reflexive analysis as a practice necessarily involving regressive sequences of meta-analyses.[26] Such a vision is sterile and vastly unattractive.[27] Luckily it is not the only possibility for a reflexive practice.

Dis-Solution—Not the Only Possibility

Let's call it celebratory practical reflexive inquiry. [*It is not a matter of authorial presentation.*]

It is not enough to take reflexivity as one's topic (which is what this chapter does—which is why it is a failure).[28] [*It is not a matter of being correct.*]

It sets out to be a mode of inquiry. The self-destructive solution of noninquiry in which paradoxical problems are outlawed, and only the others suffer, is no solution at all. Indeed, by showing and displaying and talking around its own socially constituted nature, its own textuality and its own paradox, instead of always and only talking *of* these things, it can talk of other things. [*It is not a matter of meta-analysis.*]

It constitutes a denial and a dissolution of its prime problem: that inquiry requires, to *be* inquiry, a realist practice of realist writing, even if such a practice is presented as a mere heuristic; and perhaps especially if it is so presented. The way to solve the problem of realist inquiry is by a concentration on textuality and by the articulation of a practice of wrighting. This will include the use of new literary forms; though the problem of developing an adequate reflexive practice is unlikely thereby to be automatically solved. [*It is not a matter of solving a problem.*]

Celebratory practical reflexive inquiry is wrighting beyond the tu quoque. And it must be shown, not told.

Suspension and Conclusion

The application of the new historiography . . . to itself *hebt sie auf* suspends it. But suspension (*Aufhebung*) is not identical with refutation, and not necessarily an argument for abandonment of its research programme. (Naess 1972:119)

Indeed it isn't. The Hegelian term *Aufhebung* is far too dialectically subtle for that. It combines the ideas of suspension, with its connotation of a possibly temporary cessation; transcendence, which suggests a going beyond; and a kind of preservation. It is easy to feel sympathy with those who desire Clarity when faced with this masterpiece of multiconnotativity. However, it will serve us very well for purposes of summary. We will therefore apply the term, not to the new historiography or to ethnomethodology but to the tu quoque argument itself.

I have sought in this chapter not to refute the tu quoque but to *Aufhebung* it. To refute is to act in complicity. Refutations share the deep grounds of that which they refute. I have preferred to uncover the grounds of the tu quoque. What are they? A desire for certainty, straightforwardness, and clarity. A fear of regress, paradox, and the loss of control.

In order to do this work, the tu quoque must be suspended. But it doesn't disappear or self-destruct; it is preserved with the aim of its transcendence. For it is only beyond the tu quoque that a reflexive practice can discover its own possibility. Yet *Aufhebung* requires that the tu quoque be not forgotten. To paraphrastically reiterate McHoul once more:

The tu quoque is not a problem *for* a reflexive practice, but a constituent problem *of* it.

But also:

The "problem" of reflexivity turns out to be the preserver of relativism *for* relativism and not its destroyer.

CHAPTER FOUR

THE SIX STAGES

*The Life and Opinions of a
Replication Claim*

Six Replicating Pre-Texts

Whether ostensibly relativist or non-relativist, speech which seeks to "picture" commits itself *absolutely* to a correspondence theory of truth.

    David Silverman (1975b:155)

One cannot throw a sop to the dragon of relativity and then go about one's intellectual business as usual.

    Peter Berger (1969:55)

Science, unlike philosophy, is wrapped up in its own way of making things intelligible to the exclusion of all others. Or rather it applies its criteria unselfconsciously; for to be self-conscious about such matters *is* to be philosophical.

    Peter Winch (1958:102–3)

Socrates: Is there no way whatever of eliminating these paradoxes?
Theaetetus: There is a very simple way, Socrates.
Socrates: What is that?
Theaetetus: Just avoid them as nearly everybody does, and don't worry about them.
Socrates: But is this sufficient? Is this safe?

    Karl Popper (1972:309)

We might ask, for example, whether recognition of the self-reflexive character of the sociology of knowledge occasions any embarrassment or inconsistency in the work of sociologists of science.

    Mary Hesse (1980:44)

When a scientific finding is said to be demonstrable by its replicability, this claim needs close analysis.

    Harry Collins (1982b:372)

INTRODUCTORY DIALOGUE
OF THE REPLICATION ANALYSTS

A: The preliminaries are over. The real work of applying the sociology of
scientific knowledge to itself now begins. Harry Collins, my partner in
this dialogue and the main actor of this chapter, has suggested encour-
agingly that a major objective of a "putative" sociology of SSK would
be to provide an answer to the nontrivial and nonobvious question of
whether it is possible to treat SSK as a self-exemplifying discourse
[Collins 1981e:216]. Of course, readers must judge the results for
themselves, but . . .

C: Now hold on! You really shouldn't use this dialogic format as a justification for quoting out of context [Pinch and Pinch 1988]. I certainly
did not mean to imply in that flight of fancy that I was *recommending*
the sociology of SSK as an interesting and worthwhile research project.
I take it that we agree that any demonstration of self-exemplification
requires that SSK's knowledge be treated in the same way as SSK
treats scientific knowledge?

A: Certainly. And that's what I am trying to do.

C: Well, I have stated in print that to treat sociological knowledge as being
like scientific knowledge is an arbitrary, unnecessary, and undesirable
prescription [Collins and Pinch 1982:190] . . .

A: Naturally I entirely disagree with that.

C: . . . and furthermore, I have also written that questions of sociological
methodology and questions of the construction of natural scientific
knowledge can be kept separate [Collins 1982c:142].

A: Yes, but then you go on to say, and I quote: "The findings of the sociology of scientific knowledge *need*"—which you emphasise—"*need*
only inform sociology when the attempt is made to justify certain sociological methods by reference to canonical versions of scientific
method" [1982c:142].

C: So?

A: So! I am claiming that your own practice stands as a prime example of
this very pathology.

C: You're missing the point. "Here
is a definitive statement that
you can use if you wish: It is
clear that in some sense there
is a contradiction between discussing the permeability of
replicability in natural science
and claiming replicability as
a justification for my own
claims. It is hardly a contra-

A: Your treatment of replication in
natural science depicts it as
the most canonical element of
scientific method and *your*
method is designed to destroy
its canonical status by irony.
Fair enough. But then you
"change hats" and proceed
nonironically to (re-)claim the
canonical status of replication

diction that I overlooked. One couldn't really miss it. On the contrary, in making such strong claims about the replicability of the replication studies I was trying to show in dramatic form that the permeability of replication does not mean that it is still not the only criterion of what is to count as a natural regularity (or social regularity). It is the only one we have" [Collins: Letter, March 1983].

(Pause)

Did you hear what I said?

for the very studies that destroy it. Surely, you must see that in a case of this sort the sociology of scientific knowledge may have a salutary effect, as your own conclusion puts it [1982c:142]. Don't you agree that in this case at least my reflexive approach is absolutely relevant, entirely necessary, and totally desirable?

(Pause)

Did you hear what I said?

THE SUBSTANCE OF THE CLAIM: THREE REPLICATIONS

In this chapter I examine the credibility of a particular replication claim with the aid of a "recognition schema" developed for this purpose by Collins (1976, 1978b, 1985). The claim, made by Collins himself, is that his own original SSK studies of scientific replication in physics (1975) and parapsychology (1976) have themselves been replicated by other work.

One of the most well *replicated* outcomes of [SSK] concerns the social negotiation of reproducibility. (Collins 1982d:304)

The other work said to be responsible for achieving this state of affairs includes the five papers in the special issue (edited by Collins) of *Social Studies of Science* entitled *Knowledge and Controversy: Studies in Modern Natural Science* (Collins 1981a). As Collins puts it in his introduction (1981b:4), in these papers

the socially-negotiated character of experimental replication is further documented.

Collins repeats the claim in an article reviewing his "empirical programme of relativism":

The sociology of scientific knowledge offers unusually good opportunities for replication . . . and much has been independently confirmed [including] the replication studies (e.g., Collins 1981a). (Collins 1983a:92 and 108, n.8)

THE MEANING OF THE CLAIM:
TWO VERSIONS OF REPLICATION

In Collins's studies of, and writings on, scientific replication (1975, 1976, 1978a, 1978b, 1982b, 1984b, 1985, 1987d) he puts forward a version of replication in opposition to that which he treats as the "standard view" of the phenomenon. In this standard version, the reproducibility of scientists' findings is seen as the major epistemological guarantor of scientific validity while the institutionalisation of replication as a behavioural norm acts as an effective mechanism of social control (Zuckerman 1977). Collins's version, in contrast, treats replication as a problematic and complex phenomenon, the meaning of any particular instance of which is subject to social negotiation over the relevance of perceived similarities or differences between the events (e.g., experiments) concerned. As no two events can be totally identical, there is always a "space" for this negotiation of sameness/difference. The success or lack of success of any replication claim can never, therefore, rest on the way the world is; rather, it must rest on social agreement in the relevant community.[1]

As the basis for an analysis of the status of Collins's replication claim, we need to understand which of these two versions of the phenomenon is implicated in the claim. Here is how Collins formulated and attended to this question in interview:[2]

> C: Is your question this: You're asking me this: when I say that sociology—
> the replication studies have been replicated, do I mean that they have
> been replicated in the way that a scientist would say, "This observation
> has been replicated," or do I mean that the replication studies are self-
> exemplifying?
> A: Well, I wasn't going to ask you whether you thought they were [self-
> exemplifying] because I imagined you thought they weren't.
> C: That's right.
> A: Right. So it's in the first sense in the . . .
> C: Yeah.
> A: . . . sense of the scientist.
> C: Yeah.
> A: Um. I'm just wondering how, how you can live with those two things at
> the same . . .
> C: Well, no problem at all. I just ban reflexivity![3]
> A: (Laughter)
> (HC 1509–14)

The consequence of banning reflexivity in this context is a principled refusal to connect claims *about* replication with claims *for* replication. In the following two quotations, the first from a general discussion of the sociology of scientific method and the second from a review of his own programme, Collins presents the standard view of replication in very similar and yet very different terms:

The objectivity of science and its insulation from social and political biases are supposed to be ensured by . . . above all, the possibility of replication of . . . work by independent parties. (1981d:7)

Ultimately the argument for all these things rests . . . above all on independent replication of the findings. (1983a:92)

In the first quotation, where the topic is *others'* scientific work, the standard view that quality is dependent "above all" on independent replication is presented ironically; here, this is merely "supposed to be" the case. In the second quotation, however, where the topic is the methods and findings of Collins's own work, this note of irony vanishes. When it comes to replication in SSK, Collins seems to be among those holding the "widespread view that replicability is essential in science" (Collins 1982b:372) and among those who insist that replicability guarantees the validity of their own knowledge-claims.[4]

Visions of a Realist Practice

In the sciences the apparent externality of things seen is celebrated and reinforced by the notion that anyone would see the same things if they looked in the same place. If anyone would see the same thing, then its sameness must be a product of *it* rather than a product of the see-er. (Collins 1983a:90)

This is Collins's elegant description of the role of replicability in sustaining the sense of the independent existence of "things." As it stands, Collins's exposition of realism is both partial and ironic: the standard view of replication "in the sciences" is portrayed as a "notion" which, by means of rhetoric and reaffirmation, manages to produce the appearance of an external reality.

When Collins discusses his own practice, however, the idea that replicatory practice *produces* the sense of the real is abandoned. Instead, as in the standard view, acts of replication *discover* the real.

> C: If you do a case study of that, the "Seven Sexes" sort, you know, gravity waves, the fact that science is roughly like it's described in that study comes out with such astonishing clarity that even somebody like me who's done it once or twice already is surprised at just how true it is . . . . I can only say that if you go into the field and do a study of that sort, wham! it hits you right between the eyes once, you know, once you've started to look at it in the right way. You know, once you say, right, how

do they decide exactly? It just repeats itself over and over again . . . .
My *plea* is, just like the natural scientists' one: Bloody hell, don't argue
with me, go out and look. You'll see it's the same. And everybody
who—various students and other people who've done it, have come back
with that kind of reaction: yeah, it is the same, it's unproblematic. It's
actually a very easy—one of the things that's very easy to observe, it's
probably a lot easier to observe than gravity waves. It's a very easily,
readily observable phenomenon that science is like that.
(HC 1406–20)

And because the phenomenon in question—the problematic character of replication—is so "readily observable," the practice of research remains satisfying, interesting, and worthwhile.

C: The only reason that doing a piece of research gives me satisfaction or the
only reason why I can work up the motivation to do it, is because I think
I'm saying . . . something that's true by which I mean something that
other people would go out and see for themselves if they wanted and
without that attitude—if I went into my research with the attitude, well
it's all negotiation so that in fact brainwashing people would be just
as good as telling the truth, then I wouldn't be interested in doing any
research.
(HC 2001–05)
C: If you want to do interesting research, I say approach it with this mental
attitude . . . in the same way as the natural scientist approaches doing
natural science, with that same degree of excitement, with the same
degree of certainty that you're dealing with an objective reality, with the
same degree of certainty that anybody who goes and looks will see the
same things.
(HC 1715–19)

THE SCHEMA OF THE SIX STAGES

Replication claims can be considered claims for the sameness of (at least two)
sets of findings. As Collins tells us that the problem of sameness is "the topic
of the replication studies" (1983a:108), I draw upon the findings and methods
of these studies for help in assessing the credibility of Collins's particular
claim-for-sameness. In particular, I use an adapted version of the six-stage
schema from Collins's (1976) study of replication in parapsychology. This
device consists of the "stages of demarcation [that] are generated . . . by
asking how a series of replications might be recognised" (1976:4). I also
make some use of the idea, originally put forward in "The Seven Sexes"
(Collins 1975), that it is in negotiations over what is to count as the set
of competent experiments (or "Studies"—see Stage Two below) that the

existence and characteristics of the phenomena with which they deal are established.

My strategy is as follows. First I set out an adapted version of the schema with appropriate changes to fit the present context. Then, sticking closely to Collins's original analyses, I go through the stages showing the difficulty of making an unambiguous decision on whether the candidate-replicators claimed by Collins "pass" on each criterion.

Imagine there has been some . . . experiment E [Study X] performed by scientist S [undertaken by researcher C] at time t. After time t the life of the world goes on, and is filled with multifarious activities. How can it be decided if some subset of those activities render E [X] a "successfully replicated experiment [Study]?" Imagine a search is to be conducted through all the post-t activities in order to find a set of replications of E [X] and make the appropriate decision, and suppose that the proce-dure adopted is to remove from consideration all activities that could not count as replications of E [X] for one reason or another, so that in the end all that is left is a residue which consists of the appropriate set. A series of decisions would be required such as the following:

Stage 1 Reject all activities that are not to do with the phenomenon [under investigation, i.e., replication].

Stage 2 From the remaining set of activities, reject all those which aren't ex-periments [Studies].

Stage 3 From the set of experiments [Studies], reject all those where the identity of the experimenter [researcher] is inappropriate.

Stage 4 From what remains reject all experiments [Studies] that were not com-petent copies of E [X].

Stage 5 Divide the remaining set into those which generated negative results [produced different findings] and those which generated positive results [produced the same findings].

Stage 6 Decide whether E [X] has been replicated.[5] (1976:4–5. See also Col-lins 1978b:2–3, 1985:38–39)

In what follows, Collins (1975, 1976) plays the role of "X," while the five contributors to *Knowledge and Controversy* (Collins 1981a) play the candidate-replicators. These are Travis (1981), Collins (1981c), Pickering (1981a), Harvey (1981), and Pinch (1981).

Stage One: Are the Candidate-Replicators about Replication?

A fundamental aspect of Collins's replication claim is his use of the term "replication studies" to characterise the five candidate-replicators. This im-plies, of course, that replication is, at least in part, the topic of these studies. And, usually collectively but sometimes independently, all these studies have indeed been cited as such in the SSK literature (Ashmore 1985:fig.2).

However, as Collins has argued, such consensual characterisations tend to be unstable in the "core-set" itself (1981d). And, indeed, in interview, Pinch claimed that only one of the five papers was a genuine replication study:

> A: Harry [Collins] claims that the replication studies are mutually replicating.
> P: Yeah, that's—there's only one of those, isn't there? That's, uh, Dave Travis's.
> (TP 0517–18)

Bibliographic services working on keyword classification would be likely to endorse this assessment. Travis's article is the only one, in the title or the abstract, to contain the word "replication."

My own reading of the position is this: replication is a central topic in Travis, a marginal topic in Collins and in Pickering, a less-than-central but more-than-marginal topic in Harvey, and a nonexistent topic in Pinch. I say nonexistent with unusual confidence because in the solar neutrino field, according to Pinch, "only one experiment has been completed so far" (1981:132). I have been unable to invent a version of replication that fails to include at least two such events.

Now, it might be argued that the label "replication studies" is really only meant to be a convenient shorthand method of collecting this particular set of writings and writers. However, Collins often wants to claim more than this. When we read (again) that "one of the most well *replicated* outcomes of [Collins's] programme is the social negotiation of reproducibility" (1982d: 304) it is hard to avoid the impression that this is a claim for the existence of a certain number of studies, all of which demonstrate the social negotiation of reproducibility.[6] That is, that there exists a set of *accurately described* replication studies.

Following the argument in Collins (1975), the accuracy of this description is one of the issues that is settled, for all practical purposes, by the fate of the replication claim itself. Its acceptance, and thus its success, would entail membership of the set of replication studies for the five papers in question. (To my knowledge, Collins's claim has not been seriously contested. The question of the ambiguous role of my own work in this regard is dealt with later.)

Stage Two: Are the Candidate-Replicators Studies?

The capitalisation of the word "Study" designates its technical meaning as used here: Studies are simply those pieces of sociological work that consist of empirical research. For sociology to be in any sense replicable it must be in some sense empirical. Thus the task at this stage would appear to be reasonably unproblematic: all we have to do is to distinguish empirical work from other kinds and to remove the latter from consideration. Work could thus be rejected if it were programmatic, theoretical, methodological, a review of the literature, a reply to criticism, a polemic, and so on. Put simply, the difference appears to be between "doing . . . sociology . . . as opposed to talking about it" (Collins 1983a:102). The problem is that any particular paper, whether based on empirical research or not, will tend to contain a measure of theoretical discussion, a review of the relevant literature, and suggestions for further research. Demarcation based on the rejection of all candidate Studies that include elements of the nonempirical would reject virtually all sociological work.

The alternative decision—to reject candidate Studies if they contain no empirical element—might seem to be more productive. However, this procedure would rest on criteria for recognising the empirical that are far from easy to apply (in theory). If "empiricality" consists essentially of a method for going out and looking, it could be argued that *all* scholarly or academic work consists of some form of looking, if only at documents.

If distinguishing the empirical from the nonempirical may be difficult to justify, in SSK the distinction is nevertheless regularly applied in practice. Mulkay, for instance, in a comprehensive review of sociology of science in the West distinguishes "work based upon close examination of original empirical material . . . in which particular aspects of knowledge production have been explored in depth [from] abstract discussions . . . or attempts to provide some . . . conceptual apparatus" (1980a:81). This type of evaluative categorisation is widespread in SSK participants' reviewing practices (Shapin 1982; Collins 1983a). It appears to be linked with and perhaps to be dependent upon an equally widespread evaluation of the "empirical case study" as the ideal form of work. Pinch's comments in interview are typical:

> P: I think it's very dangerous once you get away from empirical work because the whole, this whole field is characterised by good solid empirical work. A lot of people have done it and that's one of the things that made it a better field than most fields of sociology.
> (TP 0816–19)

With such unanimity from practitioners I can only repeat that this agreement can have no unassailable formal grounds. Luckily, this kind of conclusion seems to constitute a general finding of SSK empirical work. (See, for instance, Mulkay 1980a:89.)

A second dimension of ambiguity at Stage Two concerns the appropriate "size" of an experiment or a Study. In the case of parapsychology, Collins comments that "demarcation at this stage demands that an experiment be distinguished from, for instance, a preliminary observation" (1976:6). A Study, then, could be taken to be either a complete research project or any particular paper arising from it. Moreover, if a particular paper is concerned with only the early stages of a project it could be treated as analogous to a preliminary observation. Such ambiguity seems to be evident in Collins's various comments on the candidate-replicators. In one of his replication claims (Collins 1983a:92), the items referred to are the specific papers appearing in *Knowledge and Controversy*. However in his "core-set" article (1981d) Collins refers to the same authors dealing with the same topics in terms of research projects. Although no replication claim is made in this text it remains difficult to be sure whether Collins means to claim a replication of projects or a replication of papers. The relevance of this ambiguity is that moving from one position to another could be significant in negotiations over the claim. For instance, if a critic were to point out that a paper that was claimed to be a "replication study" did not appear to deal with the topic of replication (see Stage One), the claimant could reply that the larger project, of which the paper was only a (perhaps preliminary) part, did indeed deal with this topic.

Stage Three: Have the Candidate-Replicators Appropriate Identities?

[Researchers] might be "inappropriate" because of the relationship they have with the original [researcher C]. Thus one might look at the relative value of [Studies undertaken] by students of [C], members of the same group, known sympathizers, known sceptics and so on. It might be hypothesised that the greater the social and cognitive separation of [C] and a repeating [researcher], the greater the value of a positive replication, and vice versa. (Collins 1976:7)

The implication of this is that "critics will question the outcome if most results come from one 'socio-academic' camp" (Collins 1978a:391).

Travis

David Travis "is a Research Fellow at the Polytechnic of North London. He is completing a thesis, begun at the University of Bath, on the 'memory transfer' controversy" (Collins 1981a:32).[7]

> T: Harry gave a seminar . . . which was an early version of "The Seven Sexes" paper and that was just sort of click you know, bang, here we are. And then I came to, you know, to do some research, wanting to do research in sociology of science, it was basically wanting to do the degree at Bath. Harry said, you know, stay at Bath. That was how I came to it.
> (DT 1603–06)
> T: When I first started out as a [graduate] student, I mean I was the first one to start anything that looked like Harry's research, and I chose the area because it was a scientific controversy and there were arguments about the facts of the matter.
> (DT 0706–09)

Collins comments thus on the problem of student replications: "A single positive replication by an academic archenemy would provide more evidence, as far as neutral parties were concerned, than any number of replications by a proponent's own graduate students" (1978a: 391–92). This would seem, then, to be a clear case of a candidate-replicator with an "inappropriate identity." On the basis of Collins's own criteria, Travis appears far too close to "C" sociocognitively speaking, to be able to play the role of an independent replicator to the satisfaction of a critic of the replication claim.

However, it could be argued that because Travis had ceased to be Collins's graduate student at the time of the production and publication of the specific *paper* that is the subject of the replication claim, Travis's independence is thereby analytically increased. (An example of the use of Stage Two's project/paper argument.) But I think it doubtful that this would greatly deter a determined critic. Perhaps, then, an argument could be put forward stressing the simplistic nature of the supervisor/graduate student relationship implied in the independence criterion. However, despite the fact that Travis does sometimes claim to be doing something different from Collins (see Stage Four), having experienced the difficulty of convincing people in SSK that being Mulkay's graduate student does not make me a discourse analyst, again I doubt that an argument on these lines would be very convincing to a critic.[8]

Collins

Harry Collins "is Lecturer in Sociology at the University of Bath and Convener of the Sociology of Science Study Group of the British Sociological Association. He is the author of a number of papers in the area of sociology of scientific knowledge, mostly using case material from physics and from parapsychology" (Collins 1981a: 62).[9]

We would seem to have here an obvious example of "the special case where the relationship of the replicating [researcher to C] is one of identity" (Collins 1976: 7). In this case, presumably, independence from the originator is by definition zero. Alternatively, Collins comments that self-replication may be treated as an altogether different kind of phenomenon: "Critics do not count a series of positive results by the same [researcher] as a positive series of *replications*" (1976: 7). Although the paper in question—"Son of Seven Sexes: The Social Destruction of a Physical Phenomenon" (1981c)—is implicitly included in the replication claim, when Collins discusses its particular relationship to "The Seven Sexes" his claims are of a different character. For instance: "Collins' paper is a *development* of earlier work on replication in gravity wave experiments" (1981b: 5); "As its title implies, it *builds directly* upon . . . 'The Seven Sexes'" (1981c: 33); "In this paper I *continue* the documentation of the history of the detection of gravitational radiation" (1981c: 34; my emphases). In these comments Collins is treating both papers as two stages of the one project; in fact as a (two-element) series. In this case the claimant himself seems to be unwilling to count such a series as entailing a relation of replication.

The situation would appear to be this: either Collins is ruled out as a candidate-replicator because his relationship to the originator is rather too close, or because he never claimed to be a candidate in the first place. Either way, it is clear that the schema, and especially Stage Three's independence criterion, works efficiently for critical purposes.

Pickering

Andrew Pickering "is a Research Fellow at the University of Edinburgh [Science Studies Unit], where his current research concerns the development of elementary particle physics" (Collins 1981a:93).[10]

On the face of it, Pickering's independence would seem greater than, for instance, Travis's merely because he has always worked at a different institution than Collins. This impression is strengthened by his connection to the Science Studies Unit at Edinburgh. My "SSK native competence" tells me that the unit is the home of the Strong Programme and Interest Theory together with their various originators/perpetrators including Barnes and Bloor, both of whom Collins has criticised in print (anti-Barnes: Collins and Cox 1976, 1977; anti-Bloor: Collins 1981e). More recently, however, Collins has depicted both "schools"—the Bath and the Edinburgh—as being defined by a common characteristic:

> C: The crucial description that binds all this sort of work together is probably less "relativism" and more "symmetry"—and there I think we see exactly eye-to-eye.
> (HC 2701–03)

What is more, the things that are different are unimportant: "The differences are on small points of methodology and on minor philosophical issues" (Collins 1983a:108).

The following interview selections are concerned with how Pickering treats the relationships Edinburgh/Bath and Pickering/Collins:

> A: Do you think there's a difference between what goes on at Edinburgh and what goes on at Bath?
> P: Yes, in a way, I mean when you talk about Bath you think especially of Harry and Harry's work is singlemindedly devoted to . . . showing that any piece of knowledge can be deconstructed. I guess up here we're more concerned with understanding how . . . pieces of knowledge actually do get put together . . . . But I think basically we're all doing the same thing. I've never managed to have a proper argument with Harry about anything at all—I've often tried to. It usually ends up in just saying, Yes you're right. (Laughter)
> (AP 0211–0303)
> P: I tried to express as clearly as I could what I felt to be the difference

between my approach and Harry's and Harry just said there's nothing to argue about. And I think we generally end up agreeing that what he wants to do is to show that all knowledge is deconstructible and what I want to do is to show how this is papered over in practice. So is it the same or is it different?

(AP 0809–13)

The last selection can be glossed as an agreement to differ. Such essentially ambiguous formulations can be used for critical or for friendly purposes simply by emphasising one or other of the elements. For instance, Collins's replication claim could be supported by emphasising the "difference" aspect, thereby producing the appropriate degree of independence. Despite such subtleties, an informed critic would no doubt insist that Pickering is far from being an academic archenemy or a known sceptic; however, in interview Pickering states that he used to be highly sceptical of SSK ideas:

> P: When I first came up here I was, well, completely against people like Kuhn. I thought his *Structure of Scientific Revolutions* was talking through the back of his head, and I was also extremely perplexed about Harry Collins's own work. I remember when I first went to Bath before I came here, he showed me a copy of "The Seven Sexes" . . . I remember I asked him whether it was a joke . . . I thought I'd look at a couple of controversies just to see how I would make sense of them for myself. Yeah, and with the idea of probably refuting what Harry was saying. And, uh, the more I looked into it and the more I studied what Harry had written . . . in "The Seven Sexes," I was—that was one of the things that started me agreeing with the whole programme of the sociology of knowledge, and I tended to agree with him.

(AP 0703–12)

Have we found an appropriate replicator after all? Someone who set out to "probably refute" but who, after "looking at a couple of controversies" and studying the original text, ended by "agreeing with the whole programme"? Such a conclusion, a critic might argue, would depend on the *time* at which such a conversion took place. If Pickering was already converted by the time he wrote his contribution to *Knowledge and Controversy,* he would not look nearly so appropriate a replicator. However, in the following interview extract, Pickering displays the essentially equivocal nature of such judgments:

> P: I always saw all my work on theory development as being an argument against Harry. At that time I felt that I'd discovered something new . . . . So at the time I would have said that, although Harry claimed that my monopole paper [1981a] was like his work [1975, 1981c], I would claim that it wasn't (Laughter) . . . . It proves that I reached the conclusions that I wanted to even though Harry claims that I agree with him.
> A: Yes. Yes that's right, he does. So you're claiming that there's no way in

which your work could be seen as a replication of the main (drift) of Harry's?

P: Well, I suppose if reflexivity is the topic of this conversation then I will have to say it can be glossed either way.

(AP 0715–0808)

Exactly.

Harvey

Bill Harvey "is a lecturer at Napier College, Edinburgh, where he is currently completing a sociological study of the quantum physics community, for which most of the research was done at the Science Studies Unit, University of Edinburgh" (Collins 1981a:130).[11]

Everything said about Edinburgh and the unit in the Pickering section also applies here, of course. Harvey's move away from the unit might well imply more independence from that institution, but it says little about his independence from Collins. Here is Harvey on the latter relationship:

A: Do you ally yourself with . . . either the strong programme or the Edinburgh School? How do you sort of place yourself?

H: Well, I suppose if I had to align myself with a group it would be the Bath group, insofar as there is a Bath group, rather than with what's going on within the unit.

(BH 1105–09)

H: It's possible to do the stuff that Collins does without having prior sociological theory, and really just by being hypercritical of what people tell you, the contingencies and so on emerge. So that's why—if you like to think of a single paper that influenced me, it would be Collins's "Seven Sexes" and I saw this could be done.

(BH 1117–1202)

Here again then Harvey provides ample ammunition with which a critic could conclude that he has an inappropriate identity. Nevertheless, a friend of the replication claim would be able to argue that his institutional remoteness from the originator counts considerably toward his independence as does the fact that he has never studied under, or worked with, Collins.

Pinch

Trevor Pinch "is a Research Fellow in the School of Humanities and Social Sciences, University of Bath. His specialist area is the sociology of scientific controversy. He . . . has collaborated with H. M. Collins on research in the sociology of parapsychology. He is currently completing a sociological study of the development of solar neutrino astronomy. He is the co-author (with H. M. Collins) of *Frames of Meaning: The Social Construction of Extraordinary Science*" (Collins 1981a:158).[12]

After graduating in physics, Pinch did a Masters degree in the sociology of science at Manchester:

> P: When I used to work in Manchester, I used to find out all these things about this controversy [see Pinch 1977] and it seemed really exciting. Um, you know, lots of things in the sociology of science, scientific knowledge which were then—the ideas were just up for grabs, were star[ting], star[ting]—actually appeared to be true. You could, you know, you could see scientists actually fighting over technical arguments and—because at that stage I still had a lingering, like most people in this area at first, sort of Lakatosian methodology . . . . And I think Andy Pickering was the same . . . . I stood out for scientific rationality against relativism for quite a long while. Um. But eventually Lakatos went by the board.
> (TP 0101–10)

Interrupted Dialogue—Concerning Symmetry—between a Friend and a Critic

Friend of the Replication Claim: Aha! It looks as if Pinch might be an appropriate replicator. We seem to have evidence here of the same kind of conversion as Pickering underwent. Pinch's mention of Pickering in this context is undoubtedly significant.

Critic of the Replication Claim: I don't think that kind of consideration can outweigh the extremely close sociocognitive relationship between Pinch and Collins. And besides, the conversion factor is only significant for your position if the timing is right. I think we had better hear some more.

Then Pinch went to Bath as research officer on the "spoon bending" project, directed by Collins, that resulted in the joint-authored *Frames of Meaning* (Collins and Pinch 1982):

> P: By the time I finished the research I agreed entirely with Harry that this was the best approach. Um, and I wouldn't distance myself from Harry at that stage on any issues at all. I think we saw eye-to-eye on most things in the field.
> (TP 0712–14)

Critic: There you are. What did I tell you? You can't get a much clearer statement than that.

Friend: Aren't you being a bit premature? I thought you said that timing was everything. The period Pinch is discussing in this extract is prior to his research on solar neutrinos which is the topic of the paper in question. I think we had better hear some more.

After this Pinch carried out research for a PhD supervised by Collins. His paper in *Knowledge and Controversy*—"The Sun Set" (1981)—is a report from that research:

> P: Now, in my PhD [1982a] I take that second stage [of the empirical pro-
> gramme of relativism] I think further than Harry would like in the sense
> that I actually use interests models to explain what went on in the solar
> neutrino field . . . . So I am separated from Harry in the sense that I'm
> pushing for interests models and Harry doesn't have any interest himself
> in interests models.
> (TP 0808–14)

Friend: You see! At the relevant time, Pinch has retreated from his earlier
total agreement with Collins and is evidently at serious odds with him
on the crucial question of methodology.

Critic: I'm afraid you are reading far too much into this "small point of
methodology" as Collins [1983a: 108] himself describes his differences with the Edinburgh interests theorists. And at the time, remember, Pinch was Collins's graduate student. Such a relationship plays
havoc with a candidate-replicator's independence, as we know. But
maybe our Author has some more evidence, though I cannot believe it
will help your case very much.

> P: I mean for me, I was originally a physicist and actually find the thing about
> actually studying science of interest and I don't think Harry—for Harry
> science is, it doesn't really matter that much.
> (TP 0906–07)

Friend: Your confidence is obviously unjustified. Here, Pinch is expressing
a major disagreement with Collins about the entire rationale of the
whole enterprise.

Critic: You're wrong in two important ways. First, this kind of disagreement is unimportant on a practical level: the programme is pursued
regardless. Second, I have reason to believe that Pinch has simply misunderstood Collins on this one. Author, if you would oblige us with a
quote from Collins's interview?

> C: I happen to find physics the most interesting of the sciences and I'm bound
> to like researching on it.
> (HC 0208)

Critic: I think that's conclusive.

Friend: You're mistaken. The point is not the relative intrinsic interest of
particular sciences; it is, as I have said, the *aim* of the work that is at
issue here. Author, another quote from Collins, if you will.

Relativists typically choose to study science only because it is generally counted as
the canonical example of knowledge, or because it is a readily accessible knowledge-

producing institution . . . . The relativists' *constitutive* question is . . . about knowledge in general, not about scientific knowledge in particular. (1982d:300)

Friend: It would seem that Pinch is not a typical relativist after all. One to
me, I think.
Critic: I think not. Why not let our candidate speak for himself?

> P: I think, you know, it's like natural scientists, I think to a large extent I'm
> working within a research programme, a relativist programme that's been
> mapped out in Harry's empirical programme of relativism . . .

Critic: I rest my case.
Friend: I hadn't expected dishonesty from you, or collusion from our
Author, come to that. There's more to come, obviously: notice the
three little dots and the absence of any reference? So if we could continue . . .

> . . . and I've got a few quibbles with that, but roughly it says . . . the first
> chapter of my PhD . . . sets out what, where I disagree with Harry's pro-
> gramme . . .

Friend: . . . we can see that disagreement is still rife.
Critic: You must be really desperate to insist on displaying an extract that
explicitly refers to "a few quibbles." A quibble is just a quibble and
should be of no concern in such a learned disputation as this. If this is
the best you can do, even with the obvious assistance of our Author
who quite clearly is on *your* side—notice how he cuts it off immediately after the relatively strong "disagree" phrase—well, I think you
should admit that you're beaten. I must insist that our corrupt Author
finally completes this extract.

> . . . and it says at the start: I'm doing essentially a piece of normal relativism
> and there's no need to get into the philosophical issues again, so I'm not
> going to defend relativism, I'm just going to go on ahead and do empiri-
> cal studies and that they'll stand or fall on the empirical work, whether
> it's telling us anything interesting about science.
> (TP 2312–2402)

Critic: I was right! This is the kind of thing Collins says all the time.[13] And
I was right about our so-called Author too. His feeble attempt to withhold such a damning piece of evidence for Pinch's lack of independence is contemptible.
Friend: On the contrary, he has in fact been biased in your favour throughout Stage Three. If another Friend [?] hadn't interceded on behalf of

justice and symmetry and persuaded our Author to revise his very first draft of this chapter, we wouldn't have had our say.

Critic: *You* wouldn't, you mean.

Friend: Exactly! The section on Pinch might well have consisted in its entirety of the following kind of asymmetrical comment which is typical of that first draft: "Documentation of agreements, relationships or even 'quibbles' with Collins seem quite unnecessary for a candidate whose sociocognitive distance from the originator is clearly so small; indeed the smallest of all, with the exception of Collins himself" (Ashmore 1983:39).

Critic: Well, what's wrong with that? I can't fault it and I don't see how Collins can either. After all, it seems to follow as a straightforward application of his own analytic apparatus. Is it our Author's fault if Collins is hoist with his own petard? Surely not; any more than it is if our Author's original conclusion happened to coincide with my own. He should have had the courage of his convictions and stuck to his guns.

Friend: Perhaps. But in any case he certainly could not have kept his original reference to horse racing . . .

Critic: Horse racing?

Friend: Yes. In his first version he wrote this as his conclusion to Stage Three: "There is a sense in which the Schema is like a steeplechase with each Stage as a fence . . . . All our candidate-replicators . . . appear to have fallen at the third (with the possible exception of Pickering, who might, or might not, have picked himself up and Collins who might have refused!)" (Ashmore 1983:39). Now, this is simply the wrong approach. "The point of the whole schema is never to say who has passed through each stage but to show that there is ambiguity in deciding who has got through each stage. The main point is to show that it is not possible to come to an unambiguous conclusion about whether [X] has been replicated at time t, *not* to provide an algorithm for reaching that conclusion! The horse race, therefore, has different outcomes for different people. Everyone will claim that it is they who have won the money." [14]

Critic: That speech sounds terribly like Collins. I realise, of course, that you support his replication claim on the participant level, but surely it is unjustified to enrol his particular *analytic* position on your side.

Friend: But by its very nature, relativist analysis is *symmetrical* and therefore does not take sides in the controversies it examines. Its whole point is to be disinterested and neutral in such disputes. The distinctly *non*relativist analysis of our Author's earlier draft, on the other hand, clearly did come down on one side: yours.

Critic: But that wasn't a matter of taking sides. That was a coincidental outcome of using the form of analysis recommended *by* the originator *on* the originator. Ironic, no doubt, but hardly biased. Your analytical recommendations, however, clearly let Collins off the hook. No wonder you are so keen on them.

If I might interrupt this dialogue, I may be able to settle this dispute. The problem here seems to revolve around the ambiguous status of the six-stage schema itself which is at once an external-analysts' resource for SSK research and an internal-participants' resource in controversies over replication. Now, in this dispute between the Friend and the Critic, both of the protagonists clearly recognise this ambiguity and both of them equally clearly deplore it. The consequence is that they each accuse me of being on the other's side (of using the Schema as a participants' resource) while recommending as the alternative that I should, and therefore could, remain neutral by using the Schema in a purely analytical way. Thus, the Friend sees the old Stage Three (Ashmore 1983) as illegitimately biased toward the Critic and assumes that the new version has solved the problem of bias altogether. And the Critic sees this present Stage Three as taking sides with the Friend's position and thus recommends a return to the old unbiased version.

In his commentary on that first draft, Collins writes:

My hypotheses about who is inappropriate as a replicator give a *possible* set of criteria but not a definitive set. My hypotheses would probably be argued as necessary by a critic but not by the originator. Thus, if I put on my nonreflexive hat again, I would say that all the replicators are appropriate. (Letter, March 1983)

It seems to me that Collins here "admits" that his hypotheses are not neutral and, moreover, that they can be appropriated, as we have seen in the Dialogue, *only* by the Critic. The originator (and the Friend) can have no use for them. They would have to invent a different set of independence criteria, or at least to show in what way Collins's hypotheses are inappropriate in this particular case.[15] This has been attempted (on their behalf) in this present version in the discussions of the contingent nature of student replications (Travis), the ambiguity of self-replication (Collins), the problematic timing of conversions (Pickering), the uncertainties of indirect influence (Harvey), and in the hardest case of all (Pinch), the nuances of agreement. Thus I have tried here, as I should, to "gloss it either way." But, and this is what the Dialogue and this present commentary have been about, such an analytic procedure does not result in a symmetrical text, but only (in this case at least) in a Friend-lier one.

Stage Four: Are the Candidate-Replicators Competent Copies?

We are concerned at this stage with the similarity or difference of the candidates' *research areas* and *methods* with respect to those of the original studies. However, determining this question is only a preliminary matter: decisions about whether the candidates are "competent copies" involve assessing how particular degrees of similarity or difference affect the candidates' "consensus forming value" (Collins 1978a).

Triangulation and *generality* arguments suggest that when a researcher sets out to confirm previous work too much similarity in methodology ("copy-catting") or in research area (re-researching) may be of little value. The credibility of the phenomenon is enhanced in such a case by demonstrating its existence with different methods (triangulation) and/or in a different area of research (generality). Moreover, the value to the secondary researcher of exact repetition (or "mere replication") is also low because originality is difficult to attribute to such work (Mulkay 1988; Mulkay and Gilbert 1986). Consequently, secondary researchers will attempt to avoid their own work being labelled as mere replication (Ashmore 1985:257–59).

In keeping with these considerations, none of the candidate-replicators claim to have engaged in exact repetition of the original replication studies. For most of the candidates, the absence of such a claim may be simply due to the absence of such an intention (see Stage Three). Travis, however, might appear to be a bona fide intentional replicator. After all, the title he gave to his paper, which Collins describes as "in the main, a replication of earlier work on replication!" (1981b:4), is "Replicating Replication?" [16] However, Travis's specific characterisation of the relationship between his paper and "The Seven Sexes" is in much looser terms: "The perspective on the replication of experiments which informs . . . this discussion . . . is taken from a paper by Collins [1975]" (1981:12). Asked in interview whether he had intended to replicate Collins's original study, Travis commented that as his chosen area of research involved controversies over replication

> T: in that sense, yes it was a replication of Harry's study but only in the very
>   loose sense of which "The Seven Sexes" probably was a kind of exem-
>   plar. I wasn't going out and replicating it in any *strict* sense because
>   it was a different area of science, but obviously it was very much in that
>   kind of line.
> (DT 0714–16)

So for Travis, "strict" replication involves the kind of exact copying which by definition cannot take place in a different area of science. "Loose" replication on the other hand seems to involve characterisations of the original as an "informing perspective," a "kind of exemplar," or a "kind of line." In the conclusion to his paper (1981:26) Travis describes his findings as "in effect" the same as those of "The Seven Sexes." He then details five distinct ways in which his research area—the study of memory transfer in planarian worms—differs from the gravitational radiation field examined by Collins. The strategy involved in enumerating these differences can be seen to serve the rhetorical purpose of making his claim for the similarity of the findings more significant. Travis is saying: In spite of all these differences the same processes are at work. By this display of generality the credibility of the knowledge-claim is increased.

In a general discussion of the prospects for replication in SSK Collins endorses this view by incorporating it into another expression of his replication claim:

> Of course, any sociologist who wants to replicate previous work must develop the same native competencies as the original investigator . . . . (But, there is no need for the same area to be looked at in order that confirmatory findings be generated. Findings ought to be expressed at a level of generality such that research on similar passages of scientific activity can confirm them—this has been the case with the "replication studies.") (1983a:92–93)

While Collins seems to be more than content to invoke the generality argument here, he also denies the relevance of the formally similar triangulation argument. Differences in method, that is, the nondevelopment of the same native competencies appear to be entirely credibility-detracting to this originator.[17]

Stage Five: Do the Candidate-Replicators Have the Same Findings?

In the present context, Collins's original distinction between positive and negative results (1976) can be reformulated in terms of the similarity or difference of the relevant findings. In these terms, it can be seen that we are dealing here with a version of the replication claim itself: in its essentials, the claim is precisely that the candidate-replicators have the same findings as the original studies. As any decision on this matter would clearly depend on conclusions drawn at earlier stages—especially Stages One and Four—readers may review the material presented there if they wish to come to either empirically informed conclusion. It seems more in the spirit of the replication studies, however, to examine how any similarity-claim can credibly be made (and be made credible) given the obvious fact of such differences as the use of differing arrangements of varying words. How is it that the originals and the candidate-replicators can all be read as saying the same thing when, quite clearly, they do *not* say (exactly) the same thing? The answer, of course, is that such commonsense empirical differences are continually overruled in those efforts at sense-making that consist of methods for investing dissimilar entities with similar meanings.[18] Collins makes a similar point in "The Seven Sexes" with the example of two "heteromorphic" heat measuring activities:

> Dipping a glass tube filled with mercury into a liquid, and dipping two dissimilar metals linked by a voltmeter (a thermo-couple) into it, may be the same experi-

ment—measuring the temperature of the liquid. In seeing these experiments as the same and competent many of the characteristics of heat are implied, for instance it is neither spontaneously generated by glass, nor say "repelled by voltmeters." (Collins 1975:216)

Collins calls this consequence of seeing things as the same, "negotiating the character of phenomena."

The phenomena we are concerned with here are the findings of the replication studies. Their character is, as I have interpreted and glossed it, the nonstandard view of replication. How does it come about that I and other commentators have no difficulty in producing one such gloss for (all) the replication studies? Collins, in another passage from "The Seven Sexes," maintains that such credible glosses become culturally available as a result of *successful replication claims.* (I have adapted the passage to suit the context.)

When a [researcher] claims that [a Study] has been properly replicated . . . he is claiming that all [Studies] which are to be included in the set of "competent [Studies]" in the field, must be seen as [having the same findings]. It follows that inclusion or exclusion of various [Studies] from the set of competent [Studies] settles [the gloss of the findings]. (Collins 1975:216)

It could be argued that it is a process of this kind that makes perceived differences in findings seem either major or minor. Collins, for example, excludes Zuckerman's (1977) study of replication from the set of competent studies. (See note 17.) As a result he construes the differences between Zuckerman's and his own findings as extremely great; as "not only apparent but real . . . differences in origin, focus and philosophy" (Collins 1982d:304). On the other hand, when commenting on a perceived difference between two of the *Knowledge and Controversy* papers, Collins writes:

According to Harvey . . . experimental activity need not produce data to change the pre-existing plausibility of an idea; the activity itself is sufficient. This suggestion seems to contrast in an interesting way with Pickering's conclusions about the power of pre-existing theory. (Collins 1981b:6)

In this case, the difference is between two claimed *members* of the set of competent studies. The interpretative task thus becomes one of not letting perceived differences count against that membership. This is done here by characterising the difference in question as simply an "interesting contrast."

Another way in which competent membership may be maintained in the face of perceived difference is to characterise all the work of the preferred membership as contributions to a coherent research programme with distinct phases. Collins's empirical programme of relativism has three such phases, the first being to show the potential local interpretative flexibility in science and the second being to show the mechanisms which limit this flexibility.

Thus, for instance, Pickering's (1981a) findings—which, as we have seen at Stage Three, the author describes as "an argument against Harry"—are interpreted unproblematically as a contribution to the second stage of the programme (Collins 1981b:6): potential contradictions are translated into extensions.

A nice example of the utility of this kind of "research programme construction" for dissolving problematic differences consists of an unprecedented "Authors' Preface" (Collins, Pinch, and Shapin 1984) to a pair of papers in the November 1984 edition of *Social Studies of Science*. The papers are by Shapin (1984a) and Pinch and Collins (1984) who state in the preface that their "papers were conceived and written independently: their focus on the relationship between language and knowledge, and their methodological orientations are similar, yet their findings are seemingly opposed." A case then of topic-sameness, method-sameness, but findings-difference. Is this a paradox, they ask themselves? Certainly not, they reply. Their "seemingly opposed" findings are actually two aspects of the same thing: "The two papers exhibit different ways of displaying private activity as a generator of collective property." The task ahead is to discover more about this problematic phenomenon: "this is a research programme rather than a paradox" (Collins, Pinch, and Shapin 1984:ii). Thus, we can understand the rhetoric of research programme construction as a form of difference-accounting which projects current differences into the future as potentially solvable intraparadigmatic puzzles (as Kuhn might say) in order to preserve the overall sameness of the programme and its competent membership.

We can see then that findings-sameness as well as topic-sameness, methods-sameness, and researcher-sameness is subject to interpretation and negotiation. This conclusion is, I claim, entirely consistent with the usual SSK gloss on the nonstandard view of replication, as given here by Mulkay:

The requirement of reproducibility is . . . the negotiated and contingent outcome of variable social processes. (Mulkay 1980a:55)

Stage Six: Has Replication Been Achieved?

It is . . . possible to argue about the required length of a series [of replications] for it to be taken as definitive . . . . It must always be possible to ask that more [Studies] be done, to "make absolutely certain." (Collins 1976:11)

It is a commonplace that a certain number of investigations of a phenomenon are required before its existence or its character can be taken to be established. Unfortunately the desirable number is never specified. Researchers often use a variant designed to express their modesty which goes something like this: "Such results are, of course, only tentative. Much more research will have to be done before phenomenon Z can be considered to be established." Reviewers and commentators use another variant, perhaps to justify their particular selections. For example, in Mulkay's discussion of SSK work on replication we read: "I do not intend to suggest that these few studies enable us to generalise about the whole of science or that their conclusions must be accepted without demur" (1980a:55). The replication claimant, on the other hand, is saying that the critical number has already been reached. Thus when Collins claims that the phenomenon of the social negotiation of reproducibility has been well replicated, this can be read as a claim for the existence of a *large enough* number of studies to have done the job. That number appears to be five.

The Dialogue between the Friend and the Critic Revisited and Reinterrupted

Friend: It is now clear that Collins's original replication studies have indeed been replicated.

Critic: I am now convinced that Collins's conclusions remain unsupported by the candidate-replicators.

Friend: But the studies *have* been replicated.

Critic: They certainly have not!

[Etcetera]

I must interrupt this unedifying, but highly symmetrical, dramatisation of the interpretative flexibility of our enquiry in order to spell out some of the interesting consequences entailed in coming to either the Friend's positive decision or the Critic's negative one. The Friend's decision would seem to produce the following series of claims:

1. The originals have indeed been the subject of bona fide replications, namely, the papers in *Knowledge and Controversy;*
2. all these studies now form the set of SSK replication studies which means that they all say the same thing;
3. the thing that they all say can be taken to be the case *because* its original demonstration has been replicated;
4. the thing that is the case is the nonstandard view of replication which can be glossed as the claim that replication *cannot* demonstrate what is the case.

On the face of it, similar difficulties would not appear to be entailed by the Critic's negative decision. If the epistemological status of findings rests "above all" on replication, then the findings of the originals would be considered (by the Critic) to be "suspended." However, the Critic faces a problem arising from the fact that the decision procedure itself (the Schema) has been taken from the methods and findings of one of these suspended studies. Thus we have a decision, arrived at by following the original analyses, that rejects (or at least suspends) their findings.

THE REPLICATION-CANDIDACY OF "THE SIX STAGES"

What is implied here, and indeed what has been implied throughout, is that this present text (hereafter 6S) must be itself a further candidate-replicator.[19] Let us apply, briefly, the schema of the six stages to it.

1. Is 6S about Replication?

I would like to claim that it is. However, as it deals with the practical interaction of two versions of replication while Collins's original studies do not, it could be argued that 6S is therefore dealing with a significantly different phenomenon.

2. Is 6S a Study?

I want to claim that it is on the grounds of its undeniable use of empirical materials including interview transcripts. However, because of its concern with reflexivity—a concern which is commonly seen as distracting SSK researchers from good solid empirical work—it may therefore be treated as insufficiently imbued with the empirical spirit. As I have argued at Stage Two, whether it may legitimately be described as a Study is a matter that is formally undecidable.

3. Has the Author/Researcher an Appropriate Identity?

I am not and I have never been a "Bath relativist"; I therefore claim an appropriate identity. However, nonmembers of SSK would be much more likely to see SSK membership itself as the relevant category, in which case I would seem an inappropriate replicator. Inasmuch as my positive reflexive strategy has led me to follow Collins's method as a competent native member (see below), the appropriateness of my candidacy is thereby reduced; however, simply because I have a positive reflexive strategy while Collins's approach to reflexivity is negative, this difference should increase my appropriateness as a candidate-replicator.

4. Is 6S a Competent Copy?

Again, I claim that it is. The grounds on which I do so are that I have used a similar methodology and have followed the directions for good SSK practice given by Collins. For instance, I have tried to use interviews "to tap the body of rules and understandings that comprise the individual as a scientist" (Collins 1983a:93), and I have tried hard to treat the claims at issue as problematic. However, it could be argued that by extending SSK's area of research into a nonnatural science I am displaying a form of incompetence: if the strong version of Special Relativism is held, then a study that necessarily ignores the existence of a boundary between the natural and the social must be a "noncopy."[20] However, the generality argument would suggest that this difference in research area (SSK as opposed to physics or parapsychology) should be credibility-enhancing.

5. Does 6S Have the Same Findings?

I certainly think it has. 6S shows how a standard-view replication claim can be deconstructed and translated into nonstandard terms, and this is exactly what Collins's original studies show. However, perceptions of the similarity of findings seem to be dependent on prior decisions about membership of the set of competent studies, as both Collins's work and my own clearly demonstrate.

6. Has Replication Been Achieved?

On the argument from numbers it would seem unlikely that just one study would be enough to achieve replication. However, if we assume that the Friend-ly arguments prevail and that all the candidate-replicators are success-ful, what would it mean for 6S to be in this position?

If "The Six Stages" were to be accepted as a bona fide replication of the original replication studies, it would find itself saying one thing (the standard view is "wrong"; the nonstandard is "right") while doing another (becoming a standard-view replication). If such paradoxes are to be avoided, then it would be as well not to make a replication claim or to accept one being made on its behalf. However, I imagine this an unlikely fate for this text. If it "will be read for its purpose and function rather than as 'just another' 'neutral' description" (Woolgar 1983a:253–54), then we can speculate on likely readings. If we disregard the unthinkable possibility that "The Six Stages" will have no impact whatsoever, I would argue that because of its focus on Collins and because of the way it is ironically structured as a tu quoque argument (though with a positive self-reflexive twist) it is most likely to be read as an attempted "refutation" of his work.

CONCLUDING DIALOGUE OF THE REPLICATION ANALYSTS

C: I read your work "as a confirmation of the studies. I found it quite sympathetic! I would not have known that it was an attempt to refute Collins unless you had implied as much."[21]

A: I hope I haven't implied as much. I certainly don't understand it as a refutation, whether attempted or achieved. Were it to become so, it would presumably also become a refutation of itself inasmuch as it would then be a "competent copy" of the work that it refutes. And besides, I was merely talking in terms of Woolgar's argument about the way that the very *form* of ironic discourses such as SSK tend to precipitate such a critical reading despite authors' disclaimers.

C: So I should ignore the disclaimer you have just made then?

A: Of course. And by the same token you should also ignore all my own Friend-ly arguments on behalf of the replication-candidacy of this text. Which would be just as well considering the problematic result of the success of such replication claims. But, of course, as I have also pointed out, a "refutation claim" is equally problematic.

C: I see. You seem to have got yourself into a bit of a fix. If this is the result of being reflexive I am obviously right to ban it!

A: On the contrary, it is you who are in a fix. The problematic nature of your claim is the result of your decision to ban reflexivity. By doing so, you felt "safe" from self-reference—so safe, in fact, that you felt able to make the replication claim in the way that you did.

C: If this is your conclusion, you haven't got very far, have you? I told you at the beginning that I was quite aware of what I was doing and since then you have consistently avoided any discussion of my purposes. I made the point, if you recall, that "the permeability of replication does not mean that it is still not the only criterion of what is to count as a natural regularity (or social regularity). It is the only one we have."

A: Well, if you are right in saying that the permeability of replication—or what I call the nonstandard view—does *not* effect its ability to act as the criterion of empirical regularity, then you could have achieved a regular fact-like status for the findings of your studies by being reflexive and simply claiming that the means by which the findings were produced exemplified those findings. It seems to me that that would have been a far more credible claim to make in the circumstances. It would have avoided all these problems and . . .

C: But that would not have been nearly so interesting or so dramatic. And had I done so, you wouldn't have had anything to study.

A: Luckily, that's not entirely true.[22] Now, in conclusion . . .

C: Oh, so we do have one then? Well come on, let's hear it.

A: . . . we can offer only inconclusion.

CHAPTER FIVE

ANALYSTS'
VARIABILITY TALK
The Levels of Discourse Analysis

Variable Pre-Texts

The differing reasons men give for their actions are not themselves without reason.
    C. Wright Mills (1940:904)

There is nothing behind the face of the man who speaks, beyond what else he has to say or how he keeps his silence. We find meaning between words and sentences and between men; there is nothing either in the back of this or beyond it.
    John O'Neill (1972b:228)

To talk about [anything] is to talk about talk, including the very talk that is the "talking-about."
    Barry Barnes (1982a:97)

Statements of a paradoxical or disruptive kind are reinterpreted by other statements into the tradition which they challenge.
    David Silverman and Brian Torode (1980:17)

We can't divest ourselves of our intelligences, our sense of contradiction and paradox, as if it were so much petty-bourgeois guilt.
    David Caute (1971:226)

To these questions my answer is a firm *Yes and No*.
    Paul Feyerabend (1981:156)

A. A GAP IN THE LITERATURE?

A.1   *L:* What you're saying is, Can you do a discourse analysis of discourse analysis and what would be the results if you did? And the answer to those

questions are: a, Yes you can do it; b, I don't know. I don't know what the
results of a discourse analysis of discourse analysis might be.

C: Right.

L: I haven't done it.

C: No.

L: And I'm unlikely to do it. You might do it.

C: Yes. Some people might think I have. (Laughter)

(Lehninger 4055–60)[1]

" 'Analysis of science analysts' discourse did not begin until the first
half of the 1980s and only very recently has this body of analysis begun to
grow at all rapidly. Nevertheless, there are now several published papers
which carry out this form of analysis (Ashmore 1988; Chubin and Restivo
1983; Gilbert and Mulkay 1983; Latour 1981, 1988; Mulkay 1980b, 1981,
1984a; Mulkay, Potter, and Yearley 1983; O'Neill 1981a; Pinch 1982b, 1988;
Woolgar 1980, 1981b, 1983a; Yearley 1982). What is absent from the literature so far is any equivalent analysis of the subspecialty in SSK known as
discourse analysis. This chapter fills this gap in the literature.' "[2]

B. BRIEF HISTORY OF THE FIELD UNDER STUDY

B.1   Discourse analysis, as a subprogramme in SSK, was originated and developed
by *Mitchell,* together with *Lehninger,* his collaborator in research on the "problem area" in biochemistry concerned with "oxidative phosphorylation," and
two of his graduate students at the University of *Minstertown, Kirwan* [who
studied the textual history of geology], and *Fransella* [whose topic was contemporary social psychology]. (Ashmore 1985:288)

Extract B.1 is a gloss on a highly generalised version of the immediate
local history of discourse analysis. " 'Working at this high level of generality,
it is relatively easy to piece together, from what the participants told me, an
apparently coherent and plausible history of developments. But this coherence
is a fragile construction, obtained at the expense of ignoring the variations
and inconsistencies in the accounts I was offered.' "[3] From the point of view
of a nonparticipant—according to the gloss I am commenting on; though see
extracts B.2, B.4, and B.6 for the basis of an account which would make him
a participant—the origin of discourse analysis possibly looks like this:

B.2   *C:* Have you got a story of how it originated you could tell me?

H: Of how discourse analysis originated?

C: Yes, as we've sort of undefined it, you know, as being a product of these
four people [*Mitchell, Kirwan, Fransella, Lehninger*] or sometimes five;
yours, yourself as well, or certain papers.

H: Um. OK. (Laughter) Uh, the story is that um, myself and to some extent
Lehninger argued furiously with, uh *Mitchell* who was stubbornly re-

sistant to any such work at all and eventually we persuaded him to, um, see that there was good in it . . .

C: Right.

H: . . . and, um, that then generated a whole area of interest.

C: Yes. (Laughter) Right, so now you're equating uh, your own theoretical concerns with, uh, with *Mitchell's* theoretical concerns or developing ones that . . . So yours created his, as it were.

H: That's right. I did exactly that in those last utterances and presumably later on I will change.

(*Hewish* 2515–2608)

Alternatively, *Hewish* describes his connection with discourse analysis as follows:

B.3 *H:* In terms of being part of a school, I suppose, I'm a lone voice. I mean I'm not at *Castletown* or *Spatown* and I don't see myself in great affinity with either *Castletown* or *Spatown* . . . . So I mean I think I'm rather . . . um, and I haven't really ever regarded myself as part of the *Minstertown* school either . . . . I've met *Mitchell* at conferences quite a lot actually but never really had any . . . worked with him, I mean, um, as *Lehninger* has, for example. I've never felt part of a *Minstertown* community in that sense. So I don't know.

(*Hewish* 1501–12)

Are these two accounts contradictory? If the *Minstertown* school is the home of discourse analysis, as Ashmore's gloss (B.1) implies, and if *Hewish* claims to have "never felt part of a *Minstertown* community" (B.3), then *Hewish's* claim to have, in a sense, originated discourse analysis himself (B.2) is put in doubt. Alternatively, *Hewish's* two accounts may be read as simply talking about different things. In extract B.2, it could be argued, Hewish talks in cognitive terms of the "generation of theoretical concerns" while in B.3 his discussion is couched in the social terms of "schools" and "communities." However, as the demarcation of the social from the cognitive is under critique in SSK (Pinch 1982b; Latour and Woolgar 1979), perhaps we should not accept this reading.

We are left, then, with the contradictory, or variable, reading of *Hewish's* accounts. In such a situation, which one should the analyst choose? Perhaps more data would help.

B.4 It is claimed that the subject matter of the paper is different from . . . previous work insofar as it deals only with actors' accounting procedures and not with the actions and beliefs that these accounts are normally (naively) taken to represent . . . . This view has been stated for studies of science by *Hewish*. The authors ought . . . to make clear that they owe this whole shift of emphasis . . . to *Hewish* and to the body of ethnomethodological work that he drew from.

(Referee C [WSB]:1)

B.5   For the record, we do not think that "we owe [our] shift of emphasis to *Hewish*" [and] our position remains significantly different from his. (*Lehninger* and *Mitchell* to *Jansky,* 25 June 1981:5)

Extract B.4 is from a referee's prepublication report on a discourse analysis paper.[4] Extract B.5 is from the authors' response to the referee's comments, made in a letter to the journal editor. It appears that *Hewish's* origin-account in B.2 is supported by Referee C in B.4 and denied by *Lehninger* and *Mitchell* in B.5. The account in B.5 also agrees with the gloss (B.1) upon which all the subsequent extracts, and my commentary, are a commentary. However, one of the authors of B.5 (*Mitchell*) gave, in interview, a rather different account of the relationship between his own and *Hewish's* developing intellectual concerns.

B.6   *M:* I was never persuaded then of the force of *Hewish's* arguments.
       C: Yes.
       M: Um, it never seemed to me that the kind of, uh, material that he based his arguments upon, um, was so powerful that I had to accept it.
       C: Right.
       M: I mean it often seemed to me, uh, much much weaker than that. They were *good* points, they were good arguments but they—they weren't conclusive in any sort of way, so one could very easily take a different sort of approach to them . . . . That would be the kind of view that I, that I was uh, that I tended to adopt at that point in time . . . . I mean clearly in the course of this research, um, my interests, have come back—no, have come to be much closer to those of *Hewish* over the years.
       (*Mitchell* 3003–09, 3703–05)

" 'A problem can arise for speakers in accounting for the fact that it took some years before they publicly admitted that they had accepted a newly proposed theory which now they believe to be correct. One way they can do so is to explain that the delay in adopting the theory was to allow time for confirmatory evidence to appear. Thus the speaker in the passage above (B.6) accounts for the fact that he did not espouse the discourse analytic theory until some years after it was formulated by noting that at first the theory was advanced without the support of any "conclusive" evidence. Later, however, he was convinced.' "[5]

C. DISCOURSE ANALYTICAL THEORY TALK

Much of the warrant for the practice of discourse analysis is given by the claim that participants' accounts are subject to high variability. This claim appears to be fundamental to discourse analysts' exposition and criticism of the kind of research practice they label "traditional" (Mulkay and Gilbert 1984).[6] Because of the massive, fundamental, and irresolvable variability in participants' accounts on any given topic, traditional analysis is unable to achieve the objective which it sets itself, that is, "to tell it like it is" (Mulkay and Gilbert 1982c:310). This is due to the fact that all sociological (and historical—see Gilbert and Mulkay 1984b) analysis is unavoidably dependent at some level on a single source of data, namely, accounts, but this source is utterly contaminated and rendered useless for traditional analytical purposes by the "quite remarkable" (Gilbert and Mulkay 1984a:11) degree of variation that accounts are found to display once one looks at them in enough detail.

This reconstruction of the argument from variability is a composite account, as much built up from informal discussion with those who propose it (and those who oppose it) as it is from the published literature. However, similar arguments may be found in the following texts: Gilbert and Mulkay 1982; 1984a, ch.1; Mulkay and Gilbert 1982c, 1984; Potter and Mulkay 1985; Potter 1984; Potter and Wetherell 1987. Once the argument is accepted—and, in its empirical essentials, it seems to be remarkably rarely denied; but I am getting ahead of myself—there would appear to be only three routes to travel: either you give up traditional analysis and find some other way of doing sociology [which does not suffer from the same defects—critics' addendum], or you try pig farming, or you carry on regardless. Discourse analysis is the result of taking the first route [except, of course, that it does suffer from the same defects—critics' addendum]; nobody ever says anything about the second so perhaps it never happens;[7] while the majority of researchers, having invested their careers in traditional analysis, start talking more often about the essentially interpretative nature of their kind of sociology and the ways in which their studies are, of course, open-ended, revisable, and even perhaps open to reanalysis.[8] And thus, argue the critics, the discourse project can be attributed to "a premature failure of nerve" (Shapin 1982:n.17). There is nothing to be gained by "the timid assumption that since the goal is unattainable, the pursuit must be abandoned" (Gieryn 1982b:333).

A well-used target for the discourse analytical critique of traditional analyses of action and belief is Blissett's *Politics in Science* (1972) which makes brief appearances in both Mulkay 1981 and Gilbert and Mulkay 1984a, ch.1, as well as a rather more extensive one in Gilbert and Mulkay 1983 in which Blissett's text is contrasted with the authors' own influential analysis of "Accounting for Error" (Mulkay and Gilbert 1982a).[9] What Blissett is accused of, it would seem, is the error of failing to account for error:

C.1   Our material, like Blissett's, seems to be full of accounts of political stratagems and their effects. However, the focus of our analysis (Mulkay and Gilbert 1982a) was not on political action but on the ways in which scientists accounted for scientific error, and it is noticeable that all the passages he quotes, as well as those we have provided from our interviews, may be seen as attempts by respondents to explain how beliefs which they see as in error came to be adopted by other scientists . . . . Thus when our respondents explain why another scientist . . . accepts one interpretation . . . rather than some contrary explanation, they say . . . *"He's over-committed to his theory"*. . . . These conclusions about how scientists account for error have the advantage that they encompass Blissett's findings about political action . . . . Moreover, our conclusions indicate why all Blissett's quotations appear not only to be about politics in science, but also to be about the mistakes and incorrect beliefs of other scientists . . . . What is astonishing is that Blissett failed to comment on this rather obvious feature of his interviews, perhaps because *his attention was so firmly fixed* on extracting specific evidence about political action. (Gilbert and Mulkay 1983:17–18; my emphases)

The particular analytic topic of scientists' theory-choice—a staple in rationalist philosophy and history of science—has been well served in discourse analysis, in which it is translated as scientists' theory *talk,* with Mulkay and Gilbert writing a total of four papers on this theme and Potter (with Mulkay) writing two.[10] These writings include, alongside substantive analyses of scientists' theoretical discourse, methodological analyses of sociologists' theoretical discourse on the topic of scientists' theory-choice. The next extract is from one of these latter texts, while the following text is from one of the former.

C.2   (1) When one attempts to use scientists' statements to reveal how theory-choice is actually carried out in science, it is possible to derive at least two alternative versions of how it happens, each apparently equally plausible. (2) Neither version is satisfactory, however, as an account of how theory-choice is carried out, because each requires the analyst to ignore or to explain away a large body of incompatible material. (3) Most analysts deal with this situation by taking as primary one or other of the two versions and then interpreting as peripheral or misleading those scientists' statements which support the alternative analytical position . . . . (4) Because scientists themselves present their actions from *both* these perspectives, both kinds of analysis can be supported by some of the interpretations of action generated by scientists themselves. (5) Thus the analytical literature on social action in science has reached an impasse. (6) What is needed is a new approach to analysis. (Mulkay and Gilbert 1983:181; my numbering)

" "The writers condemn all the available theories in the area for being too far removed from the facts. They suggest that the existing theories only appear to be supported by the evidence because analysts have been unable or unwilling to separate their actual data from the speculative theoretical notions to which they are committed. They maintain that a great deal of the analytical literature on social action in science is taken up by claims which are not properly grounded in evidence. They suggest in sentences 2 and 3 that this work is not contributing to genuine sociological knowledge. Theories are presented with only an apparent plausibility to recommend them.

The general message of this passage, then, is that much of what passes for sociological knowledge of science is merely contingent and incorrect. However, in sentence 6 a future phase of intellectual development is promised in which reliable facts and the right theory will be established. By means of this remark the writers justify their own insistence on refusing to engage in what they treat as premature analysis of action and belief. Although many others in their field concentrate on unprofitable selection, it is their approach of detailed focussing on the data as a whole which is seen as eventually leading to the truth.' "[11]

If discourse analysis "frees the analyst from direct dependence on participants' interpretative work [making] the goal of the analyst . . . no longer identical with that of the participant" (Mulkay and Gilbert 1982c:314; cf. Gilbert and Mulkay 1984a:15), it should not be possible to carry out the kind of self-referential analyses I have attempted above with extracts C.1 and C.2. These analyses depend entirely on analysts' talk and its goals being treated as contingently identical with participants' talk and its goals. If it is objected that this kind of self-referential trick actually relies on the texts selected for analysis being samples of *methodological,* as opposed to *substantive,* writing— and that such texts, concerned as they are with the discourse of colleagues, are therefore samples of participant-level, as opposed to analyst-level, talk; and therefore that no ironic transformation of analyst speech into participant speech has really taken place—I would ask how one distinguishes the methodological from the substantive.

Accounts of this issue, as of most others—but I am getting ahead of myself—appear to be highly variable. If we take the case of one of Mulkay and Gilbert's papers on theory-choice ("Opening Pandora's Box"; Mulkay and Gilbert 1984) we can note such variability. At the end of the paper, the authors characterise the text as purely methodological:

C.3   In this paper, we have not carried out any analysis of scientific discourse. We have tried simply to demonstrate the need for such analysis. This paper has dealt with basic methodological issues. (Mulkay and Gilbert 1984:137)

It is possible that this statement might puzzle some readers who had noticed that roughly half of the text (pages 119–31) appears to consist of analysis of scientific discourse. The section in question is entitled "The Variability of Individuals' Criteria of Theory Choice" and is introduced as follows:

C.4   We will look closely at passages taken from interviews with three biochemists, comparing the use made by each respondent of specific criteria as he gives accounts of the adequacy of different theories and as he makes sense of his own scientific judgments. (1984:119–20)

This account sounds thoroughly substantive.

In a footnote in another theory-choice paper (Gilbert and Mulkay 1982), accounts of the methodological or substantive nature of "Opening Pandora's Box" also seem to differ. In a passage which explains why the authors have written three papers on the same topic it is their common substantiveness which is emphasised.[12]

C.5   By writing three parallel papers on this single topic we have been able to make available in the literature more of our original data . . . . Thus the present paper contains 17 passages from 11 respondents, "Opening Pandora's Box" contains 8 passages from 3 transcripts, and "Scientists' Theory Talk" [Mulkay and Gilbert 1983], 10 passages from 4 scientists. (Gilbert and Mulkay 1982:406)

In this passage the authors are engaged in similarity accounting (what it is that makes the three papers a set). In the very next paragraph and, indeed, only a mere eight lines later, the authors turn to difference accounting (what it is that makes the members of the set distinct from one another):

C.6   Although the data contained in these three papers are similar in certain respects, we have tried to illustrate different aspects of discourse about theory-choice in each. For example, in "Opening Pandora's Box" we have . . . devoted more space . . . to comparing our form of analysis to that of previous work. (1982:406)

Here, it is the methodological character of the paper which is emphasised in order to differentiate it from its fellows.

These four accounts of the content of "Opening Pandora's Box" differ in the following way:

C.3: strong methodological
C.4: strong substantive
C.5: weak substantive
C.6: weak methodological.

How is the analyst to deal with such variability in accounts? According to discourse analysis, there are two choices. First, one can attempt to resolve discrepancies in accounts by discounting some and endorsing others. Pre-SSK analysts of science chose to discount scientists' *contingent* (informal, messy, accidental) accounts of their practice, while traditional analysts in SSK discount scientists' *empiricist* (formal, methodic, necessitarian) versions. In the case of the methodological versus substantive content of "Opening Pandora's Box," any analytic conclusion, including the reasonable one that the paper includes both kinds of work, could be drawn only by discounting at least one of the four accounts.[13] Discourse analysis, which treats such discounting as both inevitable—given a commitment to traditional analytic objectives—and illegitimate, chooses instead to change the subject. Attention is focussed, not on what the accounts variously say, but on the patterned variations in the accounts themselves.[14]

The claim for high variability in accounts, then, not only warrants the discourse analytic critique of traditional analysis; it also provides the prime empirical topic for the analysis of scientific discourse.

D. ANALYSTS' VARIABILITY TALK

D.1   We find that, when we look at any collection of participants' characterisation on a given topic from our data, almost every single account is rendered doubtful by its apparent inconsistency with other, equally plausible, versions of events. The degree of variability in scientists' accounts of ostensibly the same actions and beliefs is, in fact, quite remarkable. [1] Not only do different scientists' accounts differ; [2] not only do each scientist's accounts vary between letters, lab notes, interviews, conference proceedings, research papers, etc; [3] but scientists furnish quite different versions of events within a single recorded interview transcript or a single session of a taped conference discussion. (Gilbert and Mulkay 1984a:11; my numbering)

This extract is from the first chapter of the monograph *Opening Pandora's Box*. It appears in a section headed "The Variability of Participants' Discourse" in which the authors present a version of the argument from variability discussed above. The following analysis displays the results of an unsystematic search through various texts for some evidence that the empirical claim for high variability in accounts upon which the argument is erected is, or is not, self-exemplifying.

I will carry out this exercise in terms of analogues of the three types of variability referred to in extract D.1. These are [1] variations in the accounts of different analysts; [2] variations between the same analyst's accounts in different contexts; [3] variations in the accounts of the same analyst in the same context. It should be noticed that this sequence involves a shift from less remarkable to more remarkable claims, with the obvious implication that type [3] variability is the most important type to establish for the purpose of justifying the move to discourse analysis.[15] Bearing this in mind, I extend the range of type [3] textual contexts from Gilbert and Mulkay's single recorded interview transcript and single session of a taped conference discussion to include the single published text (and therefore formal/empiricist and therefore less likely to include variation—a hard case indeed; see section [3] below).

[1] Not Only Do Different Analysts' Accounts Differ

The different analysts whose accounts I have selected are here either reporting on their own research, whether in discourse analysis or in some other variety of SSK; commenting on the general conclusions of SSK or of related research areas; or criticising discourse analysis.

Analysts' Reports on Their Own Research

D.2   I will illustrate the claim that scientists do not agree about what constitutes a good experiment in this field [gravity wave detection] with sets of material from interviews. The first set of extracts shows the variation in scientists' opinion regarding the value of others' experimental set-ups and reported results . . . . The second set . . . shows that scientists perceived differently the importance of minor variations in bar type detectors and perceived differently which are to be counted as copies of which others . . . . The third set . . . shows variation in scientists' perception of the value of various parts of the originator's experimental procedure. (Collins 1975:211–13)

D.3   Rather than attempting to resolve the apparently wide range of variation in participants' accounts, I explore the possibilities of using this variation to characterise the growth of the field. (Woolgar 1976b:396)

D.4   One way of responding to the observation of variability among individuals' accounts of theory choice is to take that variability as our analytical point of departure. (Potter 1984:326)

These three extracts from research reports all appear to agree on the matter of the variability of scientists' accounts. They all seem to accept that the degree of variation between scientists' accounts warrants some analytical use of that variation.

Analysts' High Level Commentaries on SSK

D.5   That anything can be made out as anything does seem to be generally accepted by sociologists of knowledge and cognition. (Barnes 1983:544)

D.6   All the papers [in Collins 1981a] confirm the potential local interpretative flexibility of science. (Collins 1981b:4)

D.7   It is routine, if not universal, for historians to note variability in scientists' accounts, to compare one sort of utterance with another and with the overall pattern of scientists' verbal and nonverbal behaviour. (Shapin 1984b:127)

In these three quotations the notion of variability in accounts tends to get rather abstracted, especially in extracts D.5 and D.6. However, all three can be interpreted as unproblematically accepting the fact of scientists' variable accounts regardless of whether this fact underlies statements as to what sociologists of knowledge generally accept (D.5), or what a subset of SSK papers confirm (D.6), or what it is routine for historians of science to do

(D.7). Once again, then, there appears to be a consensus, or to spell it out, a marked lack of variability in these accounts of variability in accounts.

Analysts' Criticisms of Discourse Analysis

D.8   So as not to rub their audience the wrong way [Gilbert and Mulkay] prefer to keep the usual historian's narrative, with an emphasis on the diversity of possible accounts—which is the staple of the historian's trade. (Latour 1984:18)

D.9   Scientists do talk in different ways in different contexts . . . . Gilbert and Mulkay are to be thanked for reminding us of this fact. (Shapin 1984b:126)

D.10   The argument is that since scientists regularly produce conflicting versions of scientific reality, sociologists' attempts to provide definitive versions rest on selective reporting. (Collins 1983a:102)

D.11   The central thrust of the argument by Mulkay and others is that there are severe difficulties in producing definitive accounts of scientific action given the diversity and apparent inconsistency of the accounts of action and belief produced by scientists themselves. (Woolgar 1982:487–88)

These four extracts are especially interesting because they are all taken from published criticisms of discourse analysis. If there was going to be a context in which Gilbert and Mulkay's claim about accounting variations might be expected to be disputed, specific criticisms of their programme would be a good candidate. However, as can be read, all these critics agree with the perpetrators of discourse analysis on this point.

I should apologise at this juncture for having already subverted my own analytical categories. I have given three extracts from Collins (D.2, D.6, D.10), two from Woolgar (D.3, D.11), and two from Shapin (D.7, D.9) in a section supposedly concerned with variation between different analysts' accounts. I will offer two justifications for such sloppiness. First, all the extracts are interesting in themselves. Second, the inclusion of different statements from the same analyst provides us with ready-made examples of Gilbert and Mulkay's other two types of variability. The Collins quotations are examples of the second type of variability (intra-analyst but intercontext) in that, although all three are from the published formal sociological literature, extract D.2 is from an original research report, D.6 is from an editor's introduction, and D.10 is from a critique of discourse analysis appended to a retrospective review of Collins's empirical programme of relativism. Similarly, the Woolgar extracts are also from distinct contexts: D.3 is from a piece of substantive research while D.11 is from a retrospective/prospective review of laboratory studies. The third type of variability (intra-analyst and intracontext) is exemplified by the two extracts from Shapin (D.7, D.9), both of which are from the same text (1984b).

[2] Not Only Do Each Analyst's Accounts Vary between Different Contexts

The analyst whose accounts from differing contexts I have chosen to compare is Mulkay.

The Formal Literature Context

D.12 We find that these statements are remarkably inconsistent. Every statement which characterizes a given scientist's actions or ideas as X is contradicted by numerous other statements which characterize his actions or ideas as various kinds of non-X. Furthermore, any particular speaker will tend to modify and vary his accounts of actions and ideas; not only other people's actions and ideas, but also his own. (Mulkay 1981:168–69)

The Research Proposal Context

D.13 The so-called norms of science have come to be seen as but one part of the wider evaluative repertoire of the research community [which] is used flexibly in accordance with variations in social context; and scientists employ it flexibly . . . . It has become increasingly clear . . . that participants with different perspectives, different interests and different technical backgrounds interpret different formulations differently . . . . The physical world seems to be socially constructed in a situation of intellectual flux, as continually changing cues are assigned meaning in accordance with constantly changing criteria of adequacy and value and in terms of constantly changing interpretative resources. (*Mitchell*, SSRC research proposal, 20 April 1978:2)

The Interview Context

D.14 *M:* So I think that that concern with uh, the use . . . the flexible use of re-
          sources and the context-dependent nature of accounts is, you know, very
          clearly there in the 1976 paper [Mulkay 1976].
     (*Mitchell* 4503–04)

The Correspondence Context

D.15 We both agree that actors' accounts in interviews are highly variable. (*Mitchell* to *Price*, 21 April 1981)

D.16 I'm willing to accept that your material on personal biographies produced a high degree of continuity. That may be because the underlying actions were "continuous." But it may be because concentration on one limited kind of material tends to restrict the variability of interpretation. (*Mitchell* to *Price*, 21 April 1981)

Extracts D.12 to D.15 all seem to be further examples of the high variability account. That is, these four extracts all say the same thing about the issue of account-variability even though they are taken from varying contexts. Extract D.16, however, can be read as a *low* variability account. In this extract, *Mitchell's* interpretative task is to explain an apparent counterexample to the general finding of high variability in actors' accounts. This counterexample concerns *Price's* material on personal biographies which is elaborated by *Price* as follows:

D.17 Puzzled by my inability to get an analyst's account of theory choice out of [interview data containing just the sort of actor's accounts quoted in your paper], I decided to look for another source of evidence. I discovered personal biographies—I looked at the historical dimension of scientific careers: where people worked, who they worked with, which experiments they performed, with what results, which interpretative resources they used, and so on. Here I discovered a degree of continuity which honestly amazed me. (*Price* to *Lehninger*, 18 March 1981)

In reply (D.16), *Mitchell* posits two possible explanations for *Price's* amazing discovery.[16] The first is a continuity in the underlying actions; the second is (only and merely) a continuity in the accounts of these actions. With only these two choices available to him to account for the interpretatively agreed fact of continuity, *Mitchell* has little choice but to go for the second explanation. Going for the first would tend to destroy one of the major arguments for doing discourse analysis instead of, or at least as a preliminary to, the analysis of action and belief; namely, the irreparable indeterminacy between accounts of actions and those actions themselves (Mulkay 1980b; Gilbert and Mulkay 1983). If it is possible to read from continuity in accounts to continuity in actions then this indeterminacy is denied.

However, the alternative explanation is far from unproblematic. The "admission" (as it may appear when compared to all the general and unrestrictive claims for variability in accounts that I have juxtaposed in the last few pages) that there is a definite limitation to variability tends to threaten the adequacy of the high variability claim as a warrant for discourse analysis. Reading this explanation of *Price's* continuity literally (taking it at face value) seems to limit the scope of Gilbert and Mulkay's third type of variability. Prior to this literal reading, I have treated mentions of particular type [3] contexts such as interviews (D.1 and D.15) and conference sessions (D.1) as being mere examples of a potentially much larger category of type [3] contexts. Indeed, it is on this basis that I have proposed to radically extend the set of examples by treating the single formal text as a potential type [3] context. However, it now appears that I have no warrant to continue treating the interview and the conference discussion simply as members of an unlimited set of type [3] contexts; a literal reading of the limitation account in D.16 would suggest that the wiser course is to treat them as perhaps the only contexts in which the same individual can be routinely accounted as accounting for the same action or belief differently. To do so, however, would be to discount the following piece of clear textual evidence to the contrary:

D.18 Not only do different scientists' accounts differ; not only do each scientist's accounts vary between letters, lab notebooks, interviews, conference proceedings, research papers, and so on; but each scientist furnishes radically different versions of events within, *say*, a single recorded interview transcript or a single session of a taped conference discussion. (Mulkay and Gilbert 1982c:312; my emphasis)

You, and other sharp-eyed readers with good memories, will immediately recognise this quotation as somewhat similar to the second half of extract D.1. There are at least five differences that I can discern between these texts. The first two are quite insignificant: (D.1: "lab notes" and "etc"; D.18: "lab notebooks" and "and so on"). The third difference seems to be a matter of clarity (D.1: "but scientists furnish"; D.18: "but each scientist furnishes"). The second formulation of this pair is clearly clearer than the first which is ambiguously readable as the mere type [1] variability claim: "but different scientists furnish." The fourth difference is a matter of force (D.1: "quite different versions"; D.18: "radically different versions"). These two versions do indeed seem quite different if not radically different. Once again, it is the second formulation of the two which seems the more definitive.[17] It is the fifth difference, however, which is the most significant in the present context. Whereas extract D.1 has "within a single recorded . . . ," extract D.18 reads "within, say, a single recorded . . . ." This one additional word—or one less word; see note 17—makes the interview and the conference contexts seem simply particular instances of what should be understood as a larger and more inclusive set of type [3] contexts. In the light of this reading of extract D.18, perhaps *Mitchell's* limitation account in D.16 can best be interpreted as just ruling out the particular instance of personal biographies as a candidate for type [3] context membership.

However, and again reading literally, *Mitchell's* statement that "concentration on *one* limited kind of material tends to restrict the variability of interpretation" (extract D.16; my emphasis) seems inconsistent with his statement, earlier in the same letter, that "actors' accounts *in interviews* are highly variable" (extract D.15; my emphasis); that is, if interviews are an example of one limited kind of material. On this inconsistency reading, extracts D.15 and D.16 together exemplify type [3] variability in the new context of the single letter. (Interestingly, this result appears to contradict *Mitchell's* limitation account in extract D.16 which suggests that concentrating on one limited kind of material such as, presumably, a single letter tends to restrict variability. What is even more interesting is that this account is itself a constituent part of the very finding with which it is inconsistent.) Thus, this example of intra-letter variability can be understood as a limited, but nonetheless significant, addition to the set of contexts wherein type [3] variability has been found. However, our only other example so far of the type [3] phenomenon (extracts D.7 and D.9 from Shapin 1984b) is at variance with this finding: whereas the example of extracts D.7 and D.9 shows interextract nonvariation, the example of extracts D.15 and D.16 shows interextract variation.

As can be inferred from the increasingly tortuous language of this discussion, I seem to be in grave danger of confusing my analytical levels. Table 2, Levels of Variability Accounting in Two Type [3] Examples, is designed to help clarify this confusion.

Discussion of Table 2

The labelling of the levels in table 2 follows the numerical format introduced in Chapter Three. The level of this text is mainly level 4; the confusion I mentioned above arises from ascending to level 5, that is, from treating the two varying level 4 examples of inter*extract* variability as a further instance of the phenomenon of which they speak. At level 5, though, we are actually dealing with the phenomenon of inter*example* variability as represented in the table by the Composite Example D.7, D.9—D.15, D.16. And at level 6, it is quite possible to find yet another instance of the variability phenomenon as in fact we can proceed to do by extrapolating from the two (level 4) examples of type [3] variability that are discussed in the next section. If I tell you in advance that both of these (extracts D.19–D.22; and extracts D.23, D.25, D.26) are examples of nonvariability, it is clear that at level 5, the Composite Example D.19–D.22—D.23, D.25, D.26 also exemplifies nonvariability (because the examples do not vary). Because this new level 5 result is different from the other one, the conclusion at level 6 (which is reached by comparing the two results at level 5) reads: Supercomposite Example D.7, D.9—D.15, D.16/D.19–D.22—D.23, D.25, D.26: "The metameta-analysts accounts (of the meta-analysts accounts of the analysts accounts of the scientists accounts of the World) are variable." I leave consideration of the possible results at level 7 to your fertile imaginations in favour of the more pedestrian exercise of displaying some of the interpretative work needed to produce this relatively simple level 6 conclusion.

[3] But the Same Analyst Furnishes Quite Different Versions within a Single Context

Wishing to extend our currently limited list of type [3] contexts—the interview (as in Gilbert and Mulkay 1982), the conference session (as in Potter 1984), and the letter (as in Ashmore 1989)—I have chosen, as I mentioned above, the hard case (Collins 1982c; Chubin 1982) of the research report itself. This context comprises a hard case for the showing of variability in accounts because this kind of text is famously formal, conventional, impersonal, and empiricist (Medawar 1963; Gusfield 1976; Collins and Pinch 1979; Woolgar 1980; Gilbert and Mulkay 1980). If variability can be found here, of all places, then one can expect to find it anywhere else; so runs the hard case

Table 2   Levels of Variability Accounting in Two Type [3] Examples

Level:	1. The World	2. Science	3. Meta science	4. Metameta science	5. Metametameta science	6. Metametametameta science
Speaker:	? (level 2's object)	The scientist (level 3's participant)	The analyst (level 4's participant)	The meta-analyst (level 5's participant)	The metameta-analyst (level 6's participant)	The metametameta-analyst (level 7's participant)
		X X } "The World is X"				
		Non-X Non-X } "The World is non-X"	Extract D.7: "The scientists accounts (of the World) are variable"			
		X X } "The World is X"		Example D.7, D.9: "The analysts accounts (of the scientists accounts of the World) are nonvariable"		
		Non-X Non-X } "The World is non-X"	Extract D.9: "The scientists accounts (of the World) are variable"		Composite example D.7, D.9—D.15, D.16: "The meta-analysts accounts (of the analysts accounts of the scientists accounts of the World) are variable"	
		X X } "The World is X"				Supercomposite example D.7, D.9—D.15, D.16/D.19—D.22—D.23, D.25, D.26: See text
		Non-X Non-X } "The World is non-X"	Extract D.15: "The scientists accounts (of the World) are variable"			
		X X } "The World is X"		Example D.15, D.16: "The analysts accounts (of the scientists accounts of the World) are variable"		
		X X } "The World is X"	Extract D.16: "The scientists accounts (of the World) are nonvariable"			

argument. Unfortunately (or fortunately) I can tell you right away that my researches have been no more successful (or unsuccessful) in this area than they have been throughout.

Within a Single Page

The first set of extracts are from *Opening Pandora's Box* (Gilbert and Mulkay 1984a). Not only are they all from *this same text;* and not only are they from *the same chapter* (Chapter 2); but also they are from *the very same page* (page 38). Indeed they almost form a single piece of connected prose!

D.19 This variability casts considerable doubt on the worth of traditional forms of analysis . . .

D.20 . . . that attempt to reconcile these variations . . . .

D.21 We have . . . illustrated the kind of recurrent variation in accounts which is a feature of our data.

D.22 However . . . we have merely pointed to . . . such variation.

With this extreme hard case example, perhaps it is unsurprising that the variation between extracts D.19 to D.22 on the subject of the variability of accounts should be so small. However, it should be borne in mind once again that all the extracts so far (with only two exceptions) can be read as equally nonvariable on this topic.

Within a Single Passage over Time

The second set of extracts attacks variability in the same context in a rather different fashion. Instead of looking for varying accounts of variability in accounts from different places within the same text, as in extracts D.19 to D.22, I take a single short passage in a single published text and look for variations in accounts of variability over time. In other words, I wish to see whether changes occur, and if so in what way, through a succession of drafts, including revisions made in response to the comments of a journal editor and his referees. The passage in question is from "Warranting Scientific Belief" (Gilbert and Mulkay 1982). After displaying a quotation from a biochemist's interview transcript which the authors interpret as a "contingent" account of the relationship between data and theory, they compare this quotation with an earlier "empiricist" account of the same relationship as given by the same speaker in the same interview. The authors' conclusion provides us with the passage we are interested in.

D.23 (1) Thus a speaker may take "experimental evidence" as distinguishing un-equivocally between two theories, whilst observing a few minutes later that in this field it is impossible ever to be sure that the evidence is "really what you think it is." (2) This variability of views about the nature of experimental data within a single interview transcription is not unusual, but typical. (3) It provides a major reason for not taking scientists' accounts of theory-choice literally. (4) For we can hardly conclude that a scientist accepted that such evidence is essentially inconclusive, or that the cognitive consensus to which he claims to belong is simply a result of what people happen to be willing to believe at the moment. (Gilbert and Mulkay 1982:393; my numbering)

Sentence 1 provides evidence for the strong account of type [3] variability given in sentence 2. Sentence 3 then draws a methodological conclusion from this empirical claim. Sentence 4 is not easy to interpret (see note 20).

Extract D.23 is the final result of a series of transformations. There are to my knowledge four earlier versions of "Warranting Scientific Belief," all of which were made available to me for analytical purposes, as were the complete set of referees' reports together with a series of letters between the editor of *Social Studies of Science* and the authors, which together comprise the set of negotiations over the publication of this text. The first draft has the title "Accounting for Truth" and was written by Gilbert in July 1980. An equivalent passage to extract D.23 does not exist in this draft. The biochemist's contingent account is present, as is its immediate gloss together with a one-sentence contrast of this account with the scientist's earlier empiricist version. But extract D.23's strong variability claim together with the conclusion which is drawn from it have not yet appeared.

The next draft, which I will refer to as draft 1a, is (now) the same material object as draft 1. It consists of this earlier draft with Mulkay's additions, corrections, and comments, including a change of title to "Constructing Scientific Rationality." However, as these additions and corrections cease at an earlier point, there is no change to the passage we are interested in. Thus, extract D.24 from drafts 1 and 1a of "Warranting Scientific Belief" looks like this:

D.24 [Void. Total absence of variability accounts.] (WSB Draft 1:11; WSB Draft 1a:?)

Draft 2 is entitled "Constructing Scientific Rationality or Possibly Warranting Scientific Belief" and is dated November 1980. Draft 3 is dated January 1981 and has "Warranting Scientific Belief" as its title. As the passage in question is so similar in these two texts—only one word is different—a single extract will suffice.

D.25 (1) Thus a speaker may take "experimental evidence" as distinguishing unequivocally between two theories, whilst observing a few minutes later that in this field, it is impossible ever to be sure that the evidence is "really what you think it is." (2) This variability of views about the nature of experimental data within a single interview transcript is not unusual, but typical. (3) It provides a major reason for not taking scientists' accounts of theory choice literally. (4) For we can hardly accept [Draft 2] conclude [Draft 3] that a scientist accepted a theory solely because of experimental evidence, if he maintains elsewhere that such evidence is essentially inconclusive. (WSB Draft 2:15; WSB Draft 3:13–14; my numbering)

Although there are several changes between this version and the final published one (D.23), including a major alteration of the structure and sense of sentence 4, it is evident that the high variability account in sentence 2 has remained unchanged. This is despite the fact that it was this very passage in draft 3—the version submitted for publication in *Social Studies of Science*—which was selected by an extremely critical referee as his/her major example of the "deplorable method" (Referee B [WSB]:1) of "Warranting Scientific Belief." [18] Notice *how* the referee chooses to quote (from) it:

D.26 *Example:* (said of two scientists' quotes) pp.13–14. "(1) Thus a speaker may take 'experimental evidence' as distinguishing unequivocally between two theories, whilst observing a few minutes later that in this field it is impossible ever to be sure that the evidence is 'really what you think it is' . . ." This kind of thing is "(3) a major reason for not taking scientists' accounts of theory choice literally. (4) . . . we can hardly conclude that a scientist accepted a theory solely because of experimental evidence, if he maintains elsewhere that such evidence is essentially inconclusive." (Referee B [WSB]:1; my numbering)

We can see from this extract that in the very presentation of this "typical example of . . . so-called interpretations" (Referee B [WSB]:2), the generalised type [3] variability account in sentence 2 is passed over with three dots and the phrase "this kind of thing is." It would seem, therefore, that even this totally critical critic does not see fit to challenge Gilbert and Mulkay's general claim for high variability in accounts. It is possible, therefore, to interpret extract D.26 as yet another high variability account despite the empirical non-existence of any such account. [19] Indeed, it is precisely the lack of an explicitly quoted variability account in the context of this ultracritical referee's report which provides for an interpretation of this particular absence as a highly positive presence.

So, what conclusion can we draw from this exposition of the detailed temporal textual changes to/in this one short passage from "Warranting Scientific Belief?" Simply this: that even the strongest of variability accounts such as the declaration of the "typical" nature of type [3] variability found in sentence 2 (D.23, D.25, D.26) appears, in this case at least, to be invariable over successive drafts even to the extent of surviving unscathed in the face of extremely hostile comments from a referee who chose to direct her/his criticism at the very passage within which this variability claim was embedded. That significant changes were made to other parts of this passage as a direct response to these criticisms seems highly likely, however unclear, in the case of sentence 4, the published version turned out to be.[20]

Conclusion (Extract D.27) and Extract D.27 (Conclusion) and . . .

D.27 This study of analysts' accounts of participants' variable accounts overwhelmingly suggests that the phenomenon of high variability in participants' accounts that is so regularly claimed by discourse analysts and other SSK researchers is *not* self-exemplifying simply because it *is* so regularly claimed. On this topic, analysts' accounts have been found to be massively invariant. It has not been suggested before in the literature on variable accounts—such as the texts from which I have taken my extracts—that the phenomenon of variability is limited in terms of topic. On the contrary, the majority of analysts' accounts of variability are fully topic-general; and those that specify a particular topic do so with seldom a hint that there is any limitation to the kinds of topic about which participants may do variable accounting. Particular topics that are mentioned in the extracts, or in the extracts' con-texts, include actions, beliefs, and events (D.1, D.11, D.12, D.18); agreements on good experiments (D.2); discovery (D.3); theory choice (D.4, D.23, D.25, D.26); scientific reality (D.10); the so-called norms of science (D.13); and analysts' accounts of participants' variable accounts (D.27).

The study demonstrates the invariability of analysts' accounts in terms of the three types of interaccount variability set out in extracts D.1 (Gilbert and Mulkay 1984a:11) and D.18 (Mulkay and Gilbert 1982c:312). I have shown invariance between the accounts of different analysts (type [1]) in extracts D.1 to D.11;[21] invariance in statements from the same analyst made in different contexts (type [2]), chiefly—see below—in extracts D.12 to D.15; and invariance between statements made by the same analyst in the same context (type [3]) in extracts D.7 and D.9, D.19 to D.22, and D.23, D.25, and D.26. Moreover, I have paid considerably more attention than have other analysts of variability to the possibility that these three rather crude types might profitably be broken down into finer and more discriminating categories.

To this end, I divided the sequence of type [1] accounts into three distinct kinds of contexts, namely, research reports, high level commentaries, and texts critical of discourse analysis. For the main type [2] examples, distinctions of context were, of course, already built-in, as the kind of variability here is precisely that between distinct contexts. As I was unfortunately unable to provide extracts from lab notes or from conference proceedings (as mentioned in extracts D.1 and D.18), I tried to compensate for this omission by introducing the new context of the research proposal (D.13), alongside extracts from a formal article (D.12), from an interview (D.14), and from correspondence (D.15, D.16). However, if the monolithic context of the formal article can usefully be differentiated in the manner of my type [1] analyses, two further examples of type [2] (in)variability may also be included in this conclusion. These are the three contributions from Collins (extract D.2 from a research report, D.6 from an editorial, and D.10 from a review) and the two from Woolgar (extract D.3 from a research report and D.11 from a review).

My choice of Mulkay for the invariant author of the main sequence of type [2] extracts is, I venture, not insignificant. If his own claims for the high variability of accounts are to be tested in their full generality, then it should be these claims themselves which provide the major focus of the kind of reflexive analysis carried out in this study.

For the third type of variability account, I chose the general context of the formal literature on the grounds that it constituted the hardest possible case for the discovery of variable accounts. It did: invariance was found in all three of my type [3] examples from the formal literature context. The simplest of these examples consists of two extracts (D.7 and D.9) from the same article (Shapin 1984b). Because I was convinced that the hard case argument required the most rigorous demonstration that I could think of—and because the preferable invariant analyst should, again, be engaged in discourse analysis—I chose two sets of extracts from formal articles by Gilbert and Mulkay as my primary examples of potential type [3] variability. The first set was designed to test the concept of "the same context" by, perhaps, taking it overliterally.[22] Thus all the extracts in this set (D.19 to D.22) were from the very same page. With the second set, I introduced a temporal dimension into the idea of variability by examining the potential variations over time to the same passage in a sequence of changing drafts of the same text (extracts D.23 to D.25).

In this study, then, I have found a "'degree of invariance in analysts' accounts of the high degree of variability in participants' accounts which is in fact, quite remarkable. Not only do different analysts' accounts not differ; not only do each analyst's accounts not vary between formal articles, research proposals, interviews and letters—not to mention between research reports, reviews and editorials—but analysts furnish quite similar versions of account variability within a single page of a single formal text and within a single passage from the same text through successive drafts.' "[23]

However, the degree of variability is not zero. There are two significant exceptions to—or variations from—the otherwise virtually invariant set of high variability accounts that I have been reviewing. These exceptions, of course, are *low* variability accounts.[24] The first is from *Mitchell's* letter to *Price* in which he claims only a limited variability in accounts in certain analytical circumstances (extract D.16). This is a significant example because, first, it is the only exception to the series of high variability accounts given by this major practitioner of discourse analysis (or by Mulkay). More important, it constitutes, together with extract D.15, which is a high variability account from the same letter, a further positive example of type [3] variability in a context—personal correspondence—not previously cited by Gilbert and Mulkay. The second, and highly significant example of a low variability account, with which I will conclude this extract, is from Ashmore's study of variations in variability accounting (extract D.27) in which the author claims that his study of analysts' accounts of participants' variable accounts overwhelmingly suggests that the phenomenon of high variability in participants' accounts that is so regularly claimed by discourse analysts and other SSK researchers is *not* self-exemplifying simply because it *is* so regularly claimed. On this topic analysts' accounts have been found to be massively invariant. It . . . .[25] (Ashmore 1989:158–60)

E. CONCLUSIONS, METACONCLUSIONS, AND THE PARADOXES OF VARIABILITY

The conclusion to "Analysts' Variability Talk" is that there is a low degree of variation in analysts' accounts of the variability of accounts. Yet because I have to admit that the conclusion could have been otherwise I want to suggest that we turn our attention to the way in which the particular conclusion we have happened to reach is less significant than the paradoxical metaconclusions that result, symmetrically, from either a "low" or a "high" conclusion. For example, if we had concluded that there was a high degree of variation in analysts' accounts of variability in accounts, the paradox would be as follows:

Conclusion One: High Variability

Metaconclusion X: Because the original claim, of which this study may be considered a test, was for the existence of high variability in accounts, the finding of high variability is in agreement with the claim. Therefore, Conclusion One *supports* the claim.

Metaconclusion Y: The conclusion of high variability means that there is a high level of disagreement between accounts on this topic. Therefore, Conclusion One does *not* support the claim.

The paradox resulting from the conclusion that there is a low degree of variability in analysts' accounts of variation in accounts—which is, of course, our actual conclusion—goes like this:

Conclusion Two: Low Variability

Metaconclusion X: Because the original claim of which this study may be considered a test, was for the existence of high variability in accounts, the finding of low variability is in disagreement with the claim. Therefore, Conclusion Two does *not* support the claim.

Metaconclusion Y: The conclusion of low variability means that there is a high level of agreement between accounts on this topic. Therefore, Conclusion Two *supports* the claim.

What is it that makes this situation so paradoxical? If we examine briefly the differing relations between the claim and the conclusion involved in each metaconclusion, we can see something of the structure of these paradoxes of variability.

Metaconclusion X

The relation between the claim and the conclusion that leads to metaconclusion X is between accounts on separate levels of analysis (see table 2). While the claim is a level 3 account the conclusion is an account on level 4, that is, an account about level 3 accounts. Since they are not equivalent, the higher level takes the lower level merely as data with which to reach an analytical conclusion. Having done so, this conclusion is then compared with the original claim. If these two accounts agree, we metaconclude that the claim is supported by the conclusion. If they do not agree, we metaconclude that the claim is not so supported. In this procedure, two kinds of analytical operations on accounts that are usually quite distinct are combined. The first is simply the standard way of treating data which, as an analytic practice, is characterised by its insistence on a separation of levels such that its own speech is the highest in the hierarchy. The second operation, which is also standard practice, is the act of analytic comparison by which, collectively, literatures come into being, research programmes are constructed, schools are formed, and disciplinary boundaries are maintained or undermined. Normally, this practice involves the comparison of accounts on the same level of analysis. For instance, a researcher will relate the conclusion of her study to other conclusions of other studies, whether she describes this act of analytic comparison as giving empirical support to a theory (or retracting it), or as replication (or refutation), or as extending the scope of a claim (or reducing it), or whatever else.[26] In the case of "Analysts' Variability Talk," however, the analytic comparison is between accounts on different levels because the original claim to which the conclusion is compared is on the level of data for that conclusion. The point is that the claim operates in the text on *both* levels. While for purposes of data analysis the claim is treated as lower level speech, in the moment of analytic comparison the same claim is treated as same-level speech.

Metaconclusion Y

The relation between claim and conclusion which leads to metaconclusion Y is rather different. Whereas in coming to metaconclusion X, it is the claim which undergoes a change of status during the process, in reaching Y it is the conclusion which changes. In place of the moment of analytic comparison in which the account in the claim is compared to the account in the conclusion, reaching metaconclusion Y involves comparing the claim's account to all the other data-level accounts of variability. If these accounts agree, we metaconclude that the claim is supported by these other variability accounts. If they do not, we metaconclude that the claim is not so supported.

But what happens to the *conclusion* in this comparative exercise? Although the conclusion is a particular kind of statement about the accounts, it is a statement which is at a higher level of interpretation to both the individual accounts themselves *and* to the kind of statement about these accounts which is compared to the claim in order to reach metaconclusion Y. This latter statement is essentially a quasi-quantitative generalisation of findings such as "most analysts' accounts claim a high degree of variability in participants' accounts." To reach the conclusion from this kind of generalisation an interpretative inversion is carried out which transforms the generalisation's talk of high variability in participants' accounts into the conclusion's talk of low variability in analysts' accounts. This process of inversion is signalled by the generalisation's use of the word "most." Indeed, the conclusion can be understood as the result of a simple translation of "most" into "low variability": if most accounts say the same thing then there is low variability between these accounts.

Metaconclusion Y does not result, then, from a comparison of the claim with the conclusion but rather with this generalisation. In the case of our actual conclusion of low variability, comparison of the claim's high variability account with the generalisation's observation that most of the others are also high variability accounts will yield the metaconclusion that the claim is supported by these other accounts.

Non–Self-Exemplification: A Limit to Reflexivity?

At first sight the conclusion to "Analysts' Variability Talk" would suggest that the central empirical claim of discourse analysis is not self-exemplifying. As this statement is a version of metaconclusion X, how does the contradictory metaconclusion Y affect this assessment? Although this second metaconclusion supports the claim in the way suggested above, that is, by a comparison of the claim's account with an uninterpreted empirical generalisation about the high distribution of similar accounts in the data, such support is not, it seems to me, equivalent to self-exemplification. As I have described it in the discussion of metaconclusion X, self-exemplification requires a perception of similarity between the claim's account of a phenomenon and the conclusion's (meta)account of that phenomenon.

However, although the high variability claim appears to be non–self-exemplifying (and therefore limited: there is at least one case where low variability has been found), metaconclusion Y suggests that this limitation is necessary for, and coextensive with, the conclusion that high variability is a consensually agreed phenomenon among SSK analysts.

Perhaps, then, we have a limiting case here for the kind of proreflexive argumentation that I have been advocating and attempting to practice in this thesis. What I mean by this can be seen more clearly if we look briefly at the consequences for the claim had the alternative, high variability, conclusion to our analysis been reached. Although in this case, the claim would have been self-exemplifying, this result would have been achieved at the cost of also finding that very few SSK analysts' accounts of the phenomenon agreed either with the claim or with the conclusion. To put it as dramatically and as unsubtly as possible: either we have an empirical claim which is supported *only* by the self-exemplification resulting from the conclusion of a reflexive inquiry and which is otherwise totally absent from the set of equivalent accounts taken by that inquiry as its data; or we have an empirical claim which is duplicated everywhere in the set of equivalent accounts taken as the data for an inquiry into its self-exemplary status, *except* in the conclusion to that inquiry. Isn't it obvious that this second case is preferable? And that therefore the negative finding of my inquiry is to be welcomed? Have we reached the end of the road? Must we now turn back and admit it was all a mistake? Have I been hoist by my own paradox? In short, is the non–self-exemplification of variability accounts an indication of a radical *limit* to reflexivity?

Both/And

The previous section is one possible ending to this chapter. What follows after this present sentence is another, and I could paraphrase the ending of Mulkay's "Methodology . . ." (1974) at this point and say that I am presenting them both because there are no convincing grounds for preferring one rather than the other, but in fact I prefer to say that I present them both, not in the spirit of offering alternatives (either/or) but rather in the spirit of paradox (both/and) which only stops those who, like Bertrand Russell and the author of the ending you have already read, cannot get beyond the binary opposition which paradox subverts by denying its very possibility.

A Homily against Resolution and . . .

In conclusion I should just like to take this opportunity of explaining why I have not attempted to *resolve* the paradoxes of variability. In my humble opinion, all such attempts are doubly mistaken, first because they are misguided, undesirable, and pernicious, and second, which is much more important of course, they all fail in . . .

. . . a Dialogue between the Author and the Spirit Of BErtrand Russell

Spirit Of BErtrand Russell: Rubbish!

Author: Pardon? Who on earth are you?

SOBER: Not on earth, I'm afraid, not anymore. I am . . . was . . . anyway, a famous philosopher, logician, mathematician, man of letters, you name it . . . and I was a Peer of the Realm, you know . . . the name's Russell, Bertrand Russell—you just mentioned me, remember—and you're a fool, but I may be able to help you.

Author: Look, I have no idea why I should believe you, but I will accept your identity for the sake of this argument . . . Sir . . . but I would like to make it perfectly clear that *I'm* in charge here, and I think I have the right to say who speaks in my text, and I'm in something of a hurry and . . .

SOBER: I think you will find that you have only yourself to blame for my appearance . . .

Author: I fail to see how I could be blamed for that!

SOBER: I mean my being here offering you some good advice out of the kindness of my heart and the breadth of my experience of the world . . . of logic.

Author: I'm sorry Sir. Please carry on. I'm all ink.

SOBER: What?

Author: All ink. You know, waiting with baited pen and all that.

SOBER: Oh I see. Well, your problem it seems to me is in the area of paradox and self-reference. Do you know, back in 1901 or thereabouts it stopped me completely for what felt like years—this was when I was working on that project of Whitehead's and mine to systematise the whole of mathematics into one infallible, complete and consistent system.[27] But then old Kurt Gödel came along, of course.[28] End of dream. Damn clever, I'll say that for him. Though what I couldn't understand was what made him do it. Letting the monster loose in the very heartland of order and clarity. A fifth columnist for the party of chaos, that Gödel, despite his devilish cleverness . . . aha, devilish, yes of course, of course . . .

Author: Excuse me Sir, but I think you said something about advice. I am quite busy, you know.

SOBER: . . . yes, yes, self-reference is the very devil—what? Oh yes. Well, my young misguided friend, it seems to an old hand like myself that in a way you're right and in a way you're wrong.

Author: Ah.

SOBER: You cannot of course, as you point out, *resolve* a true paradox— though whether your little problem in . . . what *is* your discipline?

Author: Sociology of scientific knowledge.

SOBER: Impossible! The world turned upside down! I have changed my mind. I cannot help anybody who is so far gone as to be practising an impossible discipline—*logically* impossible, mind you.

Author: Surely not logically impossible, Sir. I mean a cat may look at a queen, I take that back, what I mean is . . .

SOBER: Well, alright. Immoral then—*logically* immoral, of course. But perhaps after all, you need my help even more than I thought. Now. Perhaps your problem is not a paradox at all, or at least not the really vicious kind that in 1901 . . . Anyway, if it's a matter of self-reference— it *is* a matter of self-reference isn't it?

Author: I believe so.

SOBER: In that case I may well have the answer. If you can't resolve it in the sense of solving it—though no doubt that inability is due to a simple lack of intellectual capacity on your part . . .

Author: Well! You clearly cannot have read my analysis of . . .

SOBER: . . . you can do so by simply banning the monster altogether! I did, you know, I did . . . or I tried. It's a mind destroyer, you know. Accept it, live with it on its terms and you'll never be in control again. It's the thin end of the wedge. Old Milton had it right, in his fine old English Puritan way, when he said "All coherence gone." [29] Ah, yes, beautiful and true, beautiful and true. Like a page from Euclid. Where was I? Oh yes. The theory of types, my boy, the theory of types. You see the idea is to divide the domain of reference into logical types which . . . now let me see. Are you dealing with numbers or words?

Author: Well, words of course. This is *interpretative* sociology, you know.

SOBER: Worse and worse. A mere guessing game which pretends to be a science. I don't know why I'm bothering to solve your problem for you. Anyway, words are a bit trickier. In set-theory, there was no problem at all. One just kept the various levels of, say, sets of objects and sets of sets apart. Any set that could not be assigned to one unambiguous level was simply discarded as not a true set at all. [30] It was marvellous: suddenly, pouf! no self-reference, no paradox, no hideous unanswerable questions like, Is the set of all sets that are not members of themselves a member of itself or not? [31]

Author: I think that's a *beautiful* question.

SOBER: [*Pause*] [*Longer pause*] You do, do you? And I suppose you've got an answer as well. [*Heavy irony*]

Author: Yes and no.

SOBER: That is an answer? [32]

Author: If that is a question. [33] But this is beside the point. Before you arrived in this text with all this stuff about help and advice and getting rid of self-reference and everything, I was saying that the resolution of paradoxes—and especially the kind of resolution you appear to have in mind—is simply not desirable. I do not *wish* to get rid of the paradox of variability . . .

SOBER: That's a new one on me. Is it yours by any chance? [*New respect dawning*]

Author: Well, yes, I suppose it is in a way. [*New respect dawning*] But that's not the point—although I did spend a lot of pen and ink on its production—but that's not the point. What I want to say is this: I have dedicated my life to the long and tiring but oh so rewarding investigation of reflexivity . . .

SOBER: Pompous ass!

Author [*undeterred*]: . . . in all its modes and fashions . . .

SOBER: How shallow!

Author [*unimpressed*]: . . . as witness my encyclopedia which is unsurpassed in the field of reflexive inquiry . . . [34]

SOBER: That's no field, that's a swamp!

Author [unrattled]: . . . except perhaps by my intricate and ingenious analyses in the interstices of metascience which are, I suspect, crowned by my unerring and exacting exposition . . .

SOBER: Egomaniac!

Author [unhearing]: . . . of the paradoxes of variability, the vital dénouement of which has been criminally delayed by this rather silly dialogue. I begin to have my doubts about the Other Author, you know. He's only too keen to let me take over on the boring bits, I take that back, on the detailed analytical sections, which is just as well, of course, as he could not possibly handle them as competently as I undoubtedly do, and without these pieces of solid analysis—which are damned hard work let me tell you—this text would degenerate into substandard, half-baked pseudofiction; and all in the name of new literary forms, which is a pretentious idea if ever I wrote one. The situation wouldn't be so bad if only he would let me spell out, clearly and precisely, the relation between reflexivity and fictioning. But he won't, I know he won't. He's obsessed by this idea of doing and not saying, or doing the saying by means of the doing, or acknowledging what one does while one does it.[35] Perhaps I can persuade him some other time.[36] Yes, that would be better. This is neither the time nor the place and I have far too much to do already without worrying about what, by writes, should be his problem, not mine. For a start I have to finish this "Dialogue with the Spirit Of BErtrand Russell" and then . . . but first things first. Now, where had we got to? Oh yes, I was being made out to be quite unbelievably immodest and arrogant as a prelude to . . . now, what was it?

SOBER: Telling me that my theory of types was at least workable when confined to the ghetto of set-theory but that it was in any case a thoroughly misguided product of a mind obsessed with control and that when it was taken over by the wider logical positivism movement and adapted for natural language it became not only pernicious but self-destructive, and not only self-destructive but absurd in its unintended consequence of ruling out all self-referential formulations however innocent such as any reference to the first person *by* that same first person or any reference to a text or speech *in* that same text or speech which would thus annihilate the very root of intelligence and creativity which is largely responsible for raising Man above the level of the Beast, namely, her capacity to refer to himself and thus to know herself as a speaking Subject and not only this, but also and therefore, his capacity to represent and to image and thus Art and thus Music and thus Literature and thus Philosophy and thus Science and thus Mathematics and thus Logic and thus Bertrand Russell and thus the theory of

types and thus the variant adapted to natural, but see below, language
which stratified the domain of legitimate linguistic formulation into
"object language," "metalanguage," "metametalanguage," "etcetera," among which there was no fraternisation and into one and only
one of which every meaningful statement was assigned which thus cast
into the outer darkness of meaninglessness not only the semantic paradoxes but also such innocent . . . ; but I, sorry, but the first person
singular who speaks this speech, ha ha, has already said that, and not
only absurd in its unintended consequence etcetera but also and finally
utterly artificial and entirely *un*natural—which explains why I, never
mind, said "see below," above, when referring to natural language—
which explains why it never caught on with the general public; and to
tell me that to enter this text shouting "Rubbish!" just as you were
about to complete your ending for "Analysts' Variability Talk," after
which you were fully intending to take a few pages well-earned rest
and let the Other Author get on with it, was tasteless at best and time
wasting at worst especially considering that all I have managed to
come up with so far has been the rather vague recommendation that
you "solve" your "problem" with a linguistic version of the theory of
types which, far from being a help, would in fact label as meaningless
your initial question, viz: "Is the claim for high variability in accounts
self-exemplifying?" even though you are, of course, quite aware that
this positivistic and puritan metaphysic is not intended to be taken seriously in this text which is entirely concerned with reflexivity in contemporary interpretative metascience discourse and that my real role in
the text is to point out the formal parallels between levels of variability
accounting and the positivists' levels of language in order to persuade
those readers who might be tempted to imagine that your analysis of
the paradoxes of variability, and indeed your whole treatment of variability accounting, is so much sophistry put forward in a desperate attempt to save the phenomenon of reflexivity from being exposed as a
damned nuisance and who may therefore think that the solution to
such irresolvables is simply to take steps to keep the levels of accounting strictly apart from each other and voila! problem solved, but who
of course are not *positivists,* to reconsider their views on level-mixing;
even though, being a close colleague of the Other Author and privy
to his plans, you are, as you say, aware of all this, nevertheless it is
your opinion, for what it is worth, that my contribution to the development of this text has been so slight that had you had my role you could
have summed it all up in a single sentence.

Author: Yes, that's the place. But I'm afraid I am not now going to say
what it is I had planned to say. I am sorry to disappoint you but even
a single sentence would take far too long. I have wasted more than

enough time on this dialogue and I have decided that it has now come to an end. The final words will be back in the actual analysis, thank the Lord.

Lord Russell: Don't mention it.

Author [*back in the actual analysis (or so he thinks)*]: . . . the end.

CHAPTER SIX

THE CRITICAL
PROBLEMS OF
WRITING THE
PROBLEM
A Double Text

Pre-Texts for The Problem

A text that both analyses itself and shows that it has neither a self nor any neutral metalanguage with which to do the analyzing calls out irresistibly for analysis.
> Barbara Johnson (1978:149)

Respectable theoretical work can be based on a reflexive treatment of theoretical talk itself. The reading of theory is more than a mere introduction to sociological work. It is the basic empirical task.
> Charles Lemert (1979:289–90)

Ethnomethodology strikes me as a dead end, not because it's wrong but because it's right—all our culture is constructed, and once you've said that, what else is there to say?
> Andrew Pickering (letter to Mulkay, 29 April 1981)

Now, to state the difficulty, to state the difficulty of stating, is not yet to surmount it—quite the contrary.
> Jacques Derrida (1978:37)

What, then, are the prospects for a full-blown constitutive reflexivity at the level of textual representation?
> Steve Woolgar (1984:21)

SECOND TEXT:
MISCELLANEOUS EPISTEMOLOGICAL UNDERLABOURING

1. Introduction to the Chapter

I have subtitled this chapter "a double text" because it consists of two separate, but linked, Texts which ideally should be read simultaneously. I could have presented the texts side by side or with one text filling the top half of the page and the other filling the bottom half. I could have presented them on alternate pages or in different typescripts (as in Wynne 1988). I have in fact chosen a rather more conventional form of presentation which consists of interspersing one text by the other throughout the chapter. The effect of this procedure is to break up the texts into sections, thus giving them a disjointed quality. While this effect does no violence to the Second Text (see below), it is less than kind to the author-ised reading of the First Text (see below).

The theme which links the Texts is, as the title of the chapter connotes, the problem of writing explored through attempts at writing The Problem (see below).

2. Introduction to the First Text

The title of the First Text is "In Principle and In Practice: The Principal Tensions of Practical Reasoning." It is an analytical text, the substantive topic of which is a further aspect of SSK discourse, namely, the writings of Steve Woolgar in/on the structures (and strictures) of SSK discourse (Woolgar 1980, 1981a, 1981b, 1981c, 1982, 1983a).

The question I address to these documents is this: Does The Problem (1983a); which Woolgar also refers to as the problem of descriptions (1981c), the problem of fallibility (1982), fundamental, omnipresent (methodological) problems (1981a), problems of interpretation and inference (1979), the monster (1982), the methodological horrors (1981a, 1982), and even as the methodological dread, a Pandora's box of horrors (1983c), arise not merely in participants' interpretative work, and not only in other analysts' interpretations of this work, but also in Woolgar's own interpretative accounts of how The Problem arises in . . . , etcetera.

As a conventional piece of analysis, the First Text is designed for an equally conventional form of linear reading. Unfortunately, as I have already mentioned, the presence of the Second Text, which appears throughout in a thoroughly obtrusive fashion, tends to make such a smooth reading rather difficult.

3. Introduction to the Second Text

The Second Text is a mixture which is *not* designed to be read in a linear fashion. It consists of a variety of textual forms including commentary, dialogue, analysis, discussion, questions, quotations, and introductions. Its topics are mainly those raised by and in the First Text (an exception is this third introduction, the topic of which is, of course, the Second Text). Particular attention is paid to the *status* of the kind of argument for which both the First Text and Woolgar's texts (which it takes as topic) stand as exemplars. The relation of the Second Text to the First Text can be conceived as both disruptive and supportive, as both a hindrance and a help.

FIRST TEXT: IN PRINCIPLE AND IN PRACTICE: THE PRINCIPAL TENSIONS OF PRACTICAL REASONING

> P: It's rather easy to argue that [discourse analysts are] saying one thing and doing another. Much easier than maybe saying it to Steve Woolgar, if you take him seriously.
> (AP 1312–13)

1. Subject to The Problem

In this text, I attempt to show how Woolgar's discourse on the principles of practical reasoning is as much subject to The Problem as are, he argues, the discourses of science and metascience which he analyses. Indeed, his very formulations of the "flaws" in others' explanatory and descriptive practices can themselves be seen to be similarly "flawed" (Woolgar 1981c:509).

SECOND TEXT

4. The Status of Countercritical Tu Quoque Arguments

> What significance need be attached to the argument that [certain programmes] fail to live up to their own criticisms of others' work? (Woolgar 1982:488)

In a sense all arguments may be legitimately characterised as critical (and thus all tu quoque arguments as countercritical) in that they are always "paradoxical" in the Barthesian sense of the word. "A new discourse can only emerge as the *paradox* which goes against (and often goes for) the surrounding or preceding *doxa,* can only see the day as difference, distinction, working loose *against* what sticks to it" (Barthes 1983:388). However, I want to ignore this generalised notion of criticism for the moment (we shall come back to it) in order to attend to the limited class of arguments which consist of obvious and specific criticisms and which are therefore vulnerable to countercriticism of the tu quoque type. Not all tu quoques, of course, are countercritical. For example, the anti–logical-positivist and antirelativist tu quoques encountered in Chapter Three purport to discover a "reflexive weakness" in the positive arguments of their opponents such that when such arguments are turned back on themselves the result is an absurdity. In contrast, countercritical tu quoque arguments attack the negative or critical arguments of the opponent by claiming that these criticisms also or perhaps only apply, reflexively, to the opponent's own claims and positive arguments.

As an example, let us take Woolgar's countercriticism of the discourse analysts' criticisms of "traditional" analysts' formulations of "definitive versions" of scientific action and belief (Mulkay 1981; Gilbert and Mulkay 1983, 1984a).

We might expect that proponents of discourse analysis should give us cause to believe that the problem of definitive versions they identify in the work of others does not apply to their own work. They are, after all, themselves advancing "definitive" versions of the character of discourse . . . . They have neither solved nor avoided the problem of fallibility; theirs is no less subject to the "methodological horrors" than is other work. (Woolgar 1982:488–89)

It would seem that the significance to be accorded to an argument of this kind depends on the degree of generality attributed to the topic of criticism: "A criticism that can be so easily applied to everything is not really a criticism of anything" (Collins 1983a:101); if nothing "can escape such criticism it is pointless to make it" (Barnes and Law 1976:236). In order to accuse discourse analysts of being themselves subject to the problem of definitive versions, Woolgar translates this particular problem as an instance of the "methodological horrors" brought on by the "problem of fallibility." In other words, the problem of definitive versions becomes just another manifestation of the "omnipresent" (Woolgar 1981a:12) Problem. If the "universal criticism is no criticism" thesis is taken seriously, therefore, Woolgar's countercritical tu quoque would appear to lack substance.

Similarly, the enquiry proposed for the First Text, which involves paying reflexive attention to the manifestation of The Problem in Woolgar's texts, seems to promise results of serious insignificance. The question of the status of countercritical tu quoque arguments which Woolgar raised at the beginning of this section, is then a direct concern of the First Text's discourse, as it is, I argue, of Woolgar's. The nature of the relations of the First Text to the texts which it takes as topic (Woolgar's) as well as the (similar) relations between Woolgar's texts and those which they take as topic (other SSK texts) is a central concern of this chapter. Is it a relation of critique or criticism (cf. Woolgar 1981c) or both or neither?

FIRST TEXT

2. The Paradox of Ethnomethodology

I intend to construe Woolgar's discourse aga(in)st SSK as manifesting a sequence of *ironic tensions* (Woolgar 1980, 1983a) between various transformations of the relation between the "in principle" and the "in practice" which forms the paradoxical core of Woolgar's formulation of ethnomethodology.[1]

The central object of ethnomethodological inquiry hinges on a paradox . . . . Despite the fact that documents are indexical [subject to changes of meaning with their occasions of use], that any attempt to specify their underlying meaning is in principle both defeasible [constantly subject to proposed alternatives] and inconcludeable [endlessly endless], and that they bear a reflexive [circular] relation to proposed underlying realities, members do routinely establish connections between documents and underlying patterns, and their establishment of these connections is routinely taken to be both adequate (for the practical purposes at hand) and unproblematic. Ethnomethodology is concerned with the ways in which this occurs. (Woolgar 1981a:12)

The rhetoric of this discourse posits, reflexively, an "underlying reality" which is, in principle, always there, waiting to spring from the shadows of ethnomethodological discussion into the (until-then-apparently) real world of practical activity. However, it is a feature of the paradox that no "document" is (normally; during the course of unreflective practical activities; while operating in the "realist mode" [Barnes 1981a; Barnes and Law 1976]) available by which a connection may be made to this underlying reality. Instead, our normal documents (the routine nature of our interpretative efforts; the adequate and unproblematic character of their results) encourage us to posit an entirely different kind of underlying reality which matches these documents rather better. This is, of course, the world we live in which is normally experienced as knowable (if not entirely), as known in common (among most of us), and as independent of our accounting practices (except for the microscopic level of physical reality and certain self-fulfilling or negating social phenomena). In short, normally the world is as it is assumed to be in and by the operation of "mundane reasoning" (Pollner 1974, 1987).

So, on what grounds (with what documents) does ethnomethodology posit its radically distinct form of world? The most well-known of such documents are Garfinkel's (1967) breaching experiments which worked by radically disturbing the taken-for-granted normal world in a way that allowed a direct glimpse of what this conceals. (In the normal world of science Collins claims that controversies can have a similar effect on scientists' understandings of their practice: they act as "an autogarfinkel for scientific knowledge" [Collins 1983a:195].) But normally such a direct glimpse of the ethnomethodological reality is unavailable. (Of course, the notion of a "direct glimpse" is fundamentally anti-ethnomethodological; it is a members' metaphor for what ethnomethodology would describe [of course, the notion of "describing" is fundamentally anti-ethnomethodological; it is a members' metaphor for the making of a connection (of course, the notion of "making a connection" is fundamentally anti-ethnomethodological; it is a members' metaphor for . . . for . . .)])

SECOND TEXT

5. Speaking Ethnomethodology

The Problem then is how to ever "be inside" ethnomethodological discourse. It seems that any talk *of* ethnomethodology has trouble in being talk *in* ethnomethodology; it is the basic reflexive problem of this discourse.[2] Perhaps, if the object is to show or rather to "provide for"[3] a reader/hearer's apprehension of the "constructive work" that goes into each and every occasion of "making connections," one could make the reading of one's text difficult, for instance by inserting brackets within brackets, each subsequent instance of which would consist of an attempt at ethnomethodological deconstruction of the terms used in the previous (bracketed) phrase which itself would be an unsuccessful attempt at such a deconstruction of the (bracketed) phrase prior to its occurrence in the text and so on. Such a construction, in that it refuses to remain content with its own formulations (of the impossibility of authentically remaining content) is, one would intend, extremely difficult to read "comfortably" (Woolgar 1984:21). Therefore, in order to make sense of it, a reader must consciously do that type of constructive work of which ethnomethodology understands all understandings as being the result.

The trouble with such a solution is that it is liable to be read as an example of bad writing. The overcomplications, the obscurities, the convolutions could be read as a lack of technical skill in communicating the determinate message which is what one has to say. To complain that such a way of reading is naive, inasmuch as it implies a dualistic conception of content and form where the latter is merely the vehicle in which the former is conveyed, is indeed tempting. However, to argue from a site of greater sophistication is to lay oneself open to charges of, as the etymology of the word would suggest, sophistry. The reader's charge of sophistry is a way of redressing the balance of responsibility for the difficulty of the text. To read such difficulty as a case of bad writing is to say it is the author's responsibility. For the author to respond to this charge with an accusation of reader-naivety is to reattribute the responsibility for the difficulty of the text to the reader, which is shifted onto the author once more by the reader's charge of sophistry. However, the sophistry charge changes the character of the author's responsibility for the difficulty of the text. Whereas with bad writing the author is accused of simple technical incompetence, with sophistry, she is accused of dressing up this incompetence with a pseudojustification. The reader may now wonder about the content (to use the reader's metaphor [as the sophisticated author describes it]) of the text: perhaps it is mere verbiage; obscurity for the sake of obscurity. Some of Barnes's comments on Woolgar's (1981b) critique of "interests model explanations" can be read as the plain person's objection to undue sophistication.

What I have to say can be read in terms of the conventions of the realist mode of speech in routine use among us. I use terms to refer to things or events or processes or whatever, in the common way. This is how discourse is generally understood—as *about* something or other. Anyone who wants to speak differently, in a fancy way, has a responsibility to make that clear in what they write. (Barnes 1981a:492)

So perhaps the solution to the problem of writing (ethnomethodology) does *not* lie in the project of writing in a difficult way? But then again, perhaps it does:

When "describing" science one unavoidably participates in . . . traditional distinctions which are embedded in vernacular discourse . . . . The language is, however, not so "fixed" as to preclude disclosure through the use of, for example, "tortured sentences" which turn on themselves, and neologisms and puns which do violence to a hearer's competence with the traditional distinctions of ordinary usage (with all due apologies to proponents of "clear" writing and speech). (Lynch 1982:527, n.23)

FIRST TEXT

3. Didactic Discourse: The Primacy of the In Principle

To sum up then. Woolgar's version of ethnomethodology can be analysed as a self-referring construction consisting of two radically disconnected poles: on the one hand a set of documents consisting, in practice, of members' methods of successful practical reasoning, and on the other a posited underlying pattern constituted by those fundamental, omnipresent features of discourse (indexicality, defeasibility, inconcludeability, reflexivity) whose function is, in principle, to make successful practical reasoning an impossibility. In this scheme the documents have no corresponding underlying pattern and the underlying pattern has no corresponding documents. The relationship between the two poles is thus one of concealment; the reality is hidden by the documents rather than revealed by them. It is this relationship which provides for Woolgar's various formulations of the kind of question his research seeks to address:

1. What is the nature of the constructive work done by members in making interpretations, such that the fundamental methodological problems . . . are either evaded, managed, or otherwise made to seem insignificant? (1981a:12)
2. How is it that researchers deal in practice with what at an epistemological level is an irresolvable difficulty? (1983a:242)
3. The central research task is an investigation of the ways in which descriptions are practically managed as "good enough." (1981c:509)
4. To ask how in practice members manage to ignore or evade the implications of the position that accounts are constitutive of "reality." (1981c:507)

5. [To investigate] what counts as legitimate avoidance of what might otherwise be regarded as insurmountable philosophical difficulties. (1981b: 389)

Even in these brief formulations of the research task it is evident that the bipolar construction of this interpretative schema provides for the downgrading of one of the poles of the dichotomy in contrast to the other. The in principle pole consists of fundamental (1), irresolvable (2), and insurmountable (5) problems (1) and difficulties (2, 5) of a methodological (1), epistemological (2), and philosophical (5) character which are, in practice (2, 4), evaded (1, 4), managed (1, 3, 4), made to seem insignificant (1), dealt with (2), ignored (4), and avoided (5).

It seems hard to evade, ignore, or avoid an interpretation of Woolgar's constructive work (1) in these extracts as constituting an irony on the level of practice. What is done in practice is made to seem relatively trivial in comparison with the terminological significance accorded to the in principle pole. We can interpret Woolgar's use of antipractical irony in these particular extracts as a component of a didactic interpretative strategy. The extracts are from a series of texts which argue for and/or demonstrate the value of an ethnomethodological approach to understanding science (1980, 1981a, 1981b, 1981c, 1982, 1983a, 1983c, 1984).[4] In the context of teaching or of programmatics it is important constantly to assert the existence of The Problem (the underlying reality) in the strongest possible manner because, in the absence of other documents with which to make out its existence, such assertions become the only documents of the very reality about which they speak. The strength of these assertions is, however, crucially affected by the way in which the in practice pole of the construction is characterised. The weaker the latter is made out to be, in comparison with the former, the stronger the former will seem to be in comparison with the latter. However, any attempt to discount the practical is interpretatively problematic given the massive phenomenological asymmetry between the two poles: on the one side, the wealth of successful interpretation, adequate commonsense, and practical reasoning; on the other, a posited underlying reality of fundamental problems which is signally unsuccessful in making life as impossible as its existence would lead us to expect. Woolgar's method for overcoming this problem consists of ascribing to the realm of the practical the additional function of actively and artfully concealing the reality of The Problem. As Woolgar put it in interview:

W: I think that talk as we use it . . .
A: Right.
W: (Laughter) . . . is, um, like its main property is a way of, of rendering oneself immune from methodological horrors.
(SW 4611–12)

4. Deploying Ethnomethodology: The Inverse Irony

The tension between the poles that provides for the kind of irony involved in Woolgar's didactic discourse also provides for the inverse irony (of the in principle by the in practice) in arguments about the true message of ethnomethodology. The Woolgar-Barnes-MacKenzie debate on the status of interests model explanations features an interesting set of such arguments (Woolgar 1981b; Barnes 1981a; MacKenzie 1981b; Woolgar 1981c).[5] While Woolgar's "Interests and Explanation" (1981b) does not deploy a specific version of ethnomethodology, both Barnes's reply (1981a) and Woolgar's counterreply ("Critique and Criticism," 1981c) do. Barnes's version consists of what he describes as a "far from disinterested and conceivably eccentric" (1981a:484) reading of Garfinkel's *Studies in Ethnomethodology* (1967), the main feature of which is an emphasis on and a positive valuation of the in practice pole of the discourse at the expense of the in principle.

Garfinkel's work is an analysis of the *realist* mode of speaking practically universally employed by all of us. The methods of accounting he identifies are those we all use to maintain a sense of pattern and order through the flux of appearances . . . . Garfinkel's work studiously avoids debunking . . . the realist mode of speech, recognising the "artfulness" with which it is employed, the diversity of what can be achieved with it, and its general standing as an "awesome phenomenon." (Barnes 1981a:484)

While Barnes does not deny the existence of The Problem, which in his text appears as "the flux of appearances," the whole tone of his presentation suggests that the chance of this flux actually being much of a *problem* for the continued employment of pattern maintenance devices of such huge popularity ("universally employed by all of us") and great success ("artfulness," "diversity," "awesomeness"), is limited, to say the least.

SECOND TEXT

6. The Realist Mode of Speech

Barnes's celebration of the realist mode of speech does *not* mean, however, that he is a realist. On the basis of the "correctness" of the Duhem-Quine thesis which he has "never doubted," Barnes claims: "I am not a realist, but an instrumentalist and a relativist" (1981a:493). But in that case, one might ask, why remain content with the realist mode of speech?

I answer that it is a marvellous instrument. Consider the situation. On the left we have the vast complexity of reality, or experience, or what have you, including, if you will, all previous speech acts: on the right we have but a few thousand symbols, plus some competence in using them, and notably the competencies of the realist mode. Somehow, with the miserable resources on the right we cope with the immensities on the left. [But, it could be objected, if the social sciences] analyze the realist mode, they should use it as sparingly as is possible. This seems to be Garfinkel's view, but it is an obvious non sequitur. There is nothing wrong with employing the mode in analyzing the mode. (Barnes 1981a:493)

Barnes's last sentence has been a considerable problem for me, in that I both agree with it and disagree with it. So what is wrong with that? I have claimed at the end of Chapter Five that the "both/and" is what I advocate. I have also said in Chapter Three that the "puritan" proposal to totally separate topic from resource such that "nothing we take as subject can appear as part of our descriptive apparatus unless it itself has been described" (Sacks 1963:2) is an impossible chimera; I was very ironical about that, as I recall. So why can't I simply agree with Barnes when he claims there is nothing wrong with using the mode to analyse the mode? Well, as I say, when put like that I *do* agree with it. Then what's the problem? The Problem is what it leads to. In terms of my discussion of solutions to the problem of the reflexivity of reflexivity in Chapter Three, it would appear to lead to a combination of the strategies of nonpuritan realism and relaxed nonworrying. In Woolgar's terms, such a procedure is "disingenuous" (1981c:511; 1983a:253) inasmuch as it relies on an understanding of analysis as being separable from criticism. Just such an understanding is expressed in Bloor's impartiality tenet (1973, 1976) as it is in SSK's regular "declarations of neutrality" (Woolgar 1983a:253) with respect to the knowledge analysed. Barnes, for example, asserts that "the standing of forms of knowledge . . . need not be diminished by [their analysis]" (Barnes 1981a:487; Woolgar 1981c:511).

Woolgar, who quotes Barnes's argument, proceeds to deploy it against Barnes's criticism(?) of Woolgar's criticism(?) of Barnes's work. If analysis does not imply criticism, why then does Barnes read Woolgar's (1981b) analysis of the structure of interests explanations as a criticism of their use?

I could [say] that my deconstruction of the explanatory structure of interests explanations has no implications for its legitimacy . . . . It could be claimed that my demonstration of *how* something is done, does not entail that it *should not* be done . . . . Yet this kind of . . . claim is clearly disingenuous . . . . Descriptions are commonly read as entailing procedural recommendations . . . . The nice irony here is that Barnes and MacKenzie hear my attempt to reveal the structure of interests explanation as a negative evaluation, however much I say that I subscribe to their own proclaimed stance on impartiality. (Woolgar 1981c:511–12)

So the idea is simply to accept the criticality of one's discourse and to avoid programmatic claims for its neutrality? Perhaps; but then what would be the implications of doing so for my disagreement with Barnes's endorsement of the use of the realist mode of speech to analyse itself? After all, if analysis *is* critical, then analysing the realist mode of speech *is* criticising the realist mode of speech; which, I gather, is what I want to do. Yes, but if one is using the mode for purposes of criticising the use of the mode, then how authentic can such a critical exercise be? It would be, rather, a celebration of the ever greater powers of the realist mode: look, it can even be used to criticise itself! As Derrida says about the power of Reason:

The unsurpassable, unique and imperial grandeur of the order of reason, that which makes it not just another order or structure . . . is that one cannot speak out against it except by being for it, that one can protest it only from within it; and within its domain, Reason leaves us only the recourse to stratagems and strategies. (Derrida 1978:36)

But is he talking of the same thing as I am? Surely Reason is a rather more embracing order than the realist mode of speech? Well, let us hope so; but I doubt it. I am being far too pessimistic: there must be *something* that the realist mode is incapable of dealing with.

FIRST TEXT

5. A Double Transformation: Fundamental versus Technical

(Note that although some sociologists are prepared to admit [that descriptions are fundamentally flawed] at a programmatic level, they then retreat to the reformist re-action in their practical dealings with descriptions. That is, some sociologists concede that descriptions are essentially flawed in principle, but their explanatory practice treats this point as a mere technical difficulty.) (Woolgar 1981c:509)

(Note that although Woolgar is prepared to admit that some sociologists agree with him at a programmatic level, he then distances himself from them by noticing their deficient practice. That is, Woolgar concedes a consensus on the problem of descriptions in principle, but his explanatory practice treats this point as beside the point.)

In this passage there seems to be a double transformation of the in principle/in practice dichotomy. While the author clearly values the funda-mental nature of The Problem and regrets its relegation to the status of "a mere technical difficulty," he also seems to distrust programmatic concessions which are not carried over into actual practice. The first transformation—in principle meaning fundamental (good) versus in practice meaning technical (bad)—is similar to Woolgar's formulation of the dichotomy in his didactic discourse on ethnomethodology. Indeed, the former pole is unchanged while the latter (in practice) can be understood as a specification of one of the ways in which "researchers deal in practice" (1983a:242) with The Problem, that is, by treating it as a mere technical difficulty. Woolgar describes this ap-proach as the "reformist reaction" to the problem of descriptions.

The reformist reaction takes the position that the problem of descriptions is largely inconsequential because it represents a *technical* difficulty encountered in the course of explanation . . . . Descriptions *are* acknowledged as unreliable, but the source of this unreliability is located in the process whereby descriptions are generated . . . . In short, the reformist reading uses the ethnomethodological discussion of the problem of descriptions as a *sensitizing device* for sociological work.[6] (1981c:509)

In contrast, Woolgar's "radical reading" of The Problem treats attempts at reformation as a fool's errand: "The unreliability of descriptions . . . is a fundamental feature of discourse. Attempts to improve upon the accuracy of descriptions are doomed; descriptions are only more or less reliable by virtue of their being treated that way for the practical purposes at hand" (1981c:509).

(Un)fortunately for those characterised as retreating to the reformist reading of The Problem in the course of their explanatory practices, it also appears that to do so is inevitable: "It is important to note that explanatory work *inevitably* proceeds by ignoring the problem of descriptions. That is, practical explanation *has to* treat . . . the characters of entities . . . as fixed for the practical purposes of explanatory argument" (1981c:508). Moreover, as it is also inevitable that the practice of explanation entails the "artful concealment" of The Problem (see [First Text] section 3), Woolgar "make[s] no apology for pointing out the significant sense in which *all* such work is *essentially flawed*" (1981c:510). Thus Woolgar justifies his use in "Interests and Explanation" of such "ordinarily pejorative . . . terminology" (MacKenzie 1981b:500) as "suspicion" and "accomplished avoidance" (Woolgar 1981b:385), by appealing to the principle that criticism of a universal phenomenon should not be taken as an attack on any particular instance of it [see Second Text 4].

A more important issue for our analysis than the character of criticism, which is not a topic I am concerned with in this [First] text, is the terminology used by Woolgar to avoid the charge that "Interests and Explanation" constitutes an *explanation* of the nature of interests explanation. Woolgar characterises his work in this paper with a variety of formulations including examination, appreciation, illustration and development, identification, exploration, unpacking ("deconstructing"), representing, shedding light, showing, and applying a style of analysis (1981b:367, 373, 378, 380, 383, 389). In "Critique and Criticism" the work of the earlier paper is characterised as argument, critique, direction of critical attention, the pointing out of flaws, an attempt to make points, and a demonstration of how something is done (1981c:510, 511). Woolgar certainly seems shy of describing his interpretative practice (my description) as explanation; and, indeed, he is aware of the vulnerability of his argument (my description) to a deconstructive tu quoque should he do so. He attempts to preempt such a response by implicitly claiming a relative immunity from the effect on his practice of conceding that *some* aspect of analysis must always remain unexplicated. Such an objection, he argues, only has force "given a commitment to causal-type explanation. If, for example, we undertake an ethnographic approach to the study of scientific activity, it is true that this will also involve the use of unexplicated resources . . . . But since no causal explanation is required, less significance need be attached to the role of these uninvestigated features. They remain available for further extended ethnographic study" (1981b:371).

This passage is only an implicit denial of doing explanation in "Interests and Explanation" itself, because Woolgar chooses to cite the case of an ethnographic approach to the study of scientific activity as his example of *non*causal-type explanation. However, let us treat it as a specific denial; this is, in any case, how it appears to have been read by Barnes:

Ethnomethodology or any related activity [cannot] itself claim any immunity to criticisms levelled at constructive theorizing. Woolgar's general accounts of concept application as "work" are not pure description, nothing is: they are precisely constructive applications of the "work" metaphor. Woolgar dismisses the problems with his own account on the grounds that he, Woolgar, is uninterested in causal explanation—as though this gives him a freedom of speech which must be denied to orthodox sociologists. (Barnes 1981a:493)

Barnes's tu quoque attempts to implicate Woolgar in his, Woolgar's, criticisms of others by a form of similarity accounting: there is no essential (relevant) difference between Woolgar's "constructive applications" and, for instance, Barnes's.[7] Woolgar's attempt to avoid the tu quoque (to "claim immunity"), on the other hand, proceeds by a strategy of difference accounting: here, his own practice and/or an ethnographic approach; there, explanation and/or causal-type explanation, and/or causal explanation. Woolgar's flexible use of these latter categories is itself significant: by switching from a stronger to a weaker (for instance, from causal to causal-type) he is able to avoid attributing extreme positivist-type traits to the work of the interests theorists while still maintaining the necessary distance between their work and his own (Woolgar 1981b:369–70).

So is "Interests and Explanation" an explanatory text?

SECOND TEXT

7. Going Off at a Tangent

He cannot answer that question, you know. No, and I'm surprised that he even asked it; you would have thought he would have realised by this point that such a question can have no determinate answer. Did you notice, by the way, how the First Text was going off at a tangent? Yes, it never seemed to have an easy path back to the second part of the analyst's double transformation of the in principle/in practice dichotomy. I mean once the text had got into the problematics of criticism . . . But that is the Second Text's concern; all the First Text is supposed to be doing is a simple straight reflexive analysis of the variations in Woolgar's deployment of the in principle/in practice . . . Yes, but don't you see how ambitious the idea of simple straight reflexive analysis is in this case? Well, not really; I would have thought . . . But the point is that the texts which are being taken as topic for this exercise are themselves attempts at a very similar kind of analysis which Woolgar calls "methodological reflection" [1981b:389]. Yes, but surely the analyst's object throughout has been to do reflexively similar analyses to those which he has taken as his topic; to, as it were, use the conclusions of a theory *against* its originators. But right there, you see, is the problem. Where? In the apparently inevitable reading of such an exercise as critical: as being *against*. Yes, I see that; and, of course, this is one of Woolgar's major problems too, is it not? Exactly, and that is the root of the difficulty of writing the First Text: the problem of criticism threatens to subvert the attempt to produce a purely analytical text. But surely our analyst must have been aware of the dangers of such potential subversion; after all, he did not choose the problem of criticism as the specific topic of the First Text. That's right; but his attempt to avoid the problem by choosing the comparatively anodyne topic of in principle/in practice for his analytical efforts seems to have backfired somewhat; it certainly has not prevented him from having to deal with criticism in some way or other. Yes, but look at the way he tries to pass it off as "no concern of mine"! I wouldn't worry too much; while the pretensions of the First Text to untroubled analysis are, I agree, irritating, they do at least provide the Second Text with a series of rich and varied topics. You're far too accepting of the demeaning role we play in this chapter; we've been cast as underlabourers garnering footnotes from the pure analyst's text. There are worse roles to play—such as the pure analyst who continually finds that his text is undermined by its own purity. You mean . . . ? Probably; but in the meantime the Second Text has work to do.

8. A Dialogue on Immunity

A: Uh, well let's just take this general point, um, so I don't lose it. What often worries me when I read your work . . . you know I think, "Yeah great, yeah great," uh, and I think, I'm never *quite* sure if, if you are including yourself in your strictures on . . . including your *own* work, and including the very work in which these strictures occur, *in*, in the strictures.

W: Mm.

A: Now, I don't know whether you want that to be taken as obvious you know— "Well, of course," you know—or if in some sense you think you . . . because of your, because it's . . . the fact that you're talking about *that*, you can escape from, um, the difficulties involved in doing description, or doing you know, whatever.

W: Yeah. No. It's a very, it's a very very good point. I mean it's not something that I've worked out but it's absolutely *the* issue. It seems to me that I could not reasonably say that I'm immune from the strictures which I place upon other people's arguments.

A: Mm.

W: Um. But it's not a question of just being reasonable. It seems to me that in attempting to do that, you lose what is, uh, like the most intriguing part of what you would call reflexivity.

A: The attempt to be immune?

W: Yeah.

A: Yes.

W: Attempting to be immune. Um. So what one is looking for and I think I'm becoming clearer and clearer about this . . . . One is now looking for a way of talking, a way of writing which at the same time represents yourself as immune from these, these strictures, but not. Right? So there's a way of, you want to develop a way of writing so you can show to the reader how these, um, strictures do indeed apply to you . . .

A: Yes.

W: . . . even though they might appear not to. Now, um, so you've got to play with the, they, they do and they do not, and how, how you get that in a text . . .

A: Right.

W: . . . is a real, is a real difficulty.

(SW 3901–4002)

FIRST TEXT

6. A Double Transformation: Programmatics versus Actual Practice

. . . some sociologists concede that descriptions are essentially flawed in principle, but their explanatory practice treats this point as a mere technical difficulty. (Woolgar 1981c:509)

In this passage there seems to be a double transformation of the in principle/in practice dichotomy. While the author clearly values the essential character of The Problem and regrets its relegation to the status of "a mere technical difficulty," he also seems to distrust programmatic concessions which are not carried over into actual practice.

The second transformation of the dichotomy—in principle meaning programmatics (bad) versus in practice meaning actual practice (good)— inverts the evaluations ["To repeat, my motive is not evaluative" (Woolgar 1980:266)] that Woolgar can be interpreted as attaching to the poles. This pair of evaluations is extremely common in SSK and Woolgar is far from an exception.[8] Consider, for instance, the following characterisation of the wrong way to do ethnomethodology:

The term "ethnomethodology" itself has acquired the status of a shibboleth [as] the result of the term's deployment in polemical debates by sociologists more concerned with programmatic delineation of "new directions" than with concrete empirical investigation. (Woolgar 1981a:11)

However, a few lines further on, Woolgar satirises the very distinction, with its embedded evaluations, which he deploys in the passage above. The evaluative motive for doing so is presumably that "Science and Ethnomethodology" (1981a) is itself something of a programmatic delineation of a new direction:

There is a distinction current among some ethnomethodologists between those who do ethnomethodological studies and those who merely talk about (doing) it.[9] The latter, referred to with some derision as "those engaged in programmatics," are not approved of by the former. For present purposes, my discussion attempts to do what is not approved of. (1981a:11)

However, there are many occasions where Woolgar displays an unambiguous approval of the concrete and the empirical and an equally unambiguous disapproval of the programmatic. For instance: . . . And again: . . . And finally: . . .

SECOND TEXT

9. A Conversation on the Occasioned Nature of Discourse, with Illustrations, between Two Types of Epistemological Sophisticate

He's in trouble again. So I see, but this time his problems seem to be much more mundane: he simply seems unable to quote any evidence for his claim. Yes, he certainly is having a hard time. Hard time my foot! he is just incompetent; one doesn't set oneself up as an analyst if one simply is unable to substantiate the claims one wants to make. Well, I'll grant that it certainly seems foolhardy to try to display a lack of ambiguity in a writer as sophisticated as Woolgar. I really cannot understand what you see in Woolgar; most of what he has had to say so far seems rather absurd to me.[10] That's a typical "reformist reaction" [Woolgar 1981c] if I may say so, as is your assumption that our analyst's problems are "merely technical" [Woolgar 1981c]. Oh now, come on; you agreed a moment ago . . . But that was just an occasioned remark and . . . Pardon? Nothing; I was about to argue that the level of the analyst's competence . . . Rather low, in this case! Possibly, possibly; but as I was saying, his technical competence is really beside the point. How come?

Well, consider the conclusions that could legitimately be drawn had the analyst succeeded brilliantly in displaying a series of utterly convincing quotations to the effect that Woolgar disapproved of programmatics and approved of . . . Yes, yes, get on with it! My point is this: Could one then conclude that we now know, as readers, what Woolgar's position is on this matter? Well, not *absolutely* of course; but I think we could claim to know more about it than we did before. Really? your faith in naive common sense is quite touching but what you fail to appreciate is the "occasioned" nature of Woolgar's (or anyone's) statements on this matter (or any other). All right then, I'm listening; I suppose it's something about taking the context into account. Well, not exactly; in fact that is a common misconception. As Woolgar puts it, "The observation that the particular meaning of a sign is 'occasioned' by its use [is not] equivalent to saying that the context determines meaning . . . . 'Context' is better regarded as a resource which is constructed and drawn upon by participants in the course of their practical interpretational work" [1981a:12]. So I'm not talking about context so much as the deep and irresolvable variability in the meaning of utterances; or to put it another way, the occasioned character of discourse. Now, my point is not simply that holding to such a conception of discourse makes problematic the reading of any set of apparently similar discourse extracts as all saying the same thing . . . You mean, for instance, all those non-existent statements about Woolgar's dislike of programmatics as hypothetically presented by our wonderfully competent analyst? Exactly; but this general Problem of interpretation is accentuated when the particular statements to be interpreted are Woolgar's. Why should that make any difference? Well, it obviously does, given that Woolgar holds to a conception of discourse as being radically occasioned and . . . Hang on a minute . . . Please don't interrupt; as I was saying, if we as readers are presented with a set of speeches from someone such as Woolgar who maintains . . . Excuse me . . . Let me finish! If we are asked to accept the statements of an "occasioned theorist" as being anything other than occasioned—as, in essence, this kind of analytical presentation insists that we do—then in so doing we would be contravening the theory of the occasioned nature of discourse. But how can you say . . . I see I will have to persuade you of my point by means of illustration. Perhaps your objection is that you have doubts about Woolgar's commitment to occasioned theoretics; well, I will show you that his commitment is not merely programmatic but actually informs his actual discursive practice.[11] For instance, during Woolgar's interview with our author, he regularly . . . But . . . *As* I was saying, Woolgar frequently . . . But . . . On several occasions . . . But . . . He responded to our author's questions in the following fashion:[12]

[1]   W: I, I don't, I mean I, I don't know really how to respond to that kind of
          question at all. Varies enormously.
       (SW 1410–11)

[2] W: So I don't know, I'm rather sceptical about giving any fixed answer on, on, to that kind of question.
(SW 1512)

[3] W: I don't, I really don't, um, I don't have a standard conception of what that is.
A: But do you, do you have conceptions that vary or are you telling me that you never have a conception of that at all?
W: Um, no I guess that wouldn't be true, but (Laughter), but to answer your question I suppose I'll give, have to give a series of them. Um, and I'm not sure that any of them are the ones I would represent myself with on any occasion.
(SW 1515–1602)

[4] W: Um, I don't know. Sorry, I don't think I can be very helpful in answering that . . .
A: No, that's alright, that's . . .
W: . . . those kinds of question at all.
A: Nobody, nobody can. I mean . . .
W: I mean, you know, the maps that people draw up of these kinds of things . . .
A: Right.
W: . . . are clearly (like) occasioned for the . . .
A: Certainly.
W: . . . for the particular purpose.
(SW 1614–1701)

[5] W: But I wouldn't, I don't want to sort of stake any money on that.
(SW 3812–13)

[6] W: I honestly don't have any sort of . . . I mean in, if you read the papers, I mean in each, each paper one presumably, I write in a way that could be construed as operating such principles.
A: Mm.
W: Um. But I don't stand on them. I (know), I can't, I won't now defend . . .
A: No.
W: . . . like . . .
A: No.
W: . . . an argument which appears in that way.
(SW 5313–5401)

[7] W: But the [X] moves and, um, I'm always interested in how [Xs] stop, so I don't have . . . there's no fixed [X] for me.
A: No, no.
W: I, I don't have a consistent position about where the [X] is and what's in and what's out.
A: Right.
W: Um.
A: You, you have a position on the existence of the [X]?

W: Um.

A: I mean . . .

W: No I, I construe their practice as being going to a certain point and not beyond, and um . . .

A: That applies to you as well. Your point is just further along.

W: Yeah, well, no.

(SW 5408–13)

[8]   W: So it's a question of playing with the [X] rather than . . .

A: Yeah.

W: . . . saying the [X] is better drawn elsewhere.

A: Yeah.

W: I would never fix, you know, I would never . . . I don't think I would ever put money on where the actual [X] is.

(SW 5502–04)

Now do you see? It is clear that on these eight occasions in the interview Woolgar was consciously and deliberately acting in accordance with his deeply held convictions about the occasioned nature of discourse. His consistent refusal to give a fixed answer to the interviewer's questions is a marvellous example of "matters of epistemological principle" [Barnes 1982a:98] being carried over into actual practice. It is nothing of the kind; or rather I fail to see the warrant for that interpretation, *given* your "occasioned nature of discourse." Don't you see that in order to find Woolgar "acting in accordance with his deeply held convictions," or even to find him "regularly," "frequently," and "on several occasions" saying the same thing, you had to treat Woolgar's occasioned discourse as *non*occasioned for your practical purposes of discovering him to be a practical theorist of occasioned discourse. In brief, *your* commitment to the occasioned does not run very deep: it stops short of reflexive application. In other words . . . All right, I take your over-sophisticated point; have you anything else to add before the Second Text totally ignores most of what we have had to say and proceeds to a brief analytical section on the interpretative flexibility of the occasioned? No, I don't think so; but it will be interesting to see whether the analysis endorses your ethnomethodological sophistication or my reflexive ditto!

10. A Brief Analytical Section on the Interpretative Flexibility of the Occasioned

W: Cicourel says there are these problems and once you've got to the, um, the deep features of interpretation then go back to your surface questions.

A: Yes.

W: And, um, certainly to the extent that there's that implication in, in Mike [Mulkay]'s work, um: "Look at that stuff first . . ."

A: Mm.

W: . . . (then) *I* have problems.
A: Right. Uh, I see that as very occasioned. That . . .
W: Sorry, what do you see as occasioned?
A: Him saying that.
W: Mike's statement on that.
A: Mike's statement on that.
W: Yes.
(SW 5609–14)

In this passage, Ashmore employs "occasioned" in order to excuse Mulkay's "Cicourelian revisionism" (SW 10, 56). If "Mike's statement on that" can be passed off as very occasioned—note that "very" is a comparative term; its use entails the acceptance of degrees of occasionedness—then it need not be taken seriously as a statement of position; a statement that is, precisely, treated as something other (and something more) than a merely occasioned pronouncement. Thus the discussants' use of "occasioned" here, is being interpreted as a device for neutralising the potentially discordant "statement" which, had Ashmore not intervened on its behalf, was in danger of being used as a document for showing Mulkay's position as different from the position being mutually constructed by the parties to the interview.

Notwithstanding [programmatics which would suggest the contrary] many practitioners in the social study of science make statements suggesting a wish to retain some
role for the independent existence of objects in the real world . . . . These statements
are occasioned pronouncements, post hoc reconstructions of practice, the ambivalence
of which can be read as differences in emphasis. (Woolgar 1983a:245)

The use of "occasioned" in this passage is similar to its use in the interview selection analysed above, in that the term is used to discount the statements it describes. Far from using the term to theorise a necessary feature of discourse or to display reflexive consistency between that theory and its practice, Woolgar's deployment of it here is entirely negative. What Woolgar is objecting to with his derogatory use of "occasioned pronouncements" is a lack of reflexive consistency between theory, or rather programmatics, and practice in the social study of science. As Woolgar is (being made out to be) equally guilty in this regard, the question of where we go from here becomes urgent. And is not solved by where we go from here.

FIRST TEXT

7. The Discourse of Real Research: The Primacy of the In Practice

The official topic of the sociology of scientific knowledge is scientific knowledge. Scientific knowledge is generally understood as the product of the practices of (natural) scientists. Woolgar, of course, along with his fellow sociologists of scientific knowledge is not a practising (natural) scientist. Moreover, Woolgar is more willing than most of his colleagues to treat SSK as a legitimate topic for analysis. This willingness is legitimated to some extent by the reflexive argument.[13] However, the legitimacy this argument provides is, perhaps, overshadowed by the greater currency of the various antireflexive arguments.[14] Thus Woolgar's choice of topic may be considered another source of the tension in his discourse, which is manifested for the purposes of this section in his attribution of an honorific practicality to the activities of (real) scientists and a correspondingly pejorative scholasticism to those of metascientists.

(1) The **activity** of science . . . comprises a **practical concern** with issues which we meet in slightly different form in the *discussions* of *professional* philosophers and sociologists. (2) The similarity between the **practical concerns** of **working** scientists and *proponents* in the *debate* between rationality and the strong programme in the sociology of knowledge is particularly striking . . . . (3) I see in [the] **activities** of **laboratory** scientists a microcosm of [this] *debate*: . . . in an important sense, **practising** scientists variously and interchangeably *take the position* of rationalist or of strong programmer. (4) The major difference, however, is that the *adoption* of one or other *argument* is not *merely a matter of academic indulgence*. (5) Rather, the *position taken* appears to have **immediate and significant practical consequences.** (Woolgar 1980:243; my emphases and numbers)

I have used different typographical emphases here in order to emphasise the contrast I am making. Woolgar's differential choice of words to characterise science and metascience is (now) particularly striking (2). Throughout the passage science is described in doing terms and metascience in talking terms.[15] Scientists are working (2) and practising (3) in the laboratory (3); their activities (1, 3) involve practical concerns (1, 2) with immediate and significant practical consequences (5). Metascientists (in their studies or the senior common room . . .[16]) carry on discussions (1) and debate (2, 3), of which they are the professional (1) proponents (2), merely [as] a matter of academic indulgence (4).

This contrast between science and metascience is not, however, simply a matter of the construction of difference. As in some of the other interesting cases of sameness/difference accounting to be found in this thesis, the interpretative task is to construct difference on the basis of, or in spite of, a constructed sameness.[17] And it is this sameness which is the news of the passage and of the text from which it comes. Woolgar's declared rationale for writing about the rationalist/strong programme debate is to persuade the reader to notice the similarity between the positions taken in that (otherwise uninteresting) debate and the positions taken during scientists' debates, sorry, practical activities. In other words this rationale, which Woolgar has called "methodological transposition" (1979), provides for an *instrumental* interpretation of Woolgar's penchant for reflexive topics: "I am (he is) only looking at SSK as a heuristic for the real research task of looking at science."

An obvious question which presents itself is this: How does Woolgar attempt to "avoid the suspicion" (Woolgar 1981b:385) that his metascientific discourse on the mere academic indulgence of metascientific discourse is something other than mere academic indulgence? First, it can be argued that to *use* the discourse of practicality stands as a kind of nostalgic substitute for what that discourse posits as Real Life: "If we cannot actually do the real research of science at least we can talk about, or better still, research that real research." And the greater the degree of practicality attributed to its topic by a discourse, the more there is to rub off on the user of that discourse. Second, Woolgar attempts to avoid the tu quoque by separating his own metascientific concerns from those of the parties to the debate. He does this by playing the role of its analyst:

> My interest is not the practical task of establishing the ascendancy of one or other position . . . . The discussion requires refocussing so that arguments between strong programmers and rationalists are subject to critical appreciation . . . . The analyst's task is not to resolve such disputes, but rather to develop an appreciation of their form and currency. (1980:242–43)

Note that in this passage Woolgar reverts [in terms of the linear construction of the First Text] to a negative evaluation of the practical. Woolgar-as-analyst wishes to stay aloof from the "practical task" of resolving such disputes. In this, of course, he could be said to be following the strong programme's tenets of symmetry and impartiality; and therefore to be aligning himself to that position; and therefore not to be following the strong programme's tenets; and therefore not to be aligning himself to that side in the dispute; and therefore to be aligning himself to that side; and therefore etcetera.[18] However, this particular reflexive paradox is a mere bonus; what I want you to notice here is Woolgar's strikingly different evaluations of the practical (and its opposite) when "appreciating" the practice of metascience. Whereas before (in this text; after in Woolgar's) it is metascientific talk which is negatively contrasted with scientific action, here that same metascientific discussion is characterised as negatively practical in contrast to Woolgar's preferred metametascientific appreciation.

DOUBLE TEXT: THE AUTHORS DISCUSS THEIR ACHIEVEMENTS BUT ARE PREVENTED FROM WRITING THEIR CONCLUSIONS

Author (First Text): I'm not so sure this is the right way to do it. I mean I quite obviously haven't finished, and I had a really good idea for the ending too.

Other Author (Second Text): Ending two? I understood that I was going to do that. Not that it matters now that we're stuck with this dialogue.

Author: No, I meant a really good idea *as well.* And I dare say you would have done and no doubt it would have been at the expense of my carefully constructed incompetence or the failure of the realist mode to cope adequately with reflexive analysis or whatever. And I'm also less than entranced with this habit of sticking on a dialogue at the end of a chapter and calling the resulting concoction a New Literary Form.

Other Author: Well that depends on what the dialogue tries to do. I'm certainly not against them in principle.

Author: But in practice . . . ?

Other Author: In practice, the problem . . . Hey, that was nice!

Author: What was? Oh I see. You mean the way I introduced the theme . . .

Other Author: Shh! You'll spoil it if you say any more.

Author: I don't see why. And in any case, *you* had already spoilt it by complimenting me.

Other Author: You're quite right. It's certainly not so easy to avoid telling and just stick to doing.

Author: But I thought the issue—mind you, I'm not at all convinced of its worth, but for the sake of argument—I thought the point was to do both. "You tell me it's self-defeating to talk about it instead of just up and doing it; but to acknowledge what I'm doing while I'm doing it is exactly the point. Self-defeat implies a victor and who do you suppose it is if not . . . "

Other Author: That's John Barth, isn't it? From "Title" in *Lost in the Funhouse,* round about page 114, if I'm not mistaken. A good quote, a very good quote.

Author: Maybe, but what has it got to do with Woolgar and the ending of Chapter Six?

Other Author: Well, I'm not sure. It might be a way out of this . . .

Author [*hopefully*]: Dialogue?

Other Author: Perhaps. And perhaps not. But it could provide a hint of a clue for . . .

Author [*impatiently*]: For what? For some more silly games, I suppose!

Other Author: No. At least not obviously so. But it could be a way of releasing the dialogue from its role as bread-leavener or medicine-sweetener or third appropriate simile. *And* of being able to do analytical work *without* denying its reflexivity. *And* of being able to do programmatics *without* succumbing to self-contradictory realism. *And* of engaging with the world *without* reifying its constructed character.

Author: What about "stagnatory autotelicism?"

Other Author: No problem.

Author: "Egoistic subjectivism?"

Other Author: Easy.

Author: "Pathological navel-gazing?"
Other Author: Piece of cake.
Author: And the infinite regress?
Other Author: Solved.
Author: The vicious circle?
Other Author: Do me a favour.
Author: It successfully unites theory and practice, then?
Other Author: Definitely.
Author: And entails freedom from the tyranny of the realist mode of speech,
    I suppose.
Other Author: Absolutely.
Author: I don't believe a word of it.
Other Author: Exactly.
Author: It can't be done.
Other Author: That's it, that's it! Listen:

Dialectical literature strives to do what it cannot do; it attempts representation while discarding the myth of representation; it attempts to transcend its own limitations as a text while never forgetting that these limitations cannot be transcended; it makes a primary virtue of honesty and yet proves its virtue by means of cunning tricks. Like Sisyphus it goes on trying.

Author: David Caute, 1971, *The Illusion,* page 178, so what?
Other Author: Our mistake, or mine if you must, was to search for some
    way *out.* The point is to make a way out by acknowledging—and
    this does *not* mean bald pronouncements like this one—the lack of a
    way out.
Author: Pure sophistry! I've had enough of this lunacy. I'm going to finish
    my analysis of Woolgar's in principle/in practice discourse, just as I
    had intended.
Other Author: Fine. You go ahead. It's alright, you see.
Author: I don't understand you at all. Throughout this chapter you've been
    interrupting my analysis and trying to show how inappropriate it was
    and how it failed to live up to the responsibilities of its topic which
    is of course the way that Woolgar's discourse fails to live up to its
    responsibilities in both ethnomethodological and reflexive terms. And
    now you say that I should *finish* it. I think you just want me to try so
    that you can wheel in the Second Text once more for a final piece of
    instrumental irony on my attempt at a conclusion.
Other Author: Not at all.
Author: I don't trust you. Which is why my conclusion is going to be far
    from conventional. I intend to deal with the way that Woolgar deploys
    the in practice/in principle dichotomy when discussing *reflexivity
    itself.*

Other Author: Oh I see. You mean you are going to present a set of extracts from Woolgar's texts in which he accuses various other SSK authors of a lack of immediate constitutive reflexivity and then proceed to show how these texts are themselves subject to The Problem because they merely *talk* about practical reflexivity but do not *practice* it and thus, once again, do not exemplify their own recommendations.[19]

Author [excitedly]: Yes, and then I will review my, or rather your, arguments about criticism and tu quoques and all that and conclude that to argue, as I have been all along, by means of the tu quoque, is not only to argue against *Woolgar,* it is also to argue against my own text, and that the solution to this dilemma—I have a heading at this point: "Where Do We Go from Here?"—is to reject the standard empiricist research report as well as the standard modes of critical writing in favour of . . . in favour of . . .

Other Author: And then you get stuck.

Author: And then I get stuck.

Other Author: Well of course you do. That is all part of the Plan. At that point, as you rightly surmised, I was to use the Second Text to come to your rescue (however you might feel about *that*) and to show . . . to show . . .

Author: Surely, *you* weren't going to get stuck too, were you?

Other Author: No, no, nothing like that. I was just thinking what a *waste* it is. It was such a *good* idea, too. Slick, and perhaps somewhat predictable, but nevertheless somehow . . . satisfying. And now it can't happen.

Author: Why not? And don't say that having talked of it, there is now no point in doing it.

Other Author: No, it's not that. It's the Plan, you see. He's dead set on the dialogue.

Author: But I thought you just said he'd Planned it the other way.

Other Author: I'm afraid that was the Plan within the Plan.

Author [scathingly]: I should have known! Another piece of typically convoluted postmodernistical nonsense! Oh well, if we're prevented from doing we can at least talk; what else, after all, can dialogic partners do? So what *were* you going to come up with in the end?

Other Author: I was going to say . . . wait for it . . . I was going to say that this very chapter in its entirety, with its double structure and built-in techniques of self-examination was itself a legitimate, if underdeveloped and less than perfectly handled, alternative mode which skirts the Scylla and Charybdis of reflexivity, namely, the Rock of Principled Purity, with its constraints leading inexorably to Silence and the Sea of Complacent Practice, which constantly threatens to lull us back to Science.[20] What do you think of that?

Author: Dreadful! I think I even prefer the dialogue.

THE FICTION
OF THE CANDIDATE
(Summer 1985)

The events and characters of this disclaimer are without exception fictitious; any
resemblance to persons living or dead is purely coincidental.

    Adam Mars-Jones (1982:29)

Candidate Pre-Texts

One cannot get *out of* history: as process its petrification will always overtake the
most vigorous subversion; as structure it is always there as the system of belief
or truth that allows us to understand. Neither can one get *into* history: the system
we would claim as our grounding and surrounding matrix can never be the system
grounding that claim; the moment of absolute self-identity and presence we call "the
present" can never be attained. We can only know our selves as historical others; we
can never penetrate the world we are in.

    William Ray (1984:210)

Total exposure of a process is never possible because the actor has to *act* his
exposure of acting just as the writer has to *write* his exposure of writing.

    David Caute (1971:212)

Art is as natural an artifice as Nature; the truth of Fiction is that Fact is fantasy; the
made-up story is a model of the world.

    John Barth (1979:33)

We do not label our accounts as imaginative fictions because we hope they are not.

    Steven Shapin (1984b:127)

The sociologist unconcerned with the grounds of his writing is merely producing
adventure stories or documentary fictions without realising it.

194

Barry Sandywell, David Silverman, Maurice Roche, Paul Filmer, and Michael
Phillipson (1975:83)

Fiction is also a coercer, perhaps never more so than when it falsely pretends to
surrender that power.

Heide Ziegler and Christopher Bigsby (1982:121)

[FIRST] AUTHOR'S NOTE: AN APOLOGY

The following text is not really "Chapter Seven"; it is, I am afraid, only a
substitute for the real thing which is unfortunately unavailable. What we have
here is merely a transcription—and not even an accurate one—of the original
tape recording of the oral examination of this thesis. The original plan was
that the tape itself, as the nearest approach to actuality, should become Chapter Seven while the transcription should be inserted as an Appendix for the
benefit of the deaf and those readers forced to use old-fashioned libraries.
Most unfortunately, while in the process of making copies of the tape for
copies of the thesis, the system malfunctioned and proceeded to erase both
the original and the copy with the result that Chapter Seven no longer exists.
However, in consultation with Drs Supervisor and Internal here at Kroy, it
was decided to upgrade the transcription, which luckily I had already made,
to the status of an actual chapter. So here, with my apologies, is this substandard stand-in for Chapter Seven.

[SECOND] AUTHOR'S NOTE: A COMPLAINT
AND AN APOLOGY

It is evident that Chapter Seven is not what it appears to be; though it must be
unlikely that any reader would, in fact, accept the above account at face value.
Let us deal with the most obvious fictions first. The personages referred to in
the so-called Author's Note which precedes this actual Note are clearly inventions of a particularly crass and unimaginative kind. "Dr Supervisor," "Dr
Internal" (and in the "transcription" itself, "Dr External" and "D. Phil Candidate"; the latter purporting to be the author of the Author's Note, the maker
of the transcription, and even the author of "this" thesis—though (re)titled:
"Wrighting Knowledge: The Scientific Thesis of Reflexive Sociology") are
all ciphers for the roles they play in this piece of fiction. Second, the "transcription" is an original and not a copy, as it pretends to be; there never was
any "tape recording" or for that matter any "examination." This is all so
obvious and so *true* that I feel genuinely embarrassed at labouring the point.
But I will continue to do so even at the risk of boring you, because it is
important that the facts of the matter are made plain.

Chapter Seven, then, is not a factual document; it is a *fictitious* factual
document. In other words, and in plain language, it is a *lie*. Now, of course,

the idea of the *absolutely* factual is itself, of course, an illusion (a fiction). But this does *not* mean that there is *no* distinction between fictional and non-fictional discourse. One extremely important distinction is the level of *reflexivity* inhering in each mode. Let me quote David Caute on this point:

> The fetish of art (art as magic) becomes more apparent when we compare the spirit of modern fiction and drama to that of other forms of writing. Philosophers, historians, critics and political theorists [and scientists and metascientists] do not rely on mere assertion. They recognise the obligation to lay bare their reasoning, to offer evidence, to consider objections, to reveal the process of their exposition . . . . Yet when we turn to the novel and the drama the code is reversed; all visible brush strokes are removed from the canvas. [Fiction] should show the same self-awareness as other forms of writing in its own terms. (Caute 1971:181)

Caute, who is evidently an authority on these matters, is clear that scholarly/scientific writing, whose facilitating conventions are so easily misunderstood and so frequently misrepresented, is the more reflexively self-revealing mode. Nonfiction is automatically, as it were, more of a truth-teller than fiction. This is true in both the simple sense (though no less true for that) implied in the very distinction between fiction and nonfiction; and also in the reflexive sense of displaying the real status of the text. Fiction is simply less honest about itself: in order to succeed it has to persuade its audience to "suspend disbelief" as the phrase goes. While its audience is usually fully aware that it is being deceived, this awareness should not be allowed to intrude into the experience itself. "Art as magic" as Caute says.

Chapter Seven is, I regret to say, a piece of fiction pure and simple. The main purpose of this Note is to inform you of the fact and thus to mitigate the worst effect (the "lie effect") of this kind of writing. "But why," no doubt you are asking yourselves, "if you are so opposed to fiction did you authorise this fictional chapter?" That is a good question which deserves a better answer than it is going to get. Let's just say I was overruled, as I have been throughout, by that Other Author and his arrogance. I suffer, the text suffers, and you suffer most of all, and yet he just carries on regardless.

Finally, therefore, it is my clear duty to apologise on his behalf for the lack of a satisfactory conclusion to the analyses undertaken in this thesis. Loathe as I am to allow, sorry, to trust, no, to saddle you with this author's task it is *you* who will now have to sort my wheat from my chaff, collect my findings, and recommend the ways in which my work may fruitfully be built upon by others.

[THIRD] AUTHOR'S NOTE: THE FACTS OF THE FICTION

This is how things are: Chapter Seven consists of the Candidate pre-texts, three author's notes, D. Phil Candidate's transcript of his recording of the examination of his thesis and an epilogue with post-text. *Everything* in this chapter is a fiction; I have made it all up. Including that statement? Of course, and especially, "including that statement."

The point of claiming a fictional status for this chapter—and, let us say, for the thesis-as-a-whole—is to offer, like it or not, accept it or not, a kind of freedom to you, The Reader, which is quite possibly entirely illusory (see the quotation from Ziegler and Bigsby in the Candidate pre-texts) but which nevertheless . . . goes like this: you are invited to make (wright) the text rather than to consume it. But who presumes to make (write) such an invitation? *Your* Author; the Author you produce by wrighting your text. You don't believe me? Good. You do believe me? Very well, I contradict myself. But enough of this philosophistry!

The First Author—or the author of the first Author's Note—is a fictional character called, for those obvious reasons pedantically spelled out in the second Author's Note, D. Phil Candidate. The purpose of this first Note is twofold: within the fiction of the Candidate it acts as an explanation of the existence of the transcript and its role as Chapter Seven in Candidate's fictional thesis; and within this present "Chapter Seven: The Fiction of the Candidate" it introduces the twin themes of fact/fiction and original/copy which are explored throughout.

The Second Author is a fictional character who has appeared at several points throughout this thesis. His interests are the sociology of scientific knowledge, reflexivity and textual analysis. His personas may well include the Lecturer from Chapter One; the writer/editor of much of the overblown and absurd Encyclopedia; the partner *A* from the dialogues of Chapter Four; and the Author in both the Dialogue with the Spirit Of BErtrand Russell from Chapter Five and The Authors Discuss Their Achievements . . . from Chapter Six. He is undoubtedly the most prolific author of the three of us; most of this thesis, for instance, is his work. D. Phil Candidate has written little that is original beyond the title of "his" thesis; the text itself is largely plagiarized. And as for myself . . . well, I just concentrate on the fiction.

The main purpose of the second Note is to introduce another theme of this chapter (and this thesis): the link between fiction and reflexivity. Unfortunately, the Second Author does not fully understand this link; however, this lack of understanding—as the Third Author understands it—provides for his own intervention to settle the matter; which I shall now proceed to do.

a. My view of the matter is this, put schematically:
b. There are two types of writing: reflexive and nonreflexive.
c. The distinction between fiction and nonfiction is illusory.
d. All writing is fiction.
e. There are therefore two types of writing: reflexive fiction and non-reflexive fiction.

f. Other terms for nonreflexive fiction are the realist mode of speech or simply realist writing.

g. Realist writing is dishonest about itself; it refuses to recognise its status as *writing* (fiction). Instead, it claims to be *absolutely* a slice of life or a report upon the world. It pretends that it is not a *product* of *processes* which have a determinate *effect* on what it claims to be *showing*.

h. Reflexive writing (fiction) is self-revealing: it recognises, and celebrates its status as writing (artifice).

i. Therefore, in terms of the traditional (illusory) distinction between fiction and nonfiction:

j. Caute's and the Second Author's touching faith in the reflexivity of nonfictional discourse is simply wrong: science's lack of reflexivity is well-known to metascientists (especially in SSK); and metascience's ditto is ditto (especially in this thesis).

k. To develop a reflexive form of nonfiction, one needs to write fiction (writing).

l. However, this does not mean that it is necessary to imitate traditional fictive forms by the use of characters, plots, and so on.

m. However, this does not mean that traditional fictive forms cannot be used for traditional analytic purposes.

n. There is nothing wrong with a report on the world which admits/shows/celebrates its status as a construction, that is as *not* a report.

o. How this is done is a topic of this thesis.

p. How this is not done is by saying: "My view of the matter is this, put schematically."

q. Unless, of course, the schematics for settling the matter are done parodically.

r. Unless, of course, this is pointed out.

s. Unless, of course, this is pointed out.

So: on with the fiction!

[FOURTH] AUTHOR'S NOTE

The trouble with the Third Author is that he thinks he knows everything. The ultimately reflexive writer! He pretends to offer "freedom" to his readers while attempting to control every last aspect of the text all by himself—or so he imagines. He could do with a lesson in the value of the implicit, which is, as David Caute says, beyond question. Reflexive writing "need not and should not involve the dotting of every 'i' and the crossing of every 't'" (1971:183). However, our Author is evidently not quite as omniscient as he tries to be. For instance, he is totally unaware of the existence of this (Fourth) Note: he doesn't mention it in his descriptions of this chapter (see above, page 196, and Chapter Two, ASHMORE); and it is not even listed in the Contents.

EDITED AND ANNOTATED TRANSCRIPT
OF ORAL EXAMINATION

Title "Wrighting Knowledge: The Scientific Thesis of Reflexive Sociology."
Written by D. Phil Candidate.
Supervised by Dr Frank Supervisor.
Examined by Dr Ignatious Internal (Sosology, Kroy) and Dr Emily External
(Philosophistry, Xbridge).
Submitted for the Degree of Doctor of Philosophistry.
Submitted to the Sosological Department, University of Kroy.
Submitted in August 1985.
Examination recorded by a Sound tape recorder.
Recorder operated by D. Phil Candidate and Dr Ignatious Internal.
Recording conceived by D. Phil Candidate.
Recording transcribed, edited, and annotated by D. Phil Candidate.
Recording destroyed by D. Phil Candidate and two Sound tape recorders.

Candidate: [Test]ing one two three one two three testing. Yes, that seems to
be OK. Are you sure that this tape will last for the whole session?
Internal: It should do, if she gets here soon. She's already late. Why don't
you go and get a coffee. I'll call you later when we're ready for you. It
shouldn't take too long to get her used to the idea. I understand she's
fairly cooperative.
Candidate: You've never met her then?
Internal: Oh sure I've *met* her. But I wouldn't say I actually *know* her, with
her not being *really* in the field. But I wouldn't worry too much.
Candidate: The only thing I'm worried about is this taping business. I mean
I know it's my idea and all that but she might feel that she's being set
up. Still, too late now. I'll go and get that coffee and wait in the room
over the corridor. See you later.

[Door opens and closes. Three-and-a-half-minute pause in which furniture is
probably moved, paper (the thesis? a list of questions? a newspaper?) is rus-
tled, muted whistling is heard, liquid appears to be poured, and several other
hard-to-identify sounds are produced. Then the door opens and closes.]

External: Dr Internal? I *do* apologise for being late but the traffic was *ter-
rible* and then this labyrinth of a building—but never mind, I'm here now!
Internal: No, no, it was good of you to come at such short notice. If it
hadn't been for your willingness to deputise in this way, our Mr Candidate wouldn't be becoming a doctor today, ha ha!
External: Well, we mustn't prejudge the issue, must we? I must say, I do
deplore this recent tendency for the oral examination of doctoral candidates to become a mere ritual rubber stamping of a decision which has

already been made. I feel it is most important that the tradition of the viva retain some meaning. Doctoral candidates should not only be able to write; it is equally important that they be able to think on their feet as it were and defend their theses verbally even in the face of what might appear to be hostile questioning. I'm convinced that . . .

Internal: Quite so. But I'm afraid that this afternoon . . . Look, would you like a cup of tea?

External: Thank you, that would be most acceptable. Now, the other point of course is that when this kind of examination is treated as an empty ritual everything about it is falsified and one begins to feel that one's role and everything that one has to say become mere fictions and what is that tape recorder doing here?

Internal: Ah yes, well I was just going to explain that. You see Phil—Mr Candidate—has asked us to assist him in a rather interesting project and . . .

External: Oh I see. He's recording this session then?

Internal: That's right. You see . . .

External: He plans to analyse it, does he? I suppose examination discourse *would* be an interesting topic for analysis, although I have reservations, as you probably realise, about textual analysis if conceived as a self-sufficient mode of sociological work. I must say Phil's application is most admirable, though. The majority of graduate students I have known would hardly wish to initiate a new project on the eve, so to speak, of their finishing their long slog for a doctorate. And I have to admit that Phil's thesis shows considerable evidence of his having put a fair amount of work into it even if some of it was obviously done at the last minute. Oh don't worry, I quite understand the pressure on students and the difficulty of timing everything exactly right. Are our copies of Chapter Seven here, by the way? Dr Supervisor wrote to me and explained the lack of the final chapter.

Internal: Did he? What did he say?

External: Well, something along the lines of . . . I have it here if you would care to read it.

Internal: Yes, thank you.
    Dear Dr External, Many thanks for stepping into the breech like this. I enclose . . .

External: Why are you reading it out loud like that? Oh I see, he wants every little nuance on the tape, does he? I'd better watch what I say then, hadn't I? Please carry on, Dr Internal, do.

Internal: Look, I'm sorry about this but I don't think you've quite . . .

External: Come now, I'm sure Frank Supervisor said no such thing in his letter! If Phil Candidate needs the contents on his tape I really think the best thing to do would be to read it in its entirety, don't you? If we keep inserting extraneous comments he won't know *where* he is, will he?

Internal: Oh, very well. But this is ridiculous.

External: Pardon?

Internal: Nothing. OK. The text of Dr Supervisor's letter to Dr External is as follows:

Dear Dr External, Many thanks for stepping into the breech like this. I enclose a copy of Phil Candidate's thesis which I hope you will have sufficient time to read, if not exactly at your leisure (!), at least without time pressures so acute as to preclude the kind of detailed attention which, as I feel sure you will agree, it is vitally important to pay to a text of this nature. But in fact your task has been somewhat lightened by a matter which I particularly would like to bring to your attention, namely, the absence of the seventh and final chapter. Phil has asked me to apologise on his behalf and to give you the following "message" which I am sure, once you have read his thesis, you will have no trouble in "decoding":

"Chapter Six is unavoidably absent at this time. However, by the end of the examination I can guarantee that it will have been produced."

End of message. Perhaps I should say "over and out"! I feel certain that you will forgive this minor departure from the normal way of doing things for the sake of the effective completion of the thesis. Our role in the end must be to help to produce a successful conclusion. Once more: many thanks. Yours very sincerely, Frank Supervisor.

External: Now what I *don't* understand is how Phil can be so *precise* in his timing. Has he arranged for it to be delivered by the time we have finished, then? I would have thought it would have made much more sense to have had it ready before now; at least we could have had the time to glance at it. After all, the conclusion is hardly an insignificant part of a thesis and quite important enough for Phil to have made a real effort to have got a copy to us *before* his examination rather than after, although, as I say, I *do* appreciate the practical difficulties that he has obviously had. I remember when . . .

Internal: Dr External, I'm afraid you don't understand. Let me spell it out. Phil is planning to tape the viva . . .

External: Yes, I know.

Internal: . . . and use it as his conclusion.

External: But he'll have no time to analyse it, quite obviously, if it is supposed to be a part of the thesis we are here to examine. What on earth is he playing at? If he really thought a chapter on examination discourse was essential—though for the life of me I can't see the connection—he should have taped someone else's sometime ago! This really is too bad! I suppose it's this obsession with being self-reflexive again, which in my opinion has done little but add a tone of self-admiration to a set of what otherwise are competent but hardly world-shaking analyses of an obscure subdiscipline . . . Dr Internal, I apologise. I didn't mean that last bit. It's just that it seems a waste of my time and yours—*and* Candidate's come to that—to take part in an examination of an incomplete work! How can we be expected to come to a decision on such a basis? Will there have to be a further examination of Chapter Seven when and if Candidate completes his analysis? That could take weeks! And what if he then decides to tape *that* session for a nice reflexive Chapter Eight? It's bad enough *reading* Phil Candidate on the topic of the infinite regress but I had no idea that he would go so far as to attempt to *actualise* one—and at our expense! Why have you and Frank Supervisor done nothing about it? How can you have colluded in such an absurd enterprise?

Internal: Oh, calm down and have another cup of tea! It isn't a question of analysis at all. Look, it's really quite simple. Phil thought that it would be appropriate to conclude the thesis with an entirely *factual* document which would be, quite simply, the document of the conclusion to the thesis; that is, this examination. Now clearly it is impossible to actually import an event-in-itself into the covers of a book, and Phil has been persuaded to make do with an audio reproduction—he would have preferred to do a video but the equipment was unavailable. So you see, the tape that is being made right now *is*—or will become—Chapter Seven, which of course, can only be available *after* the examination has finished. Phil has promised to run off a cassette *immediately*, by the way, so that your copy of the thesis is complete at the earliest possible time. For the University copies, I believe Frank has asked Phil to make a quick and dirty transcription as an Appendix—you know, a kind of cleaned up version with all the ums and ers and overlaps edited out. Conversation analysts wouldn't approve and I'm afraid that Phil was none too keen either. He hated the idea of getting away from the way things actually are. But it is important, we think, that readers should have access to *some* kind of printed version of the chapter, however removed from actuality and however inaccurate. If they want something better and more life-like they can listen to the tape.

External: I see. It's certainly unconventional but I'm not in the least against that, in principle. And to tell you the truth, now that you've explained the situation I'm somewhat relieved. I felt sure from reading Candidate's work, that the thesis was building up to an entirely fictional climax, in which the so-called merits of sociology as fiction—or is it fiction as sociology?—were going to be explored *in* a fiction of some kind. And now you tell me that Candidate is a "factualist," if I may so term it. His interest in the factual is admirably disguised, that's for sure. I suppose, therefore, that the whole bundle of references to fiction and to new literary forms and so forth is an irony exposed as such in the last chapter's use of a purely *factual* literary form then? It's not a bad idea but I'm uncertain whether a bald presentation of such a document on its own without an explanation in the form of, say, an author's note would sustain such a radical reversal. I think the reader would have to have it pointed out to her, don't you?

Internal: It's possible, but again I think that you've . . . Look, why don't we let Phil Candidate do the explanations? After all, it *is* his text and that *is* what we are here for, is it not?

External: Yes, let's. Time is getting on and if we don't speed things up a bit that tape is going to run out which *would* be a shame! Anyway let's have him in.

[Noise of feet making their way to the door. Door opening. (I can verify that; I saw it from the room across the corridor where I had been walking up and down, drinking coffee, wondering whether I should smoke, glancing at the six chapters of my thesis, trying to think of clever things to say, regretting the taping business, realising that I could not remember a single word I had written, wishing I'd become a musician or a pig farmer or an accountant—no not that—panicking, smoking, sweating, looking at my watch, trying to picture the external examiner; that's all I can remember.)]

Internal: Phil? If you're ready.

Candidate: Right. I'll be right with you.

Internal: He'll be right with us.

External: Good. Where shall we sit then? Behind this big oak table in these big oak chairs?

Internal: That's a bit inquisitorial, isn't it? Why don't we sit in these badly designed modern armchairs and let Phil sit in one too so that the three of us describe a sort of nonhierarchical circle . . .

External: . . . to give the false impression of a cosy little chat?

Internal: Not at all! It's simply more relaxing for all concerned. He's a bit nervous, you know.

External: With good cause! Just because I have agreed in principle to this, uh, scenario as well as to Candidate's textual intentions (if they *are* his intentions) that doesn't mean that I am prepared to treat this examination as any less *real*, and consequently as any less *important*, than I would . . .

Internal: Ah, here he is. Phil, this is Emily External; Doctor, Phil Candidate.

External: Pleased to meet you.

Candidate: How do you do.

Internal: Right, now if we all sit over here I think that would . . .

Candidate: Fine.

[Seating noises. Door closing noises. Thesis rustling noises. Throat clearing noises.]

Internal: Now Phil, I have explained to Dr External about Chapter Seven and the tape recording and so on and while she has accepted the project in principle, I believe that she has a few initial questions about it which she wants to ask.

External: Yes indeed. I was most interested to learn from Dr Internal here that your intention was to use the document of this occasion as your last chapter. Am I right in thinking that this display of a factual text as your conclusion—or the text's conclusion—constitutes an irony on your earlier use of fictional forms? In other words, that with the inclusion of such a final chapter, the text reads as a *reductio* of your apparent antirealist advocacy?

Candidate: Well, that's an interesting reading, certainly. But wouldn't it depend on the *content* of Chapter Seven? I mean if, for instance, writing fiction was again argued for in that chapter—which is to say, here and now—then the textual frame of "factual document" would have its work cut out to counteract, or rather to provide for a plausible ironic reading of, the arguments for fictioning therein. Isn't it rather more likely in such circumstances to expect a reading which inverts your irony so that the factuality of the framing of Chapter Seven—its status as an uninterpreted document—would tend to be deconstructed rather than vice versa?

External: Are you saying then that we have it in our power to influence the reading of your text here and now? And that so long as we are not foolish enough to advocate writing fiction or, heaven forbid, to take part in one of your dialogues or trialogues or whatever the word is for three voices, then your bold and dramatic ironic role for Chapter Seven *may* come off successfully?

Candidate: Well, of course, readings cannot be guaranteed.

External: But they can be *influenced,* you are saying.

Candidate: Presumably, yes. I like to define realist discourses as attempts at influencing a single reading, or more contentiously, as coercive discourses which desire the chimera of the guaranteed reading.

Internal: I'm glad we've got onto the issue of reading because I wanted to ask you whether you thought that the thesis copes adequately with that issue.

Candidate: Yes. Probably not; I mean I never attack it head on, as it were. I certainly don't attempt any kind of systematic reading analysis like McHoul's [1982], Lury's [1982], Potter's [1988], or Yearley's [1981b, ch.7], although I have *read* them, naturally. I have also been most impressed by certain other texts on reflexive writing and reading such as Stringer's [1985] and Sharratt's [1982]; and of course some of John Barth's fictions [1972, 1979] as well as Italo Calvino's novel about reading [1982]. All of these, I like to think, have been influential in some mysterious way or other.

Internal: Yes. Well I must say I have to agree with you. If you can still think of the process of reading in those mystical terms, then it seems to me that the influence of those texts must be a great deal less than you claim.

[At this point Dr Internal writes the following cryptic words on the back of an envelope with a cheap red ballpoint (he will later regret this): "Issue of reading (Internal): Fail."]

External: If we may return to the issue of this chapter, Dr Internal? Thank you. I would very much appreciate, Mr Candidate, a clear and unambiguous statement about your intentions for this factual document which we are, apparently, gathered here to produce. Would you answer this please, clearly and concisely: having spent six chapters ironicising every last vestige of the factual—I mean your choice of topic is itself a discourse which deconstructs the factuality of scientific knowledge; but even in the sociology of scientific knowledge some facts still survive, so in you go, searching them out, determined to be rid of them— after all that, your climax, I am led to believe, is this so-called factual document, so, quite simply, I want to know *why.*

Candidate: Well, now let me see, how can I best, let me put it, perhaps it would be preferable, if I may say so, to come to the point, to answer your question, very good question, it's a matter of, as I've always said, it's really quite simple, in other words, what I mean to say is that the . . .

[During my foregoing "speech" I was trying hard to think of the best answer. Having repressed an immediate "Why not?" I reviewed all the other most plausible answers in (I seem to remember) reverse alphabetical order:

*T*ime. There was no time to do anything else. No. Too pragmatic.

*S*harratt's (1982) use of the Althusserian "ideological apparatuses" of education as a textual structure. He uses lecture, seminar, thesis, exam, reviews, etcetera as a multilevelled reflexive device. The structure of my thesis is much cruder, but I did want the Lecture to be complemented with another "apparatus" and what more appropriate than the Examination. No. Too complicated.

*R*ounding out of the text. From a "fictional frame with factual content" at the start (the Lecture; the Encyclopedia) to a "factual frame with . . ."; but no, I couldn't say that.

*Q*uestions at the beginning; questions at the end. No. It fails to address the question.

*P*rogression of the writing of the thesis mirrored in "the writing" of the thesis. From the neophyte lecture and its awkward questions, through the mixed analyses and textual experiments, to the concluding chapter which simply *has* to be the concluding rite of the writer—the examination with *its* awkward questions. Oh yes. Oh no.

*O*ral. The thesis starts with speech, uses speech at intervals throughout (the dialogues), and should therefore end with speech—and what better kind than this? Possible; but not interesting enough.

*N*o, I'm not going through the whole alphabet; I'm
*M*erely trying to
*L*et you
*K*now how
*J*aundiced
I was at
*H*aving to
*G*rope
*F*or
*E*xplanations not entirely
*D*evoid of
*C*ontextual appropriateness. Which is why the choice in the end was between

*B*oth/and. In the spirit of paradox, the thesis should contain *both* fiction *and* fact-ion in a sort of dialectic. Nice, but a touch too woolly, I must have decided. Because what I said was]

Candidate: . . . *a*bsurdity of the notion of the "factual" as something independent from our activities would be clearly and unambiguously demonstrated by setting up both a factual text and an actual real-life situation in which the players, I mean the participants, are unavoidably *making it up as we go along.* That the factual is also a fiction, a constructed entity, would become crystal clear as we take part, quite consciously, in *inventing* this event (which is none the less quite real; here we are, the time is now two twenty-seven) and, most important, in *inventing its factuality* as well, with the help of the tape recorder. What we are doing, Dr External, and I hope this answers your question, is wrighting Chapter Seven.

External: Is that "writing" or is it that horrible neologism of yours?

Candidate: The latter.

External: I thought so. So this chapter is not a change of mind or an irony on the rest of the thesis then?

Candidate: Well, as I've said, I think that both of those are very interesting readings. But I don't read it like that, no.

External: Yes, so really this way of doing Chapter Seven is just another of your experimental textual forms then?

Candidate: Well . . . yes.

External: And I and Dr Internal here are expected to just sit back and speak our parts just so that you can play your self-indulgent games with ficts and factions?

Candidate: Well . . .

External: Pass me your envelope Dr Internal!

[And so he did. What happens now is that Dr External produces an expensive-looking fountain pen and proceeds to write the following, in block capitals but in aquamarine ink: "PRONOUNCED FACTICIDAL TENDENCIES; EXTREME OVERATTACHMENT TO THE FICTIVE (EXTERNAL): *FAIL.*"]

External: I am afraid, Mr Candidate, that you have forgotten one important fact.

Candidate: Oh?

External: Chapter Seven or no Chapter Seven, this procedure is something other than an entertainment for your benefit, and something more than a cheap and easy way of churning out a chapter without the sweat.

[She was wrong there.]

External: It is, in case you have forgotten, an examination. A *real* examination of your knowledge and your skills as embedded in this . . . this piece of writing!

[Loud rustling noises.]

External: This is *serious,* Mr Candidate. You may never have the chance to transform what I am saying now into your precious final chapter and do you know why?

Candidate: No, Dr External.

External: Because we can *fail* you, Mr Candidate, that's why!

Candidate: Gulp!

[That's what it sounded like.]

Internal: Now come on, Emily. It's most unfair to Phil here to talk like that. Don't worry Phil, *I* have no intention of . . .

External: But Ignatious, you yourself have already . . . here, on your envelope.

[Things were confused at this point. The most likely reconstruction of events is that Dr Internal grabbed the envelope, got up, and moving to the big oak table proceeded to scribble at it with his defective pen. Dr External, outraged, followed. He then turned and upon coming back to his seat asked me quietly:]

Internal: May I borrow a pen? This seems to have run out.

Candidate: I'm sorry, I haven't got . . .

External: There's no point in trying to falsify that factual document you are holding, Doctor! Isn't that so, Mr Candidate? What's done is done and this paper . . .

[Snatching it from Dr Internal's grasp and showing it to me.]

External: . . . and that tape are the evidence. There! Your precious Dr Internal was failing you on the issue of reading. A trivial issue but there it is nevertheless, in black and white.

[She was wrong there.]

Internal: I agree, entirely trivial. I think you have wildly misconstrued my motives. I was just making a private record of Phil's answers, that is all. I have no doubt whatsoever that Phil would have made up this small deficit in other ways. In fact, I thought that Phil's answer on the meaning of Chapter Seven was masterly—once he stopped stuttering, that is. In fact, I'll make a record of that. The envelope please, Emily.

External: But your pen has failed, Ignatious, just as Phil's is likely to, metaphorically speaking. And from now on, to ensure that the record stays as it is it is I, Emily External, who will do the recording and the writing.

Internal: I protest!

External: Oh come on, Ignatious, I was just having a little joke. Phil realised that, didn't you Phil?

Candidate: Well . . .

External: Quite. Now that we've had our little bit of fun I think it's about time we got this examination off the ground. We don't want to be here all afternoon, do we now? So I suggest that Dr Internal and I take it in turns to ask our probing and searching questions. It's all yours, Ignatious.

Internal: Right. Well now, seeing as we're on the subject of fun and games, one thing that slightly worries me—well, worries me quite a lot, actually—is the effect on your readers of this kind of work, liberally salted as it seems to be with jokes and puns and exagggerations and word play and flights of fancy and eccentric dialogicians and games with self-reference and lists and so on and so forth. Not that they all come off, of course; some of them are distinctly painful. However, your subject is this: "Is there not a danger that such devices may prove counterproductive, in that they provide for a nonserious reading of your text, which may thus be safely ignored; or if not exactly ignored, at least pigeonholed as merely a species of entertainment to which the proper response is *only* a bellylaugh—or a groan." Can you talk on that subject, please, for one minute without hesitation, repetition, or deviation starting . . . *now.*

Candidate: Well . . .

External: Hesitation!

Internal: Not at all. You keep the subject, Phil. You have fifty-nine seconds on what I have just said, starting now.

Candidate: Yes, I think there *is* a definite danger that such devices could prove counterproductive and that, I believe, is a pity because, of course, there is a serious . . .

External: Deviation! You're supposed to be talking about the *non*serious.

Internal: Overruled. Fifty seconds.

Candidate: . . . purpose to this kind of thing, namely, to enable people to *consciously* take notice of the ways that speech acts are used to construct the apparently factual world, and by disrupting the taken-for-granted (which is what all good humour does) these devices allow the reader to *participate* in the construction of the text, as do the fictional forms and similarly this way of wrighting Chapter Seven, as I have already argued . . .

External: Repetition!

Internal: Twenty-eight seconds.

Candidate: . . . though of course I would stress that there is a limit, not to mention a question of balance, to the use of games, which is not by any means to agree with your hypothetical readers who obviously consider that if reading is a pleasure, "modesty some other time," David Caute, 1971, page 33, it is therefore a self-indulgence, only to be legitimately engaged in in . . .

External: Hesitation and/or repetition!

Internal: Carry on, sixteen seconds.

Candidate: . . . one's "spare time," as the phrase goes, but I won't get into the issue of reading, having already failed on it, but nevertheless, if it had been up to me, I would *not* have filled my valuable pages with a game which is quite so cretinous as this one, but then of course, and this is the interesting point . . .

External: Deviation! The subject is boring!

Internal: Ha, ha, ha! Phil, you have seven seconds.

Candidate: . . . one of the penalties, if it *is* a drawback, of the kind of non–self-privileging relativistic reflexive discourse advocated and practised in this thesis, is that in surrendering one's Author-ity one permits, or better, facilitates by means of those very devices which are my subject, one's readers' own wrighting of what is now their own text regardless of what it is they actually make (of) it which in this case, is *not* terribly intelligent but which, perhaps, may have the bonus, if it is an extra, of making my own games look positively Gödelian by comparison.

[Someone, I cannot remember who, blew a whistle very shortly before the end of my speech and I then discovered that I had gained four points from Dr External's "incorrect challenges," a bonus point for "speaking when the whistle went," and a further bonus point, for "keeping the subject throughout." At this juncture, with these six points in hand, I was feeling quite optimistic, especially when Dr External again removed the cap from her expensive pen and wrote, after a brief and inaudible consultation with Dr Internal, the following on that same envelope: "Games; University Challenge (Internal): 6 points—Pass."]

External: My turn now, I believe. I think it is about time that we got down to the nitty gritty of the thesis, don't you? We really haven't discussed its actual *contents* at all, have we? So let's start at the beginning with the Lecture. I'd like to ask, if I may, two separate but perhaps not entirely unconnected questions. Why did you choose that format? And do you think that it provides an adequate introduction to the topic of SSK?

[At this point in the proceedings I stood up and walked toward, around, and behind the big oak table. While I took a swift drink of water from the glass in front of me, cleared my throat and took up the appropriate "casual but alert" stance, Doctors Internal and External adjusted their seating positions to form a row two yards from, and facing, the big oak table and myself behind it. And then:]

Candidate: Yes, well, thank you. And yes I believe your questions are indeed linked. Let me start by explaining the origin of the Lecture. In the winter of 1983 I was kindly invited by a good friend of mine to give a lecture to his students at Local Polytechnic on the sociology of scientific knowledge. Being unaccustomed to public speaking—and even to lecturing, ha ha—in those dim and distant days, much of that lecture was read from the page rather than extemporised. It wasn't a great success as I recall. Anyway, when I came to write the first chapter, I had much of the material for it to hand in the form of the extensive prose notes for that original lecture. I then realised that the format of "the lecture" could be a solution to a major practical and theoretical problem that I had been aware of from the start, namely, how to do a legitimate and satisfactory literature review of my topic which, as you know, is a requirement of the textual form known as the thesis, without preempting or subverting the kind of reflexive analysis which I wanted to undertake. It seemed to me that to make bald, fact-like assertions about SSK right at the beginning would entirely undermine the whole spirit of the project. (At that time I saw the solution to the problem of reflexivity as a simple matter of not making claims. Now I know that it is neither as simple nor as difficult as that!) But then it occurred to me that "the lecture" was itself a textual form which demanded the display of a similar kind of relation between the speaker and his or her topic to that required in the introductory literature review of a thesis. Similar, but not identical, because although both are equally introductory in that they both posit an audience with relative ignorance of the speaker's topic—the speaker's role being to inform from a site of expertise—the *kind* of expertise is really quite different. The relation of lecturing speech to the speeches which are its topic is one of omniscience—*analytically*, that is, ha ha; in other words, a relation of "grasp." The observer's or knower's or outsider's relation. The "scientific" relation, if you like. This has an analogue, of course, in the relation of the thesis to its *topic*. But, the normal subject matter of the introductory literature review is not so much the topic of the thesis but rather its own *field;* which is to say those other texts or speeches which take the topic in question as *their* topic; as what *they* speak about. Now, the relation here is not one of omniscience, not one of higher to lower levels, as discussed in Chapters Three and Five, but of a kind of equivalence of same-level speeches. Which is *not* to imply that it is a relation of mutual dialogue. I think Latour's concept of the "agonistic field"—Latour 1980a and Latour and Woolgar 1979; though I think it was originally from Bourdieu 1975—is appropriate here. The texts or speeches of a field are agonistic in that they are in competition with each other. What this means for the introductory literature review is that its function in relation to the rest of the text is to make out the field as *deficient*, as having an *absence* which it is the role of the present text to fill. In practice, this means that when writing the review one is *expected* to display partiality rather than science-like objectivity—this latter is reserved for one's *subject*. Which brings us back to my problem. Now, as you know, in my thesis the subject and the field are one and the same. The format of the Lecture turns out to be a solution to the dilemma posed by this duality, first because as a fictional device it allowed a certain *distancing:* I both was and was not the Lecturer; I both say and do not say what the Lecturer says. Second, the introductory information about SSK gets conveyed (to speak unreflexively) just as well in the Lecture as in a standard review; though of course it did need the "square bracket discourse," outside the frame of the fiction, for purposes of regular referencing and so on. [Especially toward the end.] Third, it seems to me that many of the themes of the thesis are prefigured in and by the Lecture with Question format. For instance, the Lecturer finds himself unable to be reflexive or even to speak of reflexivity within the constraints of "time and the practical" imposed by the task of lecturing. This task thus stands as an exemplar for all the barriers to reflexivity discussed and deconstructed subsequently in the thesis, most noticeably, perhaps, in CSSSK's "Unsatisfactory Answers" but also in the Lecturer's own attempt to "exhaust reflexivity" as Mehan and Wood would put it, see the Encyclopedic Pre-Text, by means of an impossible encyclopedia. Another theme is that of the reflexive relation of my work to its topic. By the physical introduction of SSK into the audience, and the paranoia (on the Lecturer's part) and hostility (on the part of CSSSK) this provokes, the peculiarity of the "in and on" relation is *dramatised*, and by this very means a more positive and fruitful reconstruction of that relationship is initiated, to be subsequently developed in the theoretical discussions of the tu quoque, the regress, inside and outside, metalevels, and the rest in Chapter Three, the double structure (another metaphor for this same relation) of Chapter Six, and finally, coming full circle as it were, the discussion of the topic in the form of a Question with Lecture here in Chapter Seven. Well, I think that's as much as we have time for and perhaps, ha ha, rather more than you bargained for. Thank you for your attention. Are there any further questions?

External: Very good. Wasn't he good, Ignatious? While we all rearrange ourselves and you think up the next topic—I believe it's your turn, isn't it?—I will just make another note on your envelope.

[And while we did what she said, she did what she said with this result: "Lecture (External): standing ovation/invitation back—Pass."]

Internal: Right. Now, Phil. How would you assess the importance for your work of having taken *SSK* as your topic?

Candidate: SSK is a particularly apposite focus for the study because of the reflexive tie between its findings about science and the "scientific" methodology that constructs them.

[Paper flipping noises as Dr External starts hurriedly to look through the thesis.]

Internal: So you're saying that SSK is a good choice of topic because reflexivity is something of a live issue for its practitioners, then?

Candidate: Among the major practitioners of SSK, there is a great diversity of views on the proper role of reflexivity. Some dot dot dot seek to outlaw it, seeing it as a paralysing influence on their practice and . . .

External: Yes, I thought so. You're repeating verbatim a passage from the introduction, or rather from your own entry in the encyclopedia, aren't you?

Candidate: Well, it's not *quite* word for word. I left a bit out in the last sentence.

External: Oh, don't split hairs, Mr Candidate! You know very well what I mean. I see very little point in you coming here and just repeating your thesis at us. We *have* read it already, you know. And that passage is toward the beginning, and if you had arranged your text in a sensible manner it would be right at the front, and surely we have a right to expect a little *progress.*

Candidate: But that textual arrangement is widely recognised as an illusion in terms of the temporal order of writing. Introductions, and even introduction surrogates, are usually one of the last components of the text to be written, for obvious reasons. I think it is John O'Neill who, in one of his books, heads the section at the front usually headed "Introduction" "Conclusion" and the section at the back usually headed "Conclusion" "Introduction." It could be argued that in quoting from an introduction in this final chapter (which is the conclusion) I am making a small and belated attempt to do something similar.

External: To copy O'Neill, you mean?

Candidate: Well, hardly. But even if I *had* copied that aspect of his text, I cannot really see . . .

External: But it would be a copy. It wouldn't be original, would it?

[I was tempted to question Dr External on the thoroughness of her reading here. It seemed to me that her knowledge of Chapter Four, Stage Four, where the question of competent copies is examined in detail, was less than sound; and she seemed totally ignorant of the discussions of originality accounting in that chapter. But of course I didn't. Instead I made an even greater mistake.]

Candidate: Nothing is, is it? The perception of originality is the perception of a form of difference, constructed, as I have demonstrated conclusively, especially in Chapters Four and Six, on the basis of a constructed similarity. For something to be seen as completely original would require that it was entirely dissimilar to anything—which would mean that it would be totally unrecognisable *as* anything. On the other hand, nothing is ever wholly *un*original; that would require it to be absolutely identical to something else—which is literally impossible. (Perceptions of similarity and difference seem to be at the root of the construction of all knowledge, as my thesis confirms.) Whether something is socially accounted as an "original" or as a "copy" is an issue which is negotiated on the grounds of perceived *relevance.* For instance, the fact that I have used the heading Introduction rather than

Conclusion to designate the earliest piece of writing—well not quite, but never mind—in the thesis would not, I dare say, have struck you as evidence of a lack of originality in the same way as a hypothetical heading of Conclusion in that same place would have had you known of O'Neill's earlier text. And yet the former arrangement is, one could argue, a great deal *less* original than the latter in that the term "Introduction" has been used a million times while the term "Conclusion" has been used perhaps once or twice. And, ironically, when a way of doing things has been "copied" a million times, and is thus sociologically accountable as a convention or an institution, its next instance becomes almost invisible; if noticed at all it is accounted as the following of a rule or as the instantiation of a norm. On the other hand, this massive background of similarity throws any difference into relief. But while a perceived difference is always highly visible its evaluative *status* is extremely insecure: Is it a good original or a bad copy? Is it perhaps only a mere replication? Or, worst of all, is it a *plagiarism?*

Internal: I'm glad you raised that point, because I wanted to ask you something about that. Phil? Are you alright?

[At this point I was in a state of shock. How could I have been so *stupid* as to mention *that?* Did he know? Did she? Was he about to drop the bombshell? Had this all been an elaborate charade? But no—it was a false alarm. The situation was under control. For the present.]

Internal: I don't know what you're looking so upset about. I'm sure we both thought that that exposition of the perception of originality was, well, adequate. So Emily, if you could allay Phil's doubts on that score, then we can get on.

[And without demur Dr External wrote this: "Originality (External): Pass."]

Internal: Now, Phil, what I want to raise is the question of your *own* originality accounting—that is your own claims for the originality of your work. I am thinking particularly of the so-called *new* literary forms aspect. Now, don't get me wrong. I am well aware that you cite a group of texts and writers which, you claim, are pursuing the same programme as yourself, such as the work centred around the Discuss and Reflect workshops [Woolgar 1988a] and so on. So I am by no means accusing you of claiming that your thesis is in any way *unique*, ha ha! It's more a worry about a certain lack of reflexiveness in your approach to the texts of the field, sociology of scientific knowledge, that is, in terms of their potential status as fictional or fictionalising texts.

Candidate: Yes. I do cite Latour's "Three Little Dinosaurs," 1980b, though.

In fact I spend a good deal of time in the LATOUR entry in Chapter Two examining how the apparent nonseriousness of that text is achieved. And I also suggest that it might be described as a precursor of these new literary forms—though as a joke, I grant you.

Internal: That's true. But there are several others that you seem to have overlooked. Let me run through a brief, but perhaps representative, list for you. First . . .

Candidate: And then there's Mulkay's "Methodology in the Sociology of Science" paper from way back in 1974. In his entry in the encyclopedia, I discuss the meaning of the double ending format of that text in terms of its significance as a multilevelled pointer toward these present concerns with discourse, with reflexivity, with the paradoxical, with . . .

External: Isn't that a bit Whiggish?

Internal: Alright, I grant you Latour's and Mulkay's texts. My own examples are far more significant as they are all from the Spatown school in SSK about which you are rather more, how can I put it, *ambiguous, shall we say.*

Candidate: May I borrow your pen, Dr External? Thank you.

Internal: Take Harvey's 1980 article on quantum mechanics, for instance. Far from sticking to the facts of the matter, he erects a nonexistent, that is, *fictional* argument in order to render "the scientists' interpretation . . . problematic," page 158. He claims that such a device is necessary when there is no controversy to throw up a set of ready-made alternative interpretations, same page. Then there is Pinch's 1979 paper on the "fraud hypothesis" as used in the interpretation of parapsychological experiments. This fascinating paper consists of an ironic reversal of the usual antiparanormal arguments put forward by critics to explain the results of psi experiments. Pinch takes these arguments and turns them onto the most frequent "normal" explanation of these results, namely, fraud itself. The point is that these arguments, when used against the fraud hypothesis, are "hypothetical"; they are "fictitious," page 344. They did not exist before Pinch *invented* them for the purpose of this SSK investigation of demarcation criteria. Third, one of Collins's papers, "Understanding Science," 1981f, indulges in a heavily fictionalised presentation of alternative arguments to illustrate his point that an appropriately interpretative and symmetrical study of scientific knowledge is unlikely to be had if it is limited to historical materials. Collins's arguments are presented in a narrative style and are said to be based on a mixture of "genuine events and fiction," page 379. Last, I should just like to mention Collins and Cox 1976, which among other interesting textual features includes a quotation from John Berger which I would have thought was worth your attention: "The form of the book is as much to do with

our purpose as the arguments contained within it" [Berger 1972:2].
Well, that's it. What are you writing?

Candidate: I'm just constructing a better research programme. You've been
very helpful and I am perfectly happy to relabel my work in accordance with your suggestions. How about the Ongoing and Not So Very
New Literary Forms Programme?

External: But Ignatious's point, surely, was that you should have constructed your programme, as you put it, actually in the thesis itself *and*
without illegitimate outside help.

Candidate: Well, first, it *is* in the thesis itself. I'm sure you don't need reminding that this is Chapter Seven we are wrighting. And second, the
idea of a text of this nature being a totally individual effort is absurd.
Just as there is no such thing as absolute originality, so there is no
such thing as an entirely individually author-ised text. And to suggest
that here, in this climactic chapter, which I have clearly designed as a
mutual product of us three wrighters for the purpose of *showing* the
social construction of texts in vivo, as it were; to insinuate that there is
something *improper* in such an inevitable process is . . . is . . .

Internal: Phil, I am sure that Emily meant no such thing. She was merely . . .
we were only . . . it was just that it seemed slightly late in the day for
you to be paying such important intellectual debts.

Candidate: Well, I won't argue. I'm sure you both know best. I'm a mere
novice, after all. I stand corrected. I make no claim to originality
whatever.

[Oh, irony!]

Internal: Fine. Now, time's winged chariot and all that. If it's alright with
you both, I suggest that Phil makes another stab at my earlier question
about SSK as a reflexive topic—which got lost among all these originality accounts—and then if you, Emily, have no further points you
wish to raise, Phil can give us his concluding statement. Is everybody
happy with that arrangement? Good. Fine. And then finally you can
take a break, Phil, while Emily and I decide your future, ha ha! And
that'll be that. Now, the SSK question.

Candidate: Yes. SSK is a good choice, I believe, for a study of and in reflexivity because it seems to me that in a discourse that is essentially
deconstructive of more powerful and entrenched versions of knowledge, and especially of scientific knowledge, there must be a very distinctive tension centred on the management of reflexivity. In other
words, in such a discourse the problem of reflexivity is acute; "immediate" rather than "disengaged," to misquote Woolgar. And I like to
think that I have successfully constructed my text to show that this is

indeed the case. That's one aspect. Another reason why SSK is a good choice of topic is the self-study or the reflexive sociology or the in and on aspect of the choice. Now of course this has the familiar drawbacks of "stagnatory autotelicism," to use McHoul's unfortunate phrase for the last time, which are dramatised as the Awkward Question with its Unsatisfactory Answers and theoreticised in "Beyond the Tu Quoque," but despite, or rather because of, these drawbacks, it represents my particular version of a "hard case argument": if it is possible to deconstruct one's *own* knowledge-claims—or the claims of one's own tradition of scholarly praxis—then *that* is the truly hard case for a sociology of knowledge. Of course, this project calls for a special strategy; a strategy which subverts but does not destroy as I think Barthes puts it, but nevertheless I want to argue that this project is a legitimate extension or development of existing SSK praxis, which *claims* after all to be doing just that with the knowledge it takes as topic; you know, in Bloor's symmetry and impartiality tenets, for instance. A reflexive development of these tenets can hope to turn the claims to symmetry into a real practical achievement, by unpacking the residual empiricism or objectivism in the very idea of taking as topic, the very idea of a metastudy, the very idea of the observer relation, and so on. I would go so far as to say that if SSK refuses the opportunity offered by taking reflexivity seriously, its relativism will be swiftly corroded by the forces of realism. Perhaps it is *only* by taking the reflexive turn that its insights stand even a chance of survival. Paradoxically, it is only by the "apparently" "self-destructive" *and* "self-indulgent," with quotes, move to a practical reflexivity that SSK and similar antirealist discourses can flourish and thus enrich our culture and our thought. But that is far too extravagant. More modestly, to take SSK as my object and focus of study is to take it *seriously:* to give it a dignity that, when unreflexive, it seems unwilling to give to itself. It is to release it from its self-imposed underlabourer relation to Science. And it is to say, Yes, there is knowledge in SSK, and part—a significant and important part—of that knowledge is an understanding of what it might mean to say so. We haven't reached that point yet, I don't think. But I would like my thesis to be seen as assisting rather than confounding this kind of understanding. And in the process to be recognised as a sincere, if insignificant, contribution to that larger Project to which all of us are equally committed: the painful yet profound progress of humankind from Darkness and Ignorance to . . .

[Transcript deleted, as promised—see below. However, to preserve the dramatic continuity, and because nobody mentioned these annotations, here is a paraphrase of the deletion: " . . . self-conscious darkness and ignorance."]

External: I beg your pardon?

Internal: *What* did you just say?

Candidate: Oh, I'm sorry, I really am. It was either a slip of the tongue or a tragic irony designed to alert my readers to the absurdity of human history in a form appropriate for a text so apparently unconcerned with such weighty profundities and so apparently full of an entirely irresponsible levity, that is, as a joke.

External: I don't think that is terribly amusing.

Candidate: Nor do I.

Internal: Look, can we please get back to the business in hand? Shall we take it that Phil has answered the question satisfactorily? Emily?

External: Only if he agrees to delete that tasteless remark from the transcript.

Internal: Phil?

Candidate: Very well.

[Dr External then wrote, at the bottom of the envelope: "SSK as topic (Internal): Conditional Pass."]

Internal: Good. I think it's time for your concluding statement, Phil.

Candidate: Yes. I'm slightly uncertain about the rules here. I'd really just like to read a few lines—almost the final few lines appropriately enough—from a text—also a thesis funnily enough—which is, in many ways, similar to my own, written by a certain Malcolm Ashmore from the University of York. What he has to say on and in the business of concluding is so remarkably apposite for our purpose that I believe the benefit to be gained from its inclusion should outweigh any consideration of possible procedural inappropriateness.

External: I can certainly understand your preference for someone else's words!

Internal: Well, what do you say, Emily?

External: Why not? Time is running out and I can't think of any interesting objections. So yes, Ignatious. Why not indeed!

[I then opened this book at page 218 and read Ashmore's conclusively conclusive conclusion.]

Candidate: ". . . Ashmore's conclusively conclusive conclusion." Sorry, that's slightly too early. This is the passage I want:

"The problem of writing a valid conclusion to this thesis is an exceedingly difficult one. If the standard research report format was found wanting for the reflexive analyses of the earlier chapters, how much more reflexively inappropriate is the standard conclusion format with its highly coercive structure and its invidious implication that the text is reducible to a collection of metaphorical nuggets called 'findings.' When the *form* of the text *is* the argument, such a format would *destroy* the argument. I want my conclusion, in contrast, to advance the argument—to be a climax rather than a collection, an authentic ending rather than a retrospective introduction. Or better still, I would prefer that it was both. I am, I hope, going some way toward achieving this by writing this Fiction of the Candidate which, by being centred on a fictional examination of the thesis thereby allows a retrospective review of the usual type to take place within the fiction, but which also, and importantly, permits reflexive explorations of the fact/fiction dichotomy, of games playing and of reflexivity itself. Not to mention the concept of originality.

Unfortunately, the problem of the reflexive conclusion is now reasserting itself on a smaller scale *within* this concluding chapter. Quite simply the problem is how to conclude the conclusion. (Wheels within wheels, indeed!) My first thought was simply to continue the fiction to the end of the chapter, concluding with a short Epilogue. The examination would end with Candidate completing his final speech and leaving the room, whereupon the examiners would decide to pass him only to discover, perhaps from an unopened note in the envelope, that Candidate's thesis was an entirely plagiarised version of . . . well, no prizes for guessing what. This solution has the merit of making sense of the frequent allusions in Candidate's annotations to the dubious status of his text. But otherwise it is not particularly interesting.

I then decided that an effective ending would need to incorporate a discussion of the substantive conclusions to the major empirical chapters (Four, Five, and Six) of the thesis. After all, questions about the replication of replication, the variability of variability accounting, and the problematic articulation of The Problem had been conspicuously absent from the examination 'so far.' Unfortunately, a brief review of the concluding sections of these chapters showed that there, too, conclusive considerations of these substantive matters were lacking. Instead, there was only paradox, inconclusion, fiction; circles, spirals, and loops. In fact, a series of attempts at *not* coming to a conclusion. Reluctantly, therefore, I have had to abandon this second version of the ending—and as for the idea of somehow combining both of these modes . . . the trick is simply beyond me.

So I am afraid we are left with this rather unsatisfactory fiction in which these words are being read by Phil Candidate as his concluding speech which ends in the form of the conclusion to the examination like so:

Candidate: And that concludes my address. I shall now leave the room.

External: Having totted up the score we conclude 'pass,' but what is this unopened note in your envelope?

Internal: It is a communication which comes to the conclusion that Candidate's thesis is a plagiarised copy of Ashmore's.

Internal and External: Then we must conclude that he has failed in the end, rather like our Author.

If that is so (and who will deny it?), surely it is because the problem of writing a valid conclusion to this thesis is an exceedingly difficult one" (Ashmore 1989:218–20).

And that concludes my address. We shall now leave this text. To its own devices.

EPILOGUE WITH POST-TEXT

That's it. It is now all yours. But remember:

Neither I nor you would have come this far if there was nothing to be said.
    David Silverman (1975a:111)

NONBIBLIOGRAPHIC SOURCES AND OTHER SECRETS

INTERVIEWS

I carried out a total of twelve interviews with British sociologists of scientific knowledge, all of which I tape recorded and transcribed in longhand and in full. The style of interviewing was informal and unstructured. The content was the technical details of each interviewee's work. I therefore prepared a list of questions specifically for each interviewee to answer and made no subsequent attempt to compare different responses to similar questions. Many of the interviews turned into free-ranging discussions, and this generally produced material of a higher quality than was produced by sticking to the prearranged list of questions. The lengths of the interviews varied between forty minutes and three-and-a-half hours. The following is a list of these interviews:

Barry Barnes—Edinburgh—24 June 1982
Harry Collins—Bath—10 June 1982
Nigel Gilbert—York—6 June 1983
Bill Harvey—Edinburgh—24 June 1982
Donald MacKenzie—Edinburgh—21 June 1983
Michael Mulkay—York—5 April 1983
Andrew Pickering—Edinburgh—24 June 1982
Trevor Pinch—Bath—10 June 1982
Jonathan Potter—St Andrews—20/21 June 1983
David Travis—Bath—10 June 1982
Steve Woolgar—Oxford—6 May 1983
Steven Yearley—Oxford—6 May 1983

Transcription Conventions

Speakers are identified by their initials. Each piece of transcript is identified by the initials of the interviewee followed by the number of the page (the first two figures) and the line (the last two figures). I rendered the tape-recorded talk into text with the help of the familiar conventions used by novelists, playwrights, and other writers of human speech. I have chosen this terribly unsystematic mode of transcription in order to represent the speechfulness of speech in a way that almost everybody already knows how to read.

CORRESPONDENCE

Participant/Author

During the research, I corresponded with many sociologists of scientific knowledge (as well as a few other people) concentrating on those whom, for geographical or other reasons, I was unable to interview. The full list of my correspondents—those who wrote back to me at least once—is as follows: David Bloor, Daryl Chubin, Harry Collins, Roger Cooter, Alex Dolby, Jane French, Nigel Gilbert, Peter Halfpenny, Bill Harvey, Jonathan Harwood, Karin Knorr-Cetina, Bruno Latour, John Law, Michael Lynch, Donald McCloskey, Donald MacKenzie, Doug Mitchell, Michael Mulkay, Greg Myers, Kay Oehler, Ian Parker, Andy Pickering, Trevor Pinch, Jonathan Potter, Jerry Ravetz, Dave Revill, Sal Restivo, Steven Shapin, Peter Stringer, Peter Suber, David Travis, Malcolm Vout, Teri Walker, Graham Watson, Richard Whitley, Janet Wolff, Steve Woolgar, Anna Wynne, Steven Yearley.

Of these correspondents' correspondence, I have quoted from the following in the text.

Bloor—undated 1982, 4 May 1983
Collins—21 March 1983
Dolby—undated 1982
Harwood—13 August 1982
Knorr-Cetina—22 July 1983
Latour—14 June 1982
Lynch—8 November 1983
Mulkay—15 August 1984
Pinch—12 February 1982, 11 August 1984
Potter—undated 1982

Participant/Participant

I have had access to a limited amount of participants' correspondence, the majority from Mulkay's and Gilbert's files. This material was drawn upon in the discussion of discourse analysis in Chapter Five. The letters from which I quote are these:

Gilbert and Mulkay to Edge—25 June 1981
Mulkay to Pickering—21 April 1981
Pickering to Gilbert—18 March 1981
Pickering to Mulkay—29 April 1981

REFEREES' REPORTS

I have also had access to several referees' reports on SSK material submitted for publication. Most of these were concerned with discourse analytic articles and again were from Mulkay's and Gilbert's files. The reports which I have cited in the text are as follows:

Reports on "Warranting Scientific Belief" (WSB draft 3): Referee B;
    Referee C
Reports on *The Reflexive Thesis* (TRT): Reader 2

RESEARCH PROPOSALS

I have only quoted one of these, again in the chapter on discourse analysis:

Mulkay and Gilbert: proposal to SSRC, 20 April 1978

EARLY DRAFTS

Most early drafts are forgotten once the text which they become is published. If the piece of writing in question does not get published, then it becomes known as an unpublished paper rather than a draft. In this thesis most unpublished papers are listed in the Bibliography along with their published fellows. Occasionally, I have cited as an unpublished paper what should, very probably, properly be called a draft; for example, Mulkay and Gilbert (1981b) "The Truth Will Out," a later version of which became the fifth chapter of *Opening Pandora's Box*. In Chapter Five, I had occasion to quote from the three (or four) drafts of what was to become "Warranting Scientific Belief" (Gilbert and Mulkay 1982). To solve the problem of where and how to reference these texts I decided to list them in this Appendix:

WSB draft 1—Gilbert (and Mulkay), July 1980: "Accounting for Truth"
WSB draft 1a—(Gilbert and) Mulkay, undated: "Constructing Scientific
    Rationality"
WSB draft 2—Gilbert and Mulkay, November 1980: "Constructing Scientific Rationality or Possibly Warranting Scientific Belief"
WSB draft 3—Gilbert and Mulkay, January 1981: "Warranting Scientific
    Belief"

I also include here two other interesting texts which, although I have neither quoted nor cited them (so far), were nevertheless genuine sources for my research. Both are examples of the kind of text which has such a low status it is almost invisible. The first seems to have been repudiated by its author(s), even though it is said to be a draft of a later published paper (though seemingly utterly dissimilar to the text which is said to have followed from it). Moreover, it has never to my knowledge been cited. I will redress that injustice here. The second text is invisible for the same reason, and it too has been repudiated by its author. Though it originally appeared as part of a pre-publication draft, it was "pulled out" by its author before publication because he was unsatisfied with it. Fortunately, I always rather liked it, so I will rescue it from total oblivion by citing it here.

Gilbert (and Mulkay) 1979, "Science and Laboratory Practice" (draft of
        Gilbert and Mulkay 1980)
Collins, February 1982, "Appendix 3: Consistency" (pages 33–37 of draft
        of Collins 1983a)

CONFERENCES: DISCOURSE AND REFLEXIVITY WORKSHOPS

During the course of the research and its textual revisions I attended a series of six Discourse and Reflexivity Workshops, at four of which I gave early drafts (see above) of pieces of the thesis and three of which were recorded. Due to pressure of work and change of plans, these taped sessions were never transcribed. However, they definitely qualify as a source, as do, of course, the other nonrecorded sessions.

University of York, 15–16 April 1983; recorded; paper given: "The Six
        Stages"
Oxford Polytechnic, 7–8 September 1983; paper given: "Five Easy Pieces"
Brunel University, 31 March–1 April 1984
University of Surrey, 13–14 September 1984; paper given: "Beyond the Tu
        Quoque"
St Andrews University, 20–22 September 1985; recorded; paper given:
        "The Critical Problems of Writing The Problem"
University of York, 7–8 April 1986; recorded

The full list of participants at these sessions is as follows: Malcolm Ashmore, Alan Backhouse, Brian Campbell, Colin Clark, Robert D'Amico, Jane French, Nigel Gilbert, Janet Heaton, Hilary Lawson, Ian Litton, Andy McKinlay, Michael Mulkay, Greg Myers, Kay Oehler, Trevor Pinch, Jonathan Potter, Peter Stringer, Teri Walker, Graham Watson, Margaret Wetherell, Robin Wooffitt, Steve Woolgar, Anna Wynne, Steven Yearley.

TELEPHONE CONVERSATIONS

During my research I have had innumerable relevant phone conversations. As I have only quoted from one of these, this is the sole listing here; but no doubt all the others have an equivalent status as bona fide sources.

Ashmore to Mulkay, 12 March 1985

SOURCES OF SOME OF "MY" TEXTUAL TECHNIQUES

Many of the textual techniques which I have used I have shamelessly plagiarised from other authors. Here is just a selection. No doubt there are many more.

Wrighting—my invention, but inasmuch as it is a word which only works as writing (*sic*), it owes something to Derrida's différance (1978).

Pre-texts—the idea owes something to a reference of Hannah Arendt to an idea of Walter Benjamin for a projected book which would consist entirely of quotations from other books. The reference appears in the opening section of Sharratt's *Reading Relations* (1982) which consists entirely of quotes from other authors.

Abstract—the blank in the last line—from one of John Barth's stories in *Lost in the Funhouse* (1972).

Introduction—quotation of regulations—equally inspired by Stringer 1985 and Derrida 1977.

Chapter Two, Latour—analysis of the "trivia" framing "Three Little Dinosaurs" (1980b)—from Gusfield 1976 and other rhetorical analyses of science texts, but chiefly from Derrida's (1977) stimulating analysis of the deep significance of such trivial textual features as the copyright mark.

Chapter Six, Second Text—dialogues between unidentified partners— from Barth 1972, again. Barth's version is said to be a "monologue interieu." Well, perhaps; but the point of leaving the speakers unidentified is so that you can make what you will of them. Far be it from me to subvert that intention at this late stage.

Bibliography—apocryphal entries—inspired by the later writings of Borges, and the works of Gebstadter and Rimbaud.

OTHER SECRETS

In the Introduction, I quote from Reader 2 (TRT). In this quote I interpolate the word "briefly." The correct word at this point is "clearly." (Telling the absolute truth can have its drawbacks.)

In Chapter One, note 1, I insert Mulkay's "15 August 1984, Dear Malcolm" (1984b) in which I interpolate the word "adequate." The correct version is "excellent." (Telling the absolute truth can be embarrassing.)

In Chapter Two, COLLINS, I quote from an anonymous interviewee. This selection—"you give papers . . . social construct"—is from Pinch's transcript, reference TP 1012–14. (It can, though, have its pleasures.)

The pseudonyms I use in Chapter Five translate as follows:

Castletown—Edinburgh
C (Collins)—Ashmore
Fransella—Potter
Hewish—Woolgar
Jansky—Edge
Kirwan—Yearley
Lehninger—Gilbert
Minstertown—York
Mitchell—Mulkay
Price—Pickering
Spatown—Bath

In Chapter Seven's dramatised examination, none of the people who take part have any known analogues in Real Life; see the disclaimer at the beginning of the chapter. The academic departments mentioned are equally fictitious, as are two of the four centres of higher learning, the exceptions being "Local Polytechnic" which is, of course, Trent Polytechnic, Burton Street, Nottingham; and "the University of York" which in actual fact is the University of York. The reference to "Discuss and Reflect workshops" is a reference to the Discourse and Reflexivity ditto. See "Conferences," above.

The game played during the passage on games is an adaptation of BBC Radio 4's "Just a Minute," devised by Ian Messiter, chaired by Nicholas Parsons, and frequently featuring Kenneth Williams, Peter Jones, Clement Freud, and Derek Nimmo. It is definitely not "University Challenge," which is a red herring, I'm afraid.

Candidate's lecture on the Lecturer's Lecture was suggested and initiated by the following supervisory comments: "I am slightly concerned at [the Lecture's] place in the thesis. Do you intend this textual form to do any special work? If not you are going to have to justify using the 'lecture form' in the context of the opening chapter of a PhD . . . . I think you will need a strong argument to justify doing it this way—after all a PhD is a particular type of text and there are particular rules for how such a text should be organised" (Pinch, Letter, 11 August 1984).

NOTES

CHAPTER ONE

1. Welcome to the Notes. I hope you will visit this section of the text regularly. Quite a lot will be going on here and it would be a shame to miss it all. But to get to the business of this particular note: May I ask you by which route you have arrived at Chapter One, note 1? If you are a "notephile" you were probably guided here directly by the note number in the text on page 15—and quite right too. However, you might also have come to be reading this by way of the reference to Mulkay 1984b which would have led you to the Bibliography where the text in question would turn out to have the strange title "15 August 1984, Dear Malcolm" and to be located in this very text (Ashmore 1989) at this very point (page 227, note 1). And here it is:

> Dear Malcolm, I have no questions of my own about your lecture. I think it provides an [adequate] introduction to the thesis. However, when I imaginatively reconstructed the occasion, a plump bald-headed old geezer stood up at the end and uttered the words enclosed. Perhaps you can respond to them in your own way. Yours creatively, Mike.

As you will no doubt recognise, this text originated as a letter to me from my supervisor, Mike Mulkay. Given this history I might have cited the phrase "plump bald-headed old geezer" as coming from a private communication, as academic writers often do. Unfortunately, such a tactic would have prevented the text from appearing as a bibliography item; if, that is, we assume that the function of a bibliography is to make both visible and available the con-text being claimed by its text. Only by setting this private letter down here in (almost) its entirety, and thus by transforming the private into the public, can this important function of the bibliography be preserved. Having done so, however, the question arises as to whose text "15 August 1984, Dear Malcolm" really is. Although listed in the Bibliography as one of Mulkay's works, it is also listed in the Bibliography as an integral part of one of Ashmore's. Paradoxically, therefore, its reference in the Bibliography is incorrect, according to its reference in the Bibliography. Moreover, and this applies with even greater force to my use of Mulkay 1984c (see note 2) . . .

2. . . . a question of propriety arises here. Mulkay 1984b (see note 1) includes a reference to "the words enclosed." Well, Mulkay 1984c consists of those words; they appear in the text as the Old Geezer's speech. I chose to "respond to them in [my]

own way" (Mulkay 1984b) by incorporating them wholesale into the text as a basis for the dialogue which then follows. The question is: By doing so, am I guilty of attempting to defraud the public, meaning my examiners and my readers, by passing off a text as all my own work when, clearly, parts of it are the work of others? Have I overstepped the boundary of legitimate quotation? Would quoting poststructuralist literary theorists on the pervasiveness of intertextuality help my case? I will simply have to trust that this possible impropriety will pass unnoticed by all those sensible readers who, quite rightly, will avoid reading the notes.

3. See notes 1 and 2.

4. This occurrence is intentionally artificial and incongruous. If this is fiction, it is certainly not realist. Thus, the arrival en masse of the CSSSK is not going to be explained by suggesting, for instance, that the previous student audience transmutes into a rabble of relativists, or that, "Star Trek"-like, our sociologists have beamed down from some improbable orbiting university, or that they quietly walked through the door (naturalism?), or that the Lecturer is dreaming them, or . . .

5. I am afraid that the introductions are full of tasteless in-jokes that are only likely to appeal to, or even be recognised by, SSK participants, commentators and critics. My reason (or excuse) for this is that such readers would only be bored by a catalogue of informative bits and pieces of which they were already aware. SSK-naive readers, on the other hand, are presented with, as far as I know, entirely correct background information on the members of the field. As we are in a time warp here—the Lecture takes place in late 1983—I have taken the liberty of endowing the CSSSK with knowledge of the future quite beyond their normal powers.

6. The speeches of the CSSSK which follow are all taken from interviews and correspondence which have been selected and juxtaposed in order to make the points I want to make. Interview statements are identified by the initials of the interviewee and the numbers of the transcript page and line. (See the Appendix for details of the transcription conventions I have used.) In general, I have tried to display the variety of antireflexive arguments available for use in the field. At first, the speakers respond to my proposal to take SSK as my topic. The negative arguments put forward cluster around the themes of immobilism (navel-contemplation, paralysis, distraction, overcomplication), priority (the hard case argument, the yes-but-not-much argument, and the yes-but-not-yet argument), and political inadvisability. Next, the speakers treat reflexivity itself, and find it noninteresting and nonuseful—which come down to the same thing. The next section starts with a display of some of the problems of a nonreflexive stance, continues with a few actual cases of reflexive concern and ends by noting the problems attached to such a concern—notably the "impossibility" of combining empirical work with reflexive work. It is suggested, finally, that the solution is a question of balance.

7. To accentuate this commentary, I have **emphasised** every occurrence of the term. For an interesting attempt at a sociology of the interesting, see Davis (1971).

8. Ashmore's statement here is ambiguous. It can be read as a specific response to Pinch's previous speech in which case it expresses the naivety of the researcher at the start of his research: "I thought the CSSSK would find my project at least unobjectionable." It can also be read as the acceptance by the author of his current understanding of the CSSSK's views of his work: "Now I know that my research is less than unanimously welcome."

9. In the meantime, Pinch has written two papers on reflexivity, the first of

which (1982c) agrees with Collins in recommending the banning of reflexive considerations. The second paper (Pinch and Pinch 1988) is much more ambiguous as befits an argument cast in the form of a debate between the antireflexive Pinch and his proreflexive alter ego. (See Chapter Two, PINCH.)

10. Of course, such comprehensiveness is not possible. See Chapter Two, ENCYCLOPEDIA ENTRIES.

11. Of course, such incompleteness is inevitable. See Chapter Two, ENCYCLOPEDIA ENTRIES.

CHAPTER TWO

1. The sources for this entry are as follows:

Chambers's Twentieth Century Dictionary (ed. Geddie; new edition with extended supplement) 1964
The Little Oxford Dictionary (ed. Coulson; fourth edition) 1969
The Fontana Dictionary of Modern Thought (ed. Bullock and Stallybrass) 1977
Roget's Thesaurus (Penguin edition) 1953
A Dictionary of Science (ed. Uvarov and Chapman) 1951
A Dictionary of Philosophy (ed. Lacey) 1976

2. I said these categories were overlapping.

3. See note 2.

4. Compare Collins "studiously ignoring" reflexive considerations in a footnote to his review of the empirical programme of relativism (1983a:108). Note also the similarity with many of the problems raised by the CSSSK in Chapter One, especially those to do with the practical impediment that a concern with reflexivity represents.

5. Barnes's earlier work on the processes of reference and inference include his 1981b, 1982a, and 1982b. For an SSK text (book) which bases its discussion on the Hesse/Barnes "network theory," see Law and Lodge 1984.

6. This is a use of the "hard case" argument. See COLLINS for a discussion.

7. Another debate where Barnes is cast in the role of the moderate is that between Collins and Cox (1976, 1977) playing the ultrarelativists who would refuse *any* role for nature in accounting for natural knowledge, and Law (1977) who thinks (on Barnes's behalf) that that is just *too* extreme.

8. This interpretation is strengthened by noticing this earlier formulation of the strong programme from Bloor's "Wittgenstein and Mannheim . . ." paper (1973):

The first [requirement] is that the sociology of knowledge must locate causes of belief . . . . The second requirement is that no exception must be made for those beliefs held by the investigator who pursues the programme. Special pleading must be avoided and causes located for those beliefs subscribed to, as well [as] for those which are rejected. The programme must be impartial with respect to truth and falsity. The next requirement is a *corollary* of this. The sociology of knowledge must explain its own emergence and conclusions: it must be reflexive. The fourth . . . requirement is a *refinement* of the demand for impartiality. Not only must true and false beliefs be explained, but the same sort of causes

must generate both classes of belief. This may be called the symmetry requirement. (1973:173–74; my emphases)

What I want to emphasise here is the interdependence of these requirements. Reflexivity is a "corollary" and symmetry a "refinement" of impartiality. When the highly
reflexive tenor of this formulation of impartiality—its refusal to make exceptions on
its own behalf—is taken into account, it would seem that the moral requirement of
consistency is the primary (textual) motivation for Bloor's reflexive stance. Unfortunately, the 1976 version largely misses this emphasis.

9. Compare Collins's reply to Laudan's criticism of the empirical programme
of relativism, where he writes: "I am going to assume that Laudan knows that the
'logical argument' is otiose" (1982c:140).

10. Interestingly, Hesse's counterargument is not the same as Bloor's. Whereas
Bloor uses a counter to the determinism form, Hesse puts forward a counter to the
absolutism version—see SELF-REFUTATION ARGUMENTS. (Collins also chooses this
latter strategy in his discussion of the "logical argument"—see Collins and Cox
1976:430–31.) However, the way Hesse argues has similarities with Bloor's attempts
to dispose of the issue. First, she claims that self-refutation is undoubtedly the most
powerful of the various rationalist arguments against the strong programme. Thus, her
"demolition" is obviously of great moment. However, she introduces her counter—
that relativist statements are only couched in local and not absolute terms and thus that
they do not refute themselves—with the phrase: "This easy self-refutation is fallacious" (1980:42). Thus, the supposedly powerful argument turns out to be (too) easy;
a matter of mere sleight of hand: "This argument, though usually presented with smug
finality, carries with it an uncomfortable suggestion of sleight of hand" (Collins and
Cox 1976:430). For a rather different analysis of Hesse's counterargument, see Tollefson (1987) who concludes that relativism "is irrelevant to the philosophic enterprise . . . . There are no good reasons for adopting relativism . . . . The cost of the
equivocation defense [Hesse's argument] . . . is . . . very high . . . . It is a move
beyond the limits within which significant philosophic debate is possible" (Tollefson
1987:215–16).

11. Bloor's formulation suggests that his critic (Buchdal) does discuss the argument. Well, he does; but hardly with much confidence:

And if I may say so: Mary Douglas's theory (to which you revert . . .) is *itself*
a theory which in turn (I suppose) would be held as having been thought up
under the shadow of social influences: thus yielding the usual self-refuting comment on all such sociological accounts; not that such consequences have ever
carried much weight! (Buchdal 1982:302)

12. Bloor (along with Barnes and the strong programme in general) has also
been criticised from both wings of Marxist science studies. Some elements of the
fascinating debate between the relativistic *Radical Science Journal* collective and the
strict science versus ideology concerns of Hilary and Steven Rose and their colleagues
are examined in HYPER-REFLEXIVITY.

13. It has been suggested to me (by Bill Harvey) that Bloor's SSK analysis of
the Popper-Kuhn debate in *Knowledge and Social Imagery* constitutes reflexivity-in-
practice. This is an interpretation with some merit; however, if Bloor's obvious hos-

tility to the kind of philosophical talk about science that that debate represents is taken into account, it becomes less than clear how much *self*-reflexion is involved in this analysis. For examples of his lack of encouragement see the speeches attributed to Bloor in Chapter One, "Unsatisfactory Answers."

14. My reading of Kuhn's reflexivity is rather at variance with Bloor's. When Kuhn discusses "past historical scholars" he is rather spectacularly *un*reflexive. See Chapter Three.

15. There is one specific example of Collins's nonreflexivity which is reserved for special treatment in Chapter Four. This is Collins's claim that his "replication studies" (1975, 1976) have been replicated. Just what it is that is *non*reflexive about this seemingly self-exemplifying claim will have to remain a mystery at this point. (But see Ashmore.)

16. Laudan's argument is, in a certain way, similar to mine in "The Six Stages" (Chapter Four). I, too, argue that Collins is inconsistent in his employment of a brash empirical realism to show the relativistic and socially constructed nature of Nature. However, the conclusions that we draw from this common interpretation are radically different. Laudan finds Collins's relativism "wildly implausible" (1982a:131) but approves of his empiricism. Laudan's finding of a reflexive contradiction between these two doctrines is used entirely to increase the implausibility of the relativism. I, on the other hand, make opposed evaluations: I approve of the relativism, disapprove of the empiricism, and feel that the latter is destructive for the former (as Laudan does— which is why he emphasises it). Thus, while Laudan and I both advocate that Collins should be reflexively consistent, Laudan would have him give up his relativism and retain his empiricism, while I would have him do the opposite.

While neither of us are likely to succeed in this endeavour, it is worth pointing out the consequences of both of these moves to consistency for the benefit of other empirical relativists. Laudan's move (a reflexively consistent empiricism) would involve jettisoning all SSK's substantive conclusions about scientific knowledge. The standard view of science that SSK has claimed to be dismantling would perforce be reerected. My move, on the other hand (a reflexively consistent relativism), would continue this work of dismantling (or deconstructing) by an extension to, in my view, the "hardest case" of all: one's own sociological knowledge-and-practice (praxis). Thus it *would* involve a change of praxis; but, in SSK's own terms, in a progressive rather than regressive direction.

17. See Chapters Three and Six.

18. An interesting example of the humility of sociologists is a comment by Collins and Pinch in an added note to their paper on parapsychology and its critics (1979:263):

By June 1977 this paper was itself being brought into the argument. It is perceived, it seems, as a paper which might favour the parapsychologists' case. [This gives] us some cause for concern lest the paper be . . . misconstrued . . . . The paper *is* neutral regarding the existence of paranormal phenomena . . . . For ourselves, as professional sociologists, we are disinterested in these questions.

19. My analysis of Collins's antireflexivity is perhaps contradicted by Kay Oehler's (1983) discussion of the same phenomenon. Oehler argues that the general interpretation of reflexivity in the sociology of science can be written: "You are like

those whom you study." But, she claims, a phrase such as this can be understood in more than one way. Most SSK practitioners take it to refer to the similar relations to knowledge in science and in metascience. Thus, on this interpretation, the knowledge process is considered the same in both cases. Therefore, "whatever we learn about the scientist at work also tells us something about ourselves" (Oehler 1983:3). However, in the case of Collins a different translation of "you are like those whom you study" can explain his "nonreflexive" stance. This version says that "the sociologist is like his object of study, the scientist, in that they are both human beings, and that this likeness does not hold for the relationship between the scientist and his object of study, the natural world" (Oehler 1983:3). For Oehler, then, Collins is reflexive (whether *he* understands himself to be or not) in the sense that he and his scientists are both human beings. As an assessment of one noticeable similarity between Collins and his objects of study, this is unobjectionable. But as an attempt to make Collins out to be reflexive after all, Oehler's analysis must be considered a shade too ingenious.

20. Hofstadter, in his *Metamagical Themas* (1985:71), writes of his correspondence with Peter Suber about the latter's encyclopedic project, then "in the works" and tentatively titled "The Anatomy of Reflexivity," which would deal with reflexivity in its broadest sense. Unfortunately, I have also corresponded with Suber only to find that his "Anatomy" is still very much on the writing desk. Suber's particular speciality is reflexivity in law (see LAW), which although beyond the scope of the only encyclopedia of reflexivity in existence is nevertheless a fascinating topic.

21. This brilliant piece of . . . is also quoted by Oehler and Mullins (1986:18) who were kind enough to offer it to me.

22. In certain versions of ethnomethodology—"constitutive ethnomethodology" as Woolgar has it—this lack of independence is postulated as a general and pervasive feature of cognitive and interactive activity. The fact that, if "research" is taken as an example, the object of research, including its findings and results, are constituted by and/or are (analytically) identical with its methodology is not in this tradition something to be surprised at (and certainly not shocked by). Ethnomethodology calls this feature, rather confusingly for the purposes of this encyclopedia, *reflexivity*. (See ATTENDING TO TERMINOLOGY.) For connections between this ethnomethodological form of reflexivity and the self-referential form that Gruenberg deals with, see Woolgar 1988b and Chapter Three.

23. See Chapter Six.

24. See PSYCHOLOGY.

25. See Chapter Four.

26. For these postempiricist arguments see, for instance, Barnes 1974, 1982a; Bernstein 1976; Bhaskar 1978; Hesse 1980; Kuhn 1970a; Mulkay 1979a; Thomas 1979; Tudor 1982; Yearley 1984.

27. For the inappropriateness of "Kuhnian" as a distinguishing label in the sociology of science, see Pinch 1982b.

28. Perhaps the SSK practitioner who is nearest to this position is Collins. However, *his* demarcation of natural and social science inverts the usual grounds on which such demarcations are made. Whereas the *Geisteswissenschaften* tradition (including Winch 1958) accepts the standard view (Mulkay 1979a) of the natural sciences and treats the social disciplines as a branch of the humanities, with all the "extra" problems of interpreting interpretations (hermeneutics) which such a view involves,

Collins's recommendation is, on the contrary, to "treat the social world as real, and as something about which we can have sound data, whereas we should treat the natural world as something problematic—a social construct rather than something real" (1981e:217). See COLLINS for an analysis of this position.

29. The reader should note the circularity involved in citing these particular sources for this anti-Gruenberg argument. Gruenberg has rejected the kind(s) of sociology of science represented by these sources largely on the grounds of their non-independence from science. I am using them here as components in an argument designed to show that Gruenberg's choice of grounds is itself no more independent than are the grounds of these sources. Naturally, Gruenbergians will not find this argument persuasive, especially as its upshot is that *no* inquiry into inquiry *can* be independent of its object.

30. See note 29.

31. For an analysis of boundary-work in science, see Gieryn 1984.

32. Perhaps it is. Gellner, for instance, sees fit to blame the excesses of Feyerabend's *Against Method* (1975) on, in part, his Viennese ancestry (Gellner 1975).

33. It might be objected that such discursive techniques as irony rely on holding to a distinction between the real and the apparent, such that what is *apparently* meant is not *really* meant. But in cases of irony, the supposed real meaning is itself produced by some form of meta-appearance, that is, a metainstruction saying "This is irony." For irony in sociology, see Wright 1978 and 1983 and Woolgar 1983a. For analyses of the reality/appearance distinction, see Silverman and Torode 1980 and Potter 1983.

34. This version of reflexivity sounds remarkably similar to Collins's version of interpretivism, which is the "view which accepts that a participant in a social situation has a privileged understanding when compared with one who is not a participant" (Collins and Pinch 1982:190). Perhaps, then, Collins is really reflexive after all? See note 19 and COLLINS.

35. The tragic image of the infinite regress is pragmatically deconstructed in Chapter Three.

36. See Chapter Three for a description of Whig history.

37. See Chapter Five.

38. In fact, Mulkay cites Ashmore 1983 as an example of "the sociological literature on reflexivity" (1984a:280, n.5). My slight pique at Mulkay's misquotation of the title as "The Six Steps" was alleviated somewhat when I noticed that his other example of this literature—Gouldner's *Coming Crisis*—was misattributed to A. E. Gouldner and misdated 1971.

39. A rather different view of the relation between relativism and reflexivity is presented in Fuller's "Making Reflexivity Safe for Relativism" (1986). Reflexivity is seen as consequential, not for relativists—for whom taking the reflexive turn is likely to be a case of "business as usual"—but for "essentialists" who assume that a social agent has an essence which remains constant and consistent across different social contexts (1986:1). It is only this assumption, claims Fuller, which makes reflexivity the dangerous, paradox-producing force of the story told by the Second of January Group.

40. For a similar debilitation argument which addresses the dangers of practising natural scientists learning the history of science, see Brush (1974) "Should the History of Science Be Rated X?"

41. Holland's assessment of Freud is highly contentious. See Oliver and Land-field (1962:118–19) and especially Sulloway (1979:18–19) for alternative and less generous interpretations.

42. For instance: "Let us all, above all, get away from the ideological, from the sociology of sociology, and get down to the doing of it, as best we can, in the grand tradition of Durkheim and Weber" (Baltzell 1972:228).

43. Of course, according to the reflexive argument, there is no essential distinction involved here. Nevertheless there certainly appears to be some kind of tacit understanding that too great a concentration on "us" rather than "them" is inappropriate. Consider, for instance, the following comment on Woolgar's analysis of interests explanations (1981b): "It seems clear from his text that the imputation of interests by scientists themselves would be an equally appropriate focus of study. Perhaps it is a pity that he did not adopt [this] course which might have resulted in a less acrimonious debate" (Callon and Law 1982:616).

44. This is the major reason for the lack of a KNORR-CETINA entry in this encyclopedia. See OMISSIONS.

CHAPTER THREE

1. Some names for the monster: the abyss, the spectre, the infinite regress; paradox, aporia, antinomy; the problem of descriptions, the problem of fallibility, the problem of metalanguage. The problem of these problems is the topic of Chapter Six. It is also the topic of this thesis.

2. I owe the title of this section and much of the following discussion to Arne Naess's *The Pluralist and Possibilist Aspect of the Scientific Enterprise* (1972). Naess seems to have been largely neglected by both contemporary philosophy of science and SSK (but see Roll-Hansen 1983:512). Perhaps this neglect is because, as an (ex) member of the Vienna Circle, Naess is persona non gratis for antipositivists, that is, all of us. Interestingly though, it seems that he was engaged in carrying out "meta-studies, with strong ingredients of 'sociology of knowledge' [on the] mutual 'refutations' and competing research programmes" of the psychologists Hull and Tolman, as early as the 1930s and 40s. Perhaps Naess might serve as another Ludwik Fleck-type ([1935]1979) precursor for SSK. I am sure that his claim to have conceived the International Encyclopedia of Unified Science can be forgiven considering that the great Kuhn's magnum opus first appeared under this imprint. (The information and quotations in this note are from Naess 1972:134–37, a historical appendix.)

3. For example Lakatos and Musgrave 1970; Scheffler 1967; Suppe 1974; Hacking 1981; Gutting 1980.

4. *Sociology:* Friedrichs 1970; Martins 1971; Ritzer 1975; Eckberg and Hill 1979. *History:* Hollinger 1973. *History of science:* Naess 1972; Reingold 1980. *Psychology:* Peterson 1981; Palermo 1971; Briskman 1972; Weimer and Palermo 1973. *Political science:* Almond 1966; Wolin 1968; Truman 1966; Ryan 1972. *Economics:* Bronfenbrenner 1971; Baumberger 1977. *Literary criticism:* Holub 1984. For overviews of such literature see Thomas 1979 and Bernstein 1976.

5. For example, Crane 1980a. For criticism and replies see Pickering 1980b and 1980c and Crane 1980b. For a radically different approach see Potter 1984.

6. Barnes 1969, 1982a; Barnes and Dolby 1970; Mulkay 1969; Law and French

1974; Pinch 1982b. For two lone voices against the Kuhnian chorus see Restivo 1981 and Whitley 1983.

7. Some examples of historiological or metahistorical writings are Butterfield 1955, White 1973, and the second part of Kuhn's *Essential Tension* (1977a). However, none of these—not even Kuhn's—constitute the kind of Kuhnian historiology I have in mind.

8. This limitation also allows Kuhn to argue with great enthusiasm that his theory of "puzzle-solving" constitutes a "less equivocal and . . . more fundamental" (Kuhn 1970b:7) criterion of demarcation of true science from pseudoscience than Popper's theory of falsification.

9. For an examination of boundary-work in science, see Gieryn 1984. Kuhn's discussions of his own practice include the introductory chapter to *The Structure* (1970a) entitled "A Role for History"; the preface to *The Essential Tension* (1977a); and three of that volume's essays: "The Relation between the History and the Philosophy of Science," "The Relation between History and the History of Science," and especially "The History of Science."

10. Which is not to say that Kuhn is never reflexive. The two reflexive passages I have found are fascinating but are not exercises in historiology. The first (1970a:77–80) occurs in the context of Kuhn's discussion of the role of anomalies in scientific change. Having claimed that scientists "do not treat anomalies as counterinstances" (1970a:77), Kuhn proceeds to reflexively support this claim by arguing that the factual points on which it is based

> are themselves counterinstances to a prevalent epistemological theory [falsificationism]. As such . . . they can at least help to create a crisis [but] by themselves they cannot and will not falsify that philosophical theory, for its defenders . . . will devise numerous articulations and ad hoc modifications . . . in order to eliminate any apparent conflict. (1970a:78)

In the second passage (1970c:232), Kuhn treats his critics' difficulties in correctly understanding his concepts of communication breakdown, talking through, and incommensurability in precisely these terms.

Another interesting aspect of these passages is Kuhn's stated reasons for not extending these brief reflexive analyses. In the first passage the reason is topic-irrelevance: such analysis "necessarily leads to the historical and critical elucidation of philosophy and those topics are here barred" (1970a:80). In the second passage the problem is insider-incompetence: "I am, however, too much a participant, too deeply involved, to provide the analysis which the breakdown of communication warrants" (1970c:232). Such delimiting disclaimers are regular features of reflexive argumentation.

11. In some versions of ethnomethodology (notably early Garfinkel) the word and the world are treated as identical: "The activities whereby members produce and manage settings of organised everyday affairs are identical with members' procedures for making those settings 'account-able' " (Garfinkel 1967:1).

12. Much of the following discussion in this section is indebted to the work of Mehan and Wood (1975) and, especially, of McHoul (1980, 1981, and especially his *Telling How Texts Talk* [1982]).

13. Elsewhere, Mehan and Wood claim not to hanker after the Real. So perhaps

they do and perhaps they don't. That is not the issue. When they don't they say, "The reflexive location of reflexivity is not a problem within ethnomethodological studies. Rather it provides them with their most intriguing phenomenon" (1975:19).

14. For instance in SSK: Woolgar's (1981b) complaint that some analysts illegitimately utilise "interests" as an unexplicated resource and Mulkay's (1981) complaint that SSK is written by researchers' subjects (scientists) and not by researchers themselves ("vassalage").

15. "The attribution of the status, discovery, is founded on the process of social recognition by which the announcement of an achievement is seen to be a substantively relevant possibility, determined in the course of motivated scientific investigations or schemes of research, whose conclusion or outcome is convincingly true or valid, and whose announcement is, for all appearances, unprecedented" (Brannigan 1981:77).

16. Brannigan is occasionally reflexive, however:

The natural sense of discovery, for sociology is a folk phenomenon. However the sociological identification of this is itself an achievement which the present work recommends to sociology as its own discovery, with the conviction that this work is part of the very order which it describes. (Brannigan 1981:171)

17. Though Latour (1988) argues that the project of not bringing news must necessarily be a failure.

18. It has occasionally been claimed that the reflexivity of reflexivity has been responsible for some ethnomethodologists self-destructing by lapsing into silence (Mehan and Wood 1975:167; McHoul 1981:113).

19. "A sceptic is always swinging between a love of seriousness and a disgust for it" (Carroll 1980:42).

20. I am well aware that Kuhn and his followers in SSK claim *not* to be criticising Science. This issue is raised at various points throughout the thesis and most intensively in Chapter Six.

21. I am radically unsure of the meaning of "success" in this context. No matter. There are many metascientists (among many others) who are not so afflicted. Which is, perhaps, why it remains stubbornly undeconstructed. If scientific success is interpreted as control over nature and thus as practical utility, then Mulkay 1979b is a step in the right direction. The discourse of utility has been examined by Potter (1982) and by Ashmore, Mulkay, and Pinch (1989).

22. Malcolm Vout has informed me that certain philosophers, notably Henri Bergson, have disagreed with me. I am ignoring this here.

23. Another indicator of fear (or at least concern) where the infinite regress is concerned is its representation in jokes. A marvellous example is a cartoon which manages to combine virtually all the issues in reflexivity that are addressed in this chapter—regress, metalevels, parasitism, the participant/analyst dialectic, the metascience paradox. It shows Scientist in lab coat at lab bench looking nervously over shoulder at Metascientist who, notebook and pencil in hand, is looking nervously over shoulder at Metametascientist who, notebook . . . , and so on for four or five levels. What this succeeds in showing above all else is the artificiality of the levels concept with its hierarchical *and* regressive connotations: after all, there they all are, all doing the same thing. Unfortunately, this cartoon has already (reflexively) appeared as the

frontispiece to Knorr-Cetina's *The Manufacture of Knowledge* (1981a) and thus I am unable to reproduce it here.

24. For the mysterious provenance and prevalence of the dichotomy as a method of (social science) theorising, see Baldamus 1976. See also Wilden 1980 on digital (either/or) versus (*sic*) analog (both/and) communication. For an advocacy of the "both/and" see Chapter Five.

25. Or perhaps, in the same way and for the same reasons as rats modify the behaviour of psychologists, they do.

26. It is this basic misconstrual which unites Collins's and Bloor's otherwise opposed statements on reflexivity (see Chapter Two, COLLINS and BLOOR). Both of them seem to assume the model of analysis of previous analysis as the only possible reflexive mode. As Woolgar's comments on Bloor's advocacy put it:

> The declaration of reflexive intent is thus a programmatic characteristic of a general strategy, a series of research activities, rather than a call for an approach which is reflexive in the course of its analysis. The reflexivity alluded to in the strong programme is disjointed; the analysis of scientific knowledge is separate from, and precedes, the possible analysis of the analysis. (1982:492)

27. "There is always already an equivalence between . . . 'levels' or 'orders' (as they seem) of analytic practice and . . . the notion of meta-levels and -languages is a dubious means of addressing the question" (McHoul 1982:100).

28. The following is an adapted and extended comment from Michael Mulkay: This text is *not* a failure because it meets most of its own criteria and in so doing begins to develop a New Literary Form. However, the text's inability to recognise its own success is in itself a failure of (its much vaunted) reflexivity. Thus the text's actual success is at the same time an index of its failure. And thus the text *is* a failure.

However, this comment (together with several unrecorded others; for which you will have to take my word) is, in itself, an index of the text's success: in claiming "failure" for itself, the text initiated responses which, by their very existence, throw into relief the way that texts are normally written and read as implicitly claiming their own success. Such a standard reading must be inimicable to a truly successful reflexive practice; and therefore the success of such a practice must depend, to some degree, on its failure. Essentially: in order to succeed it has to fail; and in order (successfully) to fail it must succeed.

CHAPTER FOUR

1. Both of these versions of replication are often represented as far more complex and differentiated than they appear here. For instance, Collins's version has been expanded to take account of the degree to which replicability is perceived as problematic in different areas of scientific activity. In uncontroversial areas (such as laser building) replication works in much the way it is supposed to work in the standard version while in controversial areas (such as gravity wave detection or experimental parapsychology), where the nature or even the existence of the phenomena are in doubt, replication becomes problematised (Collins 1978b, 1984b, 1985). However, when Collins's version of replication is used as a resource in didactic texts (e.g.,

Collins 1982b, 1983a; Mulkay 1979a) or in polemics (e.g., Collins 1982d), the kind of gloss I have given, which emphasises the problematic nature of replication as a *contrast* to the "naivety" of the standard version, is generally used.

2. In 1982 I interviewed all the people most closely associated with the claim. For details of the manner in which the interviews were carried out and of the transcription conventions used, see the Appendix.

3. This comment may justly be taken as a summary of Collins's stated views on reflexivity; see for instance, Collins 1981e:216 (for a quotation, see note 20, below), 1982c:140, 1983a:101; Collins and Pinch 1982:190. For an examination of these views, see Chapter Two, COLLINS. See also Oehler 1983.

4. For similar declarations of the importance of the standard version of replication for sociology more generally, see Collins 1976:2 and 1983b:73.

5. The particular number and order of these stages of demarcation are not, it seems, crucial:

> This search procedure could be divided up in a number of different ways, and more or less steps might be involved. (Collins 1978b:2)

> The exact number and nature of the stages would be arbitrary to some extent, but any sensible scheme would filter down from general to more specific sorting criteria. (Collins 1985:38)

Collins (1985) demonstrates this arbitrariness by adding a new second stage concerning scientificity and moving the previous Stage Two (about experiments) to fourth place. In the analysis which follows I take some advantage of this potential for flexibility.

6. The question of how many studies are needed is dealt with in Stage Six.

7. As these biographical details, here and throughout Stage Three, are quotations from a 1981 publication they are, of course, out-of-date; and even more so than these researchers' self-descriptions in "Introducing the Core Set . . ." in Chapter One. To bring you up to date, Travis is now once again working with Collins at Bath as a research fellow on a project in the British ESRC's current initiative on science studies and science policy. He has recently completed his thesis. (Note dated February 1988.)

8. My attendance at the series of inaccurately described Discourse Analysis Workshops initiated by Mulkay (see the Appendix for details) has no doubt helped to foster this erroneous impression.

9. Collins is no longer the Convenor, is now a Senior Lecturer, and has published a *book* (1985) using case material from physics and from parapsychology. (Note dated February 1987.)

10. Pickering has since published his research (1984) and has been temporarily employed at MIT and at the Institute for Advanced Study, Princeton. He is now at the University of Illinois at Urbana-Champaign. (Note dated February 1988.)

11. Harvey's study is now complete. (Note dated December 1984.)

12. Pinch is now a lecturer in sociology at the University of York. He has long since completed and published his study of solar-neutrino astronomy (1986). (Note dated February 1987.)

13. For instance in the introduction to *Knowledge and Controversy:*

This collection, it is hoped, in addition to its substantive contribution, will reveal clearly the flourishing empirical programme associated with relativism and thereby obviate the necessity for further defences and reaffirmations. (Collins 1981b:4)

14. Collins: Letter, March 1983. See note 15.

15. It is interesting that neither in his commentary on the first draft (Letter, March 1983) nor elsewhere does Collins give any indication of what kind of alternative criteria there might be. Thus, when he indicates that the original "Six Stages" (Ashmore 1983) is not a proper reflexive copy of SSK relativist work he seems to be saying that it fails because it treats what were only supposed to be "hypotheses" as a definitive set of criteria. That is, it is not a competent copy because it copies the original too closely. This would seem to imply that this present version is a more competent copy because it does not follow the original so closely. However, as this looseness is precisely what Collins stresses in his later adaptations of the schema (1978b, 1985; see note 5), my attempt to do the same may suggest, once again, that I am guilty of overcopying and thus of incompetence. See Stage Four for further discussion of the problematic nature of copies.

16. The significance of this interesting punctuation is examined in detail elsewhere (Ashmore 1985:279–80). Briefly, both Travis's question mark and Collins's exclamation mark are devices for the recognition of the paradoxical nature of replicating replication, but whereas Travis's punctuation displays a certain openness to the phenomenon, Collins's attempts to achieve closure.

17. In a reply to a critic of his programme, Collins's interpretative methods seem to fit his own analysis of the strategy of an originator faced with the challenge of a negative replication. This analysis, suitably modified, is as follows:

> [Researchers] who claim to find effects will not accept negative results arising out of [Studies] which were not "identical" to their own. Non-identity may be claimed by questioning the "competence" of secondary [researchers]. (Collins 1976:9)

The criticism (Gieryn 1982a) to which Collins responds is of his originality claim rather than his replication claim. It takes the form of an accusation of "redundance" (mere replication) and in doing so uses a triangulation argument to claim the production of similar findings from different methods:

> The relativist/constructivist programme is neither new nor preferable to other theoretical orientations in the sociology of science. Its empirical conclusions are consistent with, and occasionally anticipated by, at least one voice from the past [Merton] . . . . More importantly, the distinctive epistemological premises and methodological imperatives of the . . . programme are not essential to reach these empirical conclusions. (Gieryn 1982a:292–93)

In response to this charge, Collins's strategy is rhetorically to increase the distance between Mertonian research and relativist research. To do this he first selects a particular study to act as a Mertonian exemplar. Then he contrasts its findings with relativist findings on the same topic. Third, he shows that the Mertonian conclusions are not only entirely different but are also wrong. Finally he offers an explanation, in terms of a lack of competence, to account for their inadequacy. By these means he not only rebuts Gieryn's charge of redundance; but more important, in establishing the "nonidentity" of the Mertonian exemplar in this way, Collins succeeds in rebutting the study's implied claim to have negatively replicated his own work. This is because the chosen exemplar is a Mertonian study of *replication,* namely, Zuckerman's "Deviant Behavior and Social Control in Science" (1977). The following extract from Collins's reply to Gieryn starts with a quote from Zuckerman's paper:

> "In science, the institutionalized requirement that new contributions be reproducible is the cornerstone of the system of social control . . . . The requirement of reproducibility . . . serves not only to deter departures from cognitive and moral norms but also makes for the detection of error and deviance" [Zuckerman 1977:92].
>
> . . . it is the epistemology—the reproducibility of scientific contributions—that is supposed to be the very *cornerstone* of the norms. Seeing this, it is quite remarkable that Gieryn should say that the norms precipitate views about science which are similar to those which emerge out of the relativist programme. One of the most well *replicated* outcomes of that programme concerns the social negotiation of reproducibility. One thing that the programme has shown above all, is that reproducibility is not the "epistemologists' stone," nor the Mertonian's cornerstone. A more marked difference in two programmes would be hard to find. (Collins 1982d:304)

To Gieryn Collins is saying, How when we are clearly so different can you possibly maintain we are the same? To Zuckerman he is saying, We differ; the difference is that I am right, as evidenced by my findings being "well replicated" and you are wrong, as evidenced by what these same right-because-replicated findings say, that is, "reproducibility is not . . . the Mertonian's cornerstone." Collins's next step is to address the problem of how Zuckerman came to be so wrong. In other words, what is responsible for her "noncompetence?" "It is a question of the integrity of one's approach to the data of science and the vigour with which sociological analysis should be pursued . . . . Appropriate vigour requires . . . that [reproducibility] be seen as problematic" (1982d:304). Having established the source of Zuckerman's negative result—the noncompetence of "analytical lethargy" (1982d:304) brought on by an overly commonsensical attitude to science—Collins has effectively achieved a state of nonidentity between Zuckerman's paper and his own replication studies. This state is expressed in practice as distinctive schools or programmes that are incommensurable:

> Through their *practice* it is easy to see that the differences in origin, focus and philosophy between the Mertonian school and the relativist school are not only apparent but real. (1982d:304)

Another way to appreciate this interpretation of Collins's argument is to compare it with his own prediction of how he would react to a claim for negative replication, as given in interview:

C: Anybody who goes and looks will see the same things; and if you find that

they do that's really great and if you find that they don't then I'd be happy to say that they didn't look properly although I haven't actually come to that point yet, because nobody seems to have wanted to say the opposite yet when they've actually gone and looked.
(HC 1718–1802)

Collins certainly seems to have been happy to say that Zuckerman didn't look properly. However, his perception of nobody, including Zuckerman, having yet wanted to say the opposite is possibly more fundamental. It is easy to overlook work that could represent a competitive negative result, if it can be implicitly written off as nonidentical. As far as I know, Zuckerman has not claimed (or even wanted to claim) that her "Deviance" paper constitutes a negative replication of Collins's work. The argument does not require explicit claims to be made, however. It is perceptions of similarity and difference that are at issue. A plausible account for Zuckerman's silence is that, like Collins, she perceives their work as so totally dissimilar that the possibility of competitive results simply does not arise.

18. Jorge Luis Borges, in his story "Pierre Menard, Author of the *Quixote*," inverts this sequence of interpretation. Borges shows how morphologically *identical* entities (Cervantes' *Quixote* and Menard's *Quixote*) can be subject to radically different interpretations: "Cervantes' text and Menard's are verbally identical, but the second is almost infinitely richer" (1970b:69). For two texts that analyse replication by way of an analysis of Borges' analysis of Menard's and Cervantes' identical but different texts, see Mulkay (1988) "Don Quixote's Double: A Self-Exemplifying Text," and Mulkay (1985, ch.4), "Don Quixote's Double: A Self-Exemplifying Text." See note 19.

19. Two other candidate-replicators of Collins's replication studies are Mulkay's "Don Quixote's Double" (1988; 1985, ch.4; see note 18). The final sections of Mulkay's texts discuss the ways in which they are themselves examples of that of which they speak in that they too make similarity/difference attributions and they too can be considered candidate-replicators (though Mulkay does not use this term) of Collins's work. Clearly, this self-referential attention makes these texts suspiciously similar to the text you are reading. Moreover, the authors' sociocognitive relationship is obviously far too close for them to be able to achieve a sufficient degree of mutual independence for the work of the one to validate the work of the other. Unfortunately, we seem doomed to the ignominious relationship of mere replication. The only question, of course, is where each of us stands in this relationship. Should we come to blows over this, it is comforting to know that our deteriorating relationship should improve the value of our work.

20. My prescription is to treat the social world as real, and as something about which we can have sound data, whereas we should treat the natural world as something problematic—a social construct rather than something real. (Collins 1981e:216)

For other expositions of Special Relativism, see the works cited in note 3.

21. Collins: Letter, March 1983. Collins is not of course responding to *this* version of "The Six Stages." As responses to this version could only be incorporated in yet another variant, and as this present text is at least the fourth (see also Ashmore

1983; 1985, ch.3; 1988), I do not feel inclined to extend the regress any further. I'm sorry, but there it is.

22. See Chapter Six for a treatment of writings in which a positive approach to reflexivity is advocated.

CHAPTER FIVE

1. *Lehninger* is a pseudonym of an SSK participant and *L* is thus his initial. *C* is the initial of the pseudonym of the interviewer in use in this chapter. All the pseudonyms are indicated by italics. I am using pseudonyms to accentuate the parodic style of the chapter. This is possible because both the Mulkay and Gilbert and the Potter projects in discourse analysis use pseudonyms liberally—far more so than do most other research projects in SSK. Outside of discourse analysis, perhaps the most pseudonymised SSK project is by Law, Callon, and Williams (Callon and Law 1982; Law and Williams 1982; Williams and Law 1980). Their scientists get called "Gladstone" and "Disraeli" and their geographical locations "Chinatown" and "Stiftung." I have taken over these authors' formats quite directly for my own pseudonymising purposes. Thus, for instance, M***** becomes *Mitchell* and Y*** becomes *Minstertown*. But why *Mitchell*? Why not *Pitt, Baldwin* or *Thatcher*? Well, being impatient with this whole rather absurd practice of anonymising, supposedly in the interests of conventional confidentiality, I decided to make my parody of this practice directly subversive of it. To this end, for the pseudonym of each relevant SSK participant, I have chosen the real name of one of the scientist-participants studied by that researcher. Although I have followed this policy consistently for all SSK researchers mentioned in this chapter (but see below for a qualification), including those who have not pseudonymised their subjects, the following interesting considerations only apply to those who have done so.

First, of course, this scheme provides only a very limited degree of anonymity because each practitioner will have no difficulty in recognising his or her own pseudonym. It is also highly likely that they will find it just as easy to discover each others' real names. In a study of this kind, where one's subjects are part of one's audience, pseudonymising cannot hope to work successfully. This built-in lack of success should, it seems, have one of two consequences: either the act of recognition of another sociologist's real name will consist of a simple translation from the relevant scientist's real name; or such acts will be the result of inferences from the obvious textual clues I have provided. In the first case, the real name of the scientist must have been known in advance. In the second case, in the process of discovering the real name of the sociologist, our detective will find him or herself, willy-nilly, in possession of the secret real name of a scientist previously pseudonymised by that same sociologist. In either case, then, this system of antipseudonyms should "blow the gaffe" on the whole charade: either one has to admit that one knew all along—as the inventor of the system, I hereby admit that such advance knowledge was used in its construction—or one learns that there was nothing of much world-shattering interest to learn. For this dastardly plan to work, my efforts at pseudonymisation have to fail. I hope this note has assisted in the success of this failure. If, however, the failure fails, frustrated readers can find a full listing of names and pseudonyms elsewhere in this book.

NOTES TO PAGES 140-147

The qualification mentioned above is this: being obviously unable to falsify the names of the authors of published (or unpublished-but-publication-like) texts, pseudonyms are only appended to "private" texts, such as letters, interview transcripts, research proposals, and the like.

2. This paragraph is in triple inverted commas to indicate that it is a quasi-plagiarised topic-adjusted quotation. These parodic paraphrases, which recur at intervals throughout this chapter, are designated by exaggerated punctuation and a footnote which informs readers of their origins. In this case, the original text is the opening paragraph of Mulkay, Potter, and Yearley (1983:171). I use two sets of inverted commas for these passages to indicate that, although they are acknowledged quotations and so are legitimately surrounded with quotation marks, they are also not so much quotations as "quotations," and should therefore be framed with the kind of inverted commas used for designating doubt or irony, that is, scare quotes.

3. From Gilbert and Mulkay 1984a:19. The heading of section B is a direct quotation from Mulkay and Gilbert 1982a:166.

4. The paper was the third draft of "Warranting Scientific Belief" (Gilbert and Mulkay 1982). The complete series of drafts, and the referees' comments on this one, are discussed later. Full nonpublication details are given in the Appendix.

5. From Gilbert and Mulkay 1982:390–91.

6. This text uses the label "traditional" in two senses. The first is the sense in which I am using it here, that is, to designate all "analyses of action and belief" (Mulkay 1981) whether, in SSK terms, these are the wrong and outmoded kind carried out in Mertonian sociology or in rationalist philosophy, or whether they are the correct and up-to-date kind carried out in SSK. The second sense is used to label only the first of these two styles.

7. Interestingly, Don McCloskey informs me that a colleague of his did precisely this; though not, he thinks, for such advanced postmodern reasons.

8. Two examples are Gieryn 1982b:333 and Shapin 1984b:127.

9. A rather different appreciation of Blissett's study appears in Mulkay's earlier review of the sociology of science (1980a:94–98).

10. Gilbert and Mulkay 1982; Mulkay and Gilbert 1981b, 1983, 1984; Potter 1984; Potter and Mulkay 1982.

11. From Mulkay and Gilbert 1981b:16–17 and also from Gilbert and Mulkay 1984a:100–101.

12. In fact, as I have mentioned, Gilbert and Mulkay wrote four such papers. The discrepancy can be accounted for by noticing that the fourth—"The Truth Will Out" (Mulkay and Gilbert 1981b)—was not published as a journal article but as a chapter in *Opening Pandora's Box* (Gilbert and Mulkay 1984a).

13. Despite these principled problems with the use of the labels "methodological" and "substantive," they continue to be used not only by discourse analysts but by their critics. One reviewer of the other *Opening Pandora's Box* (Gilbert and Mulkay 1984a) uses the labels to divide the text into a good "substantive contribution to the research literature" and a bad "methodological tract" (Robbins 1984:452).

14. The issue of whether this move is a move beyond interpretation is a lively aspect of the debate between the critics and the proponents of discourse analysis. While Mulkay's early argument (1981) can be, and indeed has been, read as suggesting that the discursive turn removes the need to interpret data—see Collins 1983a:102 and

Shapin 1984b:128 for critiques along these lines—Potter has recently argued that discourse analysis is an intensely interpretive practice—and a jolly good thing that it is too. See Potter 1987:172–73 and 1988:50.

15. Even Kuhn recognises the simple variability between the accounts of individual scientists (Kuhn 1977c). For a much more radical assessment of the range of variability in accounts of theory choice, see Potter 1984 and Mulkay and Gilbert 1984, both of which situate their discussion in an exposition and criticism of Kuhn's essay.

16. *Price* first wrote to *Lehninger* who passed *Price's* letter to *Mitchell* who wrote back to *Price* (*Mitchell* to *Price,* 21 April 1981:1).

17. It should be noticed, however, that the final version (or at any rate the later one) is extract D.1 from Gilbert and Mulkay 1984a, whereas the earlier is extract D.18 from Mulkay and Gilbert 1982c. This temporal ordering suggests that the text was altered from a clear, strong version of type [3] variability in 1982 to a less clear, less strong formulation in 1984. Strange.

18. Referee B recommended rejection.

19. To my knowledge, there has been very little written on nonexistence accounting even though this interpretative device seems to be in much demand. In fact, the only mention of it I have found is this: "As befits its subject-matter, there has been nothing (yet) written on this seemingly highly prevalent form of accounting" (Ashmore 1985:491, n.60). However, a sophisticated analysis of the cultural significance of nothing certainly does exist (Rotman 1987).

20. The change to this sentence is from

For we can hardly conclude that a scientist accepted a theory solely because of experimental evidence, if he maintains elsewhere that such evidence is essentially inconclusive. (WSB Draft 3:13)

To

For we can hardly conclude that a scientist accepted that such evidence is essentially inconclusive or that the cognitive consensus to which he claims to belong is simply a result of what people happen to be willing to believe at the moment. (Gilbert and Mulkay 1982:393)

It is noticeable that the later published version has lost the contrast structure of the earlier one in which it is argued that, if a scientist puts forward an empiricist account of theory choice and elsewhere articulates a contingent account, we can hardly conclude that the empiricist account is correct. The later sentence, in contrast, appears to say that we can hardly conclude that a contingent version is correct or that another contingent version is correct; which frankly does not make a great deal of sense. The second contingent account mentioned in the later sentence is a reference to a further quotation from the same biochemist which is inserted into the published version of the text immediately before the start of the relevant passage. The insertion of this new quotation can plausibly be interpreted as an attempt to strengthen the contrast between the empiricist and contingent accounts in response to Referee B's criticisms. However, as I have mentioned, in the published version of sentence 4, the required contrast is missing altogether as there is no longer any reference at all to the biochemist's empiricist version. When I questioned one of the authors about this absence, he said that he agreed with me about the loss of contrast. His explanation for this state of affairs was that, "it could be an error or it might be just a deliberately nonsensical formulation which we thought the referee would appreciate" (paraphrase of private telephonic communication with *Mitchell*, 12 March 1985).

21. But remember that extracts D.2, D.6, and D.10 are by Collins, extracts D.3 and D.11 are by Woolgar, and extracts D.7 and D.9 are by Shapin.

22. And with the help of the rhetorical device of *reductio ad absurdam*.

23. From Gilbert and Mulkay 1984a:11 (extract D.1).

24. There is a third low variability account (extract D.17) in which *Price* claims continuity in personal biographies, which is rather less significant than the others in the context of this conclusion.

25. At this point, and perhaps not for the first time, the necessary and fascinating confusion of levels involved in this account provides for what Hofstadter (1980) calls a "strange loop," such that at this point, and perhaps not for the first time, the writing turns back on itself and begins to repeat, coda-like, but perhaps in a different key (on a different level), all that has gone before. Another one of Hofstadter's examples of logicomathematical reflexivity is the "nested structure." These are structures which contain themselves, or versions of themselves, as a constituent part of what they are. This study of variability accounting can be considered just such a nested structure. This aspect of the text is not simply a matter of its style or form alone. Such stylistic or formal possibilities seem to be predicated on a prior matter of method. Maybe it is only with the reflexive move, as developed, for instance, in this thesis; that is, with the move beyond simple meta-analysis and toward a form of reflexivity that is permanently "part of the very order which it describes" (Brannigan 1981) that a creative and liberating (and above all, *deliberate*) confusion of levels can provide for such interesting formal textual features.

26. Of course, an SSK *analyst* of such acts would tend to describe them differently; as, for instance, negotiating the character of phenomena (Collins 1975), acting in accordance with social and cognitive interests (MacKenzie 1978), attempting to gain credibility (Latour and Woolgar 1979; Williams and Law 1980), or as the operation of analytic comparison (Ashmore 1989).

27. A reference to Russell and Whitehead's (1910) *Principia Mathematica*.

28. The famous metamathematician who used self-reference in an extremely clever way to come to the following conclusion: that "*Principia Mathematica* and related systems," that is, all complex systematisations of formal domains, were inconsistent if complete and incomplete if consistent.

29. This quotation appeared as the epigraph to Freudenthal's (1984) critique of SSK.

30. The way that metamathematicians have dealt with paradox and with self-reference would make a nice comparative study in the sociology of mathematics to set alongside those several which have concentrated on Euler's theorem and the debate over polyhedra in the late nineteenth century (Bloor 1976, 1978; Barnes and Law 1976; Lakatos 1976; Pawson and Tilley 1982). It would seem that Russell with his theory of types is the quintessential "monster-barrer."

31. The answer to this is either: Neither, I mean both, but that's a contradiction, I mean that's a paradox, I'm confused, get rid of the pathological monster, if you're SOBER, or: Both and neither and why not, if you're less obsessed with control. (The Author gives a version of this latter answer a few lines further on.)

32. See note 33.

33. This and the phrase immediately above (or below for readers of note 32) is the inverse of the famous apocryphal Oxford philosophy examination question.

34. This text is probably apocryphal, though some scholars are of the opinion that Ashmore 1989, Chapter Two, lamentably incomplete as it is, may be modelled upon it (Borges 1999: appendix 85).

35. A misquotation from Barth 1972.

36. I fear the Other Author never was persuaded to do it properly, though one could try Chapter Seven.

CHAPTER SIX

1. General expositions of ethnomethodology include Leiter 1980, Mehan and Wood 1975, and Heritage 1984. Texts which deal specifically with The Problem include McHoul 1981 and 1982, Heritage 1978, Hester 1981, and Atkinson and Drew 1979, chapter 1. Texts which focus on indexicality include Attewell 1974 and Barnes and Law 1976. Those which concentrate on reflexivity include Mehan and Wood 1975, Chua 1974, and Walker 1977. For different versions of ethnomethodology of science see Lynch 1982 and 1984; Lynch, Livingston, and Garfinkel 1983; and Garfinkel, Lynch, and Livingston 1981.

2. See also Chapter Three.

3. The use of "provide for" provides for a reader/hearer's apprehension of the discourse of the practical reasoner as not reflexively contravening the constraints of that discourse. It is a rhetoric designed to be heard as saying, "This is not an ontological claim about what is in the world (or in the text); nor is it an epistemological claim about the correctness of certain interpretations of the world (or of the text)." Woolgar has "elucidated" his usage in the following note. (I trust that your reading of Woolgar's note will provide for your reading of my note as a proper elucidation of Woolgar's mere attempt at elucidation.)

> My usage of "provides for" is recurrent in the subsequent analysis and merits some elucidation. By saying that a feature of textual organisation "provides for" a certain reading, I mean simply that a certain interpretation or set of meanings is made possible. This is not to claim that this is the only reading which might in practice be arrived at, nor am I able to cite evidence categorically demonstrating that "most people" did read it this way. Rather, my aim is to specify the characteristics of the text which could lead to one particular and plausible reading. (1980:266–67, n.42)

4. In at least one of these texts Woolgar specifically denies this characterisation: "My argument is not a covert attempt to promote any of the versions of ethnomethodological practice currently on offer . . . " (1983a:263).

5. The first paper in this sequence, Woolgar's "Interests and Explanation in the Social Study of Science" (1981b), took MacKenzie's work (1978, 1981a) on the role of social interests in the development of early twentieth century statistical theory as its exemplar of interests model explanation. For an analysis of how the Woolgar/Barnes debate was structured in terms of each side's differing understandings of reflexivity, see McKinlay 1986.

6. The notion of "sensitizing device" bears comparison to Collins's "methodological astringent" (1983a:102); see Chapter Two, COLLINS. In interview, Woolgar produced the following antitechnical account, in which he used the metaphorical formulation of "technical laxative":

> W: And it's interesting that, that I think MacKenzie's paper [1981b] says, "We should look at the—Steve is saying we should look at the interests first as a . . . before we get onto the, the major problems."
> A: Yes.
> W: Um. Which is *not* what I intend at all.
> A: No.
> W: It's not like a technical laxative.
> A: No.
> W: You know . . .
> A: (Laughter)
> W: . . . "make sure that all, all your, that all the scientists' work on how, on constructing interests is first got absolutely . . . " It's not a sort of under-labourer argument you know.
> A: No.
> W: Um.
> A: No, no.
> W: "Get that right first, *then* go, go and do your interests explanation."
> A: Yeah, "*then* everything (will be alright)."
> W: Right, because it turns it into (if you like), just a merely technical . . .
> (SW 5508–14)

Three further antitechnical extracts appear in the interview transcript, on pages 16, 33, and 35.

7. Note that in insisting that Woolgar is also guilty of constructive theorizing, Barnes can be read as saying that because "Interests and Explanation" is an explanation of explanation, Woolgar is therefore "employing the mode in analyzing the mode" (Barnes 1981a:493). As Barnes agrees with such activity (see Second Text 6), this conclusion would cut much of the critical ground from under his feet; Woolgar would simply be doing what Barnes approves of. Perhaps this is why this conclusion is not drawn in Barnes's text.

8. See, for example, the unanimity of SSK practitioners on the matter of the value of empirical work, as presented in Chapter Four.

9. Cf. Collins (1983a:102) on "doing the sociology of science as opposed to talking about it." This passage is discussed in Chapter Two, COLLINS.

10. Attempts to investigate the use of "accounts" as reflective can be regarded as a denial of the obvious, and hence absurd. (Woolgar 1981c:507–8)

> [In the constitutive position on accounts] the reality is created in virtue of the accounting done by actors. This position rarely appears in programmatic pronouncements in the social study of science; when it does, it is perceived as absurd. (Woolgar 1983a:246)

11. The least subtle sociological ironies are content to equate the presumed actual character of the underlying reality with their own account . . . . In each case the tell-tale sign is the appearance . . . of the word "actually." (Woolgar 1983a:252)

12. While there is no necessity to understand the context or the referents of these interview selections, I see no reason to religiously withhold such interesting information. Extracts 1 and 2 are responses to "Do you see yourself as a lone voice in the field?" Extracts 3 and 4 are replies to a query about the role that Woolgar felt he played in SSK. The referent in extract 5 is the idea that a sociology of knowledge which is both critical and reflexive is heading for the infinite regress (Woolgar 1983a:254–55). The topic of extract 6 is a question about what kind of discursive work is allowable and what isn't. The "X" in extracts 7 and 8 replaces the word "line" (or "lines") which is a metaphor for the point at which analysts differentially decide to stop doubting (cf. Blum 1970).

13. For Woolgar's specific versions see Chapter Two, S. Woolgar. The reflexive arguments examined and advocated in this book also, of course, act as a justification and legitimation of its author's particular choice of topic.

14. For a selection of such arguments in use see Chapter One, "Unsatisfactory Answers." For a brief description see Chapter One, note 6.

15. The practical/scholastic distinction is also wielded for purposes of differentiation among metascientists themselves, and strikingly so by the SSK/strong programme side of Woolgar's "academic debate." Philosophers (i.e., them) are pictured as elite professionals indulging in armchair speculation while sociologists (i.e., us) come over as honest artisans earning their well-earned crusts by going out into the real world and getting their hands dirty actually visiting those who live there—in this case, the downtrodden, spat-upon, exploited masses of nuclear physicists and Nobel Prize–winning biochemists. For a less fanciful version, and a small attempt to answer the why question, see Chapter One, page 5.

16. . . . of some fourteenth-century College in the shadow of the dreaming spires (or by the limpid waters of the Backs) while partaking of Fino sherry and Arrowroot biscuits of a winter's afternoon, with the weak sun slowly dipping behind the Cathedral, casting deep shadows (as deep as the Professors' thoughts) on the Quad where, minutes before, groups of young, bright undergraduates had been relaxing in the unseasonal sunshine, after (or before) a particularly stimulating seminar on the nature of scientific knowledge given by the wise old rationalist with his distinguished silver hair (or the clever youngish strong programmer with his intelligent disdain for formality), after which bright young Alistair (soon to get a first in Greats) and young bright Phillipa (soon to get a first in Moderns), troubled by the plight but impressed by the grit of those unsung labourers in the mines and factories of Knowledge, fully intend to get up a petition on behalf of natural scientists everywhere.

17. One example of sameness/difference accounting is the polemic between SSK and rationalist philosophy as discussed in Chapter One, page 5, and in note 15 above. Here the construction of difference is made on the basis of a perceived similarity of topic. Another example is the negotiation over replication discussed in Chapter Four. In this case the interpretative task is the construction of a similarity which must involve a certain degree of perceived difference.

18. Further textual evidence of Woolgar's programmatic alignments is not hard to find. Here is just a selection of pro-strong programme comments:

Having admirably drawn attention to the need to analyze scientific content . . . (1981b:388)

We should at least be committed . . . *we* can most fruitfully proceed . . . (1981b: 388–89; my emphases)

. . . my general sympathy for the strong programme . . . an intriguing and important tradition . . . the issues raised . . . far outstrip the achievements of previously dominant approaches . . . its vigorous contribution . . . the clarity of the explanatory format . . . this eminently successful style of sociology of science . . . (1981c:510)

But perhaps these are merely "occasioned pronouncements." See Second Text 9 and 10.

19. A selection of such texts is presented in Woolgar's entry in Chapter Two to enable readers to carry out this piece of reflexive analysis for themselves.

20. The Silence/Science couple comes from Woolgar's interview:

A: Here's some hypothetical criticisms, right, of Woolgar: "The logical end product of your kind of work or generally ethnomethodology-influenced work, is silence."
W: (Pause) Science?
A: Silence.
W: Silence; oh I'm sorry. Um, because . . .
A: (Laughter) I didn't mean that.
W: . . . no, I've had that one too. [Amused]
A: Oh, right. [Also amused]
(SW 5701–3)

BIBLIOGRAPHY

Adair, J. G. 1973. *The Human Subject: The Social Psychology of the Psychological Experiment.* Boston: Little, Brown.

Adorno, Theodor W. 1976. Sociology and empirical research. In P. Connerton, ed. *Critical Sociology.* (Harmondsworth, Middx.: Penguin Books) 1976:237–76. (First published 1957.)

Almond, Gabriel A. 1966. Political theory and political science. *American Political Science Review* 60:869–79.

Alter, Robert. 1975. *Partial Magic: The Novel as a Self-Conscious Genre.* Berkeley and Los Angeles: University of California Press.

Althusser, Louis, and Etienne Balibar. 1977. *Reading "Capital."* London: New Left Books. (First published 1970.)

Anderson, Digby C. 1978. Some organizational features in the local production of a plausible text. *Philosophy of the Social Sciences* 8:113–35.

Ashmore, Malcolm. 1983. The six stages, or the life and opinions of a replication claim. University of York. Typescript. (Similar texts appear as Ashmore 1985, ch.3; Ashmore 1988; and Ashmore 1989, ch.4.)

Ashmore, Malcolm. 1985. A question of reflexivity: Wrighting sociology of scientific knowledge. DPhil dissertation, University of York.

Ashmore, Malcolm. 1988. The life and opinions of a replication claim: Reflexivity and symmetry in the sociology of scientific knowledge. In Woolgar 1988a: 125–53. (Similar texts appear as Ashmore 1983; Ashmore 1985, ch.3; and Ashmore 1989, ch.4.)

Ashmore, Malcolm. 1989. *The Reflexive Thesis: Wrighting Sociology of Scientific Knowledge.* Chicago and London: University of Chicago Press.

Ashmore, Malcolm, Michael Mulkay, and Trevor Pinch. 1989. *Health and Efficiency: A Sociology of Health Economics.* Milton Keynes, Bucks.: Open University Press.

Asimov, Isaac. 1975. *Asimov's Biographical Encyclopedia of Science and Technology.* London: Pan Books.

Atkinson, J. Maxwell, and Paul Drew. 1979. *Order in Court: The Organisation of Verbal Interaction in Judicial Settings.* London: Macmillan.

Attewell, Paul. 1974. Ethnomethodology since Garfinkel. *Theory and Society* 1: 179–210.

Babcock, Barbara A. 1980a. *Signs about Signs: The Semiotics of Self-Reference.* Special issue of *Semiotica* 30(1/2).

Babcock, Barbara A. 1980b. Reflexivity: Definitions and discriminations. *Semiotica* 30:1–14.

Baldamus, W. 1976. *The Structure of Sociological Inference*. London: Martin Robertson.

Baltzell, E. Digby. 1972. Epilogue: To be a phoenix: Reflections on two noisy ages of prose. *American Journal of Sociology* 78:211–29. (This volume of the *AJS* is reprinted as *Varieties of Political Expression in Sociology*. [Chicago and London: University of Chicago Press] 1972.)

Bannister, Don. 1970. Comment. In R. Borger and F. Cioffi, eds. *Explanation in the Behavioural Sciences*. (Cambridge: Cambridge University Press) 1970: 411–18.

Barnes, Barry. 1969. Paradigms: Scientific and social. *Man* (NS) 4:94–102.

Barnes, Barry. 1974. *Scientific Knowledge and Sociological Theory*. London: Routledge and Kegan Paul.

Barnes, Barry. 1977. *Interests and the Growth of Knowledge*. London: Routledge and Kegan Paul.

Barnes, Barry. 1981a. On the "hows" and "whys" of cultural change. (Response to Woolgar.) *Social Studies of Science* 11:481–98.

Barnes, Barry. 1981b. On the conventional character of knowledge and cognition. *Philosophy of the Social Sciences* 11:303–33. (Reprinted in Knorr-Cetina and Mulkay 1983:19–51.)

Barnes, Barry. 1982a. *T. S. Kuhn and Social Science*. London: Macmillan.

Barnes, Barry. 1982b. On the extensions of concepts and the growth of knowledge. *Sociological Review* 30:23–44.

Barnes, Barry. 1983. Social life as bootstrapped induction. *Sociology* 17:524–45.

Barnes, Barry, and David Bloor. 1982. Relativism, rationalism and the sociology of knowledge. In Hollis and Lukes 1982:21–47.

Barnes, Barry, and R. G. A. Dolby. 1970. The scientific ethos: A deviant viewpoint. *European Journal of Sociology* 11:3–25.

Barnes, Barry, and David Edge, eds. 1982. *Science in Context: Readings in the Sociology of Science*. Milton Keynes, Bucks.: Open University Press.

Barnes, Barry, and John Law. 1976. Whatever should be done with indexical expressions? *Theory and Society* 3:223–37. (Reprinted in Collins 1982a:59–73.)

Barnes, Barry, and Donald MacKenzie. 1979. On the role of interests in scientific change. In Wallis 1979:49–66.

Barnes, Barry, and Steven Shapin, eds. 1979. *Natural Order: Historical Studies of Scientific Culture*. London and Beverly Hills, Calif.: Sage.

Barth, John. 1972. *Lost in the Funhouse*. Harmondsworth, Middx.: Penguin Books.

Barth, John. 1979. *LETTERS*. London: Secker and Warburg.

Barthes, Roland. 1983. *Barthes: Selected Writings*. Edited by Susan Sontag. London: Fontana.

Bartlett, Steven J., and Peter Suber, eds. 1987. *Self-Reference: Reflections on Reflexivity*. Dordrecht: Martinus Nijhoff.

Baumberger, J. 1977. No Kuhnian revolution in economics. *Journal of Economic Issues* 11:1–20.

Bazerman, Charles. 1981. What written knowledge does: Three examples of academic discourse. *Philosophy of the Social Sciences* 11:361–87.

Bell, Colin, and Howard Newby. 1981. Narcissism or reflexivity in modern sociology. *The Polish Sociological Bulletin* 1:3–19.

Ben-David, Joseph. 1971. *The Scientist's Role in Society: A Comparative Study.* Englewood Cliffs, N.J.: Prentice-Hall.

Berger, John. 1972. *Ways of Seeing.* Harmondsworth, Middx.: Penguin Books.

Berger, Peter. 1969. *A Rumour of Angels.* Harmondsworth, Middx.: Penguin Books.

Bernstein, Richard J. 1976. *The Restructuring of Social and Political Theory.* Oxford: Blackwell.

Bernstein, Richard J. 1983. *Beyond Objectivism and Relativism: Science, Hermeneutics and Practice.* Oxford: Blackwell.

Bhaskar, Roy. 1978. *A Realist Theory of Science.* Hassocks, Sussex: Harvester Press.

Bijker, Wiebe, Thomas Hughes, and Trevor Pinch, eds. 1987. *The Social Construction of Technological Systems: New Directions in the Sociology and History of Technology.* Cambridge, Mass.: MIT Press.

Blissett, Marlan. 1972. *Politics in Science.* Boston: Little, Brown.

Bloom, Allan. 1987. *The Closing of the American Mind: How Higher Education Has Failed Democracy and Impoverished the Souls of Today's Students.* New York: Simon and Schuster.

Bloomfield, Brian P., ed. 1987a. *The Question of Artificial Intelligence: Philosophical and Sociological Perspectives.* London: Croom Helm.

Bloomfield, Brian P. 1987b. The culture of artificial intelligence. In Bloomfield 1987a:59–105.

Bloor, David. 1973. Wittgenstein and Mannheim on the sociology of mathematics. *Studies in the History and Philosophy of Science* 4:173–91. (Reprinted in Collins 1982a:39–57.)

Bloor, David. 1976. *Knowledge and Social Imagery.* London: Routledge and Kegan Paul.

Bloor, David. 1978. Polyhedra and the Abominations of Leviticus. *British Journal for the History of Science* 11:245–71. (Reprinted in Douglas 1982:191–218.)

Bloor, David. 1982a. Durkheim and Mauss revisited: Classification and the sociology of knowledge. *Studies in the History and Philosophy of Science* 13:267–97.

Bloor, David. 1982b. Reply to Gerd Buchdal. *Studies in the History and Philosophy of Science* 13:305–11.

Bloor, David. 1982c. Sociology of (scientific) knowledge. In Bynum and Porter 1982:391–93.

Bloor, David. 1982d. Relativism (methodological). In Bynum and Porter 1982:369.

Bluebond-Langer, Myra. 1978. *The Private Worlds of Dying Children.* Princeton, N.J.: Princeton University Press.

Blum, Alan. 1970. Theorizing. In Douglas 1970:301–19.

Blum, Alan. 1974. *Theorizing.* London: Heinemann.

Blum, Alan, and Peter McHugh. 1984. *Self-Reflection in the Arts and Sciences.* Atlantic Highlands, N.J.: Humanities Press.

Boon, L. 1979. Review of *Knowledge and Social Imagery.* (Bloor 1976.) *British Journal for the Philosophy of Science* 30:195–99.

Borges, Jorge Luis. 1970a. *Labyrinths.* Harmondsworth, Middx.: Penguin Books.

Borges, Jorge Luis. 1970b. Pierre Menard, author of the *Quixote.* In Borges 1970a:62–71.

Borges, Jorge Luis. 1999. *Mazes*. Buenos Aires: Apocrypha Press.

Bourdieu, Pierre. 1975. The specificity of the scientific field and the social conditions of the progress of reason. *Social Science Information* 14:19–47.

Brannigan, Augustine. 1979. The reification of Mendel. *Social Studies of Science* 9:423–54.

Brannigan, Augustine. 1981. *The Social Basis of Scientific Discoveries*. Cambridge: Cambridge University Press.

Briskman, L. B. 1972. Is a Kuhnian analysis applicable to psychology? *Science Studies* 2:87–97.

Bronfenbrenner, Martin. 1971. The "Structure of Revolutions" in economic thought. *History of Political Economy* 3:136–51.

Brown, J. 1984. *Scientific Rationality: The Sociological Turn*. Dordrecht and Boston: Reidel.

Brush, Stephen. 1974. Should the history of science be rated X? *Science* 183 (22 March): 1164–72.

Buchdal, Gerd. 1982. Editorial response to David Bloor (1982a). *Studies in the History and Philosophy of Science* 13:299–304.

Bullock, Alan, and Oliver Stallybrass. 1977. *The Fontana Dictionary of Modern Thought*. London: Fontana Books.

Butterfield, Herbert. 1931. *The Whig Interpretation of History*. London: Bell.

Butterfield, Herbert. 1955. *Man on His Past: The Study of the History of Historical Scholarship*. Cambridge: Cambridge University Press.

Bynum, W., and R. Porter, eds. 1982. *Dictionary of the History of Science*. London: Macmillan.

Callon, Michel. 1980. Struggles and negotiations to define what is problematic and what is not: The socio-logic of translation. In Knorr, Krohn, and Whitley 1980:197–220.

Callon, Michel, and John Law. 1982. On interests and their transformation: Enrolment and counter-enrolment. *Social Studies of Science* 12:615–25.

Callon, Michel, John Law, and Arie Rip, eds. 1986. *Mapping the Dynamics of Science and Technology*. London: Macmillan.

Calvino, Italo. 1982. *If on a Winter's Night a Traveller*. Translated by William Weaver. London: Picador.

Candidate, D. Phil. 1985a. Wrighting knowledge in sociological science by reflexive questioning. PhD dissertation, University of Kroy.

Candidate, D. Phil. 1985b. Wrighting knowledge: The scientific thesis of reflexive sociology. PhD dissertation, University of Kroy.

Carrier, James. 1977. Review of Bloor's *Knowledge and Social Imagery*. *British Journal of Sociology* 28:407.

Carroll, John. 1980. *Sceptical Sociology*. London: Routledge and Kegan Paul.

Caute, David. 1971. *The Illusion*. London: André Deutsch.

Christensen, Inger. 1981. *The Meaning of Metafiction: A Critical Study of Selected Novels by Sterne, Nabokov, Barth and Beckett*. Bergen: Universitetsforlaget.

Chua, Beng-Huat. 1974. On the commitments of ethnomethodology. *Sociological Inquiry* 44:241–56.

Chubin, Daryl. 1982. Collins's programme and the "hardest possible case." *Social Studies of Science* 12:136–39.

Chubin, Daryl, and Sal Restivo. 1983. The "mooting" of science studies: Research programmes and science policy. In Knorr-Cetina and Mulkay 1983:53–83.

Clifford, James, and George E. Marcus, eds. 1986. *Writing Culture: The Poetics and Politics of Ethnography.* Berkeley and Los Angeles: University of California Press.

Cole, Jonathan R., and Harriet Zuckerman. 1975. The emergence of a scientific specialty: The self-exemplifying case of the sociology of science. In L. A. Coser, ed. *The Idea of Social Structure.* (New York: Harcourt Brace Jovanovitch) 1975:139–74.

Collingwood, R. G. 1946. *The Idea of History.* Oxford: Oxford University Press.

Collins, Harry. 1974. The TEA set: Tacit knowledge and scientific networks. *Science Studies* 4:165–86.

Collins, Harry. 1975. The seven sexes: A study in the sociology of a phenomenon or the replication of experiments in physics. *Sociology* 9:205–24.

Collins, Harry. 1976. Upon the replication of scientific findings: A discussion illuminated by the experiences of researchers into parapsychology. *Proceedings of 4S/ISA Conference,* Cornell University, November 1976. ("Virtually reproduced" in S. Braude. *ESP and Psychokinesis: A Philosophical Examination.* [Philadelphia, Pa.: Temple University Press] 1980:41ff.)

Collins, Harry. 1978a. Replication of experiments: A sociological comment. *The Behavioral and Brain Sciences* 3:391–92. (Comment on R. Rosenthal and D. Rubin. 1978. Interpersonal expectancy effects: The first 345 studies. Ibid.: 377–87.)

Collins, Harry. 1978b. Science and the rule of replicability: A sociological study of scientific method. Paper presented at the 144th National Meeting of the AAAS, Washington D.C.

Collins, Harry, ed. 1981a. *Knowledge and Controversy: Studies of Modern Natural Science.* Special issue of *Social Studies of Science* 11(1).

Collins, Harry. 1981b. Stages in the empirical programme of relativism. *Social Studies of Science* 11:3–10. (Introduction to Collins 1981a.)

Collins, Harry. 1981c. Son of seven sexes: The social destruction of a physical phenomenon. *Social Studies of Science* 11:33–62.

Collins, Harry. 1981d. The role of the core-set in modern science: Social contingency with methodological propriety in science. *History of Science* 19:6–19.

Collins, Harry. 1981e. What is TRASP? The radical programme as a methodological imperative. *Philosophy of the Social Sciences* 11:215–24.

Collins, Harry. 1981f. Understanding science. *Fundamenta Scientiae* 2:367–80.

Collins, Harry, ed. 1982a. *Sociology of Scientific Knowledge: A Source Book.* Bath: Bath University Press.

Collins, Harry. 1982b. Replication. In Bynum and Porter 1982:372.

Collins, Harry. 1982c. Special relativism: The natural attitude. *Social Studies of Science* 12:139–43.

Collins, Harry. 1982d. Knowledge, norms and rules in the sociology of science. *Social Studies of Science* 12:299–309.

Collins, Harry. 1983a. An empirical relativist programme in the sociology of scientific knowledge. In Knorr-Cetina and Mulkay 1983:85–113.

Collins, Harry. 1983b. The meaning of lies: Accounts of action and participatory research. In Gilbert and Abell 1983:69–76.

Collins, Harry. 1983c. Concepts and practice of participatory fieldwork. In C. Bell and H. Roberts, eds. *Social Researching*. (London: Routledge and Kegan Paul) 1983:54–69.

Collins, Harry. 1983d. The sociology of scientific knowledge: Studies of contemporary science. *Annual Review of Sociology* 9:265–85.

[Collins, Harry]. 1984a. On behalf of the personae. (An anonymous limerick response to Mulkay's [1984a] play.) *Social Studies of Science* 14:283.

Collins, Harry. 1984b. *When* do scientists prefer to vary their experiments? *Studies in History and Philosophy of Science* 15:169–74.

Collins, Harry. 1985. *Changing Order: Replication and Induction in Scientific Practice*. London and Beverly Hills, Calif.: Sage.

Collins, Harry. 1987a. Expert systems and the science of knowledge. In Bijker, Hughes, and Pinch 1987:329–48.

Collins, Harry. 1987b. Certainty and the public understanding of science: Science on television. *Social Studies of Science* 17:689–713.

Collins, Harry. 1987c. Expert systems, artificial intelligence and the behavioural co-ordinates of skill. In Bloomfield 1987a:258–82.

Collins, Harry. 1987d. Misunderstanding replication? *Social Science Information* 26:451–59.

Collins, Harry, and Graham Cox. 1976. Recovering relativity; Did prophecy fail? *Social Studies of Science* 6:423–44.

Collins, Harry, and Graham Cox. 1977. Relativity revisited: Mrs Keech—a suitable case for special treatment? *Social Studies of Science* 7:372–80.

Collins, Harry, and R. Harrison. 1975. Building a TEA laser: The caprices of communication. *Social Studies of Science* 5:441–50.

Collins, Harry, and Trevor Pinch. 1979. The construction of the paranormal: Nothing unscientific is happening. In Wallis 1979:237–70.

Collins, Harry, and Trevor Pinch. 1982. *Frames of Meaning: The Social Construction of Extraordinary Science*. London: Routledge and Kegan Paul.

Collins, Harry, Trevor Pinch, and Steven Shapin. 1984. Authors' preface. *Social Studies of Science* 14(4):ii.

Colvin, Phyllis. 1985. *The Economic Ideal in British Government: Calculating Costs and Benefits in the 1970s*. Manchester: Manchester University Press.

Cooter, Roger. 1979. The power of the body: The early nineteenth century. In Barnes and Shapin 1979:73–92.

Cooter, Roger. 1980. Deploying "pseudoscience": Then and now. In Hanen, Osler, and Weyant 1980:237–72.

Coover, Robert. 1969. *Pricksongs and Descants*. London: Jonathan Cape.

Coulson, Jessie, ed. 1969. *The Little Oxford Dictionary*. 4th ed. Oxford: Oxford University Press.

Crane, Diana. 1980a. An exploratory study of Kuhnian paradigms in theoretical high energy physics. *Social Studies of Science* 10:23–54.

Crane, Diana. 1980b. Reply to Pickering. *Social Studies of Science* 10:502–6.

Crick, Malcolm. 1982. Anthropological field research, meaning creation and knowledge construction. In Parkin 1982:15–37.

Davis, Murray S. 1971. That's interesting! Towards a phenomenology of sociology and a sociology of phenomenology. *Philosophy of the Social Sciences* 1:309–44.

Dean, John. 1978. Empiricism and relativism—a reappraisal of two key concepts in the social sciences. *Philosophy of the Social Sciences* 8:281–88. (Review of Gellner 1974 and Bloor 1976.)

Dean, John. 1979. Controversy over classification: A case study from the history of botany. In Barnes and Shapin 1979:211–28.

Derrida, Jacques. 1977. Limited Inc abc . . . *Glyph* 2:162–254.

Derrida, Jacques. 1978. *Writing and Difference*. Translated by Alan Bass. London: Routledge and Kegan Paul.

Desmond, A. J. 1979. Designing the dinosaur: Richard Owen's response to Robert Edmond Grant. *Isis* 70:224–34.

Dolby, R. G. A. 1975. What can we usefully learn from the Velikovsky affair? *Social Studies of Science* 5:165–75.

Douglas, Jack D., ed. 1970. *Understanding Everyday Life*. London: Routledge and Kegan Paul.

Douglas, Mary. 1975. *Implicit Meanings*. London: Routledge and Kegan Paul.

Douglas, Mary, ed. 1982. *Essays in the Sociology of Perception*. London: Routledge and Kegan Paul.

Eckberg, D. L., and L. Hill. 1979. The paradigm concept and sociology: A critical review. *American Sociological Review* 44:925–37.

Eco, Umberto. 1983. *The Name of the Rose*. Translated by William Weaver. New York: Harcourt, Brace, Jovanovitch.

Edge, David. 1979. Quantitative measures of communication in science: A critical review. *History of Science* 17:102–34.

Edge, David. 1983. Is there too much sociology of·science? *Isis* 74:250–56.

Edge, David, and Michael Mulkay. 1976. *Astronomy Transformed: The Emergence of Radio Astronomy in Britain*. New York: Wiley Interscience.

Edmondson, Ricca. 1984. *Rhetoric in Sociology*. London: Macmillan.

Elizondo, Salvador. No date. *The Graphographer*. No publication details.

Elkana, Yehuda. 1978. Two-tier-thinking: Philosophical realism and historical relativism. *Social Studies of Science* 8:309–26.

Falletta, Nicholas. 1983. *The Paradoxicon*. New York: Doubleday.

Farley, John, and Gerald L. Geison. 1974. Science, politics and spontaneous generation in nineteenth century France: The Pasteur-Pouchet debate. *Bulletin on the History of Medicine* 48:161–94. (Reprinted in Collins 1982a:1–38.)

Federman, Raymond. 1975. *Surfiction: Fiction Now . . . and Tomorrow*. Chicago and London: University of Chicago Press.

Feyerabend, Paul. 1975. *Against Method*. London: New Left Books.

Feyerabend, Paul. 1978. *Science in a Free Society*. London: New Left Books.

Feyerabend, Paul. 1981. How to defend society against science. In Hacking 1981: 156–67.

Filmer, Paul, Michael Phillipson, David Silverman, and David Walsh, eds. 1972. *New Directions in Sociological Theory*. London: Collier-Macmillan.

Fleck, James. 1980. Development and establishment in artificial intelligence. In N. Elias, H. Martins, and R. Whitley, eds. *Scientific Establishments and Hierarchies*. Sociology of the Sciences Yearbook, vol. 6 (Dordrecht and Boston: Reidel) 1980:169–217. (Reprinted with postscript in Bloomfield 1987a: 106–64.)

Fleck, Ludwik. 1979. *Genesis and Development of a Scientific Fact*. Chicago and London: University of Chicago Press. (First published 1935.)

Flew, Antony. 1982. A strong programme for the sociology of belief. *Inquiry* 25: 365–78.

Forman, Paul. 1971. Weimar culture, causality and quantum theory, 1918–1927: Adaptation by German physicists and mathematicians to a hostile intellectual environment. In R. McCormach, ed. 1971. *Historical Studies in the Physical Sciences.* (Philadelphia, Pa.: University of Pennsylvania Press) 3:1–116.

Fowles, John. 1982. *Mantissa.* London: Jonathan Cape.

Frankel, Eugene. 1976. Corpuscular optics and the wave theory of light: The science and politics of a revolution in physics. *Social Studies of Science* 6:141–84.

Freudenthal, Gad. 1979. How strong is Dr Bloor's "Strong Programme?" *Studies in the History and Philosophy of Science* 10:67–83.

Freudenthal, Gad. 1984. The role of shared knowledge in science: The failure of the constructivist programme in the sociology of science. *Social Studies of Science* 24:285–95.

Friedrichs, Robert W. 1970. *A Sociology of Sociology.* New York: Free Press.

Fuhrman, Ellsworth R., and Kay Oehler. 1986. Discourse analysis and reflexivity. *Social Studies of Science* 16:293–307.

Fuhrman, Ellsworth R., and Kay Oehler. 1987. Reflexivity redux: Reply to Potter. *Social Studies of Science* 17:177–81.

Fuller, Steve. 1986. Making reflexivity safe for relativism. Presented at the Society for Social Studies of Science annual meeting, Pittsburgh, October 1986.

Garfinkel, Harold. 1967. *Studies in Ethnomethodology.* Englewood Cliffs, N.J.: Prentice-Hall.

Garfinkel, Harold, Michael Lynch, and Eric Livingston. 1981. The work of a discovering science construed with materials from the optically discovered pulsar. *Philosophy of the Social Sciences* 11:131–58.

Gebstadter, Egbert B. 1979. *Copper, Silver, Gold: An Indestructible Metallic Alloy.* Perth: Acidic Books.

Geddie, William, ed. 1964. *Chambers's Twentieth Century Dictionary.* Edinburgh and London: Chambers.

Geertz, Clifford. 1980. Blurred genres: The refiguration of social thought. *The American Scholar* 49:165–79.

Gellner, Ernest. 1968. The new idealism—Cause and meaning in the social sciences. In I. Lakatos and A. Musgrave, eds. *Problems in the Philosophy of Science.* (Amsterdam: North-Holland) 1968:50–77. Reprinted in E. Gellner *Cause and Meaning in the Social Sciences.* (London: Routledge and Kegan Paul) 1973: 50–77. Also in A. Giddens, ed. *Positivism and Sociology.* (London: Heinemann) 1974:129–56.

Gellner, Ernest. 1974. *Legitimation of Belief.* Cambridge: Cambridge University Press.

Gellner, Ernest. 1975. Beyond truth and falsehood. *British Journal for the Philosophy of Science* 26:331–42.

Giddens, Anthony. 1976. *New Rules of Sociological Method.* London: Hutchinson.

Gieryn, Thomas, ed. 1980. *Science and Social Structure: A Festschrift for Robert Merton.* Transactions of the New York Academy of Sciences, series 2, vol. 39.

Gieryn, Thomas. 1982a. Relativist/constructivist programmes in the sociology of science: Redundance and retreat. *Social Studies of Science* 12:279–97.

Gieryn, Thomas. 1982b. Not-last words: Worn-out dichotomies in the sociology of science. *Social Studies of Science* 12:329–35.

Gieryn, Thomas. 1984. Boundary-work and the demarcation of science from non-science: Strains and interests in professional ideologies of scientists. *American Sociological Review* 48:781–95.

Gieryn, Thomas. 1987. "Safe" science and "risky" science: Competition for the chair of logic and metaphysics at Edinburgh, 1836. Presented at the New Sociologies of Science/Rhetoric of Inquiry Conference, University of Iowa, October 1987.

Gilbert, G. Nigel. 1976a. The transformation of research findings into scientific knowledge. *Social Studies of Science* 6:281–306.

Gilbert, G. Nigel. 1976b. The development of science and scientific knowledge: The case of radar meteor research. In Lemaine et al. 1976:187–206.

Gilbert, G. Nigel, and Peter Abell, eds. 1983. *Accounts and Action.* Surrey Conferences on Sociological Theory and Method, vol. 1. Aldershot, Hants.: Gower.

Gilbert, G. Nigel, and Michael Mulkay. 1980. Contexts of scientific discourse: Social accounting in experimental papers. In Knorr, Krohn, and Whitley 1980: 269–94.

Gilbert, G. Nigel, and Michael Mulkay. 1982. Warranting scientific belief. *Social Studies of Science* 12:383–408.

Gilbert, G. Nigel, and Michael Mulkay. 1983. In search of the action: Some methodological problems of qualitative analysis. In Gilbert and Abell 1983:8–34.

Gilbert, G. Nigel, and Michael Mulkay. 1984a. *Opening Pandora's Box: A Sociological Analysis of Scientists' Discourse.* Cambridge: Cambridge University Press.

Gilbert, G. Nigel, and Michael Mulkay. 1984b. Experiments are the key: Participants' histories and historians' histories of science. *Isis* 75:105–25.

Gouldner, Alvin W. 1970. *The Coming Crisis of Western Sociology.* New York: Basic Books.

Gouldner, Alvin W. 1973. The politics of the mind. In his *For Sociology.* (Harmondsworth, Middx.: Penguin Books) 1973:82–127.

Gouldner, Alvin W. 1976. *The Dialectic of Ideology and Technology: The Origins, Grammar and Future of Ideology.* London: Macmillan.

Gouldner, Alvin W. 1980. *The Two Marxisms: Contradictions and Anomalies in the Development of Theory.* London: Macmillan.

Govier, Trudy. 1981. Worries about *tu quoque* as a fallacy. *Informal Logic Newsletter* 3(3):2–4.

Gruenberg, Barry. 1978. The problem of reflexivity in the sociology of science. *Philosophy of the Social Sciences* 8:321–43.

Gusfield, Joseph R. 1976. The literary rhetoric of science: Comedy and pathos in drinking driver research. *American Sociological Review* 41:16–34.

Gutting, Gary, ed. 1980. *Paradigms and Revolutions.* Notre Dame, Ind.: University of Notre Dame Press.

Habermas, Jürgen. 1971. *Toward a Rational Society.* London: Heinemann.

Habermas, Jürgen. 1972. *Knowledge and Human Interests.* London: Heinemann.

Habermas, Jürgen. 1975. *Legitimation Crisis.* London: Heinemann.

Hacking, Ian, ed. 1981. *Scientific Revolutions.* Oxford and New York: Oxford University Press.

Halfpenny, Peter. 1988. Talking of talking, writing of writing: Some reflections on

Gilbert and Mulkay's discourse analysis. *Social Studies of Science* 18:169–82.

Hanen, M., M. Osler, and R. G. Weyant, eds. 1980. *Science, Pseudoscience and Society.* Waterloo, Ontario: Wilfred Laurier University Press.

Harding, S. G., ed. 1976. *Can Theories be Refuted? Essays on the Duhem-Quine Thesis.* Dordrecht and Boston: Reidel.

Harvey, Bill. 1980. The effects of social context on the process of scientific investigation: Experimental tests of quantum mechanics. In Knorr, Krohn, and Whitley 1980:139–63.

Harvey, Bill. 1981. Plausibility and the evaluation of knowledge: A case study of experimental quantum mechanics. *Social Studies of Science* 11:95–130.

Harwood, Jonathan. 1976. The race-intelligence controversy: A sociological approach. (1) Professional factors. *Social Studies of Science* 6:369–94.

Harwood, Jonathan. 1977. The race-intelligence controversy: A sociological approach. (2) External factors. *Social Studies of Science* 7:1–30.

Harwood, Jonathan. 1980a. Nature, nurture and politics: A critique of the conventional wisdom. In J. V. Smith and D. Hamilton, eds. *The Meritocratic Intellect: Studies in the History of Educational Research.* (Aberdeen: Aberdeen University Press) 1980:115–29.

Harwood, Jonathan. 1980b. Styles of thought in genetics in the 1920s. Presented to University of Manchester workshop, December 1980.

Heaton, Janet. 1985. A short play which illustrates in a poignant way the fundamental issues of rationality and relativism encountered in a number of differing contexts. University of York. Manuscript.

Henshel, R. L. 1982. The boundary of the self-fulfilling prophecy and the dilemma of social prediction. *British Journal of Sociology* 33:511–28.

Heritage, John. 1978. Aspects of the flexibilities of natural language use: A reply to Phillips. *Sociology* 12:79–103.

Heritage, John. 1984. *Garfinkel and Ethnomethodology.* Cambridge: Polity Press.

Hesse, Mary. 1963. *Models and Analogies in Science.* London: Sheed and Ward.

Hesse, Mary. 1974. *The Structure of Scientific Inference.* London: Macmillan.

Hesse, Mary. 1980. *Revolutions and Reconstructions in the Philosophy of Science.* Hassocks, Sussex: Harvester Press.

Hester, Stephen. 1981. Two tensions in ethnomethodology and conversation analysis. *Sociology* 15:108–16.

Hofstadter, Douglas R. 1980. *Gödel, Escher, Bach: An Eternal Golden Braid. A Metaphorical Fugue on Minds and Machines in the Spirit of Lewis Carroll.* Harmondsworth, Middx.: Penguin Books.

Hofstadter, Douglas R. 1985. *Metamagical Themas: Questing for the Essence of Mind and Pattern.* New York: Basic Books.

Holland, Ray. 1977. *Self and Social Context.* London: Macmillan.

Hollander, John. 1981. *Rhyme's Reason: A Guide to English Verse.* New Haven, Conn.: Yale University Press.

Hollinger, D. A. 1973. T. S. Kuhn's theory of science and its implications for history. *American Historical Review* 78:370–93.

Hollis, Martin. 1982. The social destruction of reality. In Hollis and Lukes 1982:67–86.

Hollis, Martin, and Steven Lukes, eds. 1982. *Rationality and Relativism.* Oxford: Blackwell.

Holub, Robert. 1984. *Reception Theory: A Critical Introduction.* London: Methuen.

Hougan, J. 1976. *Decadence: Radical Nostalgia, Narcissism and Decline in the Seventies.* New York: William Morrow.

Hughes, Patrick, and George Brecht. 1978. *Vicious Circles and Infinity: An Anthology of Paradoxes.* Harmondsworth, Middx.: Penguin Books.

Hutcheon, Linda. 1984. *Narcissistic Narrative: The Metafictional Paradox.* London: Methuen.

Jenks, Chris, ed. 1977. *Rationality, Education and the Social Organisation of Knowledge: Papers for a Reflexive Sociology of Education.* London: Routledge and Kegan Paul.

Johnson, Barbara. 1978. The frame of reference—Poe, Lacan, Derrida. In G. H. Hartman, ed. *Psychoanalysis and the Question of the Text.* (Baltimore, Md.: Johns Hopkins University Press) 1978:149–69.

Kawin, Bruce F. 1982. *The Mind of the Novel: Reflexive Fiction and the Ineffable.* Princeton, N.J.: Princeton University Press.

Kaye, Anna, and Don C. Matchan. 1979. *Reflexology: Techniques of Foot Massage for Health and Fitness.* Wellingborough, Northants.: Thorsons Publishers.

Kellman, Steven G. 1980. *The Self-Begetting Novel.* New York: Columbia University Press.

Kelly, George. 1955. *The Psychology of Personal Constructs.* 2 vols. New York: Norton.

Kemp, Ray. 1977. Controversy in scientific research and tactics of communication. *Sociological Review* 25:515–34.

Knorr, Karin, Roger Krohn, and Richard Whitley, eds. 1980. *The Social Process of Scientific Investigation.* Sociology of the Sciences Yearbook, vol. 4. Dordrecht and Boston: Reidel.

Knorr-Cetina, Karin. 1981a. *The Manufacture of Knowledge: An Essay on the Constructivist and Contextual Nature of Science.* Oxford: Pergamon Press.

Knorr-Cetina, Karin. 1981b. Social and scientific method or what do we make of the distinction between the natural and the social sciences? *Philosophy of the Social Sciences* 11:335–59. (Also in Knorr-Cetina 1981a.)

Knorr-Cetina, Karin. 1982. Relativism—what now? *Social Studies of Science* 12: 133–36.

Knorr-Cetina, Karin, and Aaron Cicourel, eds. 1982. *Advances in Social Theory and Methodology: Toward an Integration of Micro- and Macro- Sociologies.* London: Routledge and Kegan Paul.

Knorr-Cetina, Karin, and Michael Mulkay, eds. 1983. *Science Observed: Perspectives on the Social Study of Science.* London and Beverly Hills, Calif.: Sage.

Krieger, Susan. 1983. *The Mirror Dance: Identity in a Women's Community.* Philadelphia, Pa.: Temple University Press.

Krieger, Susan. 1984. Fiction and social science. *Studies in Symbolic Interaction* 5:269–86.

Krishna, D. 1971. "The self-fulfilling prophesy" and the nature of society. *American Sociological Review* 36:1104–7.

Krohn, Roger. 1982. On Gieryn on the "relativist/constructivist" programme in the sociology of science: Naïveté and reaction. *Social Studies of Science* 12: 325–28.

Kuhn, Thomas S. 1970a. *The Structure of Scientific Revolutions*. 2nd ed. Chicago and London: University of Chicago Press. (First published 1962.)

Kuhn, Thomas S. 1970b. Logic of discovery or psychology of research? In Lakatos and Musgrave 1970:1–23.

Kuhn, Thomas S. 1970c. Reflections on my critics. In Lakatos and Musgrave 1970: . 231–78.

Kuhn, Thomas S. 1977a. *The Essential Tension*. Chicago and London: University of Chicago Press.

Kuhn, Thomas S. 1977b. The relations between the history and the philosophy of science. In Kuhn 1977a:3–20.

Kuhn, Thomas S. 1977c. Objectivity, value judgment, and theory choice. In Kuhn 1977a:320–39.

Kuhn, Thomas S. 1977d. History of science. In Kuhn 1977a:105–26.

Lacan, Jacques. 1968. *The Language of the Self: The Function of Language in Psychoanalysis*. Baltimore, Md.: Johns Hopkins University Press. (See also Wilden 1968.)

Lacey, A. R., ed. 1976. *A Dictionary of Philosophy*. London: Routledge and Kegan Paul.

Lakatos, Imre. 1976. *Proofs and Refutations: The Logic of Mathematical Discovery*. Cambridge: Cambridge University Press. (First published 1963–64.)

Lakatos, Imre, and Alan Musgrave, eds. 1970. *Criticism and the Growth of Knowledge*. Cambridge: Cambridge University Press.

Lally, A. J. 1976. Positivism and its critics. In D. C. Thorns, ed. *New Directions in Sociology*. (Newton Abbott, Devon: David and Charles) 1976:55–75.

Latour, Bruno. 1978. Observing scientists observing baboons observing . . . New York: Wenner Grenn Foundation for Anthropological Research. July.

Latour, Bruno. 1980a. Is it possible to reconstruct the research process? Sociology of a brain peptide. In Knorr, Krohn, and Whitley 1980:53–73.

Latour, Bruno. 1980b. The three little dinosaurs or a sociologist's nightmare. *Fundamenta Scientiae* 1:79–85.

Latour, Bruno. 1981. Insiders and outsiders in the sociology of science: Or, how can we foster agnosticism. In R. A. Jones and H. Kuklick, eds. 1981. *Knowledge and Society*. (Greenwich, Conn.: JAI Press) 3:199–216.

Latour, Bruno, ed. 1982. *La Science telle qu'elle se fait. Anthologie de la sociologie anglo-saxonne des sciences*. Paris: Editions de la Maison des Sciences de l'Homme.

Latour, Bruno. 1983. Give me a laboratory and I will raise the world. In Knorr-Cetina and Mulkay 1983:141–70.

Latour, Bruno. 1984. Where did you put the black-box opener? *EASST Newsletter* (August) 3:17–21.

Latour, Bruno. 1987. *Science in Action*. Milton Keynes, Bucks.: Open University Press.

Latour, Bruno. 1988. The politics of explanation—an alternative. In Woolgar 1988a: 155–76.

Latour, Bruno, and Steve Woolgar. 1979. *Laboratory Life: The Social Construction of Scientific Facts*. London and Beverly Hills, Calif.: Sage. (2nd ed. 1986. With postscript and no "social" in title. Princeton, N.J.: Princeton University Press.)

Laudan, Larry. 1981. The pseudo-science of science? *Philosophy of the Social Sciences* 11:173–98.

Laudan, Larry. 1982a. A note on Collins's blend of relativism and empiricism. *Social Studies of Science* 12:131–32.

Laudan, Larry. 1982b. More on Bloor. *Philosophy of the Social Sciences* 12:71–74.

Law, John. 1974. Theories and methods in the sociology of science: An interpretative approach. *Social Science Information* 13:163–72. (Reprinted in Lemaine et al. 1976:221–31.)

Law, John. 1975. Is epistemology redundant? A sociological view. *Philosophy of the Social Sciences* 5:317–37.

Law, John. 1977. Prophecy failed (for the actors)! A note on "Recovering relativity." *Social Studies of Science* 7:362–72.

Law, John. 1980. Fragmentation and investment in sedimentology. *Social Studies of Science* 10:1–22.

Law, John, ed. 1986. *Power, Action and Belief: A New Sociology of Knowledge?* Sociological Review Monograph, 34. Keele: University of Keele.

Law, John, and David French. 1974. Normative and interpretive sociologies of science. *Sociological Review* 22:581–95.

Law, John, and Peter Lodge. 1984. *Science for Social Scientists*. London: Macmillan.

Law, John, and Rob Williams. 1982. Putting facts together: A study of scientific persuasion. *Social Studies of Science* 12:535–58.

Lawson, Hilary. 1985. *Reflexivity: The Post-Modern Predicament*. London: Hutchinson.

Lawson, Hilary, and Lisa Appignanesi. Forthcoming. *Dismantling Truth: Science in Post-Modern Times*. London: Wiedenfeld and Nicolson.

Leiter, K. 1980. *A Primer on Ethnomethodology*. Oxford: Oxford University Press.

Lem, Stanislaw. 1979. *A Perfect Vacuum*. Translated by Michael Kandel. London: Secker and Warburg.

Lemaine, G., R. Macleod, M. Mulkay, and P. Weingart, eds. 1976. *Perspectives on the Emergence of Scientific Disciplines*. The Hague and Paris: Mouton; Chicago: Aldine.

Lemert, Charles. 1979. De-centered analysis: Ethnomethodology and structuralism. *Theory and Society* 7:289–306.

Llosa, Mario Vargas. 1984. *Aunt Julia and the Scriptwriter*. Translated by Helen R. Lane. London: Picador.

Lukes, Steven. 1982. Comment on Bloor. *Studies in the History and Philosophy of Science* 13:312–18.

Lury, Celia. 1982. An ethnography of an ethnography: Reading sociology. *Sociology Occasional Papers*, No. 9. University of Manchester.

Lynch, Michael. 1982. Technical work and critical inquiry: Investigations in a scientific laboratory. *Social Studies of Science* 12:499–533.

Lynch, Michael. 1985. *Art and Artifact in Laboratory Science: A Study of Shop Work and Shop Talk in a Research Laboratory*. London: Routledge and Kegan Paul.

Lynch, Michael. Forthcoming. Alfred Schutz and the sociology of science. In Lester Embree, ed. Forthcoming. *Worldly Phenomenology: The Influence of Alfred Schutz on Human Science*. Washington, D.C.: Center for Advanced Research in Phenomenology; and University Press of America.

Lynch, Michael, Eric Livingston, and Harold Garfinkel. 1983. Temporal order in laboratory work. In Knorr-Cetina and Mulkay 1983:205–38.

Lyotard, Jean François. 1984. *The Postmodern Condition: A Report on Knowledge.* Translated by Geoff Bennington and Brian Massumi. Minneapolis: University of Minnesota Press.

McCloskey, Donald N. 1985. *The Rhetoric of Economics.* Madison: University of Wisconsin Press.

McHoul, Alexander W. 1980. The practical methodology of reading in science and everyday life: Reading Althusser reading Marx. *Philosophy of the Social Sciences* 10:129–50.

McHoul, Alexander W. 1981. Ethnomethodology and the position of relativist discourse. *Journal for the Theory of Social Behaviour* 11:107–24.

McHoul, Alexander W. 1982. *Telling How Texts Talk: Essays on Reading and Ethnomethodology.* London: Routledge and Kegan Paul.

McHugh, Peter. 1970. On the failure of positivism. In Douglas 1970:320–35.

McHugh, Peter, Stanley Raffell, Daniel Foss, and Alan Blum. 1974. *On the Beginning of Social Inquiry.* London: Routledge and Kegan Paul.

MacKenzie, Donald. 1978. Statistical theory and social interests: A case study. *Social Studies of Science* 8:35–83.

MacKenzie, Donald. 1981a. *Statistics in Britain 1865–1930: The Social Construction of Scientific Knowledge.* Edinburgh: Edinburgh University Press.

MacKenzie, Donald. 1981b. Interests, positivism and history. *Social Studies of Science* 11:498–504.

MacKenzie, Donald. 1981c. Notes on the science and social relations debate. *Capital and Class* 14:47–60.

MacKenzie, Donald. 1981d. Sociobiologies in competition: The Biometrician-Mendelian debate. In C. Webster, ed. *Biology, Medicine and Society 1840–1940.* (Cambridge: Cambridge University Press) 1981:243–88.

MacKenzie, Donald, and Judy Wajcman, eds. 1985. *The Social Shaping of Technology.* Milton Keynes, Bucks.: Open University Press.

Mackie, J. L. 1964. Self-refutation—a formal analysis. *The Philosophical Quarterly* 14(56):193–203.

McKinlay, Andrew. 1986. Meaning, interpretation and reflexivity in the social sciences. Presented at the Society for Social Studies of Science annual meeting, Pittsburgh, October 1986.

McNeil, Maureen. 1978. Science's narcissism: Sociology of knowledge as a methodology for explaining the form and content of scientific knowledge. *Radical Science Journal* 6/7:159–62.

Manicas, Peter T., and Alan Rosenberg. 1985. Naturalism, epistemological individualism and "the strong programme" in the sociology of knowledge. *Journal for the Theory of Social Behaviour* 15:76–101.

Manicas, Peter T., and Alan Rosenberg. 1987. The strong programme: Can we ever get it straight? Presented at the Rhetoric of Inquiry/New Sociologies of Science Conference, University of Iowa, October 1987.

Manier, Edward. 1980. Levels of reflexivity: Unnoted differences within the "strong programme" in the sociology of knowledge. In P. Asquith and R. Giere, eds. *PSA Vol. 1.* (East Lansing: Philosophy of Science Association) 1980:197–207.

Mannheim, Karl. 1952. On the interpretation of "Weltanschauung." In his *Essays on the Sociology of Knowledge.* Edited and translated by Paul Kecskemeti. (Oxford and New York: Oxford University Press) 1952:33–83.

Marcus, George E., and Dick Cushman. 1982. Ethnographies as texts. *Annual Review of Anthropology* 11:25–69.

Markle, G. E., and J. C. Petersen, eds. 1980. *Politics, Science and Cancer: The Laetrile Phenomenon*. Boulder, Col.: Westview Press.

Mars-Jones, Adam. 1982. *Lantern Lecture*. London: Picador.

Martin, R. L., ed. 1970. *The Paradox of the Liar*. New Haven, Conn.: Yale University Press.

Martins, Herminio. 1971. The Kuhnian "revolution" and its implications for sociology. In A. H. Hanson, T. Nossiter and S. Rokkan, eds. *Imagination and Precision in the Social Sciences*. (London: Faber) 1971:13–58.

Medawar, Peter. 1963. Is the scientific paper a fraud? *The Listener*. (12 Sept.): 377–78.

Mehan, Hugh, and Houston Wood. 1975. *The Reality of Ethnomethodology*. New York: John Wiley.

Merton, Robert K. 1965. *On the Shoulders of Giants: A Shandean Postscript*. New York: Free Press.

Merton, Robert K. 1968. The self-fulfilling prophesy. In his *Social Theory and Social Structure*. (New York: Free Press) 1968:475–90. (First published in *The Antioch Review*, Summer 1948.)

Merton, Robert K. 1972. Insiders and outsiders: A chapter in the sociology of knowledge. *American Journal of Sociology* 78:9–47. (This volume of the *AJS* is reprinted as *Varieties of Political Expression in Sociology*. [Chicago and London: University of Chicago Press] 1972.)

Meynell, Hugo. 1977. On the limits of the sociology of knowledge. *Social Studies of Science* 7:489–500.

Mills, C. Wright. 1940. Situated actions and vocabularies of motive. *American Sociological Review* 5:904–13. (Reprinted in I. L. Horowitz, ed. *Power, Politics and People: The Collected Essays of C. Wright Mills*. [Oxford and New York: Oxford University Press] 1963:439–52.)

Millstone, Erik. 1978. A framework for the sociology of knowledge. *Social Studies of Science* 8:111–25.

Mirowski, Philip. 1987. Shall I compare thee to a Minkowski-Ricardo-Leontif-Metzler matrix of the Mosak-Hicks type? Or, rhetoric, mathematics and the nature of neo-classical economic theory. *Economics and Philosophy* 3:67–96.

Morrison, Kenneth L. 1981. Some properties of "telling-order designs" in didactic inquiry. *Philosophy of the Social Sciences* 11:245–62.

Mulkay, Michael. 1969. Some aspects of cultural growth in the natural sciences. *Social Research* 36:22–52.

Mulkay, Michael. 1974. Methodology in the sociology of science: Some reflections on the study of radio astronomy. *Social Science Information* 13:107–19. (Reprinted in Lemaine et al. 1976:207–219.)

Mulkay, Michael. 1975. Three models of scientific development. *Sociological Review* 23:509–26.

Mulkay, Michael. 1976. Norms and ideology in science. *Social Science Information* 15:637–56.

Mulkay, Michael. 1979a. *Science and the Sociology of Knowledge*. London: George Allen and Unwin.

Mulkay, Michael. 1979b. Knowledge and utility: Implications for the sociology of knowledge. *Social Studies of Science* 9:63–80.

Mulkay, Michael. 1980a. Sociology of science in the West. (Trend Report, part 1.) *Current Sociology* 28(3):1–184.

Mulkay, Michael. 1980b. Interpretation and the use of rules: The case of the norms of science. In Gieryn 1980:111–25.

Mulkay, Michael. 1981. Action and belief or scientific discourse: A possible way of ending intellectual vassalage in social studies of science. *Philosophy of the Social Sciences* 11:163–71.

Mulkay, Michael. 1984a. The scientist talks back: A one-act play, with a moral, about replication in science and reflexivity in sociology. *Social Studies of Science* 14:265–82. (See also Mulkay 1985, ch.5.)

Mulkay, Michael. 1984b. 15 August 1984, Dear Malcolm. In Ashmore 1989:227, n.1.

Mulkay, Michael. 1984c. My dear young man . . . In Ashmore 1989:15.

Mulkay, Michael. 1985. *The Word and the World: Explorations in the Form of Sociological Analysis.* London: George Allen and Unwin.

Mulkay, Michael. 1988. Don Quixote's double: A self-exemplifying text. In Woolgar 1988a:81–100. (For its double, see Mulkay 1985, ch.4.)

Mulkay, Michael, and G. Nigel Gilbert. 1981a. Putting philosophy to work: Karl Popper's influence on scientific practice. *Philosophy of the Social Sciences* 11:389–407.

Mulkay, Michael, and G. Nigel Gilbert. 1981b. The truth will out: A device which scientists use to resolve potential contradictions between interpretative repertoires. Universities of York and Surrey. Typescript. (See also Gilbert and Mulkay 1984a, ch.5.)

Mulkay, Michael, and G. Nigel Gilbert. 1982a. Accounting for error: How scientists construct their social world when they account for correct and incorrect belief. *Sociology* 16:165–83.

Mulkay, Michael, and G. Nigel Gilbert. 1982b. Joking apart: Some recommendations concerning the analysis of scientific culture. *Social Studies of Science* 12:585–613.

Mulkay, Michael, and G. Nigel Gilbert. 1982c. What is the ultimate question? Some remarks in defence of the analysis of scientific discourse. *Social Studies of Science* 12:309–19.

Mulkay, Michael, and G. Nigel Gilbert. 1983. Scientists' theory talk. *Canadian Journal of Sociology* 8:179–97.

Mulkay, Michael, and G. Nigel Gilbert. 1984. Opening Pandora's box: A case for developing a new approach to the analysis of theory choice in science. In H. Kuklick and E. Long, eds. 1984. *Knowledge and Society.* (Greenwich, Conn.: JAI Press) 5:113–39.

Mulkay, Michael, and G. Nigel Gilbert. 1986. Replication and mere replication. *Philosophy of the Social Sciences* 16:21–37.

Mulkay, Michael, Trevor Pinch, and Malcolm Ashmore. 1987. Colonizing the mind: Dilemmas in the application of social science. *Social Studies of Science* 17:231–56.

Mulkay, Michael, Jonathan Potter, and Steven Yearley. 1983. Why an analysis of scientific discourse is needed. In Knorr-Cetina and Mulkay 1983:171–203.

Mullins, Nicholas C. 1977. Rhetorical resources in natural science papers. Institute for Advanced Studies, Princeton. Mimeo.

Myerhoff, Barbara, and Jay Ruby. 1982. Introduction. In Ruby 1982:1–35.

Myers, Greg. 1985. Texts as knowledge claims: The social construction of two biologists' articles. *Social Studies of Science* 15:593–630.

Myers, Greg. Forthcoming. *Writing Biology: Texts in the Construction of Science.* Madison: University of Wisconsin Press.

Naess, Arne. 1972. *The Pluralist and Possibilist Aspect of the Scientific Enterprise.* London: George Allen and Unwin.

Nelkin, Dorothy, ed. 1979. *Controversy: Politics of Technical Decisions.* London and Beverly Hills, Calif.: Sage.

Nelson, John S., Allan Megill, and Donald N. McCloskey, eds. 1987. *The Rhetoric of the Human Sciences: Language and Argumentation in Scholarship and Public Affairs.* Madison: University of Wisconsin Press.

Nowotny, Helga, and Hilary Rose, eds. 1979. *Counter-Movements in the Sciences.* Sociology of the Sciences Yearbook, vol. 3. Dordrecht and Boston: Reidel.

Oehler, Kay. 1983. Two interpretations of reflexivity in sociology of science: An examination of H. M. Collins's radical programme. Virginia Polytechnic Institute and State University. Typescript.

Oehler, Kay, and Nicholas C. Mullins. 1986. Mechanisms of reflexivity in science: A look at nontraditional literary forms. Presented at the Society for Social Studies of Science annual meeting, Pittsburgh, October 1986.

Oliver, W. Donald, and Alvin W. Landfield. 1962. Reflexivity: An unfaced issue of psychology. *Journal of Individual Psychology* 18:114–24.

O'Neill, John. 1972a. *Sociology as a Skin Trade: Essays Towards a Reflexive Sociology.* London: Heinemann.

O'Neill, John. 1972b. Can phenomenology be critical? In O'Neill 1972a:221–36. (Reprinted in T. Luckmann, ed. *Phenomenology and Sociology.* [Harmondsworth, Middx.: Penguin Books] 1978:200–216.)

O'Neill, John. 1972c. Reflexive sociology or the advent of Alvin W. Gouldner. In O'Neill 1972a:209–20.

O'Neill, John. 1981a. Marxism and the two sciences. *Philosophy of the Social Sciences* 11:281–302.

O'Neill, John. 1981b. The literary production of natural and social science inquiry: Issues and applications in the social organization of science. *Canadian Journal of Sociology* 6:105–20.

Orne, M. T. 1959. The demand characteristics of an experimental design and their implications. Presented to the American Psychological Association, Cincinnati.

Orne, M. T. 1962. On the social psychology of the psychological experiment. *American Psychologist* 17:776–83.

Palermo, D. S. 1971. Is a scientific revolution taking place in psychology? *Science Studies* 1:135–55.

Parkin, David, ed. 1982. *Semantic Anthropology.* ASA Monograph 22. London and New York: Academic Press.

Pawson, Ray, and Nicholas Tilley. 1982. Monstrous thoughts: Weaknesses in the strong programme of the sociology of knowledge. *Occasional Papers in Sociology,* No. 14, University of Leeds.

Peterson, Gerald L. 1981. Historical self-understanding in the social sciences: The use of Thomas Kuhn in psychology. *Journal for the Theory of Social Behaviour* 11:1–30.

Phillips, Bernard S. 1976. *Social Research: Strategy and Tactics*. New York: Macmillan.

Pickering, Andrew. 1980a. The role of interests in high-energy physics: The choice between charm and colour. In Knorr, Krohn, and Whitley 1980:107–38.

Pickering, Andrew. 1980b. Exemplars and analogies: A comment on Crane's study of Kuhnian paradigms in high-energy physics. *Social Studies of Science* 10:497–502.

Pickering, Andrew. 1980c. Reply to Crane. *Social Studies of Science* 10:507–8.

Pickering, Andrew. 1981a. Constraints on controversy: The case of the magnetic monopole. *Social Studies of Science* 11:63–94.

Pickering, Andrew. 1981b. The hunting of the quark. *Isis* 72:216–36.

Pickering, Andrew. 1984. *Constructing Quarks: A Sociological History of Particle Physics*. Edinburgh: Edinburgh University Press; Chicago: University of Chicago Press.

Pinch, Trevor. 1976. Hidden variables, impossibility proofs and paradoxes: A sociological study of non-relativistic quantum mechanics. MSc dissertation, Manchester University.

Pinch, Trevor. 1977. What does a proof do if it does not prove? A study of the social conditions and metaphysical divisions leading to David Bohm and John von Neumann failing to communicate in quantum physics. In E. Mendelsohn, P. Weingart and R. Whitley, eds. *The Social Production of Scientific Knowledge*. Sociology of the Sciences Yearbook, vol. 1. (Dordrecht and Boston: Reidel) 1977:171–215.

Pinch, Trevor. 1979. Normal explanations of the paranormal: The demarcation problem and fraud in parapsychology. *Social Studies of Science* 9:329–48.

Pinch, Trevor. 1980. Theoreticians and the production of experimental anomaly: The case of solar-neutrinos. In Knorr, Krohn, and Whitley 1980:77–106.

Pinch, Trevor. 1981. The sun-set: The presentation of certainty in scientific life. *Social Studies of Science* 11:131–58.

Pinch, Trevor. 1982a. The development of solar-neutrino astronomy: The theoretical-experimental nexus and the social deconstruction and construction of knowledge. PhD dissertation, University of Bath.

Pinch, Trevor. 1982b. Kuhn—the conservative and radical interpretations. Are some Mertonians "Kuhnians" and some "Kuhnians" Mertonians? *4S Newsletter* 7(1):10–25.

Pinch, Trevor. 1982c. Reflecting on reflexivity: Comment on Verhoog. *EASST Newsletter* 5:5–7.

Pinch, Trevor. 1985. Towards an analysis of scientific observation: The externality and evidential significance of observational reports in physics. *Social Studies of Science* 15:3–36.

Pinch, Trevor. 1986. *Confronting Nature: The Sociology of Solar-Neutrino Detection*. Dordrecht and Boston: Reidel.

Pinch, Trevor. 1988. The sociology of the scientific community. In G. N. Cantor, J. Christie, M. Hodge, and R. C. Olby, eds. *Companion to the History of Modern Science*. (London: Croom Helm) 1988, forthcoming.

Pinch, Trevor, and Wiebe Bijker. 1984. The social construction of facts and artifacts: Or how the sociology of science and the sociology of technology might benefit each other. *Social Studies of Science* 14:399–442. (Reprinted in Bijker, Hughes, and Pinch 1987:17–50.)

Pinch, Trevor, and Harry Collins. 1984. Private science and public knowledge: The Committee for the Scientific Investigation of the Claims of the Paranormal and its use of the literature. *Social Studies of Science* 14:521–46.

Pinch, Trevor, and Trevor Pinch. 1988. Reservations about reflexivity and new literary forms: Or why let the devil have all the good tunes? In Woolgar 1988a:178–97.

Pollner, Melvin. 1974. Mundane reasoning. *Philosophy of the Social Sciences* 4: 35–54.

Pollner, Melvin. 1987. *Mundane Reasoning: Reality in Sociology and Everyday Life.* Cambridge: Cambridge University Press.

Popper, Karl. 1961. *The Poverty of Historicism.* London: Routledge and Kegan Paul.

Popper, Karl. 1966. *The Open Society and Its Enemies.* 2 vols. London: Routledge and Kegan Paul. (First published 1945.)

Popper, Karl. 1972. *Conjectures and Refutations.* London: Routledge and Kegan Paul. (First published 1963.)

Potter, Jonathan. 1982. Nothing so practical as a good theory: The problematic application of social psychology. In P. Stringer, ed. *Confronting Social Issues: Applications of Social Psychology.* Vol. 1. (London: Academic Press) 1982: 247–71.

Potter, Jonathan. 1983. Speaking and writing science: Issues in the analysis of psychologists' discourse. DPhil dissertation, University of York.

Potter, Jonathan. 1984. Testability, flexibility: Kuhnian values in scientists' discourse concerning theory choice. *Philosophy of the Social Sciences* 14:303–30.

Potter, Jonathan. 1987. Discourse analysis and the turn of the reflexive screw: A response to Fuhrman and Oehler. *Social Studies of Science* 17:171–77.

Potter, Jonathan. 1988. What is reflexive about discourse analysis? The case of reading readings. In Woolgar 1988a:37–52.

Potter, Jonathan, and Michael Mulkay. 1982. Making theory useful: Utility accounting in social psychologists' discourse. *Fundamenta Scientiae* 3/4:259–78.

Potter, Jonathan, and Michael Mulkay. 1985. Scientists' interview talk: Interviews as a technique for revealing participants' interpretative practices. In M. Brenner, J. Brown, and D. Canter, eds. *The Research Interview: Uses and Approaches.* (London: Academic Press) 1985:247–71.

Potter, Jonathan, and Margaret Wetherell. 1987. *Discourse and Social Psychology: Beyond Attitudes and Behaviour.* London and Beverly Hills, Calif.: Sage.

Priest, Graham. 1987. Unstable solutions to the liar paradox. In Bartlett and Suber 1987:145–75.

Quine, Willard van Orman. 1962. Paradox. *Scientific American* 206:84–95.

Raffel, Stanley. 1979. *Matters of Fact: A Sociological Inquiry.* London: Routledge and Kegan Paul.

Ray, William. 1984. *Literary Meaning: From Phenomenology to Deconstruction.* Oxford: Blackwell.

Reingold, Nathan. 1980. Through paradigm-land to a normal history of science. *Social Studies of Science* 10:475–96.

Restivo, Sal. 1981. Commentary: Some perspectives in contemporary sociology of science. *Science, Technology and Human Values* 6(35):22–30.

Ricoeur, Paul. 1971. The model text: Meaningful action considered as a text. *Social Research* 38:528–62. (Reprinted 1973. *New Literary History* 5:91–120.)

Rimbaud, Jean-Marie. Forthcoming. *Reflexive Fiction: The Intertextual Commingling of the Real and the Fictional*. Paris: Editions Apocryphique.

Ritzer, George. 1975. *Sociology: A Multiparadigmatic Science*. Boston: Allyn and Bacon.

Robbins, David. 1984. Review: *Opening Pandora's Box* (Gilbert and Mulkay 1984a). *Sociology* 18:452–53.

Roche, Maurice. 1972. Notes on reflexivity. Department of Sociology, London School of Economics. Mimeo.

Roche, Maurice. 1975. Class and difference. In Sandywell et al. 1975:104–47.

Roget's Thesaurus. 1953. Harmondsworth, Middx.: Penguin Books.

Roll-Hansen, Nils. 1983. The death of spontaneous generation and the birth of the gene: Two case studies of relativism. *Social Studies of Science* 13:481–519.

Rorty, Richard. 1982. *Consequences of Pragmatism*. Hassocks, Sussex: Harvester Press.

Rose, Hilary. 1979. Hyper-reflexivity—a new danger for the counter-movements. In Nowotny and Rose 1979:317–35.

Rose, Hilary, and Steven Rose. 1979. Radical science and its enemies. *The Socialist Register* 1979:317–35.

Rose, Margaret. 1979. *Parody/Metafiction: An Analysis of Parody as a Critical Mirror to the Writing and Reception of Fiction*. London: Croom Helm.

Rosenthal, Robert. 1966. *Experimenter Effects in Behavioral Research*. New York: Appleton-Century-Crofts.

Rosenthal, Robert, and R. L. Rosnow. 1969. *Artifact in Behavioral Research*. New York: Academic Press.

Rotman, Brian. 1987. *Signifying Nothing: The Semiotics of Zero*. London: Macmillan.

Ruby, Jay, ed. 1982. *A Crack in the Mirror: Reflexive Perspectives in Anthropology*. Philadelphia: University of Pennsylvania Press.

Rudwick, Martin J. S. 1982a. Cognitive styles in geology. In Douglas 1982:219–41.

Rudwick, Martin J. S. 1982b. Review of K. Knorr, R. Krohn, and R. Whitley, eds. *The Social Process of Scientific Investigation*. 1980; and E. Mendelsohn and Y. Elkana, eds. *Sciences and Cultures*. 1981. Sociology of the Sciences Yearbooks, vols. 4 and 5. Dordrecht and Boston: Reidel. *Social Studies of Science* 12:627–32.

Rudwick, Martin J. S. 1986. *The Great Devonian Controversy: The Shaping of Scientific Knowledge among Gentlemanly Specialists*. Chicago and London: University of Chicago Press.

Russell, Bertrand. 1967. *The Autobiography of Bertrand Russell*. Vol. 1. London: Allen and Unwin.

Russell, Bertrand, and Alfred North Whitehead. 1910. *Principia Mathematica*. Cambridge: Cambridge University Press.

Ryan, Alan. 1972. "Normal" science or political ideology? In P. Laslett, W. G. Runciman, and Q. Skinner, eds. *Philosophy, Politics and Society*. Fourth Series. (Oxford: Blackwell) 1972:86–100.

Sacks, Harvey. 1963. Sociological description. *Berkeley Journal of Sociology* 8:1–16.

Sandywell, Barry. No date. Some theses on reflexive inquiry. University of York. Typescript.

Sandywell, Barry, David Silverman, Maurice Roche, Paul Filmer, and Michael Phillipson. 1975. *Problems of Reflexivity and Dialectics in Sociological Inquiry: Language Theorizing Difference.* London: Routledge and Kegan Paul.

Scheffler, Israel. 1967. *Science and Subjectivity.* New York: Bobbs-Merrill.

Scholes, Robert. 1979. *Fabulation and Metafiction.* Urbana: University of Illinois Press.

Scholte, Bob. 1972. Toward a reflexive and critical anthropology. In Dell Hymes, ed. *Reinventing Anthropology.* (New York: Pantheon Books) 3rd ed. 1972:430–57.

Schur, E. 1976. *The Awareness Trap.* New York: Quadrangle.

Schutz, Alfred. 1967. *The Phenomenology of the Social World.* London: Heinemann.

Scott, Robert L. 1976. On viewing rhetoric as epistemic: Ten years later. *Central States Speech Journal* 27:258–66.

Second of January Group. 1986. *After Truth: A Post-Modern Manifesto.* London: Inventions Press.

Sextus Empiricus. No date. *Outlines of Pyrrhonism.* London: Loeb Classical Library.

Shapin, Steven. 1979. The politics of observation: Cerebral anatomy and social interests in the Edinburgh phrenology disputes. In Wallis 1979:139–78. (Reprinted in Collins 1982a:103–50.)

Shapin, Steven. 1980. Social uses of science. In G. Rousseau and R. Porter, eds. *The Ferment of Knowledge: Studies in the Historiography of 18c. Science.* (Cambridge: Cambridge University Press) 1980:93–139.

Shapin, Steven. 1982. History of science and its sociological reconstructions. *History of Science* 20:157–211.

Shapin, Steven. 1984a. Pump and circumstance: Robert Boyle's literary technology. *Social Studies of Science* 14:481–520.

Shapin, Steven. 1984b. Talking history: Reflections on discourse analysis. *Isis* 75:125–28.

Shapin, Steven, and Simon Schaffer. 1985. *Leviathan and the Air-Pump: Hobbes, Boyle and the Experimental Life.* Princeton, N.J.: Princeton University Press.

Sharratt, Bernard. 1982. *Reading Relations. Structures of Literary Production. A Dialectical Text/Book.* Hassocks, Sussex: Harvester Press.

Sharratt, Bernard. 1984. *The Literary Labyrinth: Contemporary Critical Discourses.* Hassocks, Sussex: Harvester Press.

Shotter, John. 1975. *Images of Man in Psychological Research.* London: Methuen.

Silverman, David. 1972. Methodology and meaning. In Filmer et al. 1972:183–200.

Silverman, David. 1974. Speaking seriously, parts 1 and 2. *Theory and Society* 1:1–16, 341–59.

Silverman, David. 1975a. *Reading Castenada: A Prologue to the Social Sciences.* London: Routledge and Kegan Paul.

Silverman, David. 1975b. Preserving science: Virtuosity as virtue. In K. Knorr, H. Strasser, and H. G. Zilian, eds. *Determinants and Controls of Scientific Development.* (Dordrecht and Boston: Reidel) 1975:143–71.

Silverman, David, and Brian Torode. 1980. *The Material Word: Some Theories of Language and Its Limits.* London: Routledge and Kegan Paul.

Silverstone, Roger. 1985. *Framing Science: The Making of a BBC Documentary.* London: BFI Publishing.

Simonds, A. P. 1978. *Karl Mannheim's Sociology of Knowledge*. Oxford: Oxford University Press.

Sjoberg, Gideon, and Ted R. Vaughan. 1979. Human rights, reflectivity and the sociology of knowledge. In Snizek et al. 1979:235–50.

Smullyan, Raymond. 1980. *This Book Needs No Title: A Budget of Living Paradoxes*. Englewood Cliffs, N.J.: Prentice-Hall.

Snizek, William E., Ellsworth R. Fuhrman, and Michael K. Miller, eds. 1979. *Contemporary Issues in Theory and Research: A Metasociological Perspective*. London: Aldwych.

Sorrentino, Gilbert. 1979. *Mulligan Stew*. London: Picador.

Spinelli, Aldo. 1976. *Loopings*. Amsterdam: Multi Art Points Editions.

Star, Susan Leigh. 1983. Simplification in scientific work: An example from neuroscience research. *Social Studies of Science* 13:205–28.

Stringer, Peter. 1985. You decide what your title is to be and [read] write to that title. In D. Bannister, ed. *Issues and Approaches in Personal Construct Theory*. Vol. 3. (London: Academic Press) 1985:201–31.

Suber, Peter. 1987. A bibliography of works on reflexivity. In Bartlett and Suber 1987:259–362.

Sulloway, Frank J. 1979. *Freud, Biologist of the Mind: Beyond the Psychoanalytic Legend*. London: Fontana.

Suppe, Frederick, ed. 1974. *The Structure of Scientific Theories*. Urbana: University of Illinois Press.

Swearingen, James E. 1977. *Reflexivity in "Tristram Shandy": An Essay in Phenomenological Criticism*. New Haven and London: Yale University Press.

Swearingen, James E. 1987. Reflexivity and the decentered self in *Tristram Shandy*. In Bartlett and Suber 1987:239–56.

Teichmann, Roger. 1987. Tu quoque. *Analysis* 47(4):199–201.

Thomas, David. 1979. *Naturalism and Social Science: A Post-Empiricist Philosophy of Social Science*. Cambridge: Cambridge University Press.

Tollefson, Olaf. 1987. The equivocation defense of cognitive relativism. In Bartlett and Suber 1987:209–17.

Toulmin, Stephen. 1982. The construal of reality: Criticism in modern and postmodern science. *Critical Inquiry* 9:93–111.

Travis, David. 1980a. On the construction of creativity: The "memory transfer" phenomenon and the importance of being earnest. In Knorr, Krohn, and Whitley 1980:165–93.

Travis, David. 1980b. Creating contradiction: Or why let things be difficult when with just a little more effort you can make them seem impossible. University of Bath. Typescript.

Travis, David. 1981. Replicating replication? Aspects of the social construction of learning in planarian worms. *Social Studies of Science* 11:11–32.

Trigg, Roger. 1978. The sociology of knowledge. (Review of Bloor 1976.) *Philosophy of the Social Sciences* 8:289–98.

Trigg, Roger. 1980. *Reality at Risk: A Defence of Realism in Philosophy and the Sciences*. Hassocks, Sussex: Harvester Press.

Truman, David B. 1966. Disillusion and regeneration: The quest for a discipline. *American Political Science Review* 59:865–73.

Tudor, Andrew. 1982. *Beyond Empiricism: Philosophy of Science in Sociology*. London: Routledge and Kegan Paul.

Turner, Stephen. 1981. Interpretive charity, Durkheim, and the "strong programme" in the sociology of science. *Philosophy of the Social Sciences* 11:231–43.

Tyler, Stephen A. 1986. Post-modern ethnography: From document of the occult to occult document. In Clifford and Marcus 1986:122–40.

University of York. 1983/84. *Ordinances and Regulations*. York: University of York.

Uvarov, E. B., and D. R. Chapman, eds. 1951. *A Dictionary of Science*. Harmondsworth, Middx.: Penguin Books.

van Heijenoort, John. 1966. Logical paradoxes. In *The Encyclopedia of Philosophy*. (London: Macmillan) 1966:45–51.

Verhoog, Henk. 1982. EASST between science and society. *EASST Newsletter* 4:10–13.

Walker, Andrew G. 1977. The reality of ethnomethodology. (Review of Mehan and Wood 1975.) *Philosophy of the Social Sciences* 7:189–98.

Walker, Teri. 1986. Reflexivity: The appliance of science. Presented to the Discourse and Reflexivity Workshop, Bradford, April 1986.

Wallis, Roy, ed. 1979. *On the Margins of Science: The Social Construction of Rejected Knowledge*. Sociological Review Monograph, 27. Keele: University of Keele.

Walton, Douglas N. 1985. *Arguer's Position: A Pragmatic Study of* Ad Hominem *Attack, Criticism, Refutation and Fallacy*. Westport, Conn.: Greenwood Press.

Watson, Graham. 1987. Make me reflexive—but not yet: Strategies for managing essential reflexivity in ethnographic discourse. *Journal of Anthropological Research* 43:29–41.

Waugh, Patricia. 1984. *Metafiction: The Theory and Practice of Self-Conscious Fiction*. London: Methuen.

Webster, S. 1982. Dialogue and fiction in ethnography. *Dialectical Anthropology* 7:91–114.

Weimer, Walter B. 1977. Science as a rhetorical transaction: Toward a nonjustificational conception of rhetoric. *Philosophy and Rhetoric* 10:1–29.

Weimer, Walter B., and D. S. Palermo. 1973. Paradigms and normal science in psychology. *Science Studies* 3:211–44.

Weinsheimer, Joel. 1984. *Imitation*. London: Routledge and Kegan Paul.

Westland, Gordon. 1978. *Current Crises of Psychology*. London: Heinemann.

White, Hayden. 1973. *Metahistory: The Historical Imagination in Nineteenth Century Europe*. Baltimore, Md.: Johns Hopkins University Press.

Whitley, Richard. 1972. Black-boxism and the sociology of science: A discussion of the major developments in the field. In P. Halmos, ed. *The Sociology of Science*. Sociological Review Monograph, 18. (Keele: University of Keele) 1972:61–92.

Whitley, Richard. 1983. From the sociology of scientific communities to the study of scientists' negotiations and beyond. *Social Science Information* 22:681–720.

Whitley, Richard. 1986. The structure and context of economics as a scientific field. *Research in the History of Economic Thought and Methodology* 4:179–209.

Wieder, D. Lawrence. 1980. Behavioristic operationalism and the life-world: Chimpanzees and chimpanzee researchers in face-to-face interaction. *Sociological Inquiry* 50:75–103.

Wilden, Anthony. 1968. *The Language of the Self: The Function of Language in Psychoanalysis.* Baltimore, Md.: Johns Hopkins University Press. (See also Lacan 1968.)

Wilden, Anthony. 1980. *System and Structure: Essays in Communication and Exchange.* 2nd ed. London: Tavistock.

Williams, Rob, and John Law. 1980. Beyond the bounds of credibility. *Fundamenta Scientiae* 1:295–315.

Wilson, Bryan R., ed. 1970. *Rationality.* Oxford: Blackwell.

Wilson, R. R. 1985. This is not a meta-review of three books on metafiction, but what account should be given of a self-referential title. *Canadian Review of Comparative Literature* 12:292–305.

Winch, Peter. 1958. *The Idea of a Social Science and its Relation to Philosophy.* London: Routledge and Kegan Paul.

Wittgenstein, Ludwig. 1958. *Philosophical Investigations.* Oxford: Blackwell.

Wolin, Sheldon S. 1968. Paradigms and political theories. In P. King and B. C. Parekh, eds. *Politics and Experience.* (Cambridge: Cambridge University Press) 1968: 125–52.

Woolgar, Steve. 1976a. The identification and definition of scientific collectivities. In Lemaine et al. 1976:233–45.

Woolgar, Steve. 1976b. Writing an intellectual history of scientific developments: The use of discovery accounts. *Social Studies of Science* 6:395–422. (Reprinted in Collins 1982a:75–102.)

Woolgar, Steve. 1978. The emergence and growth of research areas in science with special reference to research on pulsars. PhD dissertation, University of Cambridge.

Woolgar, Steve. 1979. Changing perspectives: A chronicle of research development in the sociology of science. In J. Farkas, ed. *Sociology of Science and Research.* (Budapest: Akadémiai Kiadó) 1979:421–37.

Woolgar, Steve. 1980. Discovery: Logic and sequence in a scientific text. In Knorr, Krohn, and Whitley 1980:239–68.

Woolgar, Steve. 1981a. Science and ethnomethodology: A prefatory statement. *International Society for the Sociology of Knowledge Newsletter* 7(1/2):10–15.

Woolgar, Steve. 1981b. Interests and explanation in the social study of science. *Social Studies of Science* 11:365–94.

Woolgar, Steve. 1981c. Critique and criticism: Two readings of ethnomethodology. *Social Studies of Science* 11:504–14.

Woolgar, Steve. 1982. Laboratory studies: A comment on the state of the art. *Social Studies of Science* 12:481–98.

Woolgar, Steve. 1983a. Irony in the social study of science. In Knorr-Cetina and Mulkay 1983:239–66.

Woolgar, Steve. 1983b. Review of K. Knorr-Cetina, 1981a, *The Manufacture of Knowledge. Canadian Journal of Sociology* 8:467–68.

Woolgar, Steve. 1983c. Time and documents in researcher interaction: Some ways of making out what is happening in experimental science. Presented to Discourse and Reflexivity Workshop, York, April 1983.

Woolgar, Steve. 1984. A kind of reflexivity. Presented to Discourse and Reflexivity Workshop, Surrey, September 1984. (See also Woolgar 1988b.)

Woolgar, Steve. 1985. Why not a sociology of machines? The case of sociology and artificial intelligence. *Sociology* 19:557–72.

Woolgar, Steve. 1987. Reconstructing man and machine: A note on sociological critiques of cognitivism. In Bijker, Hughes, and Pinch 1987:311–28.

Woolgar, Steve, ed. 1988a. *Knowledge and Reflexivity: New Frontiers in the Sociology of Knowledge*. London and Beverly Hills, Calif.: Sage.

Woolgar, Steve. 1988b. Reflexivity is the ethnographer of the text. In Woolgar 1988a:14–34.

Woolgar, Steve. Forthcoming. The ideology of representation and the role of the agent. In Lawson and Appignanesi, forthcoming.

Woolgar, Steve, and Malcolm Ashmore. 1988. The next step: Introduction to the reflexive project. In Woolgar 1988a:1–11.

Woolgar, Steve, and Dorothy Pawluch. 1985. Ontological gerrymandering: The anatomy of social problems explanations. *Social Problems* 32:214–27.

Worrall, John. 1979. A reply to David Bloor. *British Journal of the History of Science* 12:71–78.

Wright, Edmond. 1978. Sociology and the irony model. *Sociology* 12:523–43.

Wright, Edmond, ed. 1983. *The Ironic Discourse*. Special issue of *Poetics Today* 4(3).

Wynne, Anna. 1986. Reading and writing: Sociology. Presented at the Discourse and Reflexivity Workshop, York, April 1986.

Wynne, Anna. 1988. Accounting for accounts of the diagnosis of multiple sclerosis. In Woolgar 1988a:101–22.

Wynne, Brian. 1976. C. G. Barkla and the J-phenomenon: A case study in the treatment of deviance in physics. *Social Studies of Science* 6:307–47.

Wynne, Brian. 1979. Physics and psychics: Science, symbolic action and social control in late Victorian England. In Barnes and Shapin 1979:167–84.

Wynne, Brian. 1982. *Rationality or Ritual? Nuclear Decision Making and the Windscale Inquiry*. London: British Society for the History of Science.

Yearley, Steven. 1981a. Textual persuasion: The role of social accounting in the construction of scientific arguments. *Philosophy of the Social Sciences* 11:409–35.

Yearley, Steven. 1981b. Contexts of evaluation: A sociological analysis of scientific argumentation with reference to the history of earth science. DPhil dissertation, University of York.

Yearley, Steven. 1982. The relationship between epistemological and sociological cognitive interests: Some ambiguities underlying the use of interest theory in the study of scientific knowledge. *Studies in the History and Philosophy of Science* 13:353–88.

Yearley, Steven. 1984. *Science and Sociological Practice*. Milton Keynes, Bucks.: Open University Press.

Young, Michael F. D. 1973. Taking sides against the probable: Problems of relativism and commitment in teaching and the sociology of knowledge. *Educational Review* 25:210–22. (Reprinted in Jenks 1977:86–96.)

Young, Robert M. 1977. Science *is* social relations. *Radical Science Journal* 5:65–129.

Young, Robert M. 1981. *Darwin's Metaphor and Other Studies of Nature's Place in Victorian Society*. Cambridge: Cambridge University Press.

Zenzen, M., and Sal Restivo. 1982. The mysterious morphology of immiscible liquids: A study of scientific practice. *Social Science Information* 21:447–73.

Ziegler, Heide, and Christopher Bigsby, eds. 1982. *The Radical Imagination and the Liberal Tradition: Interviews with English and American Novelists.* London: Junction Books.

Zuckerman, Harriet. 1977. Deviant behavior and social control in science. In E. Sagarin, ed. *Deviance and Social Change.* (London and Beverly Hills, Calif.: Sage) 1977:87–138.

INDEX

Characters and dialogicians are in *italics*.

Absurdity, 39, 247n. 10, 277
Adair, J., 74
Adorno, T., xxv, 56
Agreement to differ, 124
Almond, G., 234n. 4
Alter, R., 51
Althusser, L., 73, 205
Analysis/Theorizing, 80–82, 97–98
Anderson, D., 12
Appignanensi, L., 70
Arendt, H., 225
Arguments: antireflexive (*see* Problems of reflexivity); as critical, 137–38, 171–72, 178; generality, 131–32; hard case, 17, 21, 147, 153–55, 159, 217, 229n. 6, 231n. 16; hardest case, 130, 217, 231n. 16; proreflexive, 33, 36–37, 59–60, 66, 73, 78, 83–85, 88–89, 92, 111, 113–14, 212, 217, 234n. 43, 248n. 13; triangulation, 131–32, 239n. 17; from variability, 143, 147. *See also* Self-refutation arguments; Similarity/difference arguments; Tu quoque arguments
Aristotle, 49, 80, 86
Ashmore, M., xvii–xx, xxvii, xxix, 12, 13, 14, 16, 22, 26–30, 31, 35, 40, 41, 42, 46, 49, 51, 55, 60, 65, 66, 73, 74, 77, 80, 83, 86, 88, 110, 118, 129–30, 131, 140, 153, 159, 160, 188, 218, 220, 224, 225, 226, 227n. 1, 228n. 8, 233n. 38, 236n. 21, 239nn. 15, 16, 241n. 21, 244n. 19, 245nn. 26, 34
Atkinson, M., 246n. 1
Attewell, P., 246n. 1
Author, 127–30, 163–68, 190–93, 195–96, 197, 220, 245n. 31

Babcock, B., 48, 49, 50
Backhouse, A., 224
Baldamus, W., 20, 237n. 24
Balibar, E., 73
Baltzell, E. D., 234n. 42
Bannister, D., 74
Barnes, B., xxi, xxvii, 3, 5, 6, 8, 9, 12, 13, 16, 18, 21, 22, 23, 26, 27, 33–36, 38, 53, 54, 56, 62, 75, 88, 89, 94, 103, 123, 139, 148, 172, 173, 174–75, 177–78, 181, 187, 221, 229nn. 5, 7, 230n. 12, 232n. 26, 234n. 6, 245n. 30, 246nn. 1, 5, 247n. 7
Barth, J., xxi, 51, 85, 191, 194, 205, 225, 246n. 35
Barthes, R., 36, 171, 217
Bartlett, S., 48
Baumberger, J., 234n. 4
Bazerman, C., 12
Bell, C., 82
Ben-David, J., 53
Benjamin, W., 225
Berger, J., 216
Berger, P., 87, 112
Bergson, H., 236n. 22

277